GREAT W
BARCOMbE

News from a Sussex village
1914~1919

edited by Ian Hilder

COUNTRY BOOKS

Published by Country Books/Ashridge Press
in association with Spiral Publishing Ltd

Country Books Courtyard Cottage, Little Longstone,
Bakewell, Derbyshire DE45 1NN

Tel: 01629 640670
email: dickrichardson@countrybooks.biz

www.countrybooks.biz
www.sussexbooks.co.uk

ISBN 978-1-910489-61-1

© 2018 Ian Hider

email: hildergen@aol.com

British Library Cataloguing in Publication Data.
A catalogue record for this book is available from the
British Library.

Printed and bound in by Print2Demand Ltd,
1 Newlands Road, Westoning, Bedfordshire, MK45 5LD

CONTENTS

———————— ◆ ————————

PREFACE

———————◆———————

This book originated in a meeting convened by the late Derek Wise, then President of the Barcombe Branch of the Royal British Legion. Derek, an antiquarian book dealer and former naval man, had seen the "war memorial books" of Ringmer and Hamsey and determined that Barcombe should have something similar.

While researching background information on the "Barcombe men" abstracts were made of contemporary local news articles from microfilm copies of the *Sussex Express*, then held by the East Sussex Record Office at 'The Maltings' in Lewes, by Wally Hope and myself, assisted by Martyn Treasure. Later, while editing this material it became apparent that there was enough interesting material for two books, one of newspaper extracts, followed by one containing biographies of the men associated with the parish who died during the war.

Looking for illustrations, I turned to postcard collector Mike Green, who generously allowed me to scan his collection and reproduce the images. Many of these postcards were issued or posted during or immediately before the First World War and feature places and people recorded in the newspaper articles.

In order to honour Derek's wish to commemorate all the men named on the parish war memorial, it is my intention to publish the information gathered on the village during the Second World War, comprising "eye-witness" interviews, newspaper extracts and biographies of those who died.

Both Derek Wise and Mike Green have passed away since the idea for this project was first discussed, so this book is respectfully dedicated to them and to the community of Barcombe, past and present.

Ian Hilder

'The Nook', Barcombe 2018

ABOVE: The "King's Shilling"

ACKNOWLEDGEMENTS

———————◆———————

I am grateful to the many people who have assisted or supported the production of this book. To the late Derek Wise for getting the project off the ground, Wally Hope for his support and research assistance and the late Mike Green for allowing access to his unrivalled collection of Barcombe postcards. To the staff at 'The Keep' for preserving and making available copies of the *Sussex Express* and original documents relating to Barcombe parish and Chailey R.D.C. and for allowing the publication of images of documents in their care. To the editor of the *Sussex Express* for permission to reproduce extracts from wartime copies of the newspaper.

On the technical side I have Leigh Simpson to thank for his assistance with the photography of items in the Barcombe W.I. scrapbook, Sue Rowland for the excellent maps and Jonathan Taylor for the stylish layout. Both Sue and Jonathan showed endless patience with my "fine tuning" requests in order to achieve the desired result.

Wherever possible the copyright owners of the illustrations have been contacted and the relevant permissions obtained. To those who have loaned images or items for copying, your generosity is appreciated, as is the advice of Geoff Bridger, military historian, proof reading of Alison Hutchins and Barbara Cruttenden and Julia's cups of tea.

To all the people who have expressed their support for this project over the many years it has taken to gather the information, please accept my apologies for the delay! Much of the research for volume 2, the biographies of the men connected with the parish who died, is already complete. So publication should not take quite so long!

Any mistakes in the text are entirely my own. Any corrections or additions to the information would be gratefully received.

Ian Hilder

(hildergen@aol.com).

CURRENCY & WEIGHTS

——————— ◆ ———————

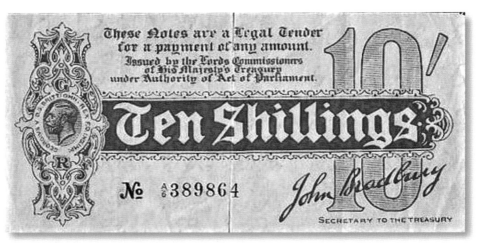

A ten shilling or "ten bob" banknote of 1914 (courtesy London Coin Auctions).

Pre-Decimal Currency *(and slang terms)*

£ Pound = 20 shillings.

s. Shilling (1/-, "Bob") = twelve pence.

d. Penny = four farthings

Half-Crown = 2 shillings and six pence.

Florin = 2 shillings.

Sixpence (6d., "tanner") = 6 pennies.

Threepence ("thrupence") = 3 pennies.

Halfpenny (½d., "hayp'ney") = 2 farthings.

Farthing (¼d.) = one quarter of a penny.

Weights *(and metric equivalent)*

Ton, 20 cwt	= 1.01 tonnes
Hundredweight (cwt)	= 50 kg
Stone (st) 14 pounds	= 6 kg
Pound (lb) 16 ounces	= 0.45 kg
Ounce (oz)	= 28 g

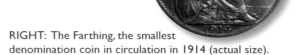

RIGHT: The Farthing, the smallest denomination coin in circulation in 1914 (actual size).

ABBREVIATIONS

———— ◆ ————

Many of the following abbreviations and initials would have been in common use during the Great War, but now require explanation. Others refer to current organisations:

A.S.C.   Army Service Corps

A.V.S.   Army Veterinary Service

Battn.   Battalion (unit of about 1,000 soldiers, commanded by a Lt. Col.)

B.E.F.   British Expeditionary Force (British Armies in France & Flanders)

Capt.   Captain (in command of a Company)

C.E.F.   Canadian Expeditionary Force

Col.   Colonel (senior administrative officer in a regiment or brigade)

Coy.   Company (approximately 225 men, commanded by a Captain)

C.R.D.C.   Chailey Rural District Council

D.S.O.   Distinguished Service Order

ESRO   East Sussex Record Office (at 'The Keep')

F.C.   Field Company (unit of Royal Engineers, commanded by a Major)

Gen.   General (the highest rank for a serving officer in the British Army)

L.B.S.C.R.   London, Brighton & South Coast Railway

L/Cpl.   Lance Corporal (non-commissioned officer ranked above a Private)

Lieut. or Lt.   Lieutenant (junior officer, ranked below a Captain)

Maj.   Major (the rank above a Captain, but below a Lt. Col.)

M.C.   Military Cross

M.E.F.   Mediterranean Expeditionary Force

M.M.   Military medal

N.C.O.   Non-commissioned officer

P.O.W.   Prisoner of War

RIGHT: Military medal, awarded to "other ranks" for acts of gallantry and devotion to duty under fire."

ABBREVIATIONS

———————◆———————

R.A.   Royal Artillery

R.A.M.C.   Royal Army Medical Corps

R.A.V.C.   Royal Army Veterinary Corps

R.D.C.   Rural District Council (Barcombe was in Chailey R.D.C.)

R.E.   Royal Engineers

Regt.   Regiment (a named body of soldiers divided into Battalions)

R.F.A.   Royal Field Artillery

R.F.C.   Royal Flying Corps (which later became the R.A.F.)

R.G.A.   Royal Garrison Artillery

R.H.A.   Royal Horse Artillery

R.M.L.I.   Royal Marine Light Infantry

R.N.   Royal Navy

R.N.D.   Royal Naval Division

R.S.R.   Royal Sussex Regiment

Sergt. or Sgt. Sergeant

Spr.   Sapper (basic rank in the Royal Engineers)

T.N.A.   The National Archives (formerly the Public Record Office)

V.A.D.   Voluntary Aid Detachment

W.A.A.C.   Women's Army Auxiliary Corps

W.I.   Women's Institute

W.L.A.   Women's Land Army

WSRO   West Sussex Record Office, Chichester

ABOVE: Royal Sussex Regiment cap badge (courtesy britishmilitarybadges.co.uk)

8

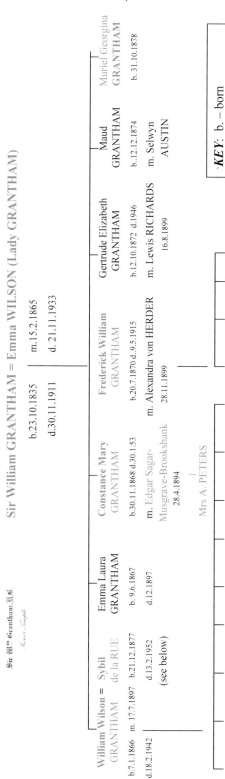

GRANTHAM 'GREAT WAR' FAMILY TREE

**Edited from a family tree kindly provided by Dave Grantham.
Names mentioned in the text are shown in red**

Sir Wm. Grantham. K.6.
James Temple

FORWARD

Sir William GRANTHAM = Emma WILSON (Lady GRANTHAM)

b.23.10.1835   m.15.2.1865
d.30.11.1911   d. 21.11.1933

William Wilson GRANTHAM = **Sybil de la RUE**	
b.7.1.1866 m. 17.7.1897 b.21.12.1877	
d.18.2.1942 d.13.2.1952 (see below)	

Emma Laura GRANTHAM
b. 9.6.1867
d.12.1897

Constance Mary GRANTHAM
b.30.11.1868 d.30.1.53
m. Edgar Sagar-Musgrave-Brooksbank
28.4.1894
Mrs A. PETERS

Frederick William GRANTHAM
b.20.7.1870 d.9.5.1915
m. Alexandra von HERDER
28.11.1899

Gertrude Elizabeth GRANTHAM
b.12.10.1872 d.1946
m. Lewis RICHARDS
16.8.1899

Maud GRANTHAM
b.12.12.1874
m. Selwyn AUSTIN

Muriel Georgina GRANTHAM
b. 31.10.1878

William Ivor	Myrtle Irene	Geoffrey Warren	John Anthony	Pauline Agnes	Thomas Elmer	Mark Edward	Frederick Andros	Nym (Kim)
b.1898	b.1900	b.1904	b.1907	b.1909	b.1911	b.1913	b.1916	b.1919

Hugo Frederick	Alexander William	Eric	Godfrey Harry
b.1895	b.1899	b.1901	b.1911

KEY: b. – born
d. – died
m. - married

A LOCAL VIEWPOINT: *THE SUSSEX EXPRESS*

◆

The
Sussex Express

With which is Incorporated Surrey Standard, Kent Mail, Hastings and St. Leonards Express, Worthing Express, West Sussex Journal, Eastbourne Observer.

In order to convey the effect of the War on the inhabitants of Barcombe, articles have been extracted from the "parish news" section of the *Sussex Express*, one of several contemporary local newspapers. This title was selected as being readily available to researchers on microfilm at East Sussex Record Office, at 'The Maltings,' Lewes during the early stages of transcription. The archives have since moved to the purpose-built facilities at 'The Keep' and images of the *Sussex Express* are now available through subscription websites, 'The British Newspaper Archive' and 'FindMyPast.'[1]

This newspaper appeared as a single county edition up to 18th February 1916, after which there were "East" and "Mid-Sussex" editions. The former title (until 1902), of the *Sussex Agricultural Express*, reflected the main source of employment in rural parishes such as Barcombe and the inland areas of the county of Sussex as a whole. Local farmers appeared at the military tribunals seeking exemption from service for their labourers, carters, wheelwrights, blacksmiths, saddlers and sons, while many of the landed estates and larger houses relinquished their trusted gardeners to form the first draft of men to volunteer for the armed forces.

The newspaper articles naturally reflect the prevailing social attitudes. There is an predictable bias towards the men going to war, while women feature in supporting roles, notably in fund-raising, clothes-making, food-processing and nursing (Red Cross and Voluntary Aid Detachments). But this was also a period of great social change, albeit sporadically. The suffragette campaign for "Votes for Women," which had been gaining support before the war, was suspended for the duration. Three daughters of Mrs TOWNER of Mount Pleasant went to work in a munitions factory in London, while the Rector's daughter, Winifred took a driving job in the Capital. The Women's Land Army was formed in January 1917 and the Barcombe branch of the Women's Institute in November 1918.

---

1   *www.britishnewsapaperarchive.co.uk and Findmypast.co.uk*

Another "sign of the times" is the prevalent attitudes towards smoking and alcohol. It was then acceptable to hold fund-raising events to raise money to buy cigarettes to send to the troops or to hold a "smoking concert", but the surviving Victorian temperance mentality prohibited alcohol in the village hall (primarily a "reading room") or club room.

ABOVE: A 1914 half crown (two shillings and six pence).

The parish was served by two Rectors during the period covered by this book, the Rev. SALMON, followed by Rev. FARRAR. Details of some of the services they performed and committees they served on are given here, but to save space references to them have usually been shortened to "the Rector."

Many articles containing lists of names (some extensive), such as those covering "whist drives," sports teams, committee meetings, wedding and funeral attendees, have been edited to allow a better flow of the text. Some representative lists have been retained to give a flavour of the local surnames and to acknowledge the work put in by particular members of the village community.

Spelling and punctuation has been transcribed as it appears in the newspaper, although minor alterations have been made (usually in brackets), where they enhance the flow of the text. Surnames have been capitalised (as in the *Sussex Family Historian* and other family history journals) to make finding them easier. The annotation "…" has been used where sections of text have been omitted.

◆

BARCOMBE is a parish, situated on the river Ouse, with a station at Barcombe Mills, on the Lewes and Uckfield branch, and another at Barcombe on the Lewes and East Grinstead section of the London, Brighton and South Coast railway; the village is 4 miles north from Lewes, 5 south-west from Uckfield and 47 from London, in the Mid division of the county, hundred of its own name, rape, petty sessional division, county court district and union of Lewes, and in the rural deanery of Uckfield, archdeaconry of Lewes and diocese of Chichester. The church of St. Mary is an ancient structure chiefly of flint stone in the Early English style, and has a tower, with spire, containing 6 bells: there are several monuments dating from the 16th century: the church was restored in 1879-80, at a cost of £2,779, and has 290 sittings. The register dates from the year 1580. The living is a rectory, net income £510, with 42 acres of glebe and residence, in the gift of the Lord Chancellor, and is at present (1915) vacant. The church of St. Bartholomew, at Spithurst, built in 1880, at a cost of £1,302, is of flint stone in the Early English style, and has a turret containing one bell: it will seat 190 persons. There is a Church Mission House in the village, erected about 1898 by the Hon. Sir William Grantham. There is also an undenominational Mission room and a Calvinistic Meeting house in Hamsey road.

A Reading room was erected in 1902 in the village by the Hon. Sir William Grantham. Conyboro, the seat of Lord Monk Bretton C.B. is a mansion in the Italian style, standing in a park of about 60 acres. Barcombe Place is the seat of Lady Grantham, and Sutton Hall the residence of Frederick S. Shenstone esq. M.A. D.L. J.P. The principal landowners are Lord Monk Bretton C.B. who is lord of the manor, Frederick S. Shenstone esq. the Rev. Francis Saunderson Sclater B.A. and William Wilson Grantham esq. The soil is a mixed loam; subsoil, clay. The chief crops are wheat, oats and beans. The area is 4,997 acres of land and 34 of water; rateable value, £9,495; the population in 1911 was 1,277.

Post, M. O. & T. Office.—Mrs. Maria Jane Holloway, sub-postmistress. Letters through Lewes arrive at 7.30 & 11 a.m. & 6 p.m.; dispatched 12 noon & 1.50 & 7.20 p.m.; sunday, arrive at 8 a.m. only; dispatched at 5 p.m. Telegraph offices also at Railway stations, open at train times

Wall Letter Boxes.—Barcombe Mills railway station cleared 12.15 & 7.5 p.m.; sundays, 5.50 p.m.; Barcombe railway station, 10.45 a.m. & 7.35 p.m. week days only

Barcombe in 1914, as described in Kelly's Sussex Directory, published 1915 (Lewes Library).

AN AGRICULTURAL COMMUNITY

◆

Barcombe's pre-war economy was based around farming and associated trades such as blacksmithing, threshing, thatching. The parish was fairly self-contained village, with a range of shops and trades, including a butcher, baker, harness maker, shoe mender and milk delivery.

BELOW: Alfred KING with 'Darling' and 'Diamond,' won 2nd prize for 'Best Turned Out Team of Horses' for F.J. CORNWELL at the 1912 Competition (courtesy the Cornwell family).

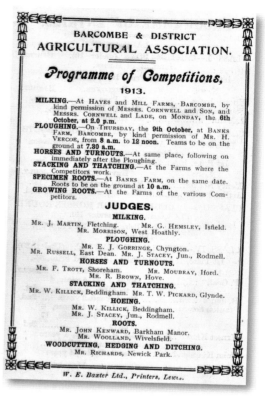

ABOVE: Barcombe & District Agricultural Association, 'Programme of Competitions' for 1913, listing some of the rural occupations, such as; milking, ploughing, thatching, woodcutting and hedging (courtesy the Cornwell family).

BARCOMBE IN 1914

◆

The two contemporary descriptions following provide a useful overview of the parish at the outbreak of the War. The first is reproduced from the annual *Kelly's Directory of Sussex*. The second was published in the *Sussex Express* on Christmas Day 1914. Illustrations have been added from contemporary local postcards.

RIGHT: A 1914 penny showing the head of the monarch, King George V on one side and Britannia ("ruling the waves") on the reverse.

PROGRESSIVE BARCOMBE

◆

An article by W. Larton Castle (*Sussex Express*, 25th December 1914).

Apart from the beauty of the immediate neighbourhood, the parish of Barcombe is deserving of notoriety by reason of the fact that it possesses two railway stations. That they are both on the same line - the London, Brighton, and South Coast Railway - rather adds to the uniqueness than otherwise, for it shows that, instead of being the outcome of commercial rivalry, the dual "linking" to the outside world results from the Railway Company having deemed the place of sufficient importance to merit two stations. It may safely be assumed that no Company, however wealthy and desirous of giving justification for its existence, would go to the trouble and expense of building an extra station just for the mere sake of bestowing a feature extraordinary upon a Sussex parish. Both "lines" are important ones, one connecting Lewes with East Grinstead, and the other - that on which the calling place is named Barcombe Mills, from the proximity of the watermills - running from the County Town to Uckfield.

IT'S SITUATION - About four miles due north of Lewes, on The River Ouse, Barcombe has at the present time a population of 1,300. The parish lies amid typical Sussex scenery - with daintily wooded copse here and there, and here and there a little

BELOW: An early colour postcard showing the signal box, platform and a steam train at Barcombe Station in the early 1900s.

Barcombe Sussex.

sylvan dell of quiet, though romantic beauty.

The district generally is so easily accessible by rail that visitors probably find it more convenient to get into the village by that means, instead of walking from a distance - say, from "headquarters" at Lewes, proceeding to "look round" after arrival in the village, in this way having the advantage of being able to secure local guidance and suggestion. There are pleasant inns where refreshment may be partaken of before the return journey is commenced…

We arrive at Barcombe Station, over whose very precincts hangs the foliage of small trees with plants thriving around the base of a telegraph pole, indeed possessing just

BELOW: The Smithy at the southern end of Barcombe High Street on a postcard by Harry Tullett of Cuckfield (Mike Green collection).

The Village, Barcombe.

that appearance of spic-and-span arrangement which characterises a well-behaved country railway station, and makes it to "the city-dweller," accustomed to his dirty-looking stations an object of interest as something extraordinary and out of the accepted order of things; rather than as an erection which belongs in these days of extensive railway travelling

ABOVE: Barcombe "Street" with the Reading Room (village hall) on the left and Ballard's Stores on the right. (Postcard from the 'Dolphin Series.' Mike Green collection).

and when air travel is a commonplace; to the world of prosaicism.

IN THE VILLAGE - Turning to the right as we leave the station, we go along a slightly-mounting road for about a hundred yards, turn to the left, and are almost at once in the "main street." The term is used advisedly, for it is a street in the full meaning of the word, and worthy of many a small town. The roadway is comparatively broad, and overgrown for a village.

Soon after turning from the station approach we pass on the left-hand side the forge - the building being of respectable dimensions, and of modern aspect-so modern, indeed, with

The Smithy, Barcombe.

ABOVE: The Reading Room & Club, photographed by Harry Tullett of Cuckfield (Mike Green collection).

seat of that well-known family being in the district. This structure is entirely of modern design, its frontal appearance being that so characteristic of some of the villas of the newer suburbs of our cities "flat" fronted and possessing a strikingly clean appearance. Before its erection, owing to the public-spiritedness of the late Mr Justice GRANTHAM, there was a small reading room just opposite, and it is interesting to note that the present Honorary Secretary, Mr

its "stiff," four-walled design and light complexion, that but for the clanging of the hammer, and the ruddy glare seen through the windows, this place would certainly not suggest itself as a smithy. And one may perhaps be excused for being practical enough to think that, however more quaint and interesting the "old original" blacksmith's establishments may appear in comparison with the present-day erection, yet the latter - with its better ventilation and general architectural improvements - is far more healthy for those whose daily toil takes them there. After all, the visitor comes and goes, but the worker remains.

Further along, on the opposite side to the forge, is the post office. Nearly at the

end on the road, on our left, is the Village Reading Room, Church Mission House, the Public Elementary School.

THE READING ROOM - The Reading Room was founded in 1901 by the late Sir William GRANTHAM, the

BELOW: 'Barcombe Castle,' also known as 'Grantham's Folly,' a viewing tower on a barn at Banks Farm. The origins of the building are unknown, but close inspection of the towers reveals a crest bearing the griffin of the Grantham family (Barcombe W.I. scrapbook, ESRO: WI 112/1/1, p.127).

Barcombe Castle   Circa 1890.

ABOVE: 'Barcombe Mills from the Crink', photographed c.1910 by Harry Tullett of Cuckfield (Mike Green collection).

A.MOON, the schoolmaster, was also Secretary of the old place, having held his position for no less than 32 years. It is perhaps needless to add that Mr MOON's experience enables him to recall many interesting reminiscences, but space forbids. Major W.W.GRANTHAM, who is now serving with His Majesty's Forces is the present president. The subscriptions are moderate and it is unfortunate that the institution has not yet become self-supporting fulfilling as it dies a great need in village life. A large proportion of its members are now with the Colours.

The Mission House is really the only Church of England meeting place at "first hand" for the people of Barcombe village. The two churches proper are both some distance out of the village. Reference will be made to them later on.

By proceeding along a turning near the School (direction will readily be given) a good view can be obtained from the neighbouring lane of an interesting building on the Banks Farm. It cannot definitely be said here how old it is or whence its origin. Probably it is not very old, for there are no apparent signs of decay anywhere, but none the less it makes its appeal to the sightseer.

About the best architectural description to give it (at least speaking externally for the interior is barren) is to liken it to a castellated church of stone and flint. There are the usual embrasures on the walls and also in the square towers, typical of the old places of defence. Yet (this is the strange thing) approach is made to the top of the tower by a door (not at all massive looking) which opens directly from the outside! There are not furnishings insides. The design of the structure is crude. But whatever its origin, and for whatever purpose intended, it is certainly an interesting monument to see.

ACROSS CRINK FIELD TO BARCOMBE MILLS

- If, when by the School, we take the road which runs to the right from the main street, we then traverse a wide lane fairly even in direction which, before long, brings us to a signpost. Just about here a few yards on the left-hand side down the road which branches off to the right is a gate which will take us through the Chink (Crink) Field to Barcombe Mills Railway Station which, like its "brother" looks as fresh as the proverbial daisy. At one time this locality was rich in relics of antiquarian interest, in the shape of arrow heads etc. Probably there are still more to be yielded up. From the field an extensive view is obtainable of the surrounding country. In the near distance are groups of swaying trees while farther away in one direction are the dark grey moors which stand sentinel-like, above Lewes…

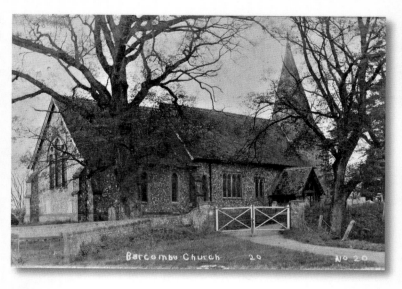

INTERESTING CHURCHES

- Reference was made above to the churches of the parish. There are two: St. Mary's and St. Bartholomew's. The last-named is at Spithurst, on the further side of Barcombe village from Lewes, and is of quite recent date. Erected in 1880, it is of Early English style. The Church of St. Mary (which is passed on the road from Lewes), on the right, some distance after passing Hamsey Railway Crossing (is of a much earlier period, but of the same style, dating from about the middle of the Sixteenth Century. Certain restorations were made about 36 years ago. There are several interesting features and objects to be seen inside. Speaking architecturally, the edifice expresses a sublime, poetical sentiment.

One cannot conclude without remarking that the parish has the advantages of its own water and drainage schemes.

ABOVE: St. Mary's Church, Barcombe on a pre-war postcard by an un-named publisher.

LEFT: St. Bartholomew's Church, Spithurst on a postcard by Harry Tullett of Cuckfield, posted in 1918.

SPRING 1914

◆

Two events taking place in April and reported in the *Sussex Express* provide a good example of the community spirit within the village.

RIGHT: Preparing for war? The Barcombe Red Cross Detachment pictured with some long-suffering Boy Scout "patients" in the "Motor House" at Barcombe Place. The inspecting officer told the members that they must consider themselves "part of the defensive forces of the country. (Barcombe W.I. scrapbook, ESRO: WI 1/1, p.172).

2nd April - RED CROSS SOCIETY – INSPECTION AT BARCOMBE – Tribute to the painstaking work which is being carried out by the Barcombe Detachment of the Red Cross Society was paid at the second annual inspection, held at the Motor House of Barcombe Place, on Wednesday afternoon

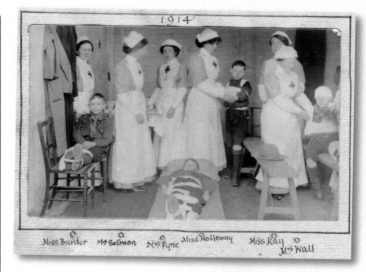

by kind permission of Lady GRANTHAM. The detachment comprises sixteen nurses and three cooks, and valuable assistance is rendered

by Miss GRANTHAM (Commandant), Mrs Musgrave BROOKSBANK (Quarter Master), and Sister LOVELL (Instructress). The motor house

The Women's Detachment of the Red Cross Society in the 'motor home' (former stables) at Barcombe Place. Left to right: The Misses; MESSAGE, MILLS, COWDREY, SHENSTONE, GRANTHAM and BROOKSBANK. Published for J. Ballard & Son, The Stores, Barcombe (Mike Green collection).

ABOVE: Beaters of the Bounds during a "luncheon" break at Balneath Manor (courtesy the Cornwell family).

had been well adapted as a hospital for the occasion, being replete with wards, operating room, kitchen, etc. Members of the Barcombe Troop of Boy Scouts made admirable patients and the Inspecting Officer, Major G.H.GODDARD, R.A.M.C., of Brighton, had an opportunity of seeing the members of the detachment at work on a variety of imaginary cases of broken limbs and other ailments…

Major GODDARD, addressing the members, said he thought they had gone through the inspection very well indeed… The work of the Red Cross was very highly appreciated by the War Office...

and that in time of war the members of the society would be of very great service indeed. "Therefore," concluded the Major, "You must consider yourselves part of the defensive forces of the country…"

16th April – BARCOMBE BOUNDS – INTERESTING CEREMONY – Barcombe has this week accomplished a task upon which it has set its heart for some time past. Residents, young and old alike, were invited by a notice worded in legal phraseology to participate in the ancient custom of beating the bounds, and so expansive is the parish that it had to be a two-day fixture,

commencing early Tuesday morning and concluding on Wednesday afternoon. Over forty years have elapsed since the boundaries of the parish were last beaten, and the number of residents now living who took part in the ceremony on that occasion is very small. The only two we have heard of are Mr J. Selby READ (the vice-chairman of the Parish Council and a great authority on Barcombe's history) and Mr TAPP. Their presence at this week's peregrinations added interest to the event, and their assistance in tracing and identifying old boundary marks was most valuable. Mr W.W. GRANTHAM (chairman

Parishioners of Barcombe pose confidently for Bliss & Co.'s camera at Seven Acre Brook, near Culver Junction, before setting out to 'Beat the Bounds' of the parish on 14th April 1914. Children sit at the front, the be-smocked squire W.W. GRANTHAM, his son Ivor and the Rector take centre stage, the few women present stand on the periphery.

of the Parish Council), was the prime mover in the ceremony, and he interested a great many Barcombe people in reviving in a fitting manner the time-honoured custom. The parishioners rose even earlier than usual on Tuesday morning, and they found the elements in a most inviting mood for a long and arduous tramp. The chief figures in the day's arrangements were entertained to breakfast at Barcombe Place, through

RIGHT: W.W. GRANTHAM (centre right) wearing a Sussex smock studies a map, while Mr BOURDILLON (far right) looks on (Mike Green collection).

the kindness of Lady GRANTHAM, and having fortified the inner man they made tracks for Seven Acre Brook, near Culver Junction,

where they were joined by a numerous and enthusiastic party. Keeping strictly to the traditions of the ceremony the claims of religion and

Beating of the Bounds 14th April 1914 – Key to Names

The contemporary numbering key on the reverse of the postcard group, has been expanded using the full names listed in W.W. GRANTHAM's printed report of the "perambulation." Many of those included were too old for military service, but served the parish in many other ways, as will be seen in the wartime newspaper articles.

1. Nancy FUNNELL
2. Harry TROWER
3. F. Burton CORNWELL
4. Arthur FLETCHER
5. William Albert TAPP
6. William HOBDEN jun.
7. Rev. W.B. LOVEBAND
8. Thomas LADE
9. W. Ivor GRANTHAM
10. Edwin G. HOLLOWAY
11. William W. GRANTHAM
12. H. John SPELLER sen.
13. Francis CORNWELL sen.
14. Rev. R.I. SALMON
15. Sydney Beard RICHARDS
16. George RHODES
17. Clarence SMITH
18. William Frederick DEAN sen.
19. Richard RHODES
20. Ernest RHODES
21. William John BUNNEY
22. William John PARRIS
23. James REED
24. Mrs Constance BROOKSBANK
25. Miss Constance BROOKSBANK
26. Frederick John DEAN *
27. Edward Walter CORKE *
28. Sydney Beard RICHARDS jun. *
29. [2 boys, possibly KEMP & KEMP]
30. Edward Harry KIRBY *
31. Jack Rhodes FUNNELL *

* Boy Scouts

Not pictured is James Selby REED who was driven in a carriage by Frederick KEMP.

the Divine Blessing were emphasised by the Rector (Prebendary SALMON), who delivered a brief address. Mr W.W. GRANTHAM called the "roll"…

Working along the south side of the parish towards Hamsey, the youthful spirits much enjoyed the ordeal of being "bumped" on the boundary stone. On reaching the blacksmith's shop, close to the Rainbow Inn, F. TAPP climbed the roof in order that the boundary line might be faithfully followed… By design or sheer good luck the party were in the neighbourhood of Balneath Manor at luncheon time. Mr (Ivor) GRANTHAM entertained a large company here and other at the Swan Inn.

After lunch the number of beaters was augmented, and on reaching the pond at Shelley's Farm a diversion was provided. Master Fred DEAN volunteered to swim the pond – a task which was safely accomplished. At the point where the parishes of Chailey, Newick and Barcombe join, the Rev. LOVEBAND read the 103rd Psalm in accordance with the practice of former days. The beaters concluded the day's march at Gypp's Farm in the Spithurst district.

The second day's proceedings were no less interesting. A large company, including many of those present on Monday, turned up at Gypp's for the resumption of the tour at 9.45 a.m. Some little difficulty was experienced in tracing the boundary, but with the help of the maps and records which were carefully kept by the late George GRANTHAM, at the beating of the bounds in 1870, the right line was eventually made clear. An exciting incident occurred early in the day; R.TAPP, one of the youthful beaters, slipped while crossing the stream and had to be extricated from an unpleasant – not to say risky – position. Sharpe's Bridge was visited and the boundary stones and trees between Barcombe parish and Isfield and Ringmer were clearly marked. At Pike's Bridge Mr Chas. HOLLOWAY walked through the river. The party finished their journey, which, allowing for all the "ins and outs" must have totalled a distance of 30 miles in the two days, about half past five, when the beaters congregated once more at the starting point and joined in an appropriate prayer…

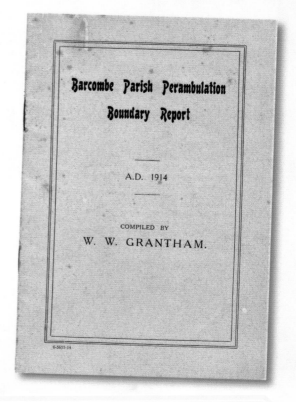

ABOVE: This printed report of the 'Barcombe Parish Perambulation' compiled by W.W. GRANTHAM and dated 4th May, was published following a meeting at Barcombe Place on 26th June (courtesy Wally Hope. A copy is also included in the Barcombe W.I. scrapbook, ESRO: WI 112/1/1, p.126).

SUMMER 1914

◆ **June** – The shortage of rural housing was under discussion.

◆ The London, Brighton & South Coast Railway were offering day trips from Newhaven to Dieppe on the steamer 'Arundel'.

◆ Petrol prices had dropped for the first time in eight years, from 1s.9d to 1s.8d per gallon for the 'best grade' and 1s.7d to 1s.6d for 'secondary quality'.

◆ A 'Ford Runabout' motorcar was advertised by a local garage for £125, or £32.2s.6d. plus 12 monthly payments of £8, "complete with full equipment, including head lamps, side and tail lamps, speedometer, horn, hood and wind-screen!"

◆ In nearby Lewes, the 'Cinema De Luxe' was screening a comedy, 'The Misadventures of a Mighty Monarch.'

◆ The 3rd Battalion, Royal Sussex Regiment were on a recruiting march across the county.

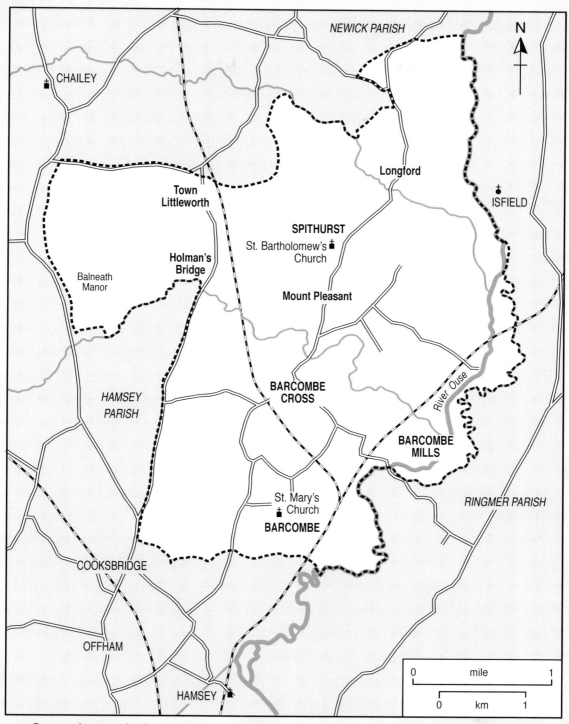

Barcombe parish, showing place-names mentioned in the text and adjoining parishes.

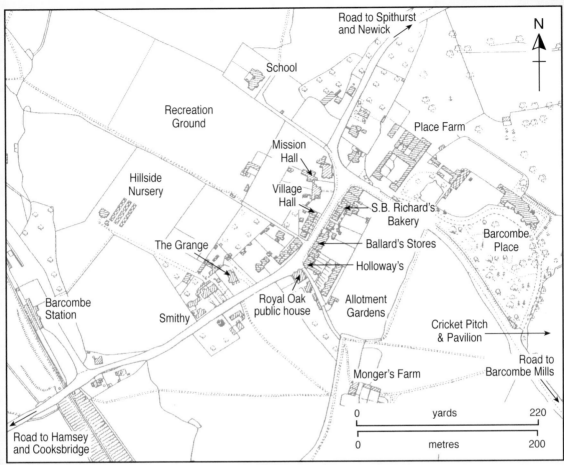

Barcombe Cross, showing some of the locations mentioned in the text.

ABOVE: Children play in the road outside Holloway's corner shop and bakery in Barcombe High Street, (from a postcard by A.M. Bliss & Co. of Lewes, posted in 1911).

9th July - CYCLE CLUB RUN – About a dozen members, led by Mr R. GRIERSON, cycled from Barcombe Cross to Danehill and back on Sunday evening.

23rd July - FLOWER SHOW – By kind permission of Lady GRANTHAM, Barcombe Flower Show will this year be held at Barcombe Place on Wednesday, August 19th. Owing to a change of secretaryship at the last moment, the arrangements are not quite as forward as usual, but no doubt lost time will now be made up, and the show will once again be worthy of the district.

NEW PARISH COUNCILLOR – Mr W.W.GRANTHAM presided at a meeting of the Parish Council on Thursday evening, and there were also present: Mr J.S. REED (vice-chair), Mr S.B.RICHARDS, Mr F.J.CORNWELL, Mr T.HAWKINS, Mr E.W.BUNNEY, and the Clerk (Mr H.TROWER). Mr T.LADE of Mill Farm was elected a member of the Council in succession to Mr A.E.DUDENEY, who has left

ABOVE: 'On War Service 1914' – These badges were issued by the Admiralty to workmen in the naval shipyards to indicate that they were engaged in essential war-work.

Barcombe for Brighton. The Clerk was directed to write to the Railway Company with reference to the bad condition of the road over the railway bridge near the church, and the footpath which crosses the line on the way to the church from Barcombe village.

FORESTERS' FETE – ...Took place at 'Handlye Farm' field yesterday (Wednesday) afternoon. The children's sports had not long been commenced when rain came on and delayed the programme for some time. In the evening the rain ceased, and the sports were continued, the remaining children's events following those for the adults...The officials were: Mr L.STEVENS (chairman), Mr J.W.BRIGGS (starter), and the Rev. G.SALMON and Mr A.MOON (judges)...The events included a 'Jingling Match' for the under 12s; Grinning through the horse collar; Sewing the button; Three-legged Race for men: 1. C.J.HOLLOWAY & P.CHARLTON, 2. WALL & F.SAUNDERS, 3. B.COLLINS & F.FAULCONER. Egg & Spoon Race for ladies: 1. Miss KING, 2.Miss DABSON, 3.Miss TOWNER; Sack race for men: 1.F. FORD, 2.F.SAUNDERS, 3.P.CHARLTON; Egg & Spoon Race for men: 1.J. FARENDEN, 2.G.BODLE, 3.H.NOAKES; Long Jump 1.F.SAUNDERS (14ft.8ins), 2.G.BODLE (14ft.4½ ins), 3.H. STEVENSON (14ft.1½ ins).

ABOVE: 'Handlye Farm,' played host to a Foresters' Friendly Society Fete on 23rd July 1914 (courtesy Anne Pearce).

30th July - CRICKET - Last Saturday, Barcombe beat Newhaven by 15 runs. Barcombe Team: S. COX, J.STANDING, F.SAUNDERS, G.M.HUBBUCK, C.J.HOLLOWAY, H.STEVENSON, W.F.RABAN, G.BODLE, E.KING, J.STEVENS, C.MUGGERIDGE.[1]

6th August - SHOW ABANDONED – The Flower Show, which was arranged to take place at Barcombe Place on Wednesday, August 19th, has been abandoned.

ANGLING COMPETITION – Barcombe Mills was alive with fishermen on Bank Holiday when the Brighton Anglers' Association held their special pegged-down competition in the upper portion of the Ouse. The

---

1   *Two members of this team, Frederick SAUNDERS and Ernest KING, were to die during the ensuing War.*

ABOVE: 'DEFENDING OLD ENGLAND - Lewes Artillery Leaving For Dover.' Local troops march past the 'Lansdown Arms' and over the railway bridge to Lewes station.

takes were rather small, no doubt owing to the clearness of the water. Mr J.S.REED (Barcombe Mills) was one of the prize donors. Results – 1.Mr A.S.C.SMITH, 2lbs; 2.Mr R.SWEETMAN, 1lb ½ oz; 3.Mr G.SAUNDERS 1lb; 4.Mr D.WILSON 13 ½ ozs; 5.Mr C.KEMPSHALL 12 ¾ ozs.

13th August - PRINCE MUNSTER'S POSITION – SUSSEX MANSION SEARCHED – Considerable excitement was caused in the Uckfield

BELOW: Town's Farewell to Territorials on their departure on Wednesday afternoon.

district on Friday afternoon by the news that Maresfield Park, the residence of Prince Munster, was being closely searched by the police. The action, which was taken by the authorities in London, was not directed against the Prince as an individual, but was part of a general plan... We have authority for stating that Prince Munster is a close friend of the Kaiser, but he does not, as has been suggested, hold an important post in his army. The Prince is not a naturalised Englishman, for the reason that he holds very extensive estates in Germany and also in Russia. His mother was a Russian Princess... That the Prince did not favour the war is certain (nothing suggesting disloyalty to England was found)...

Now is the time for marching,
  Now let your hearts be gay;
Hark to the merry bugles
  Sounding along our way.
So let your voices ring, my boys,
  And take the time from me,
And I'll sing a song as we march along
  Of Sussex by the Sea.

Chorus:
We're the men from Sussex,
  Sussex by the sea,
We plough and sow and reap and mow,
  And useful men are we.
And when you go to Sussex, whoever you may be,
  You may tell them all that we stand or fall
For Sussex by the Sea.

ABOVE: The first verse and chorus of 'Sussex by the Sea' were published in the Sussex Express on 6th August 1914. The song, which became popular during the Great War, was first published by William Ward-Higgs in 1907, and had been adopted by the Royal Sussex Regiment as a marching song.

ABOVE: Maresfield Park '(Late) the seat of Prince Munster' from a postcard c.1916.

That the Prince did not wish to engender disloyalty in the minds of his servants was apparent in his farewell remark to his Steward as he was starting for Germany last Sunday week: "Never mind me, Findlay: your first duty is to your country." On Tuesday the police again visited Maresfield Park, and brought away a number of sporting guns.

20th August – CRICKET
– Cooksbridge v. Barcombe – Cooksbridge were at home to Barcombe in Conyboro Park on Saturday and won by 22 runs…

RECRUITING AT LEWES
– "Your King and country need you" runs a circular which has been circulated in Lewes as an appeal for recruits for the Regular Army. It states that an addition of 100,000 to His Majesty's

RIGHT: Departure at Lewes Railway Station.

Regular Army is immediately necessary in the present grave national emergency, and Lord Kitchener feels confident that this appeal will be at once responded to by all who have the safety of our Empire at heart. Recruits can enlist for a period of three years or until the war is concluded, the age of enlistment being between 19 and 30…A special appeal

YOUR KING AND COUNTRY NEED YOU!
A CALL TO ARMS!

An addition of 100,000 men to His Majesty's Regular Army is immediately necessary in the present grave National Emergency. Lord Kitchener is confident that this appeal will be at once responded to by all those who have the safety of our Empire at heart.

TERMS OF SERVICE:
General Service for a period of 3 years or until the War is concluded.
Age of Enlistment between 19 and 30.

HOW TO JOIN.
Full information can be obtained at any Post Office in the United Kingdom or at any Military Depot.

GOD SAVE THE KING.

ABOVE: 'A Call to Arms,' recruiting notice published in the *East Sussex News* of 14th August 1914.

having been made for recruits for "D" (Lewes) Company 5th (Cinque Ports) Royal Sussex Regiment, Sergeant-Major R. SOUTER visited the town a few days ago and secured nearly a dozen.

SPECIAL CONSTABLES APPOINTED – The following have been appointed special constable for Lewes and district: (At least two men for each parish were sworn in at Lewes Petty Sessions, to assist the police in case of emergency. The two men appointed for Barcombe were: R. SPENCE and H. FUNNELL).[2]

FOOTBALL CLUB – In view of the present state of affairs, the Football Club's arrangements for the coming season are uncertain. A meeting will probably be held shortly to discuss the matter. It might interest members to know that the Lewes and District League will probably run as usual. At any rate, the Secretary intends calling a meeting on 1st September for the purpose of arranging fixtures.

ABOVE: Harry FUNNELL, one of two newly appointed Special Constables shoeing a horse outside his forge in this Hamilton postcard c.1910 (Mike Green collection).

CYCLING CLUB – Members of the Barcombe Cycling Club rode over to Newick on Sunday and attended evensong at the Parish Church.

MAJOR GRANTHAM's CYCLISTS – Major W.W. GRANTHAM, commanding 6th (Cyclists) Battalion Royal Sussex Regiment, writes to the "Sussex Express" – "As I am daily receiving verbal and written applications from different parts of Sussex for vacancies in the Battalion, I shall be glad if you will kindly let your readers know that the Battalion was recruited up to war establishment by midnight last Saturday week – four days after mobilisation – and that at present there are no vacancies for commissioned Officers nor for men in the ranks."

BARCOMBE'S ACTIVITY – Sixteen new members have recently joined the Barcombe Voluntary Aid Detachment and

ABOVE: A 1914 Rudge-Whitworth 'No.25' Service Roadster of the type used by the R.S.R., complete with rifle clips. Photographed at the Redoubt Museum, Eastbourne (courtesy the Online Bicycle Museum).

2 Richmond SPENCE (43) a Scotsman of "private means" appears at several meetings and entertainments in Barcombe during the war years. Where he lived is not known, but in 1911 he was living in Eastbourne with his wife Ada, daughter Lavinia and two servants. In March 1915 he left Barcombe for Ringmer.

ABOVE: Three Cyclists of the 2/6th (Cyclist) Battalion R.S.R. camped at Southwold 1st July 1915 (courtesy the Online Bicycle Museum).

useful work is being carried out with Mr George HOLLOWAY[3] as Section Leader. The fund started by Mr A.SINCLAIR[4] for equipping the detachment amounts at the present time to £2 16s. and further subscriptions will be thankfully received. The Women's Detachment, of which Miss Muriel GRANTHAM is Quartermaster,[5] and Miss SALMON hon. secretary, is also actively engaged.[6] Working parties are being held at Barcombe Place, the residence of Lady GRANTHAM. In the event of a hospital being equipped, Barcombe helpers will be required in several departments, and ladies and gentlemen willing to help should send in their names to Miss GRANTHAM.

ABOVE: 'YOUR KING AND COUNRTY NEED YOU.' Recruiting notice first published in the Sussex Express of 6th August 1914.

BOY SCOUTS – The valuable work of Boy Scouts in various directions was acknowledged at East Sussex County Council

---

2/6th (Cyclist) Battalion, Royal Sussex Regiment

The Cyclist Battalion was a unit of the Territorial Force, based at Brighton. In March 1915 they moved by train to Southwold, Suffolk for training in coastal defence (including trench digging, rifle fire and bayonet fighting). In November they joined with three other Cyclist Battalions and converted to infantry. They left Devonport for India on 4th February 1916, where they stayed until October 1918 when they moved to Vladivostok and into Serbia, before returning to England in November 1919.

Battalion War Diaries 1914-17 are available from TNA and WSRO (ref. RSR MS 6-5).

Harry FUNNELL (44) was the Barcombe-born blacksmith and wheelwright, with a forge next to his home at the southern end of the High Street.

3   *Edwin George HOLLOWAY was a baker, with a corner shop at the end of Gladstone Buildings in the High Street.*

4   *Alfred SINCLAIR of 'Place Cottages' was a grocer's assistant.*

5   *Muriel Georgina GRANTHAM (35) was the youngest child of the village squire, High Court Judge, Sir William GRANTHAM and his wife Lady Emma, of Barcombe Place, and 100 Eaton Square, London.*

6   *Miss Hilda SALMON (33) lived at 'The Rectory' with her parents the Rev. Robert & Emma SALMON.*

The handwritten annotations on the photograph read:
Mrs Cox, Miss Hewett, Mrs Haffenden, Miss Holloway, Mr G. Holloway, Miss Laughen, Miss Rhodes, Mr Fullinger, Mr Burrows, Mr Wall, Miss Kay, Miss Shenstone, Mr Funnell, Miss Salmon, Mrs Pyne
1914
Miss Message, Miss Cowdrey, Mrs Brooksbank, Miss Grantham, Nurse, Miss Burder

ABOVE: The Women's Detachment of Barcombe Red Cross Society (had been incorporated into the local Voluntary Aid Detachment). Pictured here in the motor garage at Barcombe Place, during their second annual inspection earlier in the year (Barcombe W.I. scrapbook. ESRO: WI 112/1/1, p.172).

elsewhere, probably at the Mission Room.

3rd September - RED CROSS LECTURES – A course of lectures on First Aid will be held every alternate Thursday, at eight o'clock in the Schools, commencing September 10th.

VILLAGE PATRIOTISM – A patriotic meeting has been arranged to take place on the Recreation Ground this Thursday evening, when the speaker will be Sir John BLAKER on Tuesday, and Lord MONK BRETTON, C.B. asked the Standing Joint Committee to take into consideration the question of making them some payment. He also urged that their attendance at school should be excused for the present. The suggestions will receive attention.

27th August - CRICKET – Barcombe v Castlegate

Shorthand Class (Lewes) – Castlegate beat Barcombe by a wicket and three runs at Barcombe on Saturday. The Barcombe team: C. MUGGERIDGE 0, Rev. W.B.Y. LOVEBAND 5, E.KIRBY 1, A.FLETCHER 22, A.BURDER 1, H.HENTY 0, G.BODLE 15, S.RICHARDS 1, F.BODLE 4, L.STONE 0, Miss BURDER 0.[7]

TEMPORARY HOSPITAL – The village School has been fitted up by the Red Cross Society as a temporary hospital, but the children return from their holidays next week, and we understand the Society will now find accommodation

---

7   It is unusual to see a woman in the village cricket team. Miss Florence Madeline Doris BURDER (27) lived at 'The Beeches' in Church Road with her elderly father John (81) and mother Henrietta (58), along with a cook and parlour maid.

G.   R.

YOUR KING AND COUNTRY NEED YOU!

ANOTHER 100,000 MEN WANTED.

Lord Kitchener is much gratified with the response already made to the Appeal for additional men for His Majesty's Regular Army.

In the grave National emergency that now confronts the Empire he asks with renewed confidence that another 100,000 men will now come forward.

TERMS OF SERVICE.
(Extension of age limit.)

Age on enlistment, 19 to 30, Ex-Soldiers up to 45, and certain selected Ex-Non-Commissioned Officers up to 50. Height, 5-ft. 3-in. and upwards. Chest, 34 inches at least. Must be medically fit. General Service for the War.

Men enlisting for the duration of the War will be able to claim their discharge, with all convenient speed, at the conclusion of the War.

PAY AT ARMY RATES,
and Married Men or Widowers with Children will be accepted, and will draw Separation Allowance under Army Conditions.

HOW TO JOIN.

Men wishing to join should apply in person at any Military Barrack or at any Recruiting Office. The address of the latter can be obtained from Post Office or Labour Exchanges.

GOD SAVE THE KING.

ABOVE: 'Another 100,000 Men Wanted.' This advertisement appeared in the *East Sussex News* of 4th September 1914.

London
Opinion

"YOUR COUNTRY NEEDS
YOU"

1ᴰ LONDON OPINION 1ᴰ

PRINTED BY THE VICTORIA HOUSE PRINTING CO. LTD. TUDOR ST. LONDON. E.C. SEPT 5. 1914.

LEFT: 'Your Country Needs You.' This well-known image of Lord Kitchener, the British Secretary of State for War, was originally designed by Alfred Leete as the cover of the popular weekly *London Opinion* magazine of 5th September 1914. It was later developed into a recruitment poster, but its absence from street scenes in contemporary photographs suggests that it may not have been the major enticement to recruitment that is popularly believed.[8] (Poster advertising the 'London Opinion', U.S. Library of Congress, Reproduction no. LC-DIG-ppmsca-37468).

– The village is waking up and already a number of recruits have joined Lord KITCHENER's Army.

CYCLISTS AT BARCOMBE PLACE - A second route march in connection with the 6th (Cyclist) Battalion Royal Sussex Regiment was held on Saturday. Recruits in command of Major W.W.GRANTHAM, cycled from Brighton via Haywards Heath and Chailey to Barcombe Place, where they were hospitably entertained to tea by Lady GRANTHAM.

TERRITORIALS' THANKS – Acknowledging a supply of cigarettes and tobacco sent by friends at Barcombe, per Mr SINCLAIR to the men of the 3rd (Lewes) Company, Sussex Royal Garrison Artillery, the Commanding Officer (Captain F.LOUD) states that they are very grateful for the gifts. He adds: "All are keeping very fit. This particular kind of work seems to agree with them).

10th September - Mr S.B. RICHARDS' LOSS – The loss of a horse is a serious matter at any time, but just now when there is such a scarcity it hits one all the harder. On Friday a horse belonging to Mr S.B.RICHARDS was doing the bread round, and when near Barcombe Church the driver (J.ELPHICK) left it to make a delivery. In his absence the horse by some means got its bridle off and bolted along the road. Rounding the corner by Mr J.BURDER's residence, 'The Beeches', the runaway came to grief in the ditch, and breaking its fetlock, had to be destroyed. The animal was valued at £35.

8   Copping, Jasper. " 'Your Country Needs You' – The myth about the First World War poster that 'never existed'." The Telegraph, 2nd August 2013.

PATRIOTIC MEETING

– Arranged by Lady GRANTHAM and Miss Muriel GRANTHAM, an open-air patriotic meeting was held in the Recreation Ground on Thursday evening last. Lord MONK BRETTON, C.B. presided over a big gathering, and the speakers were Sir John BLAKER (Brighton) and the Rev. H.HORDERN (St. Nicholas, Brighton). The address dealt with the origin of the War and the need for recruits, and on the motion of Mr SPENCE, seconded by Rev. George SALMON, a resoloution was passed calling on all those who are able to serve their country. Three recruits gave their names at the close of the meeting, but altogether Barcombe has provided over 20 recruits in addition to those already serving in the Territorials. Mr A.FLETCHER, who is prominently associated with the local cricket and football clubs, has joined the Sussex Yeomanry.

CYCLING CLUB CONTEST

– The free-wheel contest held at Mount Pleasant last week under the auspices of the Barcombe Cycling Club aroused much local interest, and a large number of spectators assembled on the hill to witness it. There were 22 competitors, including ladies, and the result was as follows:
1. A.OSMOND [9] (cycling lamp presented by Messrs Rice Bros., Lewes);
2. Mr HOBDEN jnr.[10] (walking stick presented by the Club); 3. A.HENTY (leather card case presented by the Club).[11] Mr JENNER and Miss SADLER (Lewes) were the judges, and Mr HOBDEN snr., acted as starter...

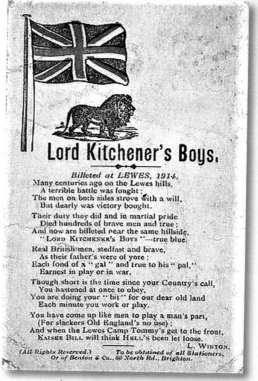

ABOVE: 'Lord Kitchener's Boys, billeted at Lewes 1914,' a poem by L. Winton on a postcard.

24th September - THE RECTOR's BIRTHDAY – Yesterday (Wednesday) the Rev. Preb. SALMON attained his 80th birthday. He has the hearty congratulations of the parishioners. Considering his age the rector is wonderfully active.

ABOVE: Mount Pleasant, Spithurst from which the Cycling Club's "free-wheel" contest started. 'Mafeking Cottages' can be seen behind the hedges to the left and the old forge to the right. (Postcard by Bliss & Co. of Lewes).

9   Arthur OSMOND (33) was working as a cowman at the time of the 1911 census, but later started a haulage business.

10   The HOBDENs lived at Mafeking Cottages, Mount Pleasant. HOBDEN junior was William (20), son of George a "threshing machine proprietor. The threshing engines were kept in the field behind the Cottages.

11   Alfred HENTY (24) was a Constable in the Metropolitan Police, retiring from the Holborn Division in 1925. His parents, William & Eliza lived in the High Street.

LEFT: 'Au revoir at the station' – The departure of a large contingent of "Kitchener's Men" from Lewes on Monday.

CHOIR OUTING – The boys of Spithurst Church Choir, accompanied by the Rev. W.B.Y.LOVEBAND (curate), spent an enjoyable day at Brighton on Saturday, the occasion being their annual outing. The journey was made by train, leaving Barcombe at 8.50 a.m. and returning by the 9.5 p.m. train. The boys visited the Aquarium among other places.

2nd October - BANKS FARM – Mr Hart VERCOE of Banks Farm, having decided to relinquish the milk business, his herd of dairy cows and heifers, together with dairy utensils and effects were sold by auction on Thursday by Messrs. Drawbridge & Ansell of Haywards Heath. The catalogue comprised 65 short-horn cows and some 36 month-old down-calving heifers and a pedigree Sussex bull was also disposed of. (A list of all the cows is given, with their names, price realised and new owner. Purchasers included Mr F.J.CORNWELL).

FIRST AID LECTURES – Commencing on October 6th, a course of lectures for women on First Aid will be held every alternate Tuesday in the Schools. The names of those wishing to join should be sent to Miss GRANTHAM (Commandant).

MISSION HALL ANNIVERSARY – The anniversary of the Barcombe Mission Hall was celebrated on Wednesday and at a special service in the afternoon Mr NOTMAN of Dr.Barnardo's Homes, preached. Tea was served at 5.30. and a special service followed in the evening

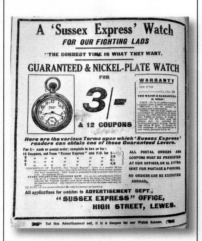

ABOVE: 'This advertisement for the 'Sussex Express Watch' encouraged readers to collect coupons to buy watches for "Our Fighting Lads," while increasing the circulation of the newspaper.

with Mr PARNELL of Hove, in the chair. Addresses were given by friends from Brighton and district, and also Mr NOTMAN. In the absence of the Secretary (Mr G.JONES) the annual report was read by Mr KNIBBS, showing credit balances on the General Sick and Sunday School funds. The musical portion of the service included a solo by Mr DOWNING of Newick, Mrs VERCOE presiding at the organ.

A DISPUTED VOTE – At the Lewes Revision Court on Monday, Mr GRAVE (Conservative Agent) raised the question of the validity of an occupier claim (service) by Henry BURNS of 'Woodside', Barcombe, on the ground that no rates had been paid in respect of the premises during the qualifying period. Mr H.TROWER (Assistant Overseer) stated that rates had not been paid during the qualifying period, as the property was returned as empty. Mr BURNS occupied a cottage on the property, and had acted as caretaker since the Rev. C.TOOGOOD gave up residence at 'Woodside'. Revising Barrister: 'Unfortunately the rates of the cottage are dependent on the rates of the house. I might regard it as a case of the rates being suspended. He added that the objection was good, although it was no fault of the man himself". After some discussion, the claim was allowed…

9th October - LOCAL PATRIOTISM - Small though it is, the village of Barcombe has made a noble response to the country's call. The following is a list of those connected with the Parish who have gone on service (some of them are already at the front) and shows also what clothing and money have been forthcoming: Regular Army: Charles Albert BRYANT, Thomas GANDER, Frederick KNIGHT, Sier MARKWICK, John TAPP, William WELLER, S. WALL, Major Frank WALKER, James EDWARDS, Harry EDWARDS. Royal Navy: Wilfred BATTEN, Francis Edward BOURDILLON, George BRYANT, William BURNS, Henry BURNS,

ABOVE: 'Don't Worry I'll Soon Be Back' – This comic postcard by Donald McGill reflects the initial optimism that it would 'All be over by Christmas.'

William FARRENDEN, Frederick FOSBURY, Frederick Wallace FOSBURY,

Charles David REYNOLDS, Frederick GREEN, Charles David REYNOLDS jnr., Harry STEVENS. Yeomanry: James DUDENEY, Arthur FLETCHER, Allan VERCOE. Territorials: David JAMES, H. BANKS, Ernest BARROW, Ben COLLINS, Frederick DEAKIN, Sidney LAKER, Albert RANN, Charles SAYERS. Public Schools' Brigade: Theodore Edmund BOURDILLON. 6th Cyclist Battalion Royal Sussex Regiment: W.W. GRANTHAM, John Fowke SINGLETON. Kitchener's Army: William BANKS, George BUCKWELL, William ARCHER, Leonard Hayward STEVENS, Archibald CROWHURST, William HATTON, Arthur MARKWICK, Bert TAPP, George STEVENS, William

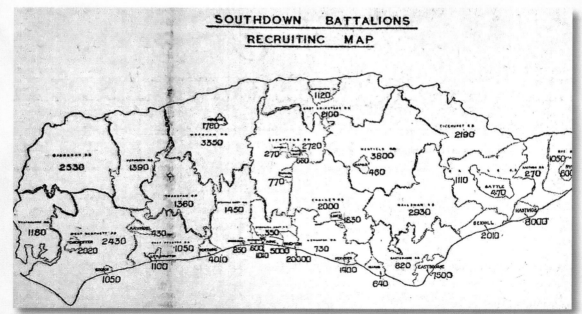

ABOVE: A rather indistinct Recruiting map published in the East Sussex News during December 1914, showing that 2,000 men had been recruited from Chailey R.D. and 1830 from Lewes for the new 'Southdown' Battalions.

ABOVE AND BELOW: These new recruits at Cooden Camp are still wearing their "civvies" as their uniforms had not yet arrived.

HAWKINS, George FORD, Cecil H. PECKHAM, Charles MARCHANT, Selby REED, Arthur EDWARDS, Frederick COX, Frederick KIRBY, Arthur FIRMINGER, Bernard PULLINGER, David WALL. Hospital Nurse: Mary BOURDILLON. The following articles have already been forwarded to the Countess of Chichester for soldiers and their dependants: Four dozen flannel shirts, 2½ dozen nightingales, 2 dozen pillow cases, 2 dozen oversleeves, 4 dozen aprons, 2 dozen calico shirts, 2 dozen caps, 2 dozen pairs of slippers, roller bandages. To date the total amount collected for the three War funds being run at Barcombe approximates £31.

SOUTHDOWNS AT COODEN – TRAINING IN FULL SWING – Now that the camp at Cooden has settled down to its regular routine and things have got shaken into their places, it will be possible to give a general survey of the whole of the activities which are proceeding at the camp, and to add a number of interesting details…[12]

The battalion now numbers 1,079 of all ranks. The men of the 'A,' 'B,' and 'C' Companies come mainly from Eastbourne, Horsham and Tunbridge Wells. Hastings and Bexhill furnishes the 'D' Company; and the remaining Companies come from Horsham, Worthing, Brighton, Bognor, Herstmonceux, etc. One of the men from Guildford rejoices in the name of Julius Caesar. Many of the men are married, and the average age of the single men is from 18 to 25 years…

THE DAY'S WORK – Drilling commences at seven o'clock in the morning, and continues for an hour; at 10.15 the men fall in again, and keep at it until 12.15, when they dismiss until 2.15, when drilling commences again, and goes on until four o'clock. After that the men are free to do as they please, but they have to all be in camp by 9.30, unless they have got a special pass…

WINTER QUARTERS – The uniforms for the men have not yet come to hand, but it is expected they will be forwarded in a short time. As it is, the men have got sufficient clothing for all their needs…

12 Cooden Camp, based around the Golf Club near Bexhill, was the training base for the 1st Southdown Battalion, raised by Lt.-Col. LOWTHER.

ABOVE: 'Major W.W.GRANTHAM, 6th Battalion, Royal Sussex Regiment, photographed by Elliott & Fry of 55 & 56 Baker Street, London (courtesy Dave Grantham).

being devoted for the purchase of cigarettes for the Royal Sussex Regiment. There was a good attendance, between 40 and 50 turning up for a capital evening's entertainment. Mr S.B.RICHARDS presided Mr J.S.REED of the Railway Inn is attending to the arrangements for the forwarding of the cigarettes for the troops, and without a doubt the efforts of the residents of Barcombe will be much appreciated by the "Tommies"[13] of the Sussex Regiment.

RECEPTION OF BELGIAN REFUGEES – It is being stated locally that although several of the residents of Barcombe and neighbourhood have informed the authorities of their willingness to give hospitality to Belgian refugees, the "willing hosts" are still awaiting developments after the lapse of weeks. In one particular instance, so it is said, an applicant for refugees was told about three weeks ago that a couple of these homeless Belgians would be sent along. A card had been filled up making the application official. But nothing further has been heard. Quite naturally, those who are anxious to extend hospitality as far as lies in their power to the poor folk from the stricken nation across the water, feel that the present is

The erection of the winter quarters for the men, consisting of three large buildings, is already in progress, and it is expected they will be complete in about six weeks' time.

16th October - FOOTBALL MATCH – Owing to the inclemency of the weather, the match between the Barcombe Cycling Club and the Barcombe Football Club (in aid of the Belgian Refugees' Fund), to have been played on Wednesday last, has been postponed until next Wednesday, the kick-off being timed for 2.45. Local feeling has risen to the occasion no less than 130 tickets having been sold.

SMOKING CONCERT – Last Saturday evening a smoking concert was held at the Railway Inn, Barcombe Mills, the proceeds £2.11s.6d.

---

13 *British soldiers had been known as "Tommies," or "Tommy Atkins" since 1815. The name became immortalised in Rudyard Kipling's poem Barrack Room Ballads, published in 1892. (www.bl.uk). See November 1915 for a verse of this poem.*

BELGIUM'S NEED.

EVERYONE MUST DO HIS PART.

Do you see the great procession
  Trailing through those grevious roads,
Weary, hungry, sad and footsore,
  Bowed beneath their piteous loads?

Mothers, fathers, children, grandams,
  Toiling, oh so wearily,
With a grim and awful patience
  Down the long road to the sea.

There to wait in countless thousands
  For a chance to board the boats,
Steamer, trawler, raft and collier,
  Anything, in fact, that floats.

For England stands across the water
  Holding out a helping hand
To a scared and hunted people
  Fleeing from their outraged land.

And she says to all her children
  " Take these strangers to your heart,
" Comfort them, and clothe and house them,
  " Everyone must do his part.

" Think what it would mean, my children,
  " If your England were stripped bare
" Of her homes, her wealth and beauty,
  " Everything she held most dear.

" If from her you had been driven,
  " Had been tortured, slain, abused,
" And you asked a friend for succour
  " Found that succour was refused.

" Open then your hearts, and purses,
  " Give, my children, then give more,
" To this brave and stricken people
  " Knocking at your England's door ! "

Blatchington.   B. H. POOLE.

ABOVE: 'Belgium's Need' – The refugee crisis expressed in poetry in the East Sussex News of 27th November 1914.

no time for delay in view of the large numbers of them who are in need of homes – at least for the time being.

23rd October - NEW CONSTABLES REBUKED – Sir, I fully endorse Mr WHITFELD's remark that those fine able-bodied men who presented themselves for enrolment in the police force on Tuesday "ought to be ashamed of themselves." We want such men in the Army. There are plenty of older men quite competent to carry out police duties intelligently and efficiently in these times.

FIRING AT NEWHAVEN – For the information of the public, the Chief Constable of East Sussex (Major LANG) notifies that there will probably be heavy gun practice at Newhaven Fort about forenoon on October 23rd, 24th, 26th, 27th and 28th.

WAR ITEMS - Mr W.W.GRANTHAM who holds the rank of Major in the 6th (Cyclist) Battalion Royal Sussex Regiment, appeared at the East Sussex Quarter Sessions on Tuesday, not in wig and gown, but khaki uniform, which is allowed in courts of law by order.

NATIONAL RELIEF FUND – For the purpose of collecting in the parish on behalf of the National Relief Fund, the Parish Council have appointed the following Committee with power to add to their number: Messrs. F.J.CORNWELL, T.N.LADE, R.RHODES, S.B.RICHARDS, G.HAWKINS and R.SPENCE. Barcombe is taking up the lead of other parishes in the arrangements made by the East Sussex County branch of the National Fund, and it is hoped there will be a liberal response to the appeal of the collectors.

ILLUSTRATED LECTURE – Mr F.MANTELL of Brighton, delivered an address on Wednesday evening at the Mission Hall, Barcombe, taking as his subject "The Great Invasion and the Price of Peace," a topic which Mr MANTELL handled with all the seriousness necessary in dealing with a matter of such grave import. The lecturer dealt with his subject in a bright and lucid manner, with that facile exposition of ideas which denotes that the speaker is master of his topic. Both the value and interest of the lecture were enhanced by the series of splendid views shown in illustration. Mr MANTELL was cordially thanked for his attendance.

FOREIGNER ARRESTED - Yesterday (Thursday) morning, about ten o'clock, a foreigner was taken into custody at Barcombe, apparently in accordance with the more stringent measures now being taken with regard to alien enemies, afterwards being conveyed to Lewes by the 10.21 train. It is understood that the man taken into charge yesterday had married into the family of a well-known local resident, and that he had been living in the neighbourhood for some considerable time, his place of residence, it is stated, being contiguous with the railway line which runs through the village. It appears he claims to be a native of Luxembourg, to have been naturalised in this country, but that he registered as a German upon the outbreak of war.

ABOVE: Cyclists vs. Footballers. A charity football match in aid of the Belgian Refugee Fund. Frederick SAUNDERS (back row, with moustache and striped jersey) was the only man in this group whose name appears on the parish war memorial. (Mike Green collection & ESRO).

VARIETY CONCERT

– There was a large and appreciative gathering at the Royal Oak, last Saturday evening, when a splendid evening's entertainment was provided by Mr Sidney LEE, of London, assisted by several other artistes. Mr LEE, who is well known to local folk, had arranged the concert with the object of devoting the proceeds the purchase of some "little luxuries" to be sent to those Barcombe men who are at present with the Colours. Mr LEE gave a conjuring exhibition, which did not fail greatly to interest the audience, and among others who helped to make the concert such a successful one were:- Mr S.LEIGHTON (London), mimic; Mr HOLLOWAY, Mr William BUNNEY, Mr H.HARRIETT, Mr HOLDEN and Miss Violet KING (patriotic songs). Mr BLAKER was at the piano.

FOOTBALL MATCH FOR REFUGEES' FUND

– The match between the Barcombe F.C. and the Barcombe Cycling Club (postponed from the previous week owing to the inclement weather) took place at the Barcombe Football Ground on Wednesday last, before a large attendance. Before the commencement of the contest there was a rendering of the National Anthem, in which the school children joined. The Cyclists had obtained assistance from Newick and Lewes, and the teams lined up as follows under Mr C.J.HOLLOWAY, who held the whistle: Barcombe F.C.: S.BLACKMAN, F.WALLS, J.PERKINS, W.HAYLER, R.DEAN, FOORD, The Rev. W.B.Y.LOVEBAND, S.COX,

DUDENEY, F.SAUNDERS and W.HOBDEN. Cyclists: J.URRY, H.STEVENSON, GODDEN, MEAD, J. STEVENS, SMITH, C.CLARK, E.RICHARDS, BAKER, E.KING and J.COTTINGHAM. Miss GRANTHAM kicked off. The cyclists had the advantage of ground at the start, but their opponents soon got to work, and pressed heavily. The score was opened for the Footballers by HAYLER, very shortly after the beginning of hostilities. A spirited reply was made by the Cyclists to the attacks made upon them, but they were forced to succumb to the "Regulars." Although the scoring was rather unequal, the spectators' interest was maintained right through. Final score: Barcombe F.C. 9 goals; Barcombe Cyclists 2 goals. COX (four goals), DUDENEY (three goals) and HAYLER (one goal) shared the honours of scoring for the Footballers, while CLARK and BAKER notched a point each for the Cyclists. The "gate" (to be placed to the Belgian Refugees' Fund) realised £5.0s.3d. and this amount is being sent to the proper quarter.

TO THE MEN OF SUSSEX.

Lord Kitchener has paid us the signal honour of asking for a second Southdown Battalion, which, together with the present Battalion, is to form part of his new Army.

Every Englishman must have followed with a just pride the glorious achievements of our men in the field.

There is no Sussex man who has not felt that his place should be by the side of those who are defending their country, their homes and their hearths against what must prove to be insuperable odds if every available man does not come forward now, and declare to the world the might of the British nation.

It is up to every one of you to prove your manhood.

There was a time when, miscalculating the strength of the enemy, you were justified in not answering the call to arms—you did not then fully appreciate the danger.

That time has passed.

To-day you can best protect your homes, your wives and your children by joining the ranks.

Let no man feel that he is not wanted. It is his bounden duty to make any sacrifice—no matter how great—to prevent the efforts of those who have already endured untold hardships from being fruitless and vain.

I therefore call upon every man with red blood in his veins to join the Second Southdown Battalion of the Royal Sussex Regiment.

You will not be separated!
Together (in your own county) you will train!
Together you will fight!
Together you will die if needs be, but
Together, pray God, you may return!

CLAUDE LOWTHER,
Lieut.-Colonel Southdown Battalion,
Royal Sussex Regiment.

Apply nearest Recruiting Office for enrolment in the Second Southdown Battalion, or to Lieut.-Col. LOWTHER, Orderly Room, Cooden Camp, Bexhill.

ABOVE: An appeal by Lt.-Col. Claude LOWTHER for volunteers to form a second Southdown (Pals) Battalion of the Royal Sussex Regt. for Lord Kitchener's "New Army." *East Sussex News*, 13th November 1914.

BARCOMBE MAN MISSING – Private Fred KNIGHT, R.A.M.C., of Spithurst, is reported missing as from August 23rd.

30th October - SUSSEX MEN ON THE "SUPERB" – List of men serving on board the H.M.S. "Superb" First Battle Squadron, Grand Fleet. Names in the 'Executive Department', include; BATTEN, R.M.A., Barcombe.

6th November - NATIONAL RESERVISTS - Nine Barcombe men have responded to the "calling up" of the National Reservists and have reported themselves at Lewes for the duties required of them.

RED CROSS NURSERY – Each evening this week two Red Cross nurses from Barcombe have been in attendance at Chailey Union in anticipation of the possible reception of forty wounded soldiers in the district.[14]

HOCKEY CLUB – The first practice match of the Hockey Club recently formed by Mrs MUSGRAVE BROOKSBANK, will take place on Wednesday next at the ground of the Barcombe Football Club. A gratifying response has been made to the efforts of Mrs BROOKSBANK, the membership now being 38.

13th November - HUNTING NEWS – The Southdown Foxhounds will meet – Monday November 16th – Barcombe Village.

NO LIGHT - Nellie FORDHAM of Barcombe was charged at the Lewes Petty Sessions on Tuesday before Mr F.B. WHITFIELD and other magistrates with failing to have a lighted lamp on a bicycle. She was riding at Barcombe at 7.30 a.m. on November 3rd. Defendant pleaded guilty and a fine of 1s. was made.

FOOTBALL MATCH – The result of last Saturday's match between Barcombe F.C. and Ballard's Brewery (Lewes) was: Barcombe 6 goals to nil.

RELIEF FUND CONCERT – Next Wednesday, November 18th, a concert will be held at

---

14 *The Chailey Union Workhouse buildings are situated on the corner beyond the current Chailey Secondary School, where Mill Lane joins Honeypot Lane. In 1914 the buildings were home to the poor or infirm from the parishes making up the Lewes Poor Law Union, including Barcombe. The buildings still are still standing, now converted to private houses.*

the Schoolroom, Barcombe, by kind permission of the Managers, the proceeds to be devoted to the Prince of Wales' Relief Fund. The concert has been arranged by the Parish Council. Doors will be open at seven o'clock for 7.30: carriages at ten o'clock. Tickets may be obtained from either of the following: Mrs HOLLOWAY, Post Office; Messrs R. RHODES, S.B.RICHARDS, A.HOLDEN, or W.J.BUNNEY (Hon. Secretary).

COLLECTIONS FOR SOLDIERS - Two special funds are being run locally in order to provide "luxuries" for soldiers who are on service and a splendid response is being made to the endeavours of those whose energies are responsible for the work. Miss WALKER of The Grange, Barcombe is inviting a subscription of 1d from all the local people with the object of sending a present of tobacco to soldiers of the Royal Sussex Regiment for Christmas. Mrs SPELLER of Barcombe Place Cottage is getting up a subscription to provide Christmas puddings for the Territorials from Lewes and district who are on duty at Dover. Donations will be welcomed at the places named.

20th November - RELIEF FUND AT BARCOMBE – Last Wednesday evening's concert at the Schoolroom, Barcombe in aid of the Prince of Wales' National Relief Fund, has to be written down

as a great success. Although disappointment was caused to many, yet it is with a feeling of pleasure one notes that the response was so hearty, and so large was the number of those who desired to be present that not a few of them were, unfortunately, unable to gain admittance.

The entertainment – a varied one – arranged by Barcombe Parish Council, was carried out by a number of well-known artistes who gave their services voluntarily. Mr E.BUNNEY presided, and said that he had to convey to those gathered there the regrets of Major GRANTHAM for inability to be with them owing to his being with His Majesty's Forces; also the apologies of Mr S.REED, Vice-Chairman of the Council, for his unavoidable absence. On the proposition of the Chairman, a cordial vote of thanks was passed to Lady GRANTHAM, who was present with Miss GRANTHAM, for her gift of flowers and flags – the hall was decorated with pleasing effect – and also to the artistes who had so generously come to their assistance for what was such a deserving cause.

The best tribute that can be paid the artistes individually is to say that all of them performed their part with ability and in a manner which won the warm appreciation of the audience. Many encores were called for and given. The artistes were: Miss Bessie WOODE. Miss HOLLOWAY, Miss KAY, Miss F.RHODES

OFFICIAL PHOTOGRAPH, (COPYRIGHT). ISSUED BY THE CORPORATION OF BRIGHTON WITH THE ASSISTANCE OF THE MILITARY AUTHORITIES.   4.   THE DOME.   A. H. FRY, PHOTO, BRIGHTON.

ABOVE: The Dome, Brighton Pavilion, converted for use as a Military Hospital for Indian troops. (Official Photograph by A.H. Fry, issued by the Corporation of Brighton).

and Miss Lily WELLER, Mrs F.BALLARD and Miss BURROWS; Messrs. A.ANDREWS, W.J.BUNNEY, H.R.DEAN, A.HOLDEN, W.HARRIOTT, C.KENT, Stuart St. John SMITH, and Frank TAYLOR.

27th November - WOUNDED INDIANS AT BRIGHTON

– Pavilion as Hospital – The people of Brighton have been honoured by the selection of their historic Royal Pavilion as a hospital for Indian soldiers wounded in the War. It is understood that this arrangement has been made in accordance with the special wishes of the King, and no doubt the Indians will feel proud to occupy the building which has so many Royal associations... Within the apartments rows of hospital beds were arranged, the neat simplicity of which contrasted with the vivid colouring of Oriental splendour above and around. The greatest metamorphosis, perhaps, is at the Dome, the large area known to concert-goers and ceremonial public functions. Under its new aspect the place looks capable of accommodating a very large number of beds. The big Corn Exchange adjoining has also been prepared for any emergency.

It is understood that the King really wanted to make provision for as many Indian wounded as possible, and the Authorities believe that so far as existing arrangements go they will be equal to the treatment of 2,000 cases.

The grounds, through which at ordinary times there is a public right of way, are to be closed. Complete quietness will be preserved, and every precaution taken to prevent inquisitive people prying into the grounds when the soldiers are able to rest outside on the exquisite carved veranda, which runs along the Eastern Front of the main building.

WAR ITEMS – Over 500 men enlisted last week at the various recruiting depots in Sussex. This number was some 400 less than the previous week, but the general total for the month will be most satisfactory.

Arrangements are being made for transference of the Brighton Workhouse and Infirmary inmates to other homes, so that the Workhouse and Infirmaries can be utilised for the reception of wounded Indian soldiers. The Workhouse and Infirmaries have between them from 1,500 to 2,000 beds.

RELIEF FUND PROCEEDS – The net amount realised for the concert last Wednesday week – arranged by the Barcombe Parish Council, and held in the Schoolroom - was £8.13.6d., and this sum has been sent on to the proper quarter.

HOCKEY MATCH – A match took place at the Barcombe F.C. ground on Wednesday last, between the teams chosen by Miss BURDER and Miss R.BROOKSBANK. The play was pretty even throughout, and resulted in 3 goals each. Mr C.HOLLOWAY, Miss N.DEAN, and the Rev. George SALMON scored one goal each for Miss BURDER's side; their opponents' scorers being Miss R.HARMAN (1), and the Rev. W.LOVEBAND (2). The teams were: Miss BURDER's: Mrs BALLARD, COWDREY and HOLDEN; Misses N.DEAN, J.HOBDEN and D.SPELLER; Messrs. HOLLOWAY, CORNWELL and Rev. G.SALMON. Miss R.BROOKSBANK: Mrs BROOKSBANK and SINCLAIR; Misses HEWITT, WATSON and R.HARMAN; Messrs. SPENCE and DEAN; and the Rev. W.G.LOVEBAND…

FOOTBALL MEETING – A special general meeting of the Barcombe F.C. was held last (Thursday) evening, among those present being: The Rev. W.B.Y.LOVEBAND and Messrs. D.DEAN, E.STEVENS, T.HENTY, C.HOLLOWAY, A.E.SINCLAIR, S.HENTY, W.HOBDEN, J. PERKINS (captain) and G. BODLE (secretary). Mr C.HOLLOWAY took the chair. The meeting was called to see if the Club should continue to run, as for the last few weeks men have been hard to find. – The Chairman said no doubt the fact was that the men were doing a greater work for their King and country, but he thought they might try to arrange two matches a month, as they did not want football to pass right away. There were several young fellows who were unable to answer the great call – The Rev. LOVEBAND proposed, and it was seconded by Mr PERKINS, that a trial should be given, and matches have been arranged as follows:- Ballard's Brewery, at Barcombe on the 5th of December; and York Place School on the 19th, at Barcombe. Newick had written trying to arrange a Charity match with the Barcombe Club, but they were unable to accept. – Mr A.SINCLAIR asked the Football Club to support him in arranging a comic football match at the end of January. – Mr BODLE (secretary of the Club) proposed that they support him in every way. – This was seconded by Mt PERKINS, and carried.

IF THE GERMANS COME – INSTRUCTIONS TO FARMERS – Mr A.K.BURTENSHAW, on taking the rostrum at the Hailsham Cattle Market on Wednesday morning, said that in the event of invasion farmers would be instructed to get their cattle over a line north of Uckfield, Heathfield and Hawkhurst, and that the main roads would not be used, only by-roads. All motor-cars and motor-cycles were to be taken there, and all farm carts and wagons were to be destroyed. Any cattle, horses or swine that were unable to be removed were to be destroyed and rendered unfit for consumption by the enemy.

4th December - Mr FRANCIS JOHN CORNWELL, AT CRINK HOUSE – Mr Francis J.CORNWELL occupies a foremost place amongst farmers of the county. He is interested in two concerns; Messrs. J.CORNWELL & Son, and Messrs. CORNWEL & LADE. For purposes of this article, his connection with the first-named firm is only dealt with. In this case the partners are sisters, though the trade name is that of "Cornwell & Son." The sisters mentioned live at 'Hayes Farm' with their mother, who was 90 last birthday.

ABOVE: Francis J. CORNWELL and sons, Burton (13) and Luther (17), photographed c.1912 (courtesy the Cornwell family).

societies, among them being the National Farmers' Union and the Sussex Dairy Farmers' Association. It has also to be noted here that he is on the Chailey Rural District Council, Barcombe Parish Council and Lewes Board of Guardians. Mr CORNWELL has two sons, the elder (Luther) assists in the business, taking charge of the cabbage plants and calf rearing. He has been connected with Red Cross work for some time, and is expecting to leave home shortly to take up duties in that sphere.

Three farms are kept going; 'Hayes' and 'Place Farms,' adjacent to each other and 'Scovells Farm' between Barcombe and Spithurst... The soil is of three distinct varieties. That at Barcombe Mills is deep loam. As soon as the rising ground is reached flints and gravel are found, in some places there being only a thin covering of soil… The

Mr CORNWELL, a tallish man, possessing grey-brown moustache and dark hair, was born at Ditton, Kent, just over half a century ago. His father, the late Mr John CORNWELL, came to 'Chamberlain's Farm,' Ringmer, in the year 1877, and to Barcombe Mills in 1892. From that time the business has been carried on under its present title.

As may be expected, Mr CORNWELL is a member of various farming

ABOVE: Francis J. CORNWELL (left) with his four sisters and brother (courtesy Jo Newman). (Courtesy the Cornwell family).

soil at 'Scovells' is very stiff and "clayey." The seasons for the past three years have been disastrous for such soils… Although the War has made a great shortage of labour, things have gone fairly well up to the present. It is felt however, that any further call will seriously hamper the business.

CRINK HOUSE – A comparatively modern structure, having been built 14 or 15 years ago to the order of the later Sir William GRANTHAM, to whose family it now belongs… It faces Brighton, and is situated on some high land, which rises towards Barcombe village from Barcombe Mills railway station…

Before the construction of the railway, the field opposite was dug practically all over to obtain flints for road making. The field adjacent is a hunting ground for archaeologists in search of arrow heads, etc.

WOMEN'S WORKING CLASS – This Class, for the making of garments for soldiers, has been restarted at Barcombe Place, the time being three o'clock on Friday afternoon.

CYCLING CLUB MEETING – A meeting of the Committee of the Barcombe Cycling Club took place at the Mission Room on Tuesday last, when there were present: Messrs. R.GRIERSON (captain), T.HENTY (vice-captain), A.SINCLAIR (hon. secretary), A.HENTY,

ABOVE: 'Crink House,' home to F.J.CORNWELL, his wife Esther and two sons (courtesy Roger Newman).

B.GOLDSMITH, A.OSMOND, and A.STEVENS. It was decided to hold a whist drive on January 6th in aid of the Belgian Relief Fund, and a fancy dress football match on the 27th of the same month on behalf of the British Red Cross work…

"LOST" SOLDIER SAFE – HAPPY SURPRISE FOR BARCOMBE PARENTS – On the 23rd of last August, Private Frederick KNIGHT (belonging to the Royal Army Medical Corps), of Barcombe, was officially reported as missing. The receipt of this news occasioning great distress

RIGHT: Frederick KNIGHT, in the uniform of the Royal Army Medical Corps.

to his parents, Mr & Mrs Alfred KNIGHT, who live at Mount Pleasant, Barcombe.

It is easy to imagine with what joy his people have now heard – after an interval of more than three months' silence, which of course, confirmed the worst fears set up by the information that he was "missing" – that he is still alive. A postcard has been received from him stating that he is slightly wounded, and is a prisoner of war in Germany. He adds the comforting message that he is being well treated, but he would like to have some money so that he might purchase cigarettes…

11th December - HUMOUR ON THE BENCH

– Mr W.W.GRANTHAM (who appeared in khaki uniform) prosecuted, and having explained that the prisoner (Reginald PITT) stole his fellow workman (Harry REED)'s boots, the Judge remarked that it was as about as mean a thing a man could do.

Pleading for leniency, accused said; "I might mention that I have very good prospects now." His Lordship – I am not so sure about that (Laughter).

Prisoner – I mean in the way of employment. His Lordship – You say you want to join the Army? Prisoner – Yes, I should like to. His Lordship – I am afraid your zeal for your country's good has come rather too late in the day. Prisoner – I have got time yet, your lordship. His Lordship – I am afraid you will get time (Laughter).

A Soldier of the KING.

AFTER the War every man who has served will command his Country's gratitude. He will be looked up to and *respected* because he answered his country's call.

The Regiments at the Front are covering themselves with Glory.

Field-Marshal Sir John French wrote in an Order of the day,

"It is an Honour to belong to such an Army."

Every fit man from 19 to 38 is eligible for this great honour. Friends can join in a body, and serve together in the same regiment.

Rapid Promotion.

There is rapid promotion for intelligence and zeal. Hundreds who enlisted as private soldiers have already become officers because of their merits and courage, and thousands have reached non-commissioned rank.

Enlist To-day.

At any Post Office you can obtain the address of the nearest Recruiting Office. **Enter your name to-day on the Nation's Roll of Honour and do your part.**

GOD SAVE THE KING.

ABOVE: 'A SOLDIER OF THE KING.' A recruiting notice for "every fit man from 19 to 38."

Sentence was then passed (eight months' hard labour).

RECTOR'S ILLNESS

– Shortly before the time for the commencement of the sermon at St.Mary's, last Sunday morning, the Rector Rev. Prebendary SALMON was suddenly taken ill. He collapsed into the arms of the curate, Rev. W.B.LOVEBAND, who at once called for help, the sidesmen rendering assistance. After a rest the reverend gentleman recovered somewhat and was able to deliver his sermon while seated in a chair. The Rector has kept in the house during the past week, but is said to be considerably improved.

SPECIAL CONSTABLES

– Another batch for Lewes District – Barcombe: William COTTINGTON, William Thomas DIPLOCK, Herbert GRIST, James REED, Henry John SPELLER, Douglas Goldie CROCKET, Sidney Beard RICHARDS, and Archibald Ernest BLAKER.

18th December - SUSSEX FARMERS AT HOME

– Mr HART VERCOE AT BANKS FARM - He is a West Countryman, who came to Sussex about seven years ago. During this period he has established himself in a strong

N.C.O's and MEN who have won the VICTORIA CROSS

Battery-Serjt.-Major *(now Second-Lieut.)* G. T. DORRELL, "L" Battery, Royal Horse Artillery.
Serjeant D. NELSON *(now Second-Lieutenant)*, "L" Battery, Royal Horse Artillery.
Corporal C. E. GARFORTH, 15th (The King's) Hussars.
Bombardier E. G. HARLOCK *(now Sergeant)*, 113th Battery, Royal Field Artillery.
Lance-Corporal C. A. JARVIS, 57th Field Company, Royal Engineers.
Lance-Corporal W. FULLER, 2nd Battalion, Welsh Regiment.
Lance-Corporal F. W. HOLMES, 2nd Battalion (The King's Own) Yorkshire Light Infantry.
Private S. F. GODLEY, 4th Battalion, Royal Fusiliers.
Private G. WILSON, 2nd Battalion, Highland Light Infantry.
Driver J. H. C. DRAIN, 37th Battery, Royal Field Artillery.
Driver F. LUKE, 37th Battery, Royal Field Artillery.

There is room for your name on this Roll of Honour.

THESE HEROES would never have won the VICTORIA CROSS by staying away from the RECRUITING OFFICE. They enlisted for their Country's sake, and fought as only brave men do.

Is *your* name to be known from one end of the world to the other as one of the Empire's *bravest* sons?

ENLIST TO-DAY.

The more men we have, the sooner the war will end.

At any Post Office you can obtain the address of the nearest Recruiting Office. Enter *your* name to-day on the Nation's Roll of Honour, and do *your* part.

GOD SAVE THE KING.

ABOVE: 'Victoria Crosses for N.C.O.s and men.' Another enticement to enlist, but the notice does not mention how many of these medals were award posthumously.

ABOVE Banks Farm c.1906. Photographed from the lawn with Alan VERCOE seated, cricket bat in hand.

position as one of the leading farmers of the county.

Mr VERCOE devotes most of his time to sheep farming and grazing cattle, having quite recently disposed of his herd of dairy cows in order that he might have more time to give to the other branch mentioned. The farm consists of 230 acres, of which approximately 120 acres are under grass, the remainder, about 110 acres, being arable...

Ten hands are employed on the farm. Until recently one of Mr VERCOE's sons, the eldest, Allan, 19 years of age, supervised a part of the work, but he is now with the Sussex Yeomanry, training for foreign service, his place having been taken by another son of 16, who was at Smithfield last week in charge of the Sussex steer which in a very strong class won honours... Mr VERCOE has had considerable success with the showing of roots, he having obtained

two first and two seconds in four years at the Barcombe Agricultural Show, which, by the way, has not been held this year, owing to the War; thus showing how a war, involving millions of men, and carried on on such a gigantic scale that the mind can hardly comprehend, if it does at all, its mighty proportions, affects

ABOVE Mr Hart VERCOE of Banks Farm,

the agricultural routine of even a remote village in an English county away from the scene of hostilities.

Many prizes have come the way of the tenant of Banks Farm...

BANKS HOUSE – Mr VERCOE's landlord is Major W.W.GRANTHAM. 'Banks House' is of comparatively modern birth and design, although it has about it the dignified, venerable atmosphere of an English country home. As is the case with 'Crink House,' it possesses a somewhat antique fireplace. On each side of the grate are two rounded pillars of solid teak, about 4½ inches in diameter (said to have come from an old ship), with a square base... The pillars are crudely decorated. The same kind of adornment is also seen above the mantelpiece, this latter being of stout wood, which harmonises both in strength and colour with the supporting columns. The house is situated in a commanding position, which gives an extensive view of the countryside. From the lawn Crowborough (about ten miles away) can be discerned, set on its exalted height, while from the front of the house, on a clear day, the view stretches as far as the coast. When the weather is particularly fine one may, with the aid of glasses, see the little steaks of smoke from ships outside Seaford and Newhaven...

SLATE CLUB – Met last Monday evening at The Reading Room. It was reported that the membership for the year had been 121. The outgoings, including sick benefit, etc., amounted to £59.6s.8d., and there was a share out of 19s.3½d. per member. Subscribers re-joined the same night to the number of 92, Mr J.STANDING being re-elected secretary.

MORE RECRUITS – As has been the case with villages generally, throughout the

RIGHT: Floods at Barcombe Mills – A horse pulls a waggon along the regularly flooded Barcombe Mills Road.

length and breadth of Sussex, Barcombe has worthily responded to the country's call and this week more men have left for service. Luther CORNWELL, the son of Mr F.J. CORNWELL of Crink House, has gone away as a member of the Army Medical Corps, while the Army Veterinary Corps has claimed A.COLLINS, who went from Barcombe on Monday, and E.JONES departed from the village yesterday (Thursday). It is interesting to note that both COLLINS and JONES were called up for service as the result of their names having been given on documents sent out by the Government a few weeks ago, so that householders could voluntarily fill in particulars as to those who were prepared to take up duty if required to do so.

ABOVE 'Is Your Name on the Roll?' Another persuasive recruiting notice.

THE FLOODS – The recent heavy rains have caused considerable flooding in the district, and at Barcombe Mills an extensive area is under water. The road from the Station to the Mills presented some unusual scenes on Monday, there being several feet of water over the highway. Despite the unpleasant conditions, drivers of vehicles traversed the road, and the Southdown Foxhounds, which were meeting in the locality, and had to pass that way. At least the riders, and some of the hounds braved the elements, but two or three of the carriages funked the water, and had to be "left till called for." A number of Artillerymen out for exercise chose this particular route, and had the experience of riding their steeds through a miniature river. For miles around the fields were under water, and the course of the River Ouse was quite indiscernible. "Alight at Barcombe Mills for boating" was the jocular remark of an engine driver to a fellow railway employee as the train pulled up in the station. But no one seemed eager to accept the invitation.

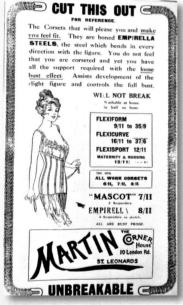

ABOVE: Fashionable corsets of 1914.

CHEQUE FOR BELGIAN FUND

– During the course of a speech at the opening of a sale of work at the Lewes Unitarian Chapel on Tuesday last the Mayor (Councillor T.G.ROBERTS), in expressing thanks for the response made to his appeals for contributions to the various relief funds, remarked that he had a few days before received a cheque for twenty guineas from Mr J.BURDER.

ABOVE AND BELOW: 'Advertisements for Christmas gifts. The apparently modern term "Xmas" had been in use since at least the mid-18th century.

GIRLS' FRIENDLY SOCIETY – At the Barcombe Reading Room on Wednesday afternoon the annual Sale of Work was held of the local Branch of the Girls' Friendly Society, of which Miss SALMON is hon. secretary. The proceeds of this Sale go to the Holiday Fund. There was a fair attendance of visitors, who made purchases from the variety of goods offered, and it is expected that the net receipts will come up to anticipation.

MOTOR VEHICLES – A census of motor vehicles of all types in the United Kingdom prepared by "The Car," shows that, compared with a year ago, there has been an increase of 111,695.

25th December - STATION INN SLATE CLUB – The annual meeting was held last Friday evening at the Station Inn, when a statement of accounts was presented for the twelve months ending December 15th. The balance brought forward from last year was 1s.5d; contributions came to £57.17s.10d. and the interest to £1.1s.10d., making a total amount of £59.1s.1d. The expenditure was £25.7s.7d. thus leaving a sum of £33.13s.6d. for distribution. 39 members each received 17s.3d., a balance of nine pence remaining. Most of the members re-joined for the coming year at a further meeting on Tuesday night.

LEFT: 'The War and the Ford Car.' Cars were becoming more affordable and easier to drive, this advertisement claims that; "Anyone can learn to drive in half-an-hour." Cars like this soon began to replace the pony and trap as the popular form of transport for the middle classes.

PRINCESS MARY'S CHRISTMAS GIFT TIN, 1914

A decorative brass tin was sent by the Princess Mary Fund to members of the British, Colonial and Indian Armed Forces for Christmas 1914. The tins contained a small Christmas card, a picture of the princess and various items including tobacco, confectionary, spices, pencils, depending on the nationality of the recipient.

The idea was the initiative of Princess Mary, the 17-year-old daughter of King George V and Queen Mary. Princess Mary organised a public appeal to raise funds so that "every Sailor afloat and every Soldier at the front" would receive a Christmas present.

Above: A Gift for the Troops – A 'Princess Mary Tin' (courtesy Roy Hunnisett).

Following strong public support £162,591 was raised, and the eligibility for the gift was widened to include every person "wearing the King's uniform on Christmas Day 1914" (about 2,620,019 servicemen and women). Due to the large number of people who were to receive

the gift they were distributed in three classes:

Class A: (received the gift on or near Christmas Day) - the Navy, troops and nurses at the Front in France, the wounded in hospitals, men on leave, prisoners (for whom the gift was reserved) and the widows or parents of those who had been killed.

Classes B & C: (received the gift during January 1915, with a "Happy New Year" card replacing the Christmas card) - all British, Colonial and Indian troops serving outside the British Isles, who were not provided for in Class A, and all troops in the British Isles.

ABOVE: 1915 – A embroidered silk postcard from France. Letters & postcards were the only way that servicemen and women could communicate with their family and friends at home. Originally hand-stitched by women in France and Belgium, these cards were later machine-embroidered, providing a novelty keepsake and a much-needed income for the civilian producers.

1st January - STORM DAMAGE AT BARCOMBE – Last Monday night's storm over such a large area wrought havoc in city and village. Considerable damage was done in the Barcombe Parish, among other things to suffer being some fine trees which had attained practically historical renown in the district. About 40 trees altogether were either blown down or injured in the neighbourhood. In the churchyard both elm and

RIGHT: 'On War Service 1915' Badge – These badges were worn by male munitions workers to make it clear that they were not shirking military service. This became important during the white feather campaign, when men in civilian clothes were presented with a white feather as a symbol of cowardice.

yew trees – veritable local "landmarks" – were made to suffer badly. One tree was uprooted bodily, in its upheaval pulling up the surrounding ground with its roots, and thereby disturbing

the gravestones. This tree of course fell completely down, and is now being dismembered. Similar damage was sustained by other stately specimens, both in the churchyard and elsewhere.

The Mission Hall was also affected. The structure, of galvanised iron, rests upon a brick foundation which comes above ground. Owing to the force of the gale, the building was moved about eight inches from its original position on the foundation, so that one side, the "ground-line" of the structure has moved to the edge of the brickwork, instead of "lying in" some distance. Temporary support has been provided by means of wooden props until repairs are made and the weakness consequent on the storm is remedied. In addition to the damage already mentioned, there was more than one minor mishap in the form of dislodged trees, etc.

BARCOMBE MAN IN FRANCE - "LIKE A HOLIDAY" – Mr A. COLLINS[1] who left Barcombe on December 14th for service in the Army Veterinary Corps has written home to his wife informing her that he is getting along nicely at the Veterinary Hospital of the Expeditionary Force "somewhere in France". He goes on to remark that is it "just like a holiday" and he can offer his recommendation

---

1 Herbert Abraham COLLINS of 'Place Cottage' was later killed in action (For his biography, see vol. 2).

to others to join that corps whose merciful duty it is to attend to the suffering of the horses injured at the Front. His communication home was received on Wednesday last and the writer makes reference to his surroundings and experiences at Christmas at the base in contrast with what they would have been in faraway Barcombe village.

ABOVE Private A. COLLINS, Royal Army Veterinary Corps.

CYCLING ACCIDENT

– While cycling along the Offham-road into Lewes on Saturday evening, Wallace KING, aged 16 of 'Thatched Cottage,' Barcombe, had an unpleasant experience. Approaching the Wallands (Lewes), he appears to have lost control of his machine, with the result that he crashed into a wall. He sustained a badly lacerated upper lip and cut nose, and also suffered considerably from shock. KING was taken to the Lewes Victoria Hospital, where he was detained.

ABOVE: Barcombe Mission Hall or "Tin Chapel," photographed by Bliss & Co. of Lewes (Mike Green collection).

HOCKEY MATCH – It says much for the enthusiasm of local hockey players that, despite the uncertainty of the weather conditions – which strongly indicated "stormy times"- a match took place on Wednesday afternoon last at Barcombe. The sides were represented by the teams of Mr Victor BOURDILLON and Mr BROOKSBANK, and lined up as follows:-
Mr V.BOURDILLON, Mr W.DEAN, the Rev. T.W.LOVEBAND, the Rev. George SALMON, Miss BROOKSBANK, Miss CURTMORE, Miss HARMAN, and Miss HOBDEN. Mr BROOKSBANK, Mr CURTMORE, Mr WATSON, Mrs BALLARD, Miss DEAN, Mrs HOLDER, and Mrs SINCLAIR. Miss Violet WALKER lent her services as referee. The result was BOURDILLONs, 8 goals;

BROOKSBANKs 4 goals.

SOLDIERS' THANKS FOR PUDDINGS – Mrs SPELLER of 'Place Cottage' collected a total sum of £7.11s.6d. towards her fund for the provision of Christmas puddings for troops, and she wishes to tender thanks to all those who generously contributed. As a result of the donations received, a large number of puddings were forwarded, principally to the members of the Lewes Company of the Royal Garrison Artillery. Some of the gifts were sent to Dover, while others reached France. Mrs SPELLER has received several letters of thanks, one of them being from Major GRANTHAM, on behalf of the men of the 6th Cyclist Battalion of the Royal Sussex Regiment, and one other from Captain Frank LOUD, of the Lewes Company Royal Garrison Artillery, who wrote: "Dear Mrs SPELLER – Puddings

LEFT: Officers of the Cyclists Battalion, R.S.R. relax around an estate gate, with their commanding officer Major GRANTHAM centre stage.

Lady GRANTHAM on the occasion of the annual Christmas treat. The children were entertained at the Garage in the afternoon, and afterwards tea was provided at Barcombe Place. About 120 were present, a most enjoyable time being spent. The boys delivered safely Christmas Eve. I think they were also safely delivered on Christmas Day, and were pronounced remarkably good by everyone. One for the officers is being kept for a day or two, as there was already one 'going' for them. On behalf of the whole Company. I want to thank you very much for the trouble you have taken in making the puddings, and to all who helped to provide us with such a nice Christmas present. With best wishes for the New Year, and many thanks, yours truly, F.LOUD."

8th January - CHRISTMAS TREAT – On Monday the younger folk of Barcombe received the hospitality of

RIGHT: The 'Ancient Yew Tree' in St. Mary's churchyard, painted by Muriel, youngest daughter of the late Sir William & Lady Emma GRANTHAM. This hallowed spot in front of the church was eventually selected as the most suitable location for the parish war memorial (the tree however is not mentioned in the Domesday Book). (ESRO: WI 112/1/1, p.48).

St. Mary's Churchyard.
THE ANCIENT YEW TREE 1906

and girls were in charge of the school teachers. The gathering broke up at six o'clock.

INJURED WHILE RABBIT HUNTING – While rabbiting with a company of friends at Newick Park on Wednesday morning, a nasty accident was sustained by Mr Harry FUNNELL of the Forge. Mr FUNNELL was hurrying along "on the scent," when his foot was caught by the protruding root or stump of a tree, causing him to fall heavily on the ground. It was at first feared that the ankle was broken, but upon examination by Dr MACKWOOD it was found that the injury was a bad sprain. Mr FUNNELL has, of course, to remain indoors for the present, but is reported to be progressing satisfactorily.

MENTIONED IN DOMESDAY BOOK – There is some belief locally that the ancient yew tree which was blown down in last week's storm is of such historic birth that it may be claimed that to it belonged the romantic distinction of being the tree mentioned in local records contained in the great classical masterpiece of William the Conqueror – Domesday Book. Be that as it may, the tree was certainly very old. Upon being dismembered it was found that the inside was cankered, and had been the sealed vault of more than one owl's nest.

VICTORIAN FANTASY PERFORMED - There were many pretty scenes at the Barcombe Place Motor House on Tuesday, when a concert was held in aid of the Barcombe detachment of the Red Cross Society, of which Miss Muriel GRANTHAM is quartermaster. Great pleasure resulted from the well-acted performance of "Iris of the Rainbow," described as an Early Victorian fantasy. All those who took part were juveniles, with the exception of Mr Lewis RICHARDS, who lent his services to complete the characters[2].

CONCERT AT BARCOMBE – An enjoyable evening was passed at the Balneath Garage last Saturday evening, when, organised by Mrs W.W.GRANTHAM, a long and pleasure-giving programme was presented for the delectation of local residents…

WHIST DRIVE – Organised by the Barcombe Cycling Club in aid of the Belgian Refugees' Fund, a very successful whist drive was held at the Garage on Wednesday evening. There were 27 tables. The various prizes had been given by Mrs WELLS, Miss A.VERRALL, Mr MUGRIDGE, and the Cycling Club… The Rev. George SALMON caused amusement when, referring to the large number present and the consequent lack of room, he said that although during the evening he had felt as though he were "packed like a sardine," yet he was able all the time to assure himself that he was really a salmon!

ABOVE: James Selby REED, landlord of the 'Station Inn' (later known as the 'Angler's Rest'), Barcombe Mills. This photograph comes from an album taken to Canada in 1910 by Mr REED's eldest daughter Marion WOOTTON when she emigrated with her husband Allen and three young sons (courtesy the great granddaughters of James S.REED).

15th January - OLDEST LICENSED VICTUALLER - FUNERAL OF Mr SELBY REED, BARCOMBE MILLS – A veteran resident of Barcombe Mills has passed away in the person of Mr James Selby REED, who had the reputation of being the oldest licensed victualler in the county. Eighty-six years of age, the deceased took over the tenancy of the Station Inn when first the house was opened in 1859 and he remained there until his death. Mr REED had been in failing health for

2   *A list of names of the performers and their characters is given in the original article, but is omitted here.*

some time and his demise late on Thursday night was not unexpected.

Deceased was a life-long resident of the parish and hand only absented himself from the district for a few days at a time during the whole of that long period. He had taken an active part in parochial affairs. He became a member of the Parish Council at its inception in 1895, and for many years he had filled the position of Vice-Chairman. Mr REED also held the office of senior overseer of the parish, a post which becomes vacant by his death. From 1864 to 1895 deceased was one of the churchwardens at St. Mary's Church, his colleague for many years being the late George GRANTHAM.

Mr REED was a familiar figure to the many visitors who find their way to picturesque Barcombe Mills during the summer months, and members of the Brighton Anglers Association had in him a genial friend. When enjoying their sport on the bank of the Ouse at Barcombe Mills they made the Station Inn their headquarters, and as a mark of their esteem for the worthy host they presented him on his 86th birthday in May last, with a silver mounted walking stick, suitably inscribed.

Deceased's father was a tenant of the late Lord LIVERPOOL, and when in the year 1850 his lordship passed away, Mr REED attended the funeral, and he used to recall how on that occasion there were about forty of the followers attired in the old Sussex smock frocks.

THE FUNERAL – The funeral took place at St.Mary's Churchyard on Monday afternoon, deceased's grave adjoining that of his wife, who predeceased him in 1907 at the age of 77. Although the veteran Rector wished to be present, ill-health prevented his attendance, but his son, Rev. G.SALMON assisted the curate, Rev. W.B.Y.LOVEBAND at the funeral service, the first portion of which was held in the Church…

TOKEN OF RESPECT – A peal of grandshire doubles (5,040 changes) was rung on St. Mary's Church bells on Monday evening, except the tenor at back stroke, deeply muffled, as a token of respect for the late Mr James Selby REED, who was formerly one of the Churchwardens. The ringers stood as follows: J.COX, treble; F.MARTIN, 2; A.ANSCOMBE, 3; Luke VERRALL, 4; E.EDWARDS, 5; A.MARTIN, tenor. The peal occupied 2 hours 43 minutes.

DAMAGE BY FALLEN TREE – Following upon the recent storm damage, a tree was being cut down in the grounds of the Barcombe Parish Church last Saturday, when it fell the wrong way, with the result that it crashed heavily on to the stable of Mr PORTER, smashing the roof in. Fortunately, although considerable material damage was done, there was no personal injury received, nor were any of the animals injured.

LETTER FROM THE FRONT – Corporal Charles A.BRYANT, who is serving with the Royal Engineers, has written another letter home to his parents, Mr & Mrs BRYANT, the communication having been received on Wednesday, in which he refers to the wet days being experienced, stating that it has been raining every day for some time. He goes on to say that in spite of this, however, they all do their best "to keep smiling and cheerful." Corporal BRYANT is engaged at present in connection with the wireless operations "somewhere or other" at the Front.[3]

YOUNG SCHOOLBOY'S ADVENTURE – Last Tuesday afternoon, about two o'clock, a five-year old lad, named BURCHELL,[4] who

3   Charles Albert BRYANT (27) was born at 11 Gladstone Cottages, Barcombe in 1887. His parents Isaac & Eliza BRYANT were still living at the same address when they received his letter in January 1915.

4   Frederick George BURCHELL was born in Newhaven in 1909. His parents Richard & Sarah and grandparents Richard & Eleanor moved to Barcombe towards the end of 1911 to take up farm labouring jobs with accommodation at 'Lower Barn' and 'Elm Cottages' respectively. In February 1912 Frederick's baby brother Sidney was buried at St.Bartholomew's, Spithurst aged 9 months.

attends Barcombe School, decided that he would take a "jaunt abroad," with the result that great anxiety was caused in his home, and a search party scouring the neighbourhood for the missing youngster. It appears that little BURCHELL, who takes his lunch with him to school, wandered away during mid-day school adjournment, and took the 1.57 p.m. motor train to Brighton – about twelve miles away! It is easy to imagine the consternation caused when he was missed from the village. About 9.30 at night a 'phone message came through to the Lewes police stating that a lad had been found wandering at Brighton, and that he made references to Barcombe. P.C. OCKENDEN, usually stationed at Ringmer, but at present doing duty in the county town, cycled to Barcombe, where, upon arrival, he saw that there were signs of activity in one house still burning lights, not often seen in the country so late at night. He went to the dwelling, guided by the illumination. Arrived there, it soon became evident that the lad found at Brighton was in all probability the missing boy for whom search was still being made in the district, a thought which brought great relief to the people. BURCHELL was restored to his home the next morning, after having spent the night in Brighton Workhouse.

BARCOMBE AND NEWICK AREA.

INSTRUCTIONS TO THE CIVIL POPULATION OF BARCOMBE AND NEWICK IN CASE IT BECOMES NECESSARY TO REMOVE THEM FROM THEIR HOMES.

Although an invasion of this country is improbable, yet it has been considered advisable to make preparations and determine what would be best to be done should such an event occur. For this reason Emergency Committees have been formed and Special Constables sworn in.

If a raid takes place and it is considered necessary for you to leave your home, you will be warned by a Special Constable, or his Messenger, and you are directed and advised to remain at home until you get this warning, notwithstanding any rumours you may hear.

Should you get this warning each person should :—

(1) Put on their warmest clothes, and as much underclothing as they can wear, and great coats. Each person should roll up a blanket, tie the two ends together with string, and carry it over one shoulder.

(2) Bring away all the food in the house, especially bread, cheese and cooked meats, that they can carry amongst them, and also one cooking pot, or saucepan, a kettle and a mug, for each family.

(3) Assemble at *Barcombe Cross.*

Those who have carts should take extra articles, like tarpaulins or rick cloths to make shelters, also food for their horses ; you would then act as directed by your Special Constables.

Any further information you require you should obtain from the Special Constables in your parish.

RICHMOND SPENCE,
Member Local Emergency Committee.

ABOVE: Invasion Precautions - A similarly worded leaflet was sent to HOLLOWAY's stores & bakery in Barcombe (ESRO: WI 112/1/1 p.167).

WHEN THE BELLS JANGLE – INVASION INSTRUCTIONS FOR LEWES RESIDENTS –

Although at the present time they do not see any grounds for fearing that it will be necessary to move the inhabitants of the town from their homes, the Lewes Emergency Committee have deemed it advisable to issue printed instructions to the civil population in the event of invasion. The notices are being delivered to every householder, and among the more nervous folk have created some alarm.

BARCOMBE READING ROOM – At the Reading Room on Monday evening, the annual general meeting took place of the Barcombe Village Club and Reading Room. In the absence of the President, Major W.W.GRANTHAM, the chair was taken by Mr BOURDILLON; and among those present were: The Rev W.B.Y.LOVEBAND, Messrs F.BALLARD, A.BLAKER, W.F.DEAN, A.FORD, A.FUNNELL, E.J. and C.J.HOLLOWAY, A.JESSOP, J.KENWARD, R.RHODES, E.STEVENS and E.WALLS, with the Hon. Secretary (Mr A.MOON). The Secretary read a letter from the Rev. R.I.SALMON, regretting that owing to a very bad cold, he was unable to be with them, and wishing the Club a prosperous New Year. – The Secretary was asked to write and thank the writer for his kind wishes, and expressing to him their hope that he would have a speedy recovery. Upon the balance sheet coming up, it was reported that there was a balance in hand of £1.8s.5d. The previous balance was £2.12s.3½d., thus showing a decrease in the past year. It was explained by Mr MOON that this was mainly due to the large number of members who were on service with His Majesty's Forces.- The usual honorarium was voted to the Hon. Secretary, who in view of the amount in hand being somewhat low, offered to take only half the

usual sum. His suggestion was however, negatived by the gathering. In the report was a record of appreciation for assistance received from Lady GRANTHAM and Major W.W.GRANTHAM. The election of officers for the coming year was next proceeded with, resulting in the re-election of all who had held positions during the past year, together with the addition of Mr Frank BALLARD on the Committee. Major W.W.GRANTHAM remains President, and Mr A.MOON the Hon. Secretary and Treasurer. Mr MOON remarked that this was his 33rd election to the position. Suggestions for the coming year were invited, but although considerable discussion took place, few definite decisions were arrived at. A Sub-Committee consisting of Mr LOVEBAND, Mr MOON, and Mr F.BALLARD, was appointed to look into the affairs of the library to see if improvements could be carried out so as to make this more popular.

22nd January - ILL IN FRANCE – Mrs JONES, of 'Spring Cottage'[5], received a telegram on Tuesday afternoon, from Headquarters in France, informing her that her husband, who joined the Army Veterinary Corps about five weeks ago, was laid up with double pneumonia. No fuller information has yet come to hand.

ARMY COMMISSIONS – Several commissions to local residents have to be recorded for Barcombe, viz.: Mr T.E.BOURDILLON has received a Second Lieutenancy in the 9th Battalion of the Royal Sussex Regiment. He has, however, not yet proceeded to take up the appointment. Mr A.FLETCHER of 'Attrees', late secretary of the Barcombe Football Club, and last year's captain, who has been away training with the Sussex Yeomanry, has been promoted to Sub-Lieutenant. Mr J.SINGLETON, only son

ABOVE: William & Bertha JONES in a faded photograph taken shortly before William's departure for France (courtesy Pamela Godley).

5   *William & Bertha JONES lived at 'Spring Cottage' on Anchor Lane. The 1911 census shows William, aged 34, as a waggoner on a local farm. See updates on William's health on 29th January, 5th & 12th February. He later returned to service as is mentioned in several later articles.*

of Captain SINGLETON of 'Panthill', has been made a Sub-Lieutenant in the Royal Army Service Corps.

FOOTBALL MATCH – Last Saturday afternoon, on the local ground, the Barcombe F.C. played the second match of the season against Brighton Railway Athletic. Barcombe had the assistance of several Territorials billeted at Lewes who had played for the Club in previous years. The team lined up as follows: A.SAUNDERS, J.KETCHELL, J.PERKINS (captain), A.FORDHAM, C.BOURDILLON, F.FORD, Rev. W.B.Y.LOVEBAND, W.FORDHAM, G.DAVIES, C.J.HOLLOWAY and F.SMITH… In the first half Mr HOLLOWAY broke away on the right, and sent in a long shot, which the keeper could not clear successfully. DAVIES, who was well up, put the ball into the net.

MISSION HALL TREAT – The annual Christmas treat for the Sunday School children was held at the Barcombe Mission Hall on Wednesday. Tea was provided in the afternoon, when about 100 scholars and their friends, with about 30 adults, sat down. Following the tea came an entertainment, which included games and extempore songs and recitations by the younger folk. The children also received a present from the Christmas tree which had been given by

Mrs FUNNELL, and a gift of fruit, on leaving. Mr G.JONES (Lewes), secretary of the Mission, presided. Mr JONES expressed hearty thanks to all those who had given their assistance, both as regards provisions and in the arrangements generally. He added that it was a pleasure to see so many there to partake of the enjoyment offered. The Chairman took occasion also to comment satisfactorily on the attendance at the Sunday School. The teachers and their friends rendered help at the tea. Amongst those who contributed various commodities were: Mrs S.FUNNELL, Mr & Mrs BALLARD, Mr & Mrs Hart VERCOE, Mrs & Mrs OSMOND, Mrs COLLINS, and Mr & Mrs WILLMORE.

LETTER FROM FRANCE – Mr A.COLLINS, who joined the Army Veterinary Corps some weeks ago, and almost immediately left Barcombe for the Continent has written another letter home stating that he is keeping quite well and comfortable. He has also written to Mr W.B.DUDENEY of 'Handlye Farm', under date January 13th from "No.2 Veterinary Hospital, Expeditionary Force," and says:

"Just a few lines to say that I am in the land of plenty, and am as happy as a sandboy – up to my knees in mud, as it keeps raining every day. Horses keep coming in and going away, so you may guess what sort of a road

ABOVE: Talking Machines & Records, available from Rice Brothers, Cycle & Motor Depot, Cliffe, Lewes.

there is. We are somewhere – but I can't tell you where. We are stopping in a brickyard not far from the sea. We are not allowed out from the Camp, and we have to be in by eight o'clock. But that doesn't trouble me much, as it is a holiday for me. Some of them who have never been in any mud before don't half make a song. I don't trouble, as long as I can keep in good health, though it is not much 'cop' sleeping in a tent at night. The work is nothing, not enough to keep you in form. We don't hear anything about the war out here. We go to bed usually about six o'clock, and up at 6.30 a.m., so we get plenty of rest. More next time when the weather gets better."

PARISH COUNCIL – At a meeting on Friday evening Mr F.J.CORNWELL (occupying the chair in the absence of Major GRANTHAM), alluded to the decease of Mr James Selby REED, who had occupied the position of

Vice-Chairman and Observer for many years and stated that his removal from their midst would be a distinct loss to his colleagues and also to the whole of the parish, the deceased gentleman having taken a life-long interest in parish affairs…

CARRYING OUT THE POLICE REGULATIONS.
(Fitting Dark Blinds to her sitting room)

ABOVE: 'Carrying out the Police Regulations. (Fitting Dark Blinds to her sitting room).' A contemporary comic postcard take on the new blackout regulations.

29th January - LIGHTS OUT! - Tuesday's order as to the lights was responded to with loyal celerity by the inhabitants. Shopkeepers generally, of course, find it rather difficult to escape the "Official eye" and yet show signs of being "alive."

A VETERINARY CORPS MAN'S IMPROVEMENT - General relief was expressed at the news received by Mrs JONES of 'Spring Cottage,' conveyed in a telegram dispatched from headquarters on Monday, stating that her husband who was reported last week as suffering from double pneumonia in France, had got through the crisis and was making satisfactory progress towards recovery.

SHOPKEEPERS AND THE WAR - It is stated that owing to the large number of men who have joined the colours from Barcombe, there is a great shortage of labour being experienced by shopkeepers. It is also remarked that whereas some districts are recompensed in at least one way for the absence of men from their families, by the billeting of troops, and consequent trade brought to the locality. Barcombe has so far not been given the opportunity so to benefit.

MORE RECRUITS – The men of Barcombe have responded nobly to the country's call, and recruits continue to leave the village. The last two to go were Mr H. VERRAL, who has joined the Motor Transport Section of the Army Service Corps, and Mr F. WALLS who has entered the Royal Field Artillery. Soon there will be another departure, Mr A. OSMOND having gone into the Army Veterinary Corps and will probably go from Barcombe next week.

ABOVE: New recruits. A group of young men, some in uniform while others wear their new cap badges on their lapels. Standing (back left) is believed to be Sidney 'Wil' BLACKMAN, carter of Mount Pleasant, Spithurst who is wearing the badge of the Royal Army Service Corps in which he enlisted in January 1915. He was discharged from the Army in June 1918 suffering from 'trench fever' and 'nervous disability' following service in Gallipoli, Egypt and Palestine (courtesy Beryl Jackson).

WHIST DRIVE – At the annual meeting of the Barcombe Reading Room the Club held a few weeks ago it was reported that owing to the numbers who had left the village on service in connection with the War, the finances, though not unsatisfactory, were not altogether in a rosy condition; and it was thought that something might be done by way of special effort in order to increase the balance of cash in hand…A whist drive was held at the Reading Room this week… Those who took part had the satisfaction of knowing not only had they themselves received and evening's enjoyment, but that they were at the same time assisting a worthy cause.

5th February - THINGS THE TROOPS WANT – People who desire to send things which are really useful to the soldiers at the Front should note that the following articles are especially welcome:- 1. Small waterproof sheets (about 2ft. Square) to sit on, the injurious effects of continually sitting on damp ground being well known. These squares can be folded up and put in the pocket, and would be a great boon in the trenches. 2. A waterproof glove. The leather and others get soaked. It was suggested a canvas one made large to slip the hand into, and treated with tar or a waterproof solution.. 3. Candles and matches. 4. The waders which are now being made should be long

ABOVE: Rubber Boots for use in the trenches. An advert by A. Russell & Son of Lewes. Albion Russell and G.F. Bromley went on to found the famous shoe shop chain bearing their surnames. The shop at 187 & 188 High Street was more recently used as the town's Tourist Information centre.

enough to come up the thighs like fishing waders, otherwise the water is apt to get in over the top.

GERMAN ATTACK ON THE "EXPRESS". BULLET PIERCES AN INTERESTING PART – How a Lewes soldier was reading the "Sussex Express" in the trenches when a German bullet came along and pierced a paragraph in which the reader was particularly interested is the piquant story told in the... letter which Corporal E.WASHER sent to the Editor.

SOLDIER'S CONVALESCENCE - Mrs JONES, of 'Spring Cottage,' has received information that her husband, who joined the Army Veterinary Corps, and who had been reported from France as suffering from double pneumonia, is making satisfactory progress toward recovery.

WOUNDED SOLDIER – It is reported that Private G.

BUCKWELL, whose mother lives at 'Vuggles Farm', has been wounded in both hands as a result of which he has entered hospital. Private BUCKWELL volunteered for service soon after the outbreak of War. He entered the Royal Sussex Regiment, and afterwards proceeded to France.

TRAP ACCIDENT – What might have been a serious accident occurred last Sunday afternoon near the Barcombe Railway Station, consequent upon the thoughtless action of a youth. It appears that at about 3.30. Miss Winnie WILLIMORE, the twelve year old daughter of Mr A.WILLMORE of 'Wootton Cottage', was driving a pony and trap in the direction of the village. Miss WILLMORE, who is an experienced horsewoman, was accompanied by a friend, Miss Violet KING. When near the bridge which crosses the railway line at this part of the road, they were met by a party of lads coming from the direction of the Station, one of whom waved his arms in front of the horse – apparently by way of a prank. The result was that the animal became frightened, and endeavoured to bolt. Miss WILLMORE, however, by her presence of mind, succeeded in pulling it up short. This caused the trap to strike the stone wall of the bridge – the parapet, by the way, being comparatively low; this, in turn, making the horse and vehicle slide for several yards. The trap was then upturned, the two occupants being thrown out. In view of the series of events which has followed the act of the boy, it is little short of remarkable that the girls received no worse injury than a few cuts and bruises. The animal, too, was fortunate, getting nothing worse than cuts about the legs.

12th February - BULL'S ESCAPADE

– On Wednesday afternoon a bull broke away in Spithurst-road. Jumping the hedge, it proceeded across the fields, knocking down three men who endeavoured to capture it. The animal remained at large, however, until the following day, when it was decoyed back into captivity.

NEWS FROM FRANCE

– Mr H.A.COLLINS, who is serving with the Army Veterinary Corps in France, in the course of his last letter to Mrs COLLINS states that he is still getting along all right. There is still plenty of mud about, but the men take things with at least a modicum of optimism.

LICENCE TRANSFERRED

– Mr E.BEDFORD, Lewes, appeared at the Lewes Licensing Sessions on Tuesday to ask that the licence of the 'Station Inn', Barcombe Mills, be transferred to Mr James REED, son and administrator of the late Mr James Selby REED. Mr BEDFORD stated that the applicant had been in charge of the house for some years.

ABOVE: 'A Kiss From France.' One of the many popular embroidered silk postcards sent home by the troops.

The transfer was granted.

CONVALESCENT IN ENGLAND

– We reported a few weeks ago that Mr W.H.JONES who joined the Army Veterinary Corps, was lying ill in France from acute pneumonia. Mr JONES has now got sufficiently well to be sent to England for convalescence, though he is still very weak. He is lying in hospital in Chester, where he arrived on Monday night, and writes home to say that he is being well looked after.

19th February - MORE TREES DOWN

– Last Saturday's stiff gale was responsible for more trees being uprooted in the Barcombe district. It will be remembered that a fine yew tree in the Parish Churchyard suffered with others on the last occasion some weeks ago, and at least one tree has been severely damaged, this time in the neighbourhood of the Parish Church.

CHOIR BOYS' PRESENT

– As the result of their carol singing at Christmas, the Barcombe Parish Choir Boys have been able to dispatch a parcel of about 1,000 cigarettes to the men of the 2nd Royal Munster Fusiliers, through Captain F. GRANTHAM, of that Regiment. The gift has been kept back some time until definite information of the men's whereabouts was obtained.

FOX HUNT

– What is stated to have been one of the longest hunts of the Southdowns for some considerable time took place on Tuesday, when the

RIGHT: '3,000,000 Destitute Belgians' – Britannia offers comfort to a Belgian mother and her children on a poster issued during 1915 by The National Committee for Relief in Belgium. The number of destitute had been amended from '1,500,000' on an earlier poster (U.S. Library of Congress, Prints & Photographs Division, reproduction no. LC-USZC4-12694).

meet started from Longford Bridge. Mr MOFFAT-SMITH acted as master. There was a large attendance. After trying several covers in vain, a fox was turned out shortly after two o'clock at Cottage Wood, and gave the hounds a good run until half-past six, when, owing to the dark, they had to be called off. Reynard had shown successful agility in eluding them all the time.

FLOODS - This week's heavy rain has brought considerable flooding to the locality. The fields to the right of the railway line near Culver Junction, going from Lewes, are inundated, in some places the water having covered the tops of the hedges and encroached almost to the metals, while the line which branches off at the junction and goes to Barcombe Mills Station has the appearance of a breakwater. The fields on either side are flooded, the tall trees rising from the waters adding to the picturesqueness. With the prevalence of wind the waters swirl and ripple like a miniature sea, the effect being intensified by the appearance of "flotsam" which has gathered here and

there. The flood has intruded into the village proper. On Wednesday the water, to a depth of about 18 inches, swept across Clappers Bridge for something like a distance of 40 yards, then falling into the "Mead," and making its way to Barcombe Mills, where it still lies over a very large area.

LECTURE ON BELGIUM – "Belgium in Peace and War" was the title of a lecture delivered on Wednesday evening by Mr MANTELL of Brighton, in the Mission Hall. Councillor G.LLOYD took the chair, and in his opening remarks briefly traced the history of the events leading up to the War; the scandalous invasion of Belgium by Germany, after pledging herself to observe its neutrality, and the fearful suffering of Belgium at the hands of Germany, and expressed a fervent hope the devastating career of the German Emperor, "this great murderer," might be speedily cut short. Mr MANTELL's lecture was illustrated by about 100 splendid lantern slides. At the close, slides were shown of the English Generals. The audience was numerous and enthusiastic and the collection amounted to £1.12s., which will be sent for the use of the distressed Belgians in Belgium…

CAPTAIN GRANTHAM'S LETTER – Mr BALLARD, of Barcombe, who forwarded cigarettes to Captain F.W.GRANTHAM for the men of the Royal Munster Fusiliers, has received the following acknowledgement, dated February 7th, from Captain GRANTHAM, who takes occasion to make interesting comment in connection with the War:

"Dear Mr BALLARD - Many thanks for cigarettes just received; the men will be delighted with them. We came down from the trenches three days ago, and are pleased to be away for a time from the ping and crack of the bullets, and from the deafening crash of a big shell when it bursts, and the whistling noise of a shrapnel shell when coming towards us. Sometimes shells burst in the air and o n the ground without hitting anyone; at other times a single shell will burst in the middle of a group, killing and wounding forty to fifty. But after men have been out here a while they take these things as a matter of course more or less, though the nerves cannot stand more than a certain amount of it. With many thanks again for the very kind present, yours truly (signed), F.GRANTHAM."

26th February - A NARROW ESCAPE - Taking the opportunity which a few days leave from the Front afforded, Captain F.W.GRANTHAM of the 2nd Royal Munsters (son of the late Mr Justice GRANTHAM) spent last week end at Barcombe Place returning to London on Monday morning en route once again for the scene of hostilities on the continent. Mr GRANTHAM first went abroad in September and this was his second time home. It appears that Captain GRANTHAM has in common with his men been experiencing a rough time. He was in the trenches for ten days extending over Christmas Day. On another occasion, two pieces of shell struck his cap which they easily pierced. Fortunately, lying inside the cap was a map, which probably saved him from injury for the splinters made holes in this also, though the stiff material checked their further progress.

Mr SINCLAIR LEAVING – By the departure from Barcombe yesterday (Thursday) of Mr Alfred G.SINCLAIR, the village has lost one of its most prominent residents. Mr SINCLAIR had lived in the village for nine years, for the last five having been a tenant of 'Teynham House'[6]. He had occupied the position of manager in the branch grocery establishment of Mr BALLARD, and by reason of this, became intimately acquainted with many of the surrounding people, among whom he made and retained not a few friends, and with whose best wishes he left the district to enter a similar sphere of duty near Ashford, Kent. Mr SINCLAIR was the originator of the Barcombe Cycling Club, for which Society he has done excellent service, having, on occasion, organised special events under the Club's auspices in the nature of whist drives, etc. It was just twelve months ago – in March of last year – that Mr SINCLAIR called together a few friends at his residence, mooted his proposal with regard to the formation of a Cycling Club, with the result that the organisation came into existence. Until about two years ago Mr SINCLAIR was in the choir of the Parish Church, also being a teacher in the Sunday School.

---

6   *The 1914 Electoral Register shows Alfred SINCLAIR at 'Place Cottages', which would have been part of 'Place Farm'. Was 'Teynham House' an alternative name for one of the cottages? There is a house of the same name in Saltdean. Did a previous occupier come from Teynham in Kent?*

CYCLING CLUB - At the Mission Room, on Tuesday, the second annual general meeting was held of the Barcombe Cycling Club. Mr C.H.HOLLOWAY occupied the chair, and others present were: Messrs. E.BROWN, C.BODLE, G.HOBDEN, J.SPELLER, F.FORD, W.HOBDEN, R.PARSONS, H.STEVENSON, S.HENTY, A.FUNNELL, B.GOLDSMITH, E.STEVENS, R.GRIERSON (captain), T.HENTY (vice-captain), and W.SINCLAIR (hon. secretary). The reports showed a balance in hand of £1. Reference was then made to the depletion of the Club's active membership owing to a large proportion of the members having joined the Colours, and it was decided to lower the age limit to fifteen years. Mr W.HOBDEN, jun., was chosen hon. secretary in succession to Mr SINCLAIR, who has now left the village. Mr E.STEVENS was elected the new Captain, and Mr PARSONS Vice-Captain. Messrs. G.HOBDEN, T.HENTY, A.HENTY, and R.GRIERSON were placed on the Committee. – Prizes for making the most attendances at runs were taken by Messrs. A.OSMOND, E.STEVENS and J.SPELLER.

5th March - 5th SUSSEX IN THE TRENCHES – Many homes in East Sussex have been thrilled by the news that the 5th Battn. Royal Sussex Regiment served in the trenches for the first time last Sunday. Seeing that these Territorials only landed in

COURT BARCOMBE, No. 7672. Ancient Order of Foresters.

ABOVE: The Ancient Order of Foresters were a 'Friendly Society' providing a form of private health insurance in the days before the National Health Service (taken from the cover of a 1904 Rules Amendment booklet, author's collection).

France ten days before, the speedy manner in which they have got to work speaks well for their military efficiency and the confidence that is reposed in Colonel LANGHAM's men.

WORKERS WANTED - In connection with the Red Cross Society, working parties are held every Friday afternoon at Barcombe Place, the residence of Lady GRANTHAM and notices in the village state "all those willing to work will be welcome".

12th March - CRICKET CLUB - Monday evening next has been fixed for the annual meeting of the Barcombe Cricket Club. Among other business will be the appointment of a new honorary secretary, as Mr Richmond SPENCE who now holds the position, will be leaving the village at the end of March for Ringmer.

STEAMERS TORPEDOED OFF THE SUSSEX COAST – At six o'clock on Tuesday morning, the steamer "Blackwood," 1,230 tons, owned by the Tyneside Line (Ltd.), North Shields, was sunk without warning by a torpedo from a submarine off Hastings. The crew of seventeen were all saved, and were landed at Newhaven...

19th March - BARCOMBE FORESTERS – THE YEAR'S WORK – The twenty-seventh annual report of Court "Barcombe" No.7,672, Ancient Order of Foresters, records that the total number of benefit members on December 31st last was 149, 21 being 16 years of age; 34 between 16 and 20; 78 between 20 and 50; 15 between 50 and 65; and one over 65.

The sickness experienced during the year has been £94.0s.2d., compared with £54.16s.5d. for 1913, the increase upon the funds during the year amounting to £140.10s.11d. The valuation, which was necessary in consequence of the National Insurance Act, shows the great prosperity of the Court, the valuer having certified that the Court can safely reduce the contributions of all members of ten years' membership in the adult section. The Executive Council having sanctioned same, and also the transfer of £60 from the Sick and Funeral Fund for management purposes, as soon as the necessary new rule is registered the reduction can take effect. The difficulty regarding medical benefit to juvenile and uninsured members has not yet been overcome. The Medical Association, which it was hoped to have formed in the district, has in consequence of the War, been postponed. As soon as peace is proclaimed, it is hoped to bring the matter to a successful issue, when the disadvantages which the junior section is suffering from will disappear. Junior members can now be admitted from 3 years of age and adults from 16 years upwards. A wide range of benefits are provided; a copy of the tables will be sent free on application. No medical examination is necessary when benefits are less than 7s.6d. per week, merely a declaration of health, which must be witnessed by an adult member. It is a pleasure to note that members have taken advantage of the members' surplus fund; 4 per cent. Has been allotted as interest during the past year. It should be clearly understood that the whole of the sum invested can be withdrawn at any time by giving a few days' notice. The Court continues to subscribe to the Lewes Victoria, Sussex County, Newick Cottage, and Brighton Ear and Throat Hospitals, but as the applications for letters are in excess of the supply, it is not always possible to supply them when required. Application should be made to Bro. C.CHATFIELD or the Secretary (Mr J.W.BRIGGS).

The accounts have been audited by Bros. W.EDWARDS, P.C.R., and F.EDWARDS, P.C.R. Rev. Preb. SALMON and Mr W.W.GRANTHAM are Trustees of the Court, and Bro. G.HILLMAN, Chief Ranger, while Bro. J.W.BRIGGS of Lewes, carries out the secretarial duties. The total worth of the funds is now £2,545.14s.6½d.

NEW COMERS – The attractions of Barcombe as a residential village are many, and new comers may be expected shortly. "Hill Brow" has been let to Mr WORSLEY, a London gentleman, and Dr John McCUTCHEON, assistant school medical officer for East Sussex, has taken "Fern Hill."

INDIANS & SCHOOL GIFTS – Two Barcombe girls – Lena KING and Annie JONES – are amongst those who have been "doing their bit" by making knitted articles for soldiers. Each of them has now received a kindly letter of acknowledgement from officers of Indian regiments thanking the girls for their gifts, and expressing the Indian's appreciation.

STARLING & CHURCH ORGAN – When Mr G.GASSON, the organist of the Parish Church, attempted to work a certain "stop" one day last week, it became apparent that "something was wrong." Investigations followed, and it was then found that by some means a starling had entered the pipe, with the result that the "stop" had been interfered with. The bird had suffered the penalty of death for its daring.

CHILDREN ON THE LAND – Barcombe, in common with other districts, is feeling the labour shortage, so many of the local men having joined the Forces. In one instance at least the school children have come to the rescue, for on Saturday morning twenty five boys and girls were engaged stone picking on Lady GRANTHAM's estate. The children worked with a will, and not only rendered useful service but made a little pocket money for themselves. They were paid by the hour, and the "picking" operations were something unique.

BARCOMBE TRAGEDY - COWMAN'S SAD END - Last Monday afternoon an employee working for Mr John GURR of 'Curds Farm', seeing that the cows had not been fed by the man who did the work, went into a barn to obtain the food. He there discovered his workmate, William Henry MILLS,[7] dead as a result of hanging. Deceased, a comparatively young man, lived at 'Lewes

---

7   William's surname was actually MILES (ref. GRO death indexes). He was 27 when he died and had lived in Barcombe for at least twenty years with his parents William & Louisa.

ABOVE: 'Curds Farm,' home of John GURR. Photographed by A.M. Bliss & Co. of the County Studios, Lewes (Mike Green collection).

SINGLETON at the annual meeting of the Cricket Club... and with this idea generally prevalent, the members have decided to continue operations during the coming season...

26th March - DEPARTED RESIDENTS - Mr SINCLAIR, who left Barcombe some weeks ago, has written to a former neighbour stating that he is getting along comfortably in his new surroundings. This week another well-known resident has left the village in the person of Mr Richmond SPENCE, who had occupied positions on several local organisations. Mr SPENCE, however, has not gone very far afield – only to Ringmer.

PHOTO FROM THE FRONT - During the past week several of the London papers have contained a

Land Cottages', Barcombe. He was well known in the neighbourhood, the news of the tragedy coming with a shock to the villagers... (Further details of the Coroner's inquest are given).

VILLAGE CRICKET – BARCOMBE CLUB TO CONTINUE – "A little homely, manly cricket here won't hurt anybody," remarked Captain

ABOVE: George DAVIES (seated, middle row, left) in the 1910-11 Barcombe F.C. team. Seated next to him (centre) is team captain, Fred SAUNDERS who was to die at the Somme in November 1916. Standing (back left) is the Club's President, Sir William GRANTHAM who died in 1912 (Barcombe Football Club archive; ESRO: AMS 7290/4/1).

photograph showing a soldier "cooking under difficulties" and it was almost needless for attention to be drawn to the fact that he is smiling during his domestic labours. Nor was it difficult for local people to recognise the photo - as that of Corporal George DAVIES of Barcombe, a popular member of the Football Club, who is now at the Front. It is apparent that the Corporal has been busy in one direction or another, for the knees of his breeches are in the condition popularly known as "out." Corporal Davies went to the Front with the 5th Royal Sussex Regiment (Territorials).[8]

2nd April - BILLIARDS SEMI FINAL

– In connection with the competition for the 150-up billiard tournament, for which Mr A.BLAKER offered a prize, Mr S.B.RICHARDS (owing 75) played with Mr BLAKER (owing 100) in a semi-final at the Reading Room on Tuesday, the latter winning by 45. Mr BLAKER and Mr W.HOBDEN are thus matched to meet in the final. There is therefore, a possibility that the trophy may be entered for re-competition. There were 18 entrants altogether.

READING ROOM MEETING

- The adjourned monthly meeting of the Committee of the Barcombe Reading Room was held on Tuesday evening. Mr S.B.RICHARDS occupied the chair, others present being Mr F.BALLARD, Mr W.F. Dean, Mr J.KENWARD, Mr

SUNLIGHT SOAP.

IN France you called this "Savon," Tommy, dear!
And the meaning of the word is very clear.
What saved the shirt you have on?
Why, good old Sunlight Savon.
It's the SAVON that you SAVE ON—Tommy, dear!

£1,000 GUARANTEE OF PURITY ON EVERY BAR.

LEVER BROTHERS LIMITED, PORT SUNLIGHT.

ABOVE: Sunlight Soap – Advertising would use war-related images whenever they felt it would draw attention to their product. Here an image of an injured 'Tommy' is used to advertise soap.

E.STEVENS, Mr W.WALL and Mr A.MOON (Hon. Secretary). It was reported in the minutes that the reduction in the charge for billiards had been attended with satisfactory results during a month's working and it was decided that it should be continued until further notice. An application was heard from the Barcombe Cricket Club asking for permission to use the Reading Room on the occasion of whist drive proposed to be held on April 8th in aid of the funds of the Club. It was agreed that permission should be granted without a charge being made in view of the special circumstances; but the opinion was expressed that this present instance should not be regarded as a precedent for granting the use of the Room without a fee.

9th April - BARCOMBE VESTRY - Mr BOURDILLON'S RESIGNATION

- Barcombe Vestry is one of the few attended by ladies and there was no exception to this local rule on Monday morning's meeting. The Rector (the Rev. Prebendary SALMON) presided and there were also present Mrs SINGLETON, Mrs BURDER, Miss SHENSTONE, Miss BURDER, the Rev. G.SALMON, the Rev. W.B.Y.LOVEBAND, Captain SINGLETON, Mr W.F.DEAN, Mr BOURDILLON and Mr W.H. REECE. The Rector expressed his thanks to the churchwardens for their kind help in the past year. They met under exceptional circumstances. The War had no doubt interfered more or less with their parochial work and it had necessitated the absence of Major GRANTHAM a good deal owing to his military duties. The Rector also thanked the district visitors, sidesmen, organists and choirs of both churches. They were indebted too to the Verger (Mr J.KING).

---

8   George Thomas DAVIES was a member of the Barcombe F.C. Lewes & District League Division 2 and Charity Cup winning team of the 1910-11 season. Then living with the BEST family at Brewery Cottages, Cooksbridge (1911 census), he later moved to 'Forge Cottage,' Barcombe after marrying blacksmith's daughter Winifred FUNNELL at St.Mary's in 1917.

The Rector again nominated Captain Singleton as his Warden and paid a warm tribute to his willing and cordial help in connection with everything affecting the well-being of the Parish.

On the motion of Mr REECE, seconded by Mr BOURDIULLON, Major W.W.GRANTHAM was re-elected Peoples' Warden.

The following sidesmen were re-elected - St. Mary's Church, Messrs. BOURDILLON, BEST, DEAN, LADE and VAUGHAN, with Mr JESSUP in place of Mr SINCLAIR, who has left the district. St. Bartholomew's Church – Messrs. REECE, R.RHODES and LUCAS with the addition of Mr O.FUNNELL.

WORK FOR ALL - Mr BOURDILLON did not seek re-election as a sidesmen as he did not like holding sinecures. There were no duties to perform. He was not quite accustomed to the system in vogue at Barcombe and could not fall into line with it. The Rector hoped that Mr BOURDILLON would re-consider his decision. He did not regard him as a mere figurehead. Duties could always be found for the sidesmen in the way of collecting, showing people to their seats and maintaining order.

Mr BOURDILLON regretted that he was not able to get about sufficiently.

The Churchwardens' accounts were not presented, and Mr BOURDILLON asked whether they ought not to be submitted for approval? The Rector "I don't think it is necessary. They have been posted up outside the church, and published in the Parish Magazine. The accounts show a balance in hand at both churches."

BEAUTIFYING THE CHURCHYARD – The Rector mentioned that they had suffered a great loss and blessing by the storm which recently levelled the dear old yew tree to the ground in the Churchyard, and also one of the elm trees. It had also been necessary to cut down other trees. As Rector, he believed the timber belonged to him, but he had devoted the proceeds of the sale, about £14.10s., to wiping out the deficit on the upkeep of the Churchyard. That would only leave about 3s.9d. standing over from last year. In the future he thought they should try and start a small fund for beautifying the Churchyard.

A vote of thanks was accorded the Rector for his services in the chair and before the meeting dispersed Mr BOURDILLON suggested that another year they should meet in the body of the church instead of the small vestry. It would be more dignified, and would not be derogatory to the building.

AMPUTATED HAND - Private GANDER, of the Coldstream Guards, who was reported missing some time ago, has had the misfortune to lose a hand. It was found necessary to amputate the limb.

CYCLING CLUB'S RUN – As with so many other things, the Barcombe Cycling Club has been adversely affected by the War. But endeavours are being made – and made successfully – to "carry on business as usual." The first run of the season took place on Easter Monday evening. A start was made from Barcombe Cross at six o'clock, the riders going to the Hippodrome, Brighton, via Lewes and Falmer, returning over the same route. The distance travelled altogether was thus about 25 miles. The second run has been fixed for next Wednesday, further information being obtainable at Barcombe.

16th April - A CALL FOR COMPULSION – The adoption by the Sussex Territorial Force Association of a resolution in favour of some kind of compulsory military service must be regarded as extremely significant. It may mark the approaching end of voluntary means for recruiting, at least so far as the county is concerned..

ABOVE: 'At the Front, Cycles' from G. Sands of Heathfield, in another example of war-related advertising.

23rd April - ANNUAL COUNCIL MEETING – Barcombe Parish Council held its annual meeting on Friday in the Mission Room, when there were present: Mr E.W.BUNNEY (in the chair), and Messrs. F.J.CORNWELL, G.T.HAWKINS, T.N.LADE, S.B.RICHARDS, and E.RHODES, with the Clerk (Mr H.TROWER). The elections resulted: Chairman – Major W.W.GRANTHAM; Vice-Chairman – Mr W.BUNNEY; Overseers; Messrs. F.J.CORNWELL, R.RHODES, and S.B.RICHARDS (Mr RICHARDS taking the place of the late Mr J.S.REED). Mr RICHARDS was appointed school manager and also the representative of the parish on the Drainage Committee. An application was considered from the Clerk for leave of absence to enable him to join the "Industrial Firing Line" as an Engineer. It was unanimously decided to grant this, pending the appointment of a substitute.

CONCERT – Last Friday and Saturday evenings large attendances were drawn to the Barcombe Place Motor House for the entertainment, organised by Mrs BROOKSBANK and Mr A.BROOKSBANK, in aid of Lady JELLICOE's Fund. Those taking part had been put through their rehearsals, and they all acquitted themselves with pleasing distinction on the two occasions. The programme – a varied one – was the same each evening, and it testifies much to its presentation that many of those who were at the "house" the first time the entertainment was given attended the following day. Perhaps the best thing among items of general merit was the farce, entitled "A Rest Cure." As a result of the effort, a sum approximating £6 is available to be handed over to the Fund mentioned. The programme, in two parts, was as follows:- Pianoforte solo, "Gipsy Love," Miss BURDEN; National Anthems, Rev. G.SALMON, supported by Boy Scouts; songs, "Land of Hope and Glory" and "Agnes Macdonald" Mrs F.BALLARD; dances, Miss K.HOLLINGS; choruses, "Here we are", "Sister Susie", "The Barcombe Rag", "Mary's Age" and "My Word!" by "The Pierrots"; half-minute stories; Mr Richmond SPENCE; comedy "Miss Honey's Treasure" Miss M.RHODES and Miss L.HOLLOWAY; farce "A Rest Cure" Miss HOPWOOD, Miss CARPMAEL, Miss BROOKSBANK, Mr Richmond SPENCE, Mr V.BOURDILLON, and Mrs A.BROOKSBANK.

WEDDING OF CORPORAL SAYERS – A wedding of interest to local residents took place on Saturday at Christ Church, Freemantle, near Southampton. The bride was Miss Edith Olive MASTERS, daughter of Mr William Edward MASTERS of Richmond road, Freemantle, and the bridegroom Mr Charles SAYERS of Barcombe. The bridegroom is a popular member of the Lewes Company of the Sussex Royal Garrison Artillery, now stationed at Dover, and holds the rank of Corporal. The bride, who was given away by her brother (Mr Charles MASTERS), wore a dress of pale grey silk pollin[9] with hat to match, and she carried a white Prayer Book, the gift of the bridegroom. Miss Eleanor MASTERS attended as bridesmaid and was also attired in pale grey pollin with pink sash and pink hat to match. Mr Alfred KNIGHT, of Brockenhurst, acted as best man. The Rev. H.L.ATKINS of Freemantle, was the officiating clergyman. The wedding presents included the following: Bride to bridegroom, gold ring; bridegroom to bride, gold military badge: Sussex R.G.A... A marble clock presented to the bridegroom bears the inscription: "Presented to Corporal SAYERS by the N.C.O.s and Gunners of the Lewes Company Sussex R.G.A...

30th April - MOTOR & FELLED TREE – What looked like being a rather nasty accident was narrowly averted near the Rectory, yesterday (Thursday) afternoon, a few minutes before four o'clock, a motor car being pulled up just in time to avoid collision with a tree which had been felled. The car – which carried the letters "O.H.M.S., R.A.M.C." – was being driven towards the village. It had negotiated a bend and was proceeding at a fairly moderate pace, when one of the woodsmen shouted out a warning. By the time his calls were heard the tree had descended too far towards the ground to be drawn back. The driver of the motor, in which was also a uniformed occupant, applied the brakes so suddenly that the vehicle skidded some distance, only coming to a standstill as the front wheels and the bonnet touched the boughs. About five minutes' delay occurred while the workmen, in very business-like and smart manner, cleared a passage. But for the look-out kept by the woodmen, and the promptitude exercised in pulling up the car, the consequences must have been more serious.

7th May - NEW RATES – The Lewes Magistrates have allowed a special rate of two pence in the £ in connection with the expenditure for drainage in the parish of Barcombe for the ensuing half year, and also a poor rate of 3s. in the £.

SOLDIER WOUNDED - Well known in the Lewes District Private F.GORRINGE who is in the 3rd Infantry Battalion of the Canadian Regiment has been wounded at the Front. He left this country some time ago to take up farm work in Canada and it will be remembered that previous to his departure he held the position of Clerk and Assistant Overseer for the Barcombe Parish. He was one of those who enlisted in the land of the maple leaf following the outbreak of war. While in England prior to going to France, he took the

ABOVE: Remarkable Lewes Accident – in a more serious accident, a steam lorry crashes into railings in Lewes, much to the interest of soldiers in the town (photographer C. Bunce).

9   'Silk pollin' - no description could be found in any of the standard dictionaries.

ABOVE: 'Some of the "Fearless Fifth" ' – The Machine Gun Section of the 2nd/5th Battn. R.S.R. to whom half of the proceeds of the May Day Collection were sent for cigarettes.

opportunity of paying a visit to the County town.

MAY DAY COLLECTION
– It was a happy idea to make the occasion of a May Day procession at Barcombe last Saturday the opportunity for having a collection with which to purchase cigarettes for the soldiers. The contributions gathered during the proceedings amounted to 23s. One half of this sum is being sent to Captain COURTHOPE, for the men of the 5th Royal Sussex Regiment, and the other half to Captain F.GRANTHAM, for the 2nd Battalion of the Royal Munster Fusiliers. Miss B.STANDING was chosen Queen…

NEWICK SOLDIER RECOVERED - Private George BUCKWELL, 2nd Royal Sussex Regiment, of Vuggles, Newick "has just recovered from wounds received in the fighting in France."[10]

OUR LITTLE CONTRIBUTORS' COLUMN - …The prize winners included Frances GANDER (13), Spithurst Private School, for her anecdote.

14th May - SCHOLARS' HELP – Barcombe school children have been doing their "bit" in this time of War. They have been taught in school (according to the Parish Magazine) the way to make worn garments into clothing for children among the Belgian refugees. As a result a considerable number of small garments have been forwarded to the Central Clothing Depot in London, from which organisation has come thanks in acknowledgment. The scholars are now on other, but similar useful work; and pieces of material – such as flannel and linen – likely to be serviceable, would be gladly received by Miss ATKINS at Barcombe School.

CHURCH FUNDS – In this month's Parish Magazine appears the following paragraph with reference to the funds of the two churches: "On looking over the accounts Lord MONK-BRETTON took exception to the grant of £7 made by the District Church to the Parish Church. To alter that would have entailed a complete revision of the two balance sheets, already printed and circulated; so to counteract the deduction from St.Bartholomew's Funds, Lord MONK-BRETTON most generously sent a cheque for £7 to Captain SINGLETON to be

---

10 George Henry BUCKWELL's parents George & Ellen lived in a cottage on 'Vuggles Farm' on the northern boundary of Barcombe with Newick. Although there was a boundary change (and land swap) in that part of the parish, 'Vuggles' is still listed under Barcombe in both the 1911 census and 1914 electoral roll.

devoted to St.Bartholomew's expenses. This liberal offering is most acceptable, as there are many little things wanted in St.Bartholomew's, and we are greatly indebted to Lord MONK-BRETTON for his kindness."

CHURCH LIFE IN THE VILLAGES – BARCOMBE

…There are many offsprings of the parent church in the form of different societies. A troop of Boy Scouts is in existence, Miss DUVAL at present carrying on the duties of Scoutmaster in the absence of Mr LAKER, who is with H.M. Forces. Then there are stoolball, football and cricket clubs, though there has been, inevitably, a certain amount of interference by the War, with the "carrying on." Of another nature is the Clothing and Coal Club, and the Boot Club for Sunday School children, in which Miss SALMON and Lady GRANTHAM are respectively interested, Miss SALMON also being the Secretary of the Society for the Propagation of the Gospel. Then there is the branch of the Girls' Friendly Society, the Nursing Association (with which Lady GRANTHAM and Mrs BURDER are associated), a

Red Cross detachment (of which Miss Muriel GRANTHAM is commandant), and the Mothers' Guild (with which the names of Lay GRANTHAM, Lady MONK-BRETTON, Mrs BURROWS, and Mrs SINGELTON have been connected), and the Band of Hope…

ABOVE: 'Enlisted for the Duration' – A National Egg Collection poster (U.S. Library of Congress, Prints & Photographs Division, reproduction no.LC-USZC4-11169).

EGGS FOR THE WOUNDED – With the full approval and grateful appreciation of the War Office, the National Egg Collection for the Wounded has been established, and is now in active operation. The object of that collection is briefly to collect and deliver new-laid eggs free of cost to our wounded soldiers and sailors.

We have appointed Depot Managers and collectors for Lewes, Ringmer, Barcombe and surrounding districts, and as such we appeal for the gifts of new-laid eggs, which may either be brought to us here, or they may be carefully packed in suitable boxes labelled "National Egg Collection" and sent to us by railway, carriage forward. All empty boxes will be returned free of charge. On receipt of a postcard from poultry keepers residing in this district, we or an official collector will call and collect the eggs at any time, and will do so regularly if, as it is earnestly hoped, contributions are made weekly…

S.ELPHICK, Corn & Seed Stores, Lewes.

21st May - CYCLE RUN – Wednesday, May 26th, has been fixed for the next meet of the Barcombe Cycling Club, when it is hoped to have a "run" to Uckfield, via Maresfield, returning by Shortgate.

CAPTAIN F.W.GRANTHAM – Local residents will regret to learn that there is reason to fear that Captain GRANTHAM, of the Royal Munster Fusiliers, has met with mishap at the front. The name of Captain GRANTHAM - who is, of course, a member of the prominent Barcombe family – appeared in the official list of officers "wounded and missing" published this week. Enquiries have been set on foot, but, unfortunately, without success up to the present.

ABOVE: Lance-Cpl. Reginald John Pooley JESSUP, 3rd Battn. Royal Sussex Regt. The twenty-year-old son of Albert & Minnie JESSUP of Barcombe Place Lodge, had worked as a railway clerk at Hever Station in Kent, before moving to Barcombe with his parents when they took jobs as head gardener and house servant for Sir William GRANTHAM at Barcombe Place.

NO FLOWER SHOW – A meeting of the Barcombe Horticultural Society was held at the Reading Room last Friday, Mr A.JESSUP presiding, when there were also present: Mr H.TROWER (hon. Secretary), Rev. W.B.Y.LOVEBAND, and Messrs. W.BANKS, A.FLEET, J.FARRENDEN, E.KING, A.MARTIN, J.MORTBY, S.B.RICHARDS, W.SAVAGE, J.VAUGHAN, and J.WEBB. It was decided that, owing to the War, it would be desirable, as was the case last year, not to hold a Flower Show this summer. It was also decided not to collect subscriptions, but the hope was expressed that activities would be resumed and the event held when conditions became normal once more. The accounts, presented by Mr TROWER, showed that there was a balance in hand of £28.9s.2d.

28th May - DEATH OF THE RECTOR OF BARCOMBE – After fifty-seven years' service in the Church, twenty-seven of which were spent at Barcombe, the Rev. Prebendary SALMON died at the Rectory on Tuesday morning, at the advanced age of 80. In spite of his years, the reverend gentleman carried out his duties almost up to the end, sometimes delivering his sermon seated…In his earlier years, at least, deceased was a follower of athletics, and when at Oxford he had the honour of rowing in such a classic contest as the Varsity Boat Race. It is related that

ABOVE: The Rev. R.I.SALMON, signs the burial register of St. Mary's Church for the last time on 12th June 1914, before his own name was added on 29th May 1915 (ESRO: PAR 235/1/5/2).

when he went to Oxford his College boat was "at the bottom of the river," but when he left, after being stroke, it had risen to top position. In after years he devoted attention to things agricultural, particularly the breeding of horses, and towards the end of the 90's he gained two medals from the Hunters' Improvement Society for two of his horses at a Sussex Show.

CAPTAIN F.W.GRANTHAM – General satisfaction will be felt at the news that Captain F.W.GRANTHAM of the Royal Munster Fusiliers may be still alive. The Captain's name was published in the list of missing after some heavy fighting recently; and it was at first feared he was lost. On Wednesday morning, however, the following reassuring telegram was received by Lady GRANTHAM from a member of the family who has been prosecuting enquiries; "Red Cross report received gives hope Fred taken prisoner."

ABOVE: The Rev. R.I. SALMON, who died on 25th May 1915.

4th June - LATE RECTOR OF BARCOMBE – IMPRESSIVE FUNERAL SERVICE [11] – In the picturesque churchyard of St. Mary's, the late Rector of the parish, Robert Ingham SALMON, Prebendary of Selsey, was laid to rest on Saturday afternoon (29th May), the deceased being buried in the same grave as his wife, who predeceased him several years ago.

BARCOMBE CRICKET CLUB – A meeting of the Committee of the Barcombe Cricket Club was held last (Thursday) evening. The Rev. W.B.LOVEBAND presided, and there were also present: Messrs. G.HOLLOWAY, W.DUDENEY, C.MUGGERIDGE, J.STANDING, and S.B.RICHARDS (Hon. Secretary).

The Secretary reported that home and away matches had been arranged with Cooksbridge and Offham, and it is hoped to fix other games later, preferably on the home ground. Several of the Clubs challenged were not playing this season, and others had not replied to his letter.

A letter was read from the Ringmer C.C. cancelling their fixtures, owing to the death of members at the Front.

Practice nights are Mondays, Wednesdays, and Fridays, when the nets will be put up in readiness by the Groundsman.

The Secretary emphasised the need of funds, new tackle being required and the rent to be met.

11th June - AT THE DARDENELLES - In January Mr Alfred KNIBBS of Barcombe enlisted in the Naval Service as a saddler and after a short period at the Crystal Palace left for a destination abroad. He has sent the following letter home: "We went up to the Dardanelles and saw the terrible bombardment on May 1st. It was awful. They landed a party of us; with Jim BLACKMAN (another local man who has joined since the outbreak of war) three saddlers in all. One of the party was shot. We were marched about sixty miles, and now we have come back to --- and are camped on the beach by the plain. It is lovely on the borders of the Sahara plain. There are camels for transport. We have got the afternoon off and are sitting in the Soldiers' Home writing. I am in splendid health. It is very hot here in the day."

Barcombe.

Bliss Series. No 6.

ABOVE: The Barcombe branch of Curtis & Co., with saddles and harness on display. This was the pre-war workplace of Alfred KNIBBS and Jim BLACKMAN. The shop was later used as the village fire station and a bank (Postcard by Bliss of Lewes).

---

11 A full newspaper column is dedicated to a long report of the funeral service and a list of mourners.

Curtis & Co. Saddlers & Harness Makers of Barcombe & Lewes

BARCOMBE,

Nov 18 1914

Dr. to CURTIS & CO.,

SADDLERS AND HARNESS MAKERS.

Rick Cloths and Waggon Covers.   Ropes, Lines and Twines.

MARQUEES, TARPAULINS AND SACKS ON HIRE.

. . . . AND AT CLIFFE, LEWES. . . . .

ABOVE: Billhead of the Barcombe branch of Curtis & Co., 1914.

Alfred KNIBBS (35) was the manager of the Barcombe branch and Jim BLACKMAN (21) worked for the company as a saddler. The shop was located in Gladstone Buildings, next to Holloways the bakers.

Alfred, a native of Birmingham, had moved to Barcombe from Rochester, Kent late in 1910, with his wife Alice and three children. They lived behind the shop at 13 Gladstone Cottages. One of his early decisions as the new branch manager of Curtis & Co. was to employ Jim BLACKMAN as an apprentice saddler.

James Thomas BLACKMAN, to give him his full name, had been born in Barcombe in 1894, and baptised at St. Mary's to Alfred & Sarah. After leaving school he worked as a waggoner on a local farm for a couple of years, before joining Curtis & Co., as an apprentice saddler.

Both men joined the army as saddlers, to service the equipment of the many thousands of horses pressed into military service. Jim's employer was asked to write a character reference for him to present to the recruiting officer at Hove when he attested in November 1914, he wrote; "*we can recommend him as quite trustworthy & obliging & has been used to the all round trade & we found him in every way reliable having been with us 4 years.*"

(Service Papers for J.T.BLACKMAN; TNA: WO 363, on Ancestry)

18th June - RESIDENT OFFERED TOWN'S FREEDOM – On the occasion of the Jubilee of the Incorporation of Dudley, the Corporation sent a message of congratulation to Mr F.S.SHENSTONE, of Sutton Hall, Barcombe, who was the first Mayor of Dudley. We understand a desire was expressed to confer the freedom of the borough on Mr SHENSTONE, but that owing to advancing years he was unable to accept the proffered honour.

ARRIVED FROM CANADA – Mr Kenneth GORRINGE, son of Mr & Mrs F.GORRINGE of Hampden Park, and formerly of Barcombe, recently arrived in England with a contingent of Canadian troops. Mr Kenneth GORRINGE is, of course, well known in this locality, and is a brother of Mr F.GORRINGE, who passed through this country some time ago en route to the Front from the Land of the Maple Leaf, and who has since been wounded.

SOLDIERS' THANKS - As the result of children's efforts on May Day, a sum of money was collected for the purchase of cigarettes for despatch to soldiers at the Front. Mr S.B. Richards is now receiving cards of acknowledgement, among others writing to express their thanks being E. BUTTON, Hugh J.BROCK, I. DIPLOCK and C.SPIRES of the Royal Sussex Regiment. The following is a typical communication: "Many thanks for the cigarettes and tobacco received this morning (Sunday last). It may interest you to know that they reached the Sussex boys, many of us coming from Lewes and other places in Sussex."

FIRST MAYOR CONGRATULATED – Mr F.SHENSTONE, of Sutton Hall, Barcombe, was formerly chief mining agent to the Earl of Dudley in Staffordshire and Worcestershire, and in 1865 was elected first Mayor of the borough of Dudley in the latter county. Last week Dudley celebrated the jubilee of its incorporation, and it had been decided to mark the occasion by conferring the freedom of the borough on Mr SHENSTONE, but he was obliged to decline the honour, being unable on account of his age – he is 91, though enjoying fairly good health – to travel so far away from home. On the day of the celebration, however, he was not forgotten, for he received the following telegram: "Corporation of Dudley sends hearty greetings and congratulations to the first Mayor on the occasion of its jubilee." Mr SHENSTONE forwarded this reply: "The first Mayor of Dudley thanks the Mayor and Corporation for their kind remembrance of him, and regrets that his great age prevents his being present on this memorable occasion, but sends best wishes to old friends."

Knowland's Farm.   Barcombe, Sussex.

ABOVE: 'Knowlands Farm', home to Richard & Alice RHODES and visited by wounded soldiers from Brighton. A pre-war coloured postcard by the Mezzotint Co. of Brighton.

25th June - HEALTH CRUSADE OUTING – LEWES CHILDREN'S FIRST VISIT TO BARCOMBE – To-day (Friday) the annual outing takes place in connection with the Lewes Branch of the Juvenile Health Crusade. The scholars of the various schools visit Barcombe. The Crusade is part of the movement against consumption, having originated about three years (ago) under the auspices of the Women's Imperial Health Association.... All being well to-day, the children, to the number of about 320, and mainly under the charge of their respective day-school teachers, leave Lewes for Barcombe by the 11 a.m. train and return is intended to be made at 7.40 p.m. Lady GRANTHAM is kindly allowing the use of her fields, and also the motor house for the reception of the children's coats, and the various commodities which must necessarily be taken.

The Managers of the Barcombe School are granting the use of the school and offices for the provision of tea if the weather should become wet. Teachers' lunch will take place in the Reading Room, the Committee having offered it for that purpose. Miss FOWLER-TUTT acting as hostess. Each of the children has been provided with a programme outlining the day's events, and instructing them on such matters as the assembling, etc. Upon arriving at Barcombe, they will be marched to the school playground for the distribution of light refreshments. Among the amusements scheduled to take place are swings, peddling, rambles and races.

SOLDIERS' VISIT - Barcombe was visited yesterday by a number of wounded soldiers from the hospitals at Brighton. Their host and hostess were Mr & Mrs RHODES (Knowlands Farm), who received the assistance of friends in the dispensing of hospitality. The day was a fine one, and the visitors expressed deep satisfaction at the pleasures of the drive through the picturesque countryside.

Rev. Herbert W.FARRAR, M.A.

2nd July - BARCOMBE'S NEW RECTOR – The Rev. Herbert W.FARRAR, M.A., of All Saints' Vicarage, Shooters Hill, Woolwich, has been appointed to the Rectory of Barcombe, near Lewes, in succession to the Rev. Prebendary Robert Ingham SALMON, deceased. He comes to the district with many recommendations, and is already known in Sussex. His elder son has fallen in the War.

The new Rector is the son of the late Rev. W.FARRAR, M.A., who was Vicar of Castleside, county Durham, for 28 years, and who died seven years after his retiring at Llandudno in 1898. Mr FARRAR took his degree at Queen's College, Cambridge. He was ordained Deacon and Priest by Dr. HARVEY, Bishop of Carlisle, in 1879 and 1880. From 1879 to 1882 he was Curate of St.Mark's, Barrow-in-Furness. In 1882 he was appointed Chaplain to the Missions to Seamen on the Tyne, and served under Bishops LIGHTFOOT and WESTCOTT for eleven years. In 1885 Mr FARRAR married Florence Margaret, daughter of the late Mr Annandale TOWN, J.P., of Allansford House, county Durham, and Chairman of the Consett Bench of Magistrates. By the marriage he has four children, two daughters and two sons. The elder son, Ronald H.FARRAR, B.A., was gazetted to the Leicesters on the outbreak of the War, and in October was attached to the 2nd Manchesters, taking out a draft of 220 Manchesters in October. He went up to the Front with them, and fell in action on Christmas Eve, being buried in Belgium on Christmas Day... In 1893 Mr FARRAR was appointed Vicar of St. James', Carlisle, where he built a Mission Church, and was twice elected on the School Board. In 1898 he was asked to return to the Missions to Seamen Society, as Superintendent for the South Coast, which post he held for twelve years, living in Dulwich. It was during these years that he became so well known in Sussex and adjacent counties when preaching for our sailors. Many generous gifts were given in response to these appeals, one of £1,000 being sent anonymously in a registered envelope. The growing and important port of Newhaven was under Mr FARRAR's jurisdiction in these days. In July 1910, Mr FARRAR was appointed Vicar of All Saints', Shooters Hill, Woolwich, a parish of 6,000, with large Church Day Schools. Here again Mr FARRAR, aided by Mrs FARRAR, has done yeoman service in this large and important parish, with church, mission hall, men's club, iron room, and day schools, which have been brought up to the modern requirements as to class rooms and staffing…

16th July - GRANDSON OF SIR WILLIAM GRANTHAM KILLED – Second-Lieut. Hugo Frederick GRANTHAM, 1st Essex Regiment, eldest son of Captain F.W.GRANTHAM and Mrs F.W.GRANTHAM, of Beeleigh Abbey, Essex, and grandson of the late Mr Justice GRANTHAM, who was born on April 15th, 1895, was killed at the Dardanelles on

ABOVE: Lieut. Hugo GRANTHAM (1895-1915), grandson of the late Sir William & Lady GRANTHAM of Barcombe Place.

June 28th. He was educated at Cheltenham, where he obtained his football colours. He was also a very promising cricketer, making his century at an excellent match at the Witham Cricket Club, and carrying out his bat. He was gazetted in March of this year from Sandhurst, and commended for exceptional gallantry and coolness under most trying conditions in the action of June 4th by his Colonel, and the Brigadier mentioned him in his dispatch.

23rd July - CAPTURED BY GERMANS

There recently returned to his home at Spithurst, Barcombe, Private Frederick KNIGHT [12] a member of the RAMC, who was taken prisoner by the Germans in September last, after being wounded at Candog. He was home on a fortnight's leave, and returned to duty last Saturday.

30th July - FOOTBALL CLUB

At the annual meeting of the above-named Club the Secretary, Mr G. BODLE, announced that there was a balance in hand of 12s.6d., which was handed to Captain SINGLETON "to use at his discretion." Mr C.HOLLOWAY, who presided, moved a resolution, which was agreed to, congratulating the Club on the large number of members who had enlisted.

6th August - NO REAR LIGHTS

Edward PARSONS of Barcombe was at Lewes Police Court, on Tuesday, fined 2s.6d. for riding a bicycle without a red rear light at Offham on 24th July at 11 p.m.

REGISTRATION ENUMERATORS

On Wednesday at the special Parish Council meeting the following were appointed enumerators under the Registration Act: - Messrs. J.GURR, R.RHODES, E.RHODES, S.B.RICHARDS, E.W.BUNNEY, G.T.HAWKINS, and F.CORNWELL.

13th August - RECTOR'S LETTER

The Rev. Herbert FARRER, the recently appointed Rector of Barcombe, who will be inducted to the living on August 18th, has addressed the following letter to his parishioners – "My dear friends and future parishioners – I want to send you a few words in the August number of your Parish Magazine. Though not actually your Rector yet, I want your prayers for my ministry among you. In so wide and scattered a parish, and with two churches, it will take some time before I and my wife can know you all personally in your homes. The settling into a new home al takes time, and I know you will allow for this...

20th August - NEW RECTOR OF BARCOMBE

– INSTITUTION AND INDUCTION – A large congregation assembled in the Barcombe Parish Church on Wednesday evening, on the occasion of the institution and induction of the Rev. Herbert William FARRAR to the Rectorate. The institution was conducted by the Right Rev. The Lord Bishop of Lewes, and the induction ceremony was performed by the Rev. Prebendary SANDERSON, Rural Dean. The Bishop was attended by the Rev. F.PARTRIDGE of Brighton, and the Churchwardens, Captain M.SINGLETON and Major W.W.GRANTHAM. Among the congregation were Lady GRANTHAM, the Hon. Ethel DODSON, the Hon. Mildred DODSON, Miss GRANTHAM, Mrs SINGLETON, and Mr F.W.BOURDILLON...

He (the Bishop) could not pass on without expressing great

---

12 *Fred KNIGHT enlisted before the war, in January 1912, so was sent to France with the first wave of British troops as part of the British Expeditionary Force (B.E.F.) on 13th August 1914. His time at The Front was short, as he was wounded and taken prisoner three weeks later on 2nd September, while on medical detachment with the 4th Middlesex Regiment. He was wounded again in India during the later years of the war and invalided home in August 1918.*

Barcombe Parish Magazine.

SEPTEMBER, 1915.

Burial.

Aug. 19—Charles George Baker, aged 55 years, by the Rector.

FORM OF SERVICE

TO BE USED AT

THE INSTITUTION

OF THE

REV. HERBERT WILLIAM FARRAR, M.A.,

TO THE

RECTORY OF BARCOMBE.

BY THE

RIGHT REV. THE LORD BISHOP OF LEWES,

AND

INDUCTION TO THE SAME

BY THE

REV. PREBENDARY SANDERSON, M.A., RURAL DEAN,

AT 7 P.M., ON

Wednesday, August 18th, 1915.

ABOVE: Rev. FARRAR's Induction as Rector (Barcombe Parish Magazine, September 1915).

ABOVE: Rev. Walter Beauchamp Yerburgh LOVEBAND (1886-1915) at the Beating of the Bounds in April 1914. His uncle, Lieut.-Colonel Arthur LOVEBAND, C.M.G., of the 2nd Royal Dublin Fusiliers had been killed at Ypres on 25th May 1915.

DEATH OF THE Rev. W.LOVEBAND – Parishioners have learnt with deep regret of the death, which occurred at Haywards Heath, of the Rev. Walter Beauchamp LOVEBAND, who had been Curate in the village for some time. The deceased gentleman, who was the eldest son of the Rev. W.LOVEBAND, R.D., Vicar of Ifield, was on a visit to his fiancée, Miss LANGTON, making arrangements for their approaching marriage, when he was taken ill. The deepest sympathy is felt for the lady and the deceased's family. The funeral took place at Ifield on Monday.

A BARCOMBE FAMILY SQUABBLE – UNCLE AND NEPHEW AT LOGGERHEADS – "I expect

sorrow at the loss the parish had sustained in the sudden death of another priest who had been working up to last week among them. He referred to the Rev. W.B.Y.LOVEBAND, and said he died in the full vigour of life. He was ordained in 1909, and came to Barcombe after being two years at Burgess Hill and Heathfield. Their sympathy went out to those he had left behind...The Rev. FARRAR,

the new Rector, is well known in the locality. For some years he worked as Chaplain in connection with the Mission for Seamen, and then became Vicar of St. James's, Carlisle. The Rector was for some time Superintendent of the Seaman's Mission, and at the time he was appointed to the Rectory of Barcombe he was Vicar of All Saints', Shooters Hill, Woolwich...

there were faults on both sides; and the Magistrates dismiss the case. It is a pity they can't settle this family squabble." So spoke Mr F.B.WHITFELD, the presiding Magistrate at the Lewes Petty Sessions on Tuesday at the conclusion of the evidence in a case in which Sier MARKWICK, of Barcombe, was summoned by his nephew, Aubrey Markwick COPPARD, for an alleged assault on August 11th.

Complainant said that at about eight o'clock on the evening of the day named he went to 'Delves Farm' to pay a bill. As he was leaving, a carter named KING, said to him, "If you want a job you had better go and help your father." Complainant replied, "I don't think (so); I shall let those who are paid to do it go and do it." Complainant stood talking by the stable door when defendant remarked, "Men don't know how to work." Complainant replied, "You can't expect two old men to work like two younger men. I expect they have done their share." Defendant then struck him with his open hand twice and told him to "clear off home." Complainant stood talking to his brother, and then defendant struck him several more times and also kicked him. Complainant's father worked for defendant's mother. The following evening he again saw the defendant, who threatened to "throw him into a slush hole and tread him in." Complainant

ABOVE: The 6 H.P. "Baby-Peugeot" car, £147 complete, Eastgate Garage, Lewes

denied striking defendant in the face with a basket. He swung the basket to protect himself from the defendant.

Amos MARKWICK (15) gave corroborative evidence. Defendant denied the assault, and called Horace KING, a carter, as a witness. KING protested that it was a shame "to fetch us down here when four horses which should be corn cutting are idle at home." He denied that defendant struck his nephew. All defendant did was to take him by the shoulders and push him away after complainant had struck his uncle in the face with a fish basket. As stated above, the case was dismissed.

27th August - BARCOMBE MILLS VISITORS –
Barcombe Mills is well known as the rendezvous of many visitors in the summer, and this year, we are informed, the influx is as good as previous years. Therefore many residents who let apartments can say, like their seaside contemporaries "full up".

WOUNDED SOLDIER'S TREAT – Last Friday Lady GRANTHAM generously entertained a number of wounded soldiers from the School Hill Hospital, Lewes. The men arrived at about two o'clock in the afternoon, and returned to Lewes by the 6.17 train in the evening. The party consisted of about thirty men, including two Belgian soldiers.

STILL "FALLING IN" – It is claimed that Barcombe has given as many men to the Army as any district with a proportionate population. The latest recruits to be added to the list are: Frank FOORD[13] and Sidney HENTY, who have joined the Royal Garrison Artillery; Victor and Stanley KEMP, Reggie WALL, Arthur TROWER, and George KING have all joined the Marines.

JUVENILLE CRICKET – As is customary during the cricket season, Miss WALKER of Barcombe and Miss REECE of Spithurst, arrange cricket matches for each Saturday. It is a form of friendly rivalry between the two districts. The scratch teams consist of boys under fourteen, who, fired with enthusiasm, are no mean batters and bowlers.

CRICKET – Last Wednesday, members of the Barcombe Cricket Club journeyed to Preston Park and played the Royal Army Service Corps, but were badly beaten. Barcombe only scoring 64 to their opponents' 132. The members of the Club were entertained to tea by the Colonel of the Corps. To-morrow (Saturday) the Club will play Offham, the match starting at 2.30.

ANGLING – If you possess rod and line and other necessary equipment, visit the stream and you will not return home with an empty bag. Plenty of good fish are being hooked, particularly trout. Victor KING, for instance, who is only a small boy, landed during the week a roach weighing 1 lb.2 ozs.

and George WILMOUR two fine trout. Furthermore, Mr Alfred STEVENS, who is a noted local angler, had the felicity of catching four fine specimen trout, and the annoyance of losing a "monster" which completely broke his tackle.

LATE RECTOR'S WILL – The Rev. Prebendary SALMON left estate of the gross value of £5,491. He bequeathed £10 to his coachman, John BANKS, and a similar sum to his gardener, John VAUGHAN.

ABOVE: Captain Frederick GRANTHAM (1870-1915)

LATE CAPTAIN GRANTHAM – Captain Frederick William GRANTHAM, Royal Munster Fusiliers, second son of the late Sir William GRANTHAM, who was reported wounded and missing on 9th May, is now reported killed. Forty-four years of age, the deceased officer was Clerk of Assize in

the Oxford Circuit. He served in the South African War, and had taken part in a good deal of fighting in Flanders.

3rd September - A DECENT JACK – The pleasure of capturing a Jack weighing 3½ lbs. fell to the rod of Mr Thomas REED this week.

JUVENILLE CRICKET – The usual match between the boys of Barcombe and Spithurst was played on Saturday, the conqueror's on this occasion being those playing for Spithurst.

STILL "FALLING IN." – To be added to the already long list of recruits from this district are Thomas STEVENS and Harry FURMINGER[14], who have both enlisted in the Royal Garrison Artillery.

10th September - FATHER AND SON KILLED – We recently recorded the death in battle of Captain F.W. GRANTHAM, second son of the late Sir William GRANTHAM of Barcombe and we have now heard that the gallant Captain's son 2nd Lt. Hugo GRANTHAM has been killed at the Dardanelles. Thus the honoured family of GRANTHAM sustains a grievous double blow which has aroused the most

---

13 *Killed 1st September 1917 near Ypres, Belgium.*

14 *Harry Albert FURMINGER, a farm carter, originally from Forest Row, was just seventeen when he signed up. He survived the war and re-enlisted at Lovinich, Germany, for a further two years in March 1919, as a driver in the Royal Field Artillery.*

sincere sympathy among the inhabitants of Barcombe and throughout the County generally. Soon after the father gave his life for King and country in France, his gallant son fell on the other front in the Gallipoli peninsular, a family sacrifice which will always be recalled with mingled sorrow and pride in the history of the War. Captain GRANTHAM who was 44 years of age was first reported wounded and missing on May 9th and recently his name was included in the official list of killed. He was serving with the Royal Munster Fusiliers. His son, 2nd Lt. Hugo GRANTHAM was killed in the fighting at the Dardanelles. He was in the Essex Regiment. The oldest son of Captain GRANTHAM, he was only 20 years of age.

SERVICES IN MISSION ROOM & SPITHURST – The

evening services are to be held in the Mission Room, but on the third Sunday in each month there will be evening prayers and a sermon at St.Bartholomew's.

LIGHTS TOO CONSPICUOUS – The

evening services which have been held at 6.30 in the Parish Church on Sundays are now to take place at three o'clock in the afternoon. The alteration applies to both churches.

THANKS – The Rector refers in the Parish Magazine, to his recent Institution and Induction, and thanks the Churchwardens for their foresight and excellent arrangements for the occasion. He also tenders his thanks to

ABOVE: 'There's Room For You…' – Recruiting poster issued by the Parliamentary Recruitment Committee during 1915 (U.S. Library of Congress, Prints & Photographs Division, reproduction no. LC-USZC4-11023)

the ringers for "ringing him in"; the choir, and all those who decorated the church. He writes sympathetically of the

late Rector and the Rev. Walter LOVEBAND.

17th September - LAST POST AT BARCOMBE - LADY GRANTHAM'S LOSS - A memorial service for the late Captain F.W. GRANTHAM, second battalion Royal Munster Fusiliers, younger son of Lady GRANTHAM of Barcombe Place, Barcombe and the late Mr Justice GRANTHAM was held at St. Mary's Church, Barcombe on Wednesday afternoon.

The deceased officer, who was 44 years of age, was leading some of the Fusiliers in an attempt to take an enemy trench in Flanders on May 9th when he was shot while on the parapet. He fell into the trench and it is believed that his death was instantaneous. The Fusiliers took the trench but could not hold it and the Germans recovered it. Later however the Fusiliers made another charge and recaptured the trench but the Captain's body was not then in the trench. On May 9th he was reported missing and wounded and there was no further news of him until August when he was officially reported to have been killed. Deceased lived at Beeleigh Abbey, Maldon, Essex, and is survived by a wife and two sons. He had three sons, but the eldest, Lt. Hugo GRANTHAM, 1st Essex Regiment was killed at the Dardanelles sometime

ABOVE: Motorised transport of the 6th (Cyclists) Battalion, RSR, who were stationed at Southwold, Suffolk for most of 1915. Photographed by A.W. Coen of Norwich.

after the falling of his father.

The service which was attended by the bereaved families and many parishioners was conducted by the Rector and the Rev. C.TOOGOOD of Burpham, a former curate, also took part. The surpliced choir was also present. The hymns sung were "For All the Saints" and "Peace Perfect Peace", while Psalm xci was rendered and the 'Nunc Dimittis' was sung kneeling. The lesson was from I Corinthians, xv.

Reference had been made by the Rector to the deceased in prayers but not in the pulpit and at the close of the service the Organist (Mr G.H.GASTON) played "The Dead March" and Drummer W.J.ALLEN 10th Middlesex Regiment beat a tattoo on the drum. Finally Drummer G.W.BROWN, also of the 10th Middlesex Regiment, sounded the Last Post…

THE FIGHTING GRANTHAMS - Mr Ivor GRANTHAM, a grandson of Lady GRANTHAM of Barcombe Place is about to become a Private in the 6th Royal Sussex (Cyclists) Regiment.

NEW RECRUITS - To be added to the already long list of recruits from this district are: Leslie WILLMORE, William CROUCHER and Joseph COTTINGHAM who have enlisted in the Royal Garrison Artillery.

ON LEAVE - Corporal Arthur PRATT, who joined the Army Veterinary Corps as a Private, and is now promoted, has returned from the Front, having been granted leave for a short period.

CRICKET - The match which was to have taken place last Saturday between Barcombe and Newick was scratched at the last moment, and it is unlikely now, seeing that the season is drawing to a close, that the teams will meet.

LEWES CADETS – Barcombe was visited on Sunday by the above Cadets. There were about fifty members, and the peaceful village was soon thronged with people when the bugle band was heard approaching in the distance.

NOTICE TO QUIT – At Lewes County Court on Monday, before his Honour Judge MACKARNESS, Frederick ARCHER, now in the Sussex Regiment; was summoned to show cause why he should not give up possession of a cottage in Barcombe, the property of Edwin Walter BUNNEY. His Honour read a letter from the defendant (who was not present), and asked plaintiff's son: "Did you give him notice because his sons had enlisted?" – Mr BUNNEY: "No. We want possession of the cottage." – An Order was made for defendant to give up possession in 14 days.

HUNTSMEN AND HOUNDS – At about half-past five on Wednesday morning, the Southdown Huntsmen met in the centre of the village, and later proceeded to the Rough. Reynard (the fox), however, was not located there, so the huntsmen and hounds, together with many of the villagers, wended their way to Beachy Wood.[15] Whilst there, the cry of "Tally Ho" was sounded from the road, which Reynard had been observed slinking across and making for the Rough. Here with the aid of the little fox terriers, he was located in a hole, and after a full hour's digging, he became the hounds' prey.

---

15 *Beachy Wood lies on the Hamsey side of the Town Littleworth road, to the north of 'Gallybird Hall'.*

24th September - BARCOMBE PARTNERS AND THE PIGS – Charles PUTT and Arthur DAY, two young men, were summoned at Lewes Petty Sessions on Tuesday for failing to deliver up movement licences of swine, and also for moving swine during period of detention. They pleaded guilty in both cases.

P.S.GOODSELL, who is an inspector under the Diseases of Animals' Act, stated that on August 21st he granted a movement licence for five pigs to come from Norfolk to Chailey, but as he did not receive the licence from the defendants he called upon them

ABOVE: Southdown Foxhounds 'In Full Cry' at Cooksbridge. A collectable card given inside a packet of Franklyn's cigarettes c.1925.

at Caveridge Farm. PUTT admitted receiving the pigs from Norfolk, and he produced the licence. Witness told him that it should have been delivered up, but he said that he did not know that. Witness then asked him where the pigs were, and he replied that they had sold them at Lewes Market. Witness told him that they should have been kept on the premises for 28 days, and he replied that he did not know anything about that, adding "I was totally unaware of the conditions, and hope you will accept my plea of ignorance."

In reply to the Chairman (Mr F.R.WHITFELD), witness said he could produce evidence that the pigs did go into the Lewes Market. PUTT – We had only been there two months and had not been farming before. We had not had pigs before. Each were fined £1.

DEATH OF A VETERAN PLOUGHMAN – Mr Richard PARSONS, famous in his time as an unrivalled ploughman, passed away at his residence in Barcombe last Monday.[16] He had reached his 89th year, and only retired from work two years ago. This was on the occasion of Mr DUDENEY, for whom the deceased had worked for twenty years, relinquishing his farm.[17] He

---

16 *F Richard PARSONS lived "near Clappers" bridge on the road between Barcombe Cross and Spithurst (1914 electoral register, ESRO: C/C70/201).*

17 *Arthur Ellis DUDENEY farmed 'Handlye Farm' on the Cooksbridge Road, before moving along the road to 'Stepney Farm' c.1913.*

ABOVE: Ploughing at 'Mongers Farm' (Mike Green collection).

and his wife, whose age is 87, have been living on their old age pensions. He was the father of four daughters and three sons, grandfather to twenty-four children, and great-grandfather to sixteen. Deceased – who was born at Barcombe – about a fortnight ago was the victim of a stroke, which was the herald of his death. The funeral took place yesterday (Thursday) afternoon.

GIFT FOR CHOIR BOYS – Lady GRANTHAM has this week presented a little gift to each of the choir boys for their excellent singing at the memorial service which was recently held on the occasion of the death of her son.

YESTERDAY'S FARM SALE – By order of Mr S.DIPLOCK, who is relinquishing farming, Messrs. Drawbridge and Ansell, of Haywards Heath , conducted a sale at the Bradness and Beaks Farms, Longford, yesterday,

RIGHT: Recruits and Railway Staff at Cooksbridge Station (courtesy Sue Rowland).

when there was a large attendance and good prices were realised.

ANGLING – You have not long to wait for a bite if you visit the stream. Mr William LANE, a well-known local angler, hooked about twenty roach last week, and not one weighed under 10 ozs. A visitor had the pleasure also of landing a pike weighing about 7 lbs., which he caught on live bait.

NEW RECRUITS - It is said there is hardly a young man to

be found in the district now. This week two more men have helped to swell the already big list. Thomas FAULKNER known as "Cann" FAULKNER who worked for Mr MUGGERIDGE the butcher has joined the Army Service Corps whilst Bert KING who was in the employ of the Blacksmith Mr FUNNELL, has enlisted in the Royal Field Artillery as a farrier.

ANNIVERSARY CELEBRATION – The members of the Barcombe Mission Hall, which was founded about eighteen years ago, had their annual celebration on Wednesday afternoon and evening. Mr Gerrard LLOYD occupied the chair, and an address was delivered in the afternoon by Mr William TAYLOR of Hove. In the evening, after tea had been served, the members were addressed by a number of other person, and later Miss

BRIDGE of Brighton, rendered three sacred songs, whilst Mrs VERCOE accompanied her on the organ. There was a good attendance, many persons having come from Chailey, Brighton, etc.

FUNERAL OF MISS TROWER

– The funeral of Miss Edith Mercy TROWER, who died at the Lewes Victoria Hospital from heart disease on Tuesday, the 14th inst., took place at Barcombe cemetery on Friday afternoon. Deceased had been six weeks in hospital, and was thirty-two years of age. She was the daughter of the late Mr William Luther TROWER, and had resided with her sister at 'Crink View.' She was well known and highly respected, and her demise was the occasion of much sympathy. There were many floral tributes, and the principal mourners who attended the funeral were:- Mrs W.L.TROWER (mother), Miss TROWER (sister), Mr & Mrs W.L.TROWER, Mr & Mrs H.TROWER, Mr & Mrs J.TROWER, Messrs. W. & H.TROWER (nephews), Miss E.DIPLOCK, Miss GOODE, and Miss DITTON.

1st October - BY AUCTION

– Mount Pleasant & Spring Farm, Hamsey (Opposite Gallybird Hall, Barcombe).

A BARCOMBE CRACK

- Sergeant HAWKINS of the 9th Battalion Royal Sussex Regiment, son of Mr HAWKINS of 'Sole

ABOVE: Sunlight Soap – Lever Brothers' advertising with a military twist: "The British Line is firmly held by the Cleanest Fighter in the World. The clean, chivalrous, fighting instincts of our gallant Soldiers reflect the ideals of our business life."

Cottage', Barcombe enlisted on September 13th 1914 and went to the Front three weeks ago, and during the previous week was awarded first prize for marksmanship in the firing test. He was made a Sergeant last December. He went through the Boer War as a private in the 2nd Battalion, Royal Sussex Regiment and for this service he has two medals. His wife, who lives at High Street, Barcombe, is a Lewes woman, being a daughter of Mr & Mrs W.BARROW of 16 St. John's Terrace.

SHORT LEAVE - Captain BROWNE who has been serving with a Manchester Infantry Regiment, was granted two days leave and returned

to his Regiment again last Monday. The Captain has been home twice before, but on each occasion he had been wounded. The Captain's wife was (formerly) Miss HOPWOOD of 'Scobells' Barcombe.

HARVEST FESTIVAL – These services take place next Sunday, and sermons will be delivered by the late Curate, the Rev. C.TOOGOOD, who is now Rector at Burpham. The offerings will be divided between the men who are now prisoners in Germany and the Royal Agricultural Benevolent Society, whilst the fruit and vegetables will be dispatched to the men of the Fleet.

FOUND COMPETENT - Bert KING, who, as announced in our last issue, has joined the Royal Field Artillery as a farrier, had to undergo a stiff examination in his trade at the Brighton Barracks. This was for the purpose of elucidating whether one so young (KING is but 18) could be classed as a special shoeing-smith. Four sergeant-majors and a veterinary surgeon stood by when KING was ordered to make four shoes and affix same. The job was accomplished so capably and rapidly that he was congratulated and of course will in future be designated as a "special". This speaks well for his late employer Mr FUNNELL, to whom KING was apprenticed.

RGHT: Ben COLLINS, seated far right, in a tug of war team, during training with the 3rd Lewes Company of the Territorial Battalion, Sussex Royal Garrison Artillery. The two officers in the centre (corporal, centre and sergeant-major, below) had been taking part (note white trousers), but had put their tunics and caps on for the photograph to show their rank (courtesy Beryl Jackson).

SUSSEX. R.G.A. (T) 3RD LEWES COY. TUG OF WAR TEAM.

PATRIOTIC BROTHERS - Mrs WALL of 'Place Lodge', has the proud distinction of having five of her six sons with the Colours. Harry is in the Army Service Corps as a motor driver; David in the Kents; Fred in the Royal Field Artillery; Sidney in the Bantams and Reg in the Royal Navy. The sixth son Jack, who is not yet old enough to enlist, is a keen member of the Barcombe Troop of the Boy Scouts. Mrs STEVENS of Thatched Cottage, has four sons serving, Frank in the Canadians; Harry in the Marines and Ernest and Leonard in the Royal Garrison Artillery. Mrs COLLINS, of Spithurst, has three sons: Ben and George in the Royal Garrison Artillery, and Bert in the Royal Marines. A brother, Ben SAYERS, is in the National Reserve; and a nephew Charles SAYERS, is in the Royal Garrison Artillery.

A DREADFUL NIGHT – At the latter end of last week Barcombe was invaded by Companies of the Hants, Wilts, Surrey, Royal Medical Corps, Royal Horse Artillery, etc. Regiments, and it is questionable if the district had ever so many visitors before. They arrived in the morning, and so great was the attraction that scarcely any of the district children made their appearance at school. The soldiers were out on manoeuvres, and at night they sojourned in the fields for rest. They possessed no tents, so their dilemma can be readily imagined when the torrential rain began to fall. The men were soon in a pitiable condition, and hundreds of them wended their way back to the village, where they knocked at the doors of the houses and begged admittance, which was promptly granted. Another feature of the visit was the intermingling of the Barcombe Boy Scouts, who had gained permission to camp out with the soldiers. They, fortunately, had protection from the rain, inasmuch as they were tucked away snugly beneath the many wagons. The boys furthermore, had been granted permission to march next morning with the soldiers to Lewes, from which destination they returned home. The Scouts, it may be added, have been granted twenty-eight days' leave, and are now helping the district farmers in the fields of mangles.

8th October - THE LAST CHANCE – MAJOR COURTHOPE, M.P., ON THE VOLUNTARY SYSTEM – "Slackers, Scrimshankers and Cowards." – At a recent recruiting demonstration at Hastings on Saturday, Major G.L.COURTHOPE, M.P. for the Rye Division, who has been serving with the 5th Battalion Royal Sussex Regt. at the Front, delivered a very candid speech with regard to the Voluntary system and the men who ought to be serving in the Army and are not. He confessed he would not be sorry if the recruiting rally were a failure, as it would force several millions to realise the duties of citizenship... Sgt. NICHOLLS, who has lost a foot in the war, said: "... It is the last chance given to the Voluntary System to find the men we want... They can come in under the voluntary system, they can come in with some little credit to themselves... but if the recruiting rally which is going on now is a failure, they will still come in, but as conscripts, and they will probably come in without pay. It will serve them right."

MAJOR GRANTHAM UPSETS A LORD – Major W.W.GRANTHAM, commanding the Sussex Cyclists Battalion, gave evidence at Bexhill on Tuesday in a case in which Lord Francis HERVEY was summoned for having shown too much light at his house in Sussex square.

Major GRANTHAM said he was passing the house of Lord Francis, and saw a very bright light, which was visible from the sea. When the defendant was told of the light by the police he replied, "I have been a barrister; I know what the law is."

A servant said that she went into the room complained of and turned on the light. She wrote a postcard, and in five minutes she turned the light out again.

While the Magistrates were consulting there was a passage of words between Lord Francis and Major GRANTHAM, in which Lord Francis said, "You did not give your name, but forced yourself into my house."
Major GRANTHAM – No, I came in at the invitation of your servant.

Lord Francis (heatedly) – You committed a breach of law.
Major GRANTHAM – You can summons me if you like.
Lord Francis – I will.
Defendant was fined 20s.
Lord Francis HERVEY, who is an uncle of the Marquis of Bristol, was a Conservative Member of Parliament from 1874 to 1880 and from 1885 to 1892.

HARVEST FESTIVAL – The collections at the Barcombe churches last Sunday, when the Harvest Festival services took place, amounted to over £12.

SUFFERING FROM SHOCK – Sergeant Ernest WATSON, who has been serving with the Royal Army Medical Corps, has been suffering from shock. He has been at the Dardanelles, and this is his second visit home. He resides at 'The Bungalow'.[18]

WOUNDED – Second-Lieut. Theodore BOURDILLON, of the 9th Royal Sussex Regiment, has been wounded in the arm. He is now at Guy's Hospital, London. He had only been in France about a month, and took part in the recent big battle there.

HE FEARED NOTHING – On the occasion of the death of Captain F.W.GRANTHAM, Lady GRANTHAM received a letter from the Commanding Officer, in which he said: "It was largely owing to the gallant leading of your son that we were the only regiment in the Brigade to reach the German trenches. I can assure you that all the men in his Company loved him, and his is a great loss to the Regiment. One of the Officers once said to me, speaking of your son: 'He is the bravest man in the Regiment, and fears nothing.'" The late Captain's widow received a telegram from Their Majesties the King and Queen.

15th October - MRS MARKWICK MEETS WITH AN ACCIDENT – Mrs MARKWICK, who up to last week occupied Delves and Gallops Farms, and who only removed to Plumpton last Monday, has had the misfortune to break her thigh. Fuller information will be found in our Plumpton news.

ANGLING – Fishing is excellent at the present time. Mr William LANE, of 'Wootton Lodge', caught twelve nice roach on Sunday, and Mr George STANDING of Brighton, had the pleasure of hooking and landing a tench weighing 3lbs. The stream was

---

18 *The WATSON family continued to live at 'The Bungalow' after the war. The 1939 Electoral Register shows Fanny and Constance Jessie WATSON at this address, but there is no sign of Ernest.*

visited on Sunday afternoon by two Brighton Angling Clubs, the purpose being to hold a competition, the losing Club having to "stand" a mutton supper.

LATEST RECRUIT - Mr James STANDING has joined the Army Service Corps and leaves the district on Monday. He is well known having been for the past 9 years employed by Mr RICHARDS the baker. He was Secretary of the Slate Club for a number of years and at a meeting of the members of that body held on Wednesday evening at the Reading Room, it was decided that Mr J.G.HOLLOWAY would act in Mr STANDING's stead till the end of the season.

OCTOGENARIANS DEATH - Mr William VERRALL, a native of Barcombe, passed away at his son's residence, in Patcham, on Tuesday last. Deceased, who was 86 years of age last August, was much respected in the village. Senile decay was the cause of death, but up to the last five weeks, when he visited his son, he had been hale and hearty throughout his life. His wife died about five years ago, and from that period he has keenly felt the bereavement, for the pair lived a loveable and inseparable life. In his younger days he acted as a farm bailiff, and held several positions in the district. Of flowers he was passionately

fond, and their cultivation, together with gardening generally, was his great hobby. The remains of the deceased were removed from Patcham to Barcombe to-day (Friday), when he was buried, as was his wish, beside his wife. The principal mourners were: Mr & Mrs George VERRALL, Mr & Mrs William VERRALL, Mrs Alfred VERRALL, Mr A. and Miss VERRALL, and Mr & Mrs Thomas VERRALL. A fair

ABOVE: "Sussex Star Turns" At Sea – "A Sussex Quartet on H.M.S. Superb," including (standing right) W.E. BATTEN of Barcombe, Royal Marine Artillery and (seated right) Seaman G. REEVES of Newick.

number of friends visited the Cemetery, and there were many floral tributes.

FARM SALES – DELVES AND GALLOP'S FARMS – Mrs S.MARKWICK is quitting these farms, which have been in the occupation

of the family for 30 years, and on Saturday there was a sale on the premises of the stock, machinery, implements, etc., by Messrs. Drawbridge and Ansell. The ingoing farmer is Mr REVELL, jun. of Balcombe, and Mrs MARKWICK is removing to a smaller acreage at Plumpton. There was only a moderate attendance at the sale. The luncheon was catered by Mrs CLARE, of the 'Elephant & Castle', Lewes. [Details of the animals sold, their names, prices and purchasers are given].

22nd October - ON LEAVE – Seaman William BATTEN, serving on H.M.S. 'Superb' and Seaman Harry STEVENS, serving on a transport ship, have been granted short leave.

QUITE WELL – The many friends of Private William BANKS, the Barcombe bell-ringer and choirman, who is serving at the Front with the 9th Royal Sussex Regiment, will be glad to learn that, according to a letter received by a friend, he is in the best of health.

TRAFALGAR DAY – The ladies attending the sale of flags were: Miss Muriel GRANTHAM, Mrs S.BURROWS, Mrs BROOKSBANK, Miss HOLLOWAY, Mrs George HOLLOWAY, Mrs J.FUNNELL, Miss DAY, and

ABOVE: Alfred MOON (far left) and infants' class photographed at Barcombe School, c.1905 (ESRO: WI 112/1/1, p.162).

Miss VAUGHAN. The sale, as far as can be gleaned, was exceptionally good.

WHIST DRIVE RESULT – The inaugural whist drive of the season took place at the Reading Room on Wednesday evening, 22 tables being occupied. The lady prize winners were: 1st, Miss KENWARD and Miss WELSH, 172 each; Miss KENWARD won the cut; 3rd, Miss HAFFENDEN 139. The gentlemen winners were: 1st, Mr J.STEVENS 172; 2nd Mr Ernest RHODES 171; 3rd Mr A.FULLER of Newick 135.

29th October - RETIREMENT OF MR MOON – On the 31st of December Mr Alfred MOON,

who has been headmaster at the Church of England School, for nearly forty years, relinquishes his position. During that period no fewer than seventeen to eighteen hundred boys and girls have passed under his tuition. Mr MOON loves his school and his children; and after the uninterrupted lengthy period he has become so inured to school life, and endeared to its every detail, that it is with profound regret he severs his connection. He has reached his 65th year; his resignation therefore becomes compulsory, that being the age limit, according to the Education regulations.

His first school was at Chipping Ongar, Essex,

and it was in 1876 that he was installed as headmaster at Barcombe School… Mr MOON has ever been keenly interested in all matters connected with the village, and has acted in the capacity of Secretary for five or six clubs at a time, such, for instance, as the Cricket Club, Agricultural Society, Reading Room, Juvenile Foresters, etc. He is greatly attached to the Reading Room. In his early days, previous, of course, to compulsory education, he had known as few as five children make an appearance at school on a wet day, and at that time there were more children on the books than there were at present, whereas now, should it

RIGHT: Women of Britain Say 'Go!' - Poster produced during 1915 by the Parliamentary Recruiting Committee.

prove a wet day, there would be an attendance of about 150.

Mr MOON was connected with the Sunday School for about 33 years, and for most of that period acted as Superintendent. He resigned the position however, in 1909, and on that occasion was the recipient of an illuminated address, together with a gold watch, which the late Sir William GRANTHAM, at the request of the many subscribers, selected in London. The presentation was made by Lady GRANTHAM. Mr MOON remembers the railway to East Grinstead being made, and recalls the heavy snowstorm which occurred in 1881. The snow on that occasion lay ten feet deep, and the roads had to be cleared by the many navvies who were engaged working on the railway, most of whom were Yorkshiremen. At that period he had a night school, and a number of the men, some for the purposes of improving themselves, and others to while away the time, attended. They were always deferential and quiet pupils, but in the open would at times fight between themselves like lions. These navvies lived in huts. Brick-making was quite an industry at Barcombe at the period, and many bricks were made on the ground on which the station now stands.

About three years ago one of Mr MOON's sons died in Canada; another is in Gloucestershire, and his daughter is acting as his housekeeper at Barcombe. Mr MOON, who is liked and respected by everybody in the village, will leave the school with the best wishes of all.

ON LEAVE - Private Sidney BECK has been granted short leave and is at home. He is connected with the Norfolk Regiment, which shortly leaves for India.[19]

19 Sidney A. BECK (34) was born in the Fulham registration district in 1881, moving to Barcombe by the time he was twenty.. By 1911 he had married Edith FUNNELL and was living with their first three children in the High Street home of his brother-in-law John FUNNELL. He survived the war and was buried in St. Mary's churchyard in 1953.

WOUNDED - Private Frederick KING of the 9th Royal Sussex Regiment has been in hospital for some time having been wounded in the arm and foot. He is now home. He has two brothers, Ernest and George serving in the Royal Marines and the former Ernest is at the Dardanelles.

LATEST RECRUITS - Private Frederick BLACKMAN who worked for Mr W.BUSSEY builder of Malling Street, Lewes, has joined the Royal Garrison Artillery and Private Henry CROUCH, lately connected with Mr MUGGERIDGE the butcher has joined the Royal Field Artillery. He has two brothers serving with the Colours, one of whom was wounded early in the war whilst serving with the 3rd Royal Sussex Regiment.

SURGEON LEAVES THE DISTRICT – Surgeon J.M. McCUTCHEON, who has been living at 'Fern Hill', for the last six months, left the district last Tuesday. He was assistant doctor on the Education Committee of the Borough of Lewes, and was previously surgeon on the super-Dreadnought 'Thunder'. He sails for India to-day (Friday), where he is taking up a position under the Government. Surgeon McCUTCHEON has a brother who is Sergeant-Major of a Canadian Contingent, and his father,

it may be stated, is a professor at one of the Scotch Universities.

5th November - KICKED BY A MULE – The many friends of Special Shoeing-smith Bert KING, who only joined the Royal Field Artillery a few weeks ago, will be sorry to hear that he was kicked in the face by a mule. It necessitated his removal to hospital for a few days, but we are pleased to state that he is progressing favourably.

LATEST RECRUIT - So many men have joined the Colours from this district that the inhabitants believe there are no more to enlist. Another man, however, in the person of Mr Ernest WATTS (of 'The Stables, Croft Ham'), who has been acting as chauffeur to Mr James Arthur Ley BIDEN has joined the Mechanical Transport Section. He leaves the district tomorrow (Saturday).

FUNERAL OF MRS COTTINGHAM – The funeral of Mrs COTTINGHAM took place yesterday (Thursday) afternoon at the Parish Church Cemetery, the officiating clergyman being the Rector. Deceased, who was forty years of age, and was the wife of Mr Harry COTTINGHAM, succumbed, after a lingering and painful illness, lasting about three years, to pernicious anaemia. She had been for twelve months in

Brighton Hospital, and about six weeks in Guy's Hospital, London.

BARCOMBE NURSING ASSOCIATION - The balance-sheet for the year ending September 30th shows a balance in hand of £8.6s. Mrs BURDER, who has acted as hon. secretary for a period of twenty-three years, is now resigning her position. Lady GRANTHAM has kindly consented to act in her stead, so those requiring medical and surgical nurses must apply to that lady. If maternity nurses are required, application must, as heretofore, be made to Miss J.DYKE.

NEARLY BLINDED WITH SHOTS - Official news has reached the mother of Private Stanley CLARK, who has been serving with the 1/4th Essex Regiment, that he is suffering from gunshots in the eyes. Private CLARK is now at a convalescent camp at Alexandria. He has been fighting at the Dardanelles, and only a few days ago a neighbour of Private CLARK's mother who had called on Private CLARK at Alexandria, had stated in a letter that his eyes were bad, that he was very deaf, and had become thin. He is now stated by the doctors to be medically unfit for further service, so he will therefore, it is expected, reach home for Christmas.

BARCOMBE ROLL OF HONOUR.

—:o:—

Leonard Stevens, Royal Garrison Artillery.
Charles Sayers, Royal Garrison Artillery.
Charles Stanley, Royal Navy.
Ernest Stevens, Royal Navy.
Albert Tapp, Royal Sussex Regiment.
John Tapp, Lancashire Regiment.
Ernest Trigwell.
Arthur Trower, Royal Navy.
Horace Verrall, Army Service Corps (Motor Transport).
Allan Vercoe, Sussex Yeomanry.
Henry Wall, Army Service Corps (Motor Transport).
David Wall, Royal West Kent Regiment.
Frederick Wall, Royal Field Artillery.
Sidney Wall, 12th Suffolk Regiment.
Reginald Wall, Royal Navy.
George Waller, Royal Sussex Regiment.
William Ward, Royal Sussex Regiment.
James Ward, Royal Sussex Regiment.
Thomas Ward, Royal Sussex Regiment.
Stanley Weller, Royal Sussex Regiment.
Selby Reed, Royal Sussex Regiment.
Albert Rann, Royal Garrison Artillery (F.T.).
Reginald Rhodes, Royal Army Medical Corps.
William Ridley, Royal Field Artillery.
H. Stanley Pullinger, Royal Sussex Regiment.
Bernard Pullinger, Royal Sussex Regiment.
Percy Pullinger, Irish Fusiliers.
James Pettit, Royal Field Artillery.
Cecil Peckham, Royal Sussex Regiment.
Jabez Pratt, Army Veterinary Corps.
Frederick Prevett.
Henry Prevett.
Charles Osborne, Royal Sussex Regiment.
John Oliver, Royal Sussex Regiment.
James Morley, Sussex Yeomanry.
Frederick Martin, Royal Garrison Artillery (T.F.).
Frank Martin, Royal Garrison Artillery (T.F.).
Ernest King, Royal Marines.
Frederick King, Royal Sussex Regiment.
Frederick Knight, Royal Army Medical Corps.
Alfred Knight, Royal Army Medical Corps.
George King, Royal Marines.
Stanley Kemp, Royal Marines.
Victor Kemp, Royal Marines.
Frank S. Henty, Royal Navy.
Gilbert Howell, Royal Sussex Regiment.
Albert Howell, Royal Sussex Regiment.
Reginald Jessup, Royal Sussex Regiment.
Charles Elphick, Royal Sussex Regiment.
Ernest Elphick, Royal Garrison Artillery.
Jack Elphick, Army Service Corps.
Albert Englefield.
Arthur Edwards, Royal Field Artillery.
James Edwards, Canadian Army.
Harry Edwards, Royal Sussex Regiment.
Frederick Fosbery, Royal Navy.
William Farenden, Royal Navy.
George Foord, Royal Sussex Regiment.
Alfred Foord, Army Service Corps.
Frank Foord, Royal Garrison Artillery (T.F.).
Arthur Furminger, Royal Garrison Artillery (T.F.).
Frederick Deacon.
Frederick Day.
Ernest Diplock, Army Service Corps (M.T.).
Benjamin Collins, Royal Garrison Artillery (T.F.).
George Collins, Royal Garrison Artillery (T.F.).
Reginald Chatfield, Cycle Corps.
John Cox, Royal Garrison Artillery (T.F.).
Thomas Cruse, Royal Sussex Regiment.
Frederick Cox, Royal Sussex Regiment.
Jack Baldwin, Royal Navy (T.P.).
George Bryant, Royal Engineers.
Charles Bryant, Royal Sussex Regiment.
George Buckwell, Royal Garrison Artillery (T.F.).
Ernest Barrow, Royal Garrison Artillery (T.F.).
James Blackman, Army Service Corps.
Sidney Blackman, Army Service Corps.
Alfred Blackman, Royal Marines.
John Blackman, Royal Sussex Regiment.
Frank Baker, Royal Sussex Regiment.
Albert Baker, Royal Sussex Regiment.
Frank Burne, Royal Navy.
Donald Burne, Royal Army Medical Corps.
William Banks, Royal Sussex Regiment.
David Banks, Territorials.
John Banks, Royal Sussex Regiment.
Arthur Brown.
Charles Brown.
William Burne, Royal Navy.
Frederick Green, Royal Navy.
Albert Collins, Royal Marines.
Albert King, Royal Field Artillery.

12th November - BARCOMBE (SCHOOL) ROLL OF HONOUR - (A list of 110 former pupils is given, along with the units in which they were serving).[20]

Arthur Skerrett.
Frederick Dobson.
Frederick Banfield, Royal Sussex Regiment (T.F.).
Leonard Chatfield, Royal Sussex Regiment (T.F.).
Charles Moon.
Sidney Henty, Royal Garrison Artillery.
Frank Austen, Canadian Army.
Trayton Austen.
Alfred Sandles, Royal Sussex Regiment.
Walter Edwards, Royal Sussex Regiment.
Arthur Martin, Royal Field Artillery.
Wallace King, Royal Sussex Regiment.
William Hawkins, Royal Sussex Regiment.
John Austen, Canadian Army.
Joseph Cottington, Royal Garrison Artillery (T.F.).
William Payne, Royal Navy.
Lloyd Ashdown, Royal Sussex Regiment.
Frederick Blackman, Royal Garrison Artillery.

We shall be pleased to publish any Sussex School Roll of Honour sent to us by the Headmaster.

"YOU OUGHT TO BE A SOLDIER."

(Addressed to the Eligible and Fit.)

—:o:—

Young man, you ought to be a soldier!
And wear a khaki suit!
Why do you stay? Your King is calling!
Can you that call dispute?

You knew the cruel and ruthless foeman,
With cunning skill and might,
Is waging war on Truth and Freedom!
So now defend the Right!

LEFT AND ABOVE: Barcombe School Roll of Honour – ex-pupils serving as of November 1915.

ON LEAVE - Private Frederick DAY, who is serving with the Sussex Regiment, has been granted leave, and is now at home.

PARISH CHANGE RINGERS - Three of the (bell) ringers are serving with His Majesty's Forces, namely Private Plummer STEVENS, Private William BANKS and Private Alfred MARTIN.

CANVASSER FOR RECRUITS APPOINTED – Mr H.WELLER, who holds the position of Sanitary Inspector for the Chailey Rural District Council, has been chosen as canvasser for recruits for the district.

RUSSIAN DAY – The arrangements for the collection in this district were in the hands of Mrs Gerard LLOYD. The result was excellent, about £6.5s. being collected. The school children contributed about 9s., and the lady collectors were: The Misses GODFREY, BOURNE, HEWITT, HALTER, Lena KING, D.HOLDEN, and K.VERCOE and Mrs Frank BALLARD.

WHIST DRIVE – There were eighty players at the whist drive on Wednesday evening. The prizes were given by Messrs. MOON and BLAKER. Results: Ladies: 1.Mrs E.RHODES 171; 2.Mrs BEAUCHAMP 167; 3.Miss A.HILLYER 129. Gentlemen: 1.Mr BLAKER 180; 2.Mr E.RICHARDS (Newick) 170; 3.Mr FORDHAM (Isfield) 127.

METROPOLITAN POLICEMAN AT HOME - Sergeant George FLEET, a member of the Metropolitan Police, is spending a week at home. At one time the

---

20 *One of the names on this list is Selby REED, a grandson of James Selby REED of the 'Station Inn,' Barcombe Mills (see obituary 15th January 1915). He had moved to Tunbridge Wells with his parents Hector & Rose and enlisted in the 5th Battalion, R.S.R. Selby "died of wounds" at Bethune Casualty Unit, France on 2nd May 1915, aged 19 (ref. Margaret Wootton, email 3rd September 2018).*

Sergeant worked for Mr RICHARDS as a baker's boy. He has been attached to the Police for the last eleven years, and was promoted to Sergeant after eight years' service. His father is gardener at 'Barcombe House', the residence of Colonel BICKNELL.

CIGARETTES FOR "TOMMIES" - Messrs. BALLARD & Son, grocers, have on three occasions dispatched cigarettes to the boys at the Front, numbering 1,000 each time. Payment for these cigarettes has been attained, not by asking for donations, but by simply placing a collecting box on the counter. This speaks well for the generosity of their many clients. The two first donations were consigned to the late Captain GRANTHAM, who used to see to the distribution. The last lot has been acknowledged by Captain J.R. Stokes.

19th November - A BARCOMBE EXAMPLE – A Letter from Rev. FARRAR, Barcombe Rectory: "Referring to the splendid record of Sussex men who have responded to the call of their King and Country in this our hour of need", may I send you the following from the parish, alike as an interesting record, and also as an incentive for others to follow: Mr & Mrs Isaac BRYANT, 'Gladstone Cottages' –

RIGHT: 'Barcombe House', Barcombe Mills, where George FLEET's father Fred worked as a gardener.

eldest son, Alfred Wallace BRYANT, as a soldier served at home and in India, where he died 23rd September 1897 at Dutta Khel. Second son, Henry BRYANT, serving in the Home Defence, London. Third son, George BRYANT, Warrant Officer of H.M.S. "Sparrow Hawke." Fourth son, Charles Albert BRYANT, Sergeant in the Engineers, serving at the Front. Sons-in-Law, Frederick FOSBERY, Chief Petty Officer on H.M.S. "Edgar," and his son Frederick Wallace FOSBERY, Signaller on

H.M.S. "Magpie." Charles William REYNOLDS, Air Craft Gun Instructor, at the Front; and his son, Charles David REYNOLDS, A.B. on H.M.S. "Queen Mary." Henry BARROW, Home Defence, Mayfield.

I would like to add that the four sons of this family were all educated in our Church Day Schools at Barcombe, under Mr Alfred MOON, and from which school so many have responded to their country's call, to the credit alike of their Headmaster and his staff and also to all who

Barrack Room Ballads

O it's Tommy this, an' Tommy that, an' "Tommy, go away";
But it's "Thank you, Mister Atkins," when the band begins to play,
The band begins to play, my boys, the band begins to play,
O it's "Thank you, Mr. Atkins," when the band begins to play.

Rudyard Kipling, 1892

have helped to maintain the efficiency of these schools.

LATEST RECRUIT - Seaman Jack BUCKWELL who worked for Mr Frederick S. SHENSTONE, J.P. on Vuggles Farm, has joined the Marines.

SINGING TO SOLDIERS – Miss Florrie RHODES,[21] who is attached to a Lewes troop of entertainers, known as the "Yellow Dominoes," sang at Eastbourne last Saturday night. The troupe, it may be pointed out, was organised for the purpose of entertaining soldiers.

ANOTHER VOLUNTEER - Mr Charles MUGGERIDGE, the butcher, has presented himself for enlistment and has passed the doctor. He intends joining the Sussex Yeomanry, and will become attached to that body when he disposes of his business.

ILLNESS OF MR SPELLER – Mr J.SPELLER of 'Place Cottage', who is bailiff to Major W.W.GRANTHAM, has been in ill health for the past twelve months. He has been suffering from sciatica, and is expecting to become an in-patient at one of the hospitals shortly…

WEDDING – The marriage of Miss Esther ROGERS and Mr Joseph HOBDEN was solemnised at the Chapel, Newick on Wednesday afternoon. The bride, who was given away by her father, is the youngest daughter of Mr Alfred ROGERS of 'Longford Farm', Spithurst, and the bridegroom belongs to Croydon. The best man was the brother of the bridegroom, and the bridesmaids were: Miss Ruth ROGERS (sister of the bride), Miss Doris GANDER (niece), and Miss Alice ROGERS (niece).

PARISH COUNCIL MEETING – The monthly meeting of the members of the Barcombe Parish Council was held on Tuesday evening at the Mission Room, Mr BUNNEY occupying the chair. Messrs. CORNWELL, RHODES and RICHARDS were present. The repairing of the gates of the glebe land was mentioned, but it was pointed out that the Footpaths Committee could not entertain the cost of same, and it was maintained that it was the landlords who should keep them in repair. The pathway at Barcombe Mills Station, which in the wet season becomes flooded, was also under discussion, and the Clerk was instructed to write and refer the Railway Company to previous letters sent by the Council in relation to the matter, and further, to invite the Company's Engineer to make an appointment, so that the matter could be dealt with at once. Mr RHODES called the attention of the Council to the big hole at the side of the road by Clappers Bridge, and the Clerk was instructed to write to the County Surveyor.

26th November - "*THE SIGNPOST*" - Mrs SYBIL GRANTHAM's USEFUL BOOK – ...We feel sure that this thoughtful work by a Sussex lady, whose earlier volume of poems, *Through Tears to Triumph* met with so much appreciation, will be received with real pleasure and gratitude.[22] The Bishop of Chichester has written an introduction.

NEW RECRUIT – The latest to join the forces is Mr Frank COPPARD,[23] who has been in the employ of Mr S.B.RICHARDS, the baker, for the last twelve years. He has joined the 3rd Royal Sussex Regiment.

Mr MOON'S SUCCESSOR – It was arranged that Mr CANNON, who was assistant teacher at the Elementary Schools, Mayfield, was to succeed Mr Alfred MOON as schoolmaster at the beginning of the New Year. Mr CANNON, however, has accepted a position at the Schools at Forest Row. The post, in consequence, is still vacant.

---

21 *Florence RHODES (19) was the daughter of Richard RHODES of 'Knowlands Farm'.*

22 *Sybil GRANTHAM (33) lived at Balneath Manor, Chailey with her husband W.W.GRANTHAM.*

23 *Frank COPPARD (25) lived at 'Slate Cottage' (1918 electoral register).*

W. Corke F. Cox R. Wall Dudeney E. Kirby Approximately 1912-1914
Sidney Richards Ron Kemp Laker Jack Bodle Wilfred Tapp Chinney Tapp
Tom Reed Fred Dean Jack Funnel

ABOVE: Barcombe Boy Scouts c.1913-1915, with their first Scoutmaster Sidney LAKER. The young scouts named include: W. CORKE, F. COX, Sidney RICHARDS, R. WALL, DUDENEY, E. KIRBY, Sydney RICHARDS, Tom REED, Fred DEAN, Ron KEMP, Jack BODLE, Jack FUNNELL, Wilfred & 'Chiney' TAPP (ESRO: WI 112/1/1, p.205).

CONSECRATION OF BOY SCOUTS' FLAGS – At the Parish Church on Sunday afternoon, the flags of the Barcombe Boy Scouts were consecrated.[24] The service was conducted by the Rev. FARRAR. There was a fair congregation, including a number of the Scouts from Glynde and Lewes. After the ceremony the boys were entertained to tea at the residence of Mr LAKER, 'Holmbush'.[25]

24 *Barcombe scout troop had been founded in late January 1913 at an inaugural meeting arranged by Mr W.W. GRANTHAM of Barcombe Place, "who had persuaded Mr LAKER to become Chief Scout Master." Also present at the meeting were neighbouring estate owner and Scout District Commissioner, Lord MONK BRETTON of Conyboro' and Mr Warrington BADEN POWELL K.C., brother of the founder General Robert BADEN POWELL whose cousin Thomas lived at 'High Hurst', Newick (Sussex Express, 31st January 1913)*

TESTIMONIAL – On Friday, the 19th inst., a meeting was held at the Reading Room to inaugurate a testimonial to Mr

25 *Sidney Joseph LAKER joined the Territorial Army in October 1914, before becoming a Lieutenant in the R.G.A. While he was away one of his step-daughters, Miss DUVAL took temporary charge of the Scout Troop, until he was invalided out of the Army in July 1915. The following year he was declared bankrupt (see Sussex Express, 26th May), at which time the incoming Schoolmaster William CARTER took over his roll as Scoutmaster.*

ABOVE: A Wartime Romance - May DAY of 'Willow Cottage' writes to Sgt. Thomas PYNE at Langdon Battery, Dover during 1915. Sgt. PYNE is named as one of the prize-winners at the 'Whist Drive' in the village hall in the article of 24th December. The couple eventually married at St. Mary's Church in September 1918 (courtesy Gwen Cannings).

Alfred MOON, who has been nearly forty years headmaster at the Barcombe School. The chair was occupied by the Rector, who read letters of apology for non-attendance from Miss SHENSTONE, correspondent for the school; Lord MONK BRETTON, Major W.W.GRANTHAM, Col. BICKNELL and Mr A.B.DEALTRY, who promised their support. The following committee were appointed to carry on the scheme: Lady GRANTHAM, Miss SHENSTONE, Captain SINGLETON, Messrs. BOURDILLON, BUNNEY, CORNWELL, H.C.DIPLOCK, R.RHODES, S.B.RICHARDS, and G.SMITH. Many of the old boys, it was pointed out, had joined the Army and Navy, and a good number of them

were at present fighting "somewhere in France," and it was hoped that many of these men would contribute.

TWO WEDDINGS – The marriage of Miss Winnie STRIVENS and Mr Harold KING was solemnised at the Parish Church on Wednesday afternoon, the Rev. FARRAR officiating. The bridegroom belongs to West Hoathly, and the bride, who is the youngest daughter of the late Mr Arthur STRIVENS, of 'Gypps Farm', was given away by her uncle, Mr Alfred BROWN of Cuckfield. She was attired in a grey costume, with black hat and carried a bouquet of white chrysanthemums. The best man was Mr Horace O'CONNOR, of Fittleworth, Pulborough. The bridesmaid was Miss Winnie BROWN,

cousin of the bride, and she was clad in saxe-blue and wore a black hat. The happy pair was the recipients of numerous presents.

– A quiet wedding took place last Saturday at the Parish Church, the contracting parties being Miss Elizabeth Frances OSBORNE, only daughter of Mr George OSBORNE, of Church House Farm and Mr Frederick Charles TURK, of Southover, Lewes. The bride was given away by Sergeant George TOWNSHEND, a cousin. The best man was Mr George FUNNELL, of Glynde, and the officiating clergyman was the Rev. FARRAR. The bride, who was clad in khaki and pale blue, with hat to match, and carried a bouquet of white chrysanthemums, was attended by Miss Eva WICKS, cousin of the bride, who wore a grey dress, a hat to match, and whose bouquet was of red and white chrysanthemums. The couple received many useful presents.

3rd December – VILLAGE CLUB – The 33rd annual meeting of this Club was held on Saturday, when there was a fair attendance considering the number of members who are serving with the Colours. Major W.W.GRANTHAM presided, and was supported but the Rector, Mr E.BOURDILLON, Mr MOON (hon. secretary), and the others. The balance-sheet showed a balance in hand. It was pointed out that this balance was due to the fact that the honorarium voted to the Hon. Secretary had been given back to the Club by Mr MOON, who was very cordially thanked for this generous act. The Rector and Mr BOURDILLON were added to the Committee. It was decided to repair the bagatelle table for the younger members. Major GRANTHAM very kindly gave £1 towards this object. After the election of the Committee and the re-election of the Hon. Secretary, Major GRANTHAM said a few words of good wishes for the success of the Club, and the hope was expressed the Major might be with them at the next annual meeting. The Major is now under orders for foreign service. It was decided to place a list of members on service in the Club Room.

10th December – SCHOOL GARDENING – The following estimates were approved by the East Sussex Education Committee at their meeting at Lewes, on Tuesday, for gardening requisites for the year which began on November 1st: Barcombe Church of England School – manure 12s., seeds and potatoes £1 0s.7d; total £1.12s.7d.

ON LEAVE – Three soldiers have been home on leave in the village. They are: Sergeant George DAVIES and Lance-Corporal Bernard PULLINGER of the 5th Royal Sussex Regiment; Private WALL, also attached to a Sussex Battalion, who has four brothers serving with the Colours; Reginald is in the Navy, Harry (who is now at the Front), Sidney, and Frederick are in the Army.

ABOVE: Bernard PULLINGER, photographed by the Wykeham Studios, London (courtesy Anne PEARCE).

PLUM PUDDINGS FOR "TOMMIES" – Mrs SPELLER together with her daughter, is making Christmas puddings for all Barcombe men who are at the different theatres of war. This is a big undertaking for two ladies; nevertheless, both are imbued with the desire of adding a little cheer to the fighting boys of the district, and their labour is encouraged by the people in the village, who readily subscribe.

Last year, it may be mentioned, over 20 Christmas puddings were made and despatched to soldiers, through the aid of Mrs SPELLER.

HEADMASTERSHIP – The Elementary School Sub-Committee reported to the East Sussex Education Committee, at Lewes on Tuesday, that the secretary of Barcombe Church of England School had submitted a letter, dated 15th November, from the Correspondent, stating that the Managers had not secured the Headmaster required, and enquiring whether, in the circumstances, the local Education Authority would be prepared to support an application to the Board of Education for an extension of the recent Master's certificate, which in the ordinary course, would expire on the 31st December. It was resolved that the Managers be informed that the Education Committee will be prepared to support an application to the Board for the extension of Mr MOON's certificate in the event of the Managers failing to secure the head teacher required by the 31st December.

17th December – POUND DAY – Yesterday (Thursday) was recognised as Pound Day for the Hospitals in the district. Messrs. BALLARD and Son were the receivers of goods, and Mr S.B.RICHARDS has undertaken to convey and deliver same to the Victoria Hospital, Lewes.

CHRISTMAS 1915.

The giving of presents at the Christmas Season is a good old custom that the passing of the years leaves untouched. But under existing circumstances we shall all feel that the national necessity for reasonable economy will oblige us to confine our gifts to articles that will be of real practical value and service to the recipients. Many of us also have friends and relatives in the Forces, either at the Front or with the Fleet, or in the Training Camps at home.

BROWNE & CROSSKEY

Have been successful in securing a variety of articles particularly suitable for gifts and remembrances, but which combine utility with beauty, and which are in many cases well within the reach of slender purses.
An inspection of the goods exhibited at the

High Street & Eastgate Street Establishments
AND AT THE
Furnishing Showrooms in Friars' Walk, Lewes,
will be a pleasure to the eye and solve many a difficulty in selection.

ABOVE: Christmas 1915 – Gifts "within the reach of slender purses" from Browne & Crosskey of Lewes.

BACK FROM HOSPITAL

- Mr SPELLER has been an inmate at the Sussex County Hospital for about a fortnight, where he has been undergoing an electrical massage treatment for sciatica. His many friends will be glad to learn that he has returned home this week greatly improved in health.

JAM FOR THE WOUNDED

- Lady GRANTHAM and her many willing workers deserve great praise on the result of their efforts at making jam for the sick and wounded soldiers. No less than 1,394 lbs of jam were sent from Barcombe to the following hospitals: Barons Down and School Hill House, Lewes; Brighton, Eastbourne, Westmeston and Hurst. Fruit was sent by Mr

BUNNEY, Mr GEARING, Mrs WALKER, Mrs T.TAYLOR, Mrs BURDER, Mrs WRIGHT, Mrs POCOCK, Miss SHENSTONE, Mrs O.FUNNELL, Mrs J.KING, Mrs H.VERRALL, Mrs CHATFIELD, Mrs HEASEMAN, Lady GRANTHAM, Lady MONKBRETTON, Mrs ELDRIDGE, Mrs MORLEY and Mr G.BODLE. The jam was made at Coneyboro', Barcombe Place, The Grange and Sutton Hall.[26]

SLATE CLUB – The members

of the Barcombe Slate Club assembled at the Reading Room on Monday evening for the purpose of receiving the annual "share out." The amount received by each member was 21s.1d., and there were 92 recipients, so the total amount was £96.19s.6d. Major W.W.GRANTHAM was re-elected President, Mr JESSOP chairman, Mr George HOLLOWAY as secretary, and Mr S.B.RICHARDS as treasurer…

SALE OF WORK – The Barcombe Girls' Friendly Society held their annual sale of work at the Reading Room on Wednesday afternoon. There were some exceptionally nice goods displayed, comprising gloves, mufflers, mittens, and numerous other articles, all of which had been made by the Barcombe girls. The lady workers have included the Misses DEALTRY, Mrs BURROWS and Miss SALMON, the late Vicar's daughter. Lady GRANTHAM, who is interested in the Society, paid the sale a visit. Independent of the stalls, where the girls' work was displayed, there were a cake stall, one for flowers, and one on which there was a bran dip for children. The latter was managed by young girls under fourteen years of age, who, connected with the Society, are known as "candidates". The Girls' Friendly Society, as

---

26 *The three largest houses in the parish had opened their kitchens to the jam makers. Coneyboro' was the home to Lord MONK BRETTON, Barcombe Place to Lady GRANTHAM and Sutton Hall to Frederick SHENSTONE and his daughter Adela.*

L. B. & S. C. RY.
PRIVILEGE TICKET.
This half available for One
week including date of issue

Newhaven Town to
BARCOMBE M'LS
5d. Third Class.
See conditions on back.
0446

ABOVE: Privileged Rail Travel – 'Privilege' return tickets were issued at the cost of a single fare to soldiers on short leave. This return half of a 3rd Class ticket was issued for a journey from Newhaven to Barcombe Mills on Boxing Day 1915.

is well-known, is world-wide, and the object of the sale was to create funds whereby sickly girls from London, etc., can visit the country to recuperate. The Barcombe branch of the Society consists of about thirty members, exclusive of the twenty candidates.

24th December - ON LEAVE - Sergeant William HAWKINS, who is attached to the 7th Royal Sussex Regiment, is home on leave. He returns to duty today (Christmas Eve).

RIGHT: 'A Merry Xmas and A Happy New Year. From the Staff of the Sergts Mess. R.F.A. Brighton 1915.' A note on the back says "From a few old pals to another." Mr MUGGERIDGE the butcher and Bert KING, blacksmith both joined the Royal Garrison Artillery during the later part of 1915 (courtesy Beryl Jackson).

POUND DAY – The aggregate weight of goods contributed in this district was about 3 cwt., which, considering the high prices of goods at the present time, is deemed fair.

SALE OF WORK – The sale of work which took place in the Reading Room on Wednesday, 15th inst., and which was under the auspices of the Girls Friendly Society, realised over £7, which was better than previous sales held in normal times.

BARCOMBE MILLS SLATE CLUB – The members of the Club received

A Merry Xmas and A Happy New Year. from the Staff of the Sergts Mess. R.F.A. Brighton. 1915

ABOVE: Christmas Greetings 1915-16 – A seasonal, embroidered silk postcard with a military aviation theme.

their annual "share out" last Friday evening, the amount received by each being 14s. The number of members was 27, and the small amount paid out to the members was owing to the large amount (£22) having been drawn for sick pay during the year.

RECTOR'S KINDNESS – The Rev. FARRAR is showing his kindly spirit this Christmas. He has given an order for 32 cwts. of coal, which are to be delivered to sixteen poor widows in the district. Each widow will therefore receive 2 cwt. It is needless to mention that the kindly action is much appreciated by the villagers.

WHIST DRIVE – A drive took place at the Reading Room, fifteen tables being occupied. The prizes were presented by Lady GRANTHAM, to whom Mr MOON proposed a vote

of thanks, seconded by Mr RICHARDS. Results:- Ladies: 1, Miss Elsie RHODES 189; 2, Mrs Harry FUNNELL 175; 3, Miss DAY 138. Gentlemen: 1 Mr J.SPELLER 178; 2 Mr A.FULLER 170; 3 Sergeant PYNE 139.

31ˢᵗ December - BARCOMBE GIRLS' FREAK, "EXCHANGE NO ROBBERY" - Two Barcombe sisters appeared at Lewes Petty Sessions on Tuesday, one being charged by the other with the theft of a coat, a skirt, a petticoat, and a hat.

The defendant was Alice Edith GANDER,[27] and she was charged with stealing these articles, which her sister, the owner, Fanny PRATT, valued at £1.11s.6d.

Prosecutrix, who occupies a cottage at Mill Lane, and is the wife of Jabez PRATT, of the Army Veterinary Corps in

France, said that both she and the defendant stopped with their parents at Barcombe until the 17ᵗʰ inst., when the defendant left without giving any reason. Witness gave her the cottage key, the rent book, and 3s., and asked her to go and pay the rent to Mr BUNNEY. She did not return, and when, three days later, witness went to the cottage and got in with one of her father's keys, she missed the articles which formed the subject of the charge. In their place had been left similar articles of clothing, excepting a hat. These her sister wore when she left her father's home. Defendant returned home on Christmas Day.

In reply to the Chairman, the witness said she knew, when she reported the matter, that the defendant was the only person who could have got into the cottage, as she had the key. The Chairman – We don't think there is sufficient evidence in the case, and we dismiss it. (To prosecutrix): Exchange is no robbery. Prosecutrix – I don't wish her to be treated harshly, but I would like it to be a lesson to her.

27 Alice GANDER (19) and her sister Fanny (24) moved to Barcombe from Herstmonceux c.1907 with their parents George & Ellen. Fanny had married Jabez PRATT at St.Mary's church in November 1911 and moved into a cottage in Mill Lane, where Jabez was working as a mill carman. Alice lived with her parents at 'Pond Plat' in front of St.Mary's church.

7628-L.   ROTARY PHOTO.E.C.

LEFT: 'Good Luck!' – A contemporary postcard promoting the 'On War Service' badge and wishing "Good luck to the fair munitioneer."

VALUED WORK – Mrs SPELLER and her daughters, according to the current issue of the Parish Magazine, collected £7.15s.9d. for the purpose of making plum puddings and sending same to the soldiers and sailors and prisoners of war in Germany. 52 plum puddings and gifts were sent to the Barcombe men abroad and at sea, and 20 to the prisoners. Mrs SPELLER and daughters have already received some deeply touching letters from the men.

WHIST DRIVE – The whist drive which was inaugurated by the ladies connected with the Red Cross Society took place at the Reading Room on Tuesday evening, when there was a good attendance.

BELOW: 'On War Service, 1916' – This badge was issued by the Ministry of Munitions to women engaged on war work. The badges were individually numbered on the back, but the whereabouts of the registers naming their recipients are unknown.

7th January - SUBSCRIPTIONS - A sum of £20.14s. has been subscribed towards the Barcombe Nursing Association.

JAM FOR THE WOUNDED - In addition to those already mentioned as contributing to the collection of jam for the military hospitals, it should be mentioned that nearly every cottager in the Parish gave a pot or pots of jam or fruit.

CHILDREN'S GARDENING CLASS – Mr MOON has received an encouraging letter from the East Sussex County Council Education Department about his gardening class: "I must congratulate you on your sales during the year, the amount realised being next to the highest in the county."

The lady winners were: 1 Mrs T.HENTY (brush and comb); 2 Miss CHATFIELD (tea caddy); hidden number prize, Mrs WALL (Japanese purse); booby, Miss E.RHODES (Iron Cross). Gentlemen: 1 Mr William DIPLOCK (hair brushes); 2 Mr J.KING (match stand); booby, Mr Thomas LADE (Iron Cross).

SUNDAY SCHOOL TREAT
– The annual children's treat took place at Lady GRANTHAM's residence, Barcombe Place, on Tuesday afternoon, when between 50 and 60 children participated. Amongst those present were: The Rev. Herbert FARRAR, Mrs FARRAR, Miss VAUGHAN and Miss Doris WALDER (teachers), Mr and Mrs BOURDILLON, Mr and Mrs REECE, Mrs BROOKSBANK and Mr & Mrs L.RICHARDS. The children thoroughly enjoyed the treat, and were very interested spectators of the tableaux, which were historical representations of such well-known events as King Alfred and the burning cakes, Queen Elizabeth and Sir Walter Raleigh, the Princes in the Tower, etc., and also representations of the characters from those ever-interesting children's stories; "Bo-peep", "Cinderella", "Sleeping Beauty", "Blue Beard", "Babes in the Wood" and "Queen of Hearts." The tableaux were formed by Mr and Mrs L.RICHARDS' children – Misses Nancy, Barbara, Gwenydd, and

Masters Norman and Trevor; also Miss Maud BOURDILLON, and Master REECE. They were, of course, in character costume, and undoubtedly made excellent pictures.

14th January - LIEUTENANT COLONEL F.H. WALKER - KILLED AT THE DARDENELLES - We regret to announce the death of Lieut. Col. Frank Hercules WALKER, who was killed whilst fighting at the Dardanelles. The official information was sent first to Isfield, where the deceased at one time resided, but was forwarded on Wednesday night to The Grange, Barcombe, which is the residence of his mother.

SOLDIERS ENTERTAINED
– A concert took place at 'The Grange,' the residence of Mrs WALKER, on Wednesday evening, there being a good attendance, including wounded soldiers from 'Hickwells' Convalescent Home, Chailey. Amongst others present were

ABOVE: 'Hickwells' Convalescent Home, Cinder Hill, Chailey c.1915. Home to 'Sussex 54 V.A.D.' from March 1915 to June 1916, when they moved to 'Beechlands,' Newick (courtesy, www.chailey1418.blogspot.com).

Mrs WALKER, the Misses WALKER, Miss MARSHALL, Mrs BOURDILLON, Miss PEEBLES, Mrs REECE, and Mrs & Miss BROOKSBANK. Those who entertained the company with songs, etc., were: Mrs CARPMAEL, Mrs BALLARD, Mr FARRAR, Miss Mabel KAY, who was encored: Mr CROWHURST, Mr HOLDEN, who together with his little daughter Doris, delighted the company; the Misses HENTY and BOAKES, who were encored; Miss HOLLOWAY, whose singing is always enjoyed, and who was encored; Miss FARRAR, Miss Venus Victoria (encored) and Miss R.TAPP.[1]

---

1 *The identity of Miss 'Venus Victoria' is a mystery. Possibly a stage name?*

MOTORS COLLIDE – A collision between two motors occurred on Wednesday near the 'Five Bells Inn', Chailey, and several persons, including a number of wounded soldiers from 'Hickwells' Convalescent Home', Chailey, were severely shaken and bruised. Mrs WALKER, of 'The Grange', Barcombe, had arranged for a concert to take place at her residence for the soldiers at 'Hickwells' and East Chiltington Convalescent Homes. Only those of 'Hickwells', however attended, together with the Matron, Miss MARSHALL. On their way home at night, in a motor, they collided with a motor van belonging to Mr S.B.RICHARDS, baker, Barcombe. The two vehicles were badly damaged, and the occupants much shaken and bruised, one soldier having his artificial leg smashed. The driver of Mr RICHARDS' van was Mr Jack ELPHICK, whose chest was hurt, and Mr Sidney BEST, the driver of the other vehicle, was hurt about the knees.

21st January - HOW TO GET FARM HANDS "STARRED" (or "Reserved") – Farmers would be well advised to make themselves acquainted with the steps that they can take to prevent their skilled men from being called up for service in the Army. By special arrangement between

2 A "marsh-looker" was a shepherd, often self-employed, in places such the Romney Marshes and Pevensey Levels.

Chailey Rural District Council - Military Service Tribunal

The Military Service Act of January 1916 introduced conscription for certain ages and categories of men. All single men and widowers between the ages of 18 and 41, without children were now liable to serve in the Armed Forces. Military Service Tribunals were established to hear appeals for exemption from individuals or their employers. Tribunal members included Barcombe farmer Mr Francis J.CORNWELL, later joined by market gardener and nurseryman Edwin W. BUNNEY. Meetings took place at West Street in Lewes.

A minute book for the Chailey Local Tribunal (1917-1918) is one of only three such records known to survive for East Sussex, following a government instruction that the records should be destroyed after the War.

the War Office and the Board of Agriculture, the following classes of skilled workmen have been either put into "Starred Classes" or "Reserved Occupations":

STARRED CLASSES – Farm bailiffs, foremen, wagoners, ploughmen, horsemen, carters, stockmen, cowmen, dairymen, milkmen, shepherds, marsh-lookers, thatchers, engine drivers, and machine attendants.

RESERVED OCCUPATIONS – Timber carters, wood fellers, mill sawyers, farriers (horse shoeing), fruit, hop and market gardeners – foremen in all departments. The War Office has undertaken not to enlist for immediate service any man who comes under any of the above classes, even if he offers himself for that purpose. Nor will any of these men be called up under Lord Derby's Scheme if the farmers take the necessary steps to see that

their workmen who are entitled to come under any of these classes have been properly marked on the Army Register....

INDISPENSABLES NOT ENTITLED TO BE "STARRED" OR "RESERVED"... In considering a claim made by a farmer on the ground that one of his men is indispensable, the Tribunal will require evidence that the man is willing to continue in his civil employment. The employer then has to show; 1) good reason why he is individually indispensable, 2) that every effort has been made temporarily to replace him, and 3) that reasonable facilities for enlistment have been given to other men (if any) in his employment.

SCHOOL MANAGERS MEET – At a meeting of the School Managers, which took place last week, it was decided that Mr MOON, the

LAST WORDS

◆

Soldiers often wrote a letter home before going "over the top" and out of their trenches. Their army papers carried the name of their next-of-kin to whom news of any injuries, capture or fatalities would be communicated, if necessary. It was also suggested that it they make a simple will so their wishes would be known. This article including a letter from a Wadhurst man to his family back home serves as a sad example:

"SOLDIER'S FAREWELL LETTER – Mrs STANDEN, of 'Durgates,' Wadhurst, has received a very pathetic letter (found unposted by a fellow soldier), written by her husband, Private H.G.STANDEN, of the Royal Sussex Regiment, who has been missing since the Battle of Hulinch:

Dear wife and children, just a few lines to wish you all good-bye, in case I get bowled over in the attack we are about to make. You know we have to do it as well as the others, but we shall all do our best whichever way it goes. We all hope, however, to come out safely. I have your photos with me, and I am kissing you all before we start on this job. Now I hope God will look to you and the children and guide you safely through if anything happens to me. Well cheer up. With my fondest love and kisses to you and the children, and best of luck. I remain your loving hub. George."

Private G/4845 Henry 'George' STANDEN of the 2nd Battalion, Royal Sussex Regiment died on 25th September 1915, aged 30. His parents lived at 'Durgates,' and his wife Emily Frances and children lived at 'The Platt,' in nearby Frant, where she died in June 1925, aged 37, leaving children; Henry George (14) and Emily Lily (10).

---

headmaster, should be invited to retain his position till the end of March. Mrs ELPHICK, the caretaker, having resigned, Mrs FIGG was appointed as her successor.

COINCIDENCE AT WHIST DRIVE – There were twenty tables engaged at the drive which took place at the Reading Room on Tuesday evening, and the result was an extraordinary coincidence, as the two gentlemen winners, also the two lady winners, won by 175 each. The cards, needless to say, had to be cut for the first prizes, and the final result was:- Gentlemen:

1. Mr Richard RHODES, who received a gold watch; 2. Mr James TAPP, a gold tie pin; booby, Mr Charlie HOLLOWAY, an imitation stuffed duck. Ladies: 1. Miss Nancy FUNNELL, silver brooch with stone in centre; 2. Miss N.JESSUP, case of enamel buttons; booby, Miss Ivy HOBDEN, a little white bone elephant as a charm.

PARISH COUNCIL MEETING – The members of the Parish Council met on Saturday evening at the Mission Room, Mr E.W.BUNNEY in the unavoidable absence of Major

W.W.GRANTHAM, occupying the chair. Others present were: Mr Frank CORNWELL, Mr Richard RHODES, Mr Thomas HAWKINS, Mr Thomas LADE, Mr S.B.RICHARDS, and the Clerk, Mr PARIS. Correspondence between the L.B. & S.C. Railway Company and the Council was read regarding a public footpath at Barcombe Mills – a path for pedestrians when the road is flooded: and it was pointed out that an agreement had been arranged. It was stated that all the allotments in the district were being utilised to the very best advantage.

Barcombe Mills Station.

LEFT: Barcombe Mills Station with a covered goods waggon in the siding to the right, where Sydney RICHARDS' workmen unloaded corn and coal. (Dolphin Series postcard, Haywards Heath).

28th January - COUNTY COURT CASE – At Lewes County Court, on Monday, the L.B. & S.C. Railway Company failed in their claim for 8s.6d. against Sydney B. RICHARDS, corn and coal merchant, for the cost of repairing a truck lever used for propelling railway trucks along sidings by hand. Mr RUTHERFORD, solicitor for the plaintiffs, argued that at Barcombe Mills Station the defendant's workmen improperly used the lever for knocking out the pins of the truck doors, and that it was afterwards found lying broken across the rails…

---

3 *Alice & William FIGG lived at 'Slate Cottages.'*

4 *Thomas BOURDILLON (26) was born at Bloemfontein, Orange Free State in 1890. He came back to England for schooling at Tonbridge, before returning to Africa, where he made his first-class cricket debut for the Rhodesia in 1910. After the war he played once for Sussex in 1919, before returning to Rhodesia where he played a further three matches. He died in Salisbury, Rhodesia in 1961.*

4th February - EXTENSION OF SERVICE – The Board of Education have consented to an extension of the certificate of Mr A.MOON, Headmaster of the Church of England School, Barcombe, up to and including March 31st, 1916.

STATIONMASTER LEAVING – Mr Frederick James BONE, stationmaster at Barcombe Mills, is shortly taking up similar duties at Ardingly; and Mr Arthur HOLDEN, stationmaster at Barcombe, is to have the dual position. Mr HOLDEN was previously chief clerk at Lewes Station. He has been at Barcombe for about three years, during which period he has, through his amiable and obliging nature, made himself popular. Mr HOLDEN has often figured as an entertainer at concerts, etc.

BELL RINGERS – A sum of £12.10s.6d. was contributed for the bell ringers at Barcombe at Christmas…

PATRIOTISM – Mr Thomas Edmund BOURDILLON, son of Mr Edmund BOURDILLON,[4] has for the last six years, been in Rhodesia, South Africa, conducting a farm, together with a partner, Mr Gerald CALLENDER. Although Mr BOURDILLON has been through the German West African campaign, so imbued is he with patriotism that he has returned home, as also has his partner, for the purpose of enlisting in the Army. Mr BOURDILLON has two brothers serving their King and Country, one Lieut. Theodore BOURDILLON, attached to the 9th Royal Sussex Regiment, and the other Sub. Lieut. Francis BOURDILLON, who is in the Navy, and at present in the Cameroons.

DEATH OF Mrs PATCHING – The death of Mrs Catherine Jane PATCHING, a lady who was well known and highly respected, took place at her residence, 'Spithurst House,' on Monday evening. The deceased lady, who was 87 years of age, succumbed after an attack of pneumonia. She was a Quakeress, and devotedly attached to the Mission in the district for many years, which, in a large measure, she installed at Spithurst. She inaugurated a school in the district, which was attended by thirty scholars.

SPITHURST HOUSE

ABOVE: Spithurst House – Mrs PATCHING and her successor ran a boarding house from here (ref. Kelly's Directory). The writer of this postcard describes a stay at this "beautiful spot" in April 1916. "We sit in the parlour all day, the sun is quite hot & violets and primroses are blooming everywhere."

The governess of this school was Miss MOULE, who now, after a period of over twenty years, has left the district. The deceased, like the majority of her denomination, was sincerely religious, and the object of starting the school was for the purpose of giving the local children, as chief part of the curriculum, a thorough knowledge of Scripture. The school, however, after a lengthy

existence, ceased last summer, and the children now attend at Barcombe. The deceased lady, who was predeceased by her husband about thirty years ago, was buried yesterday (Thursday) at the Friends Burial Ground, Blackrock, Kemp Town, Brighton.

11th February - MILITARY SERVICE TRIBUNALS FOR CHAILEY RURAL DISTRICT – Chailey Rural District Council met specially on Tuesday afternoon at Lewes to consider the question of appointing a Tribunal for their area to hear appeals under the Military Service Act. It was decided that for this purpose the members of the Tribunal elected under Lord Derby's Recruiting Scheme – Colonel G.A.MONEY, J.P., Mr H.SCARLETT, J.P., Mr J.KENWARD (members of the

Council), Major TOWERS CLARK, and Mr MOFFATT SMITH – should act in conjunction with the Rev. H.S.MUSGRAVE, Messrs. H.M.H.WOODS, J.WOOLLAND, F. MARTIN, C.L.ANDREW, E.C.KNIGHT, E.W.BUNNEY, F.J.CORNWELL (members of the Council), J.PAGE (Ringmer), J.G.HARMER (Hamsey), and C.W.ELLIS (Streat).

BARCOMBE PASSENGER – TROUBLE AT LEWES STATION – At the Lewes Petty Sessions on Tuesday, Esther Elizabeth WRIGHT,[5]

BELOW: The Military Service Act (1916) introduced conscription in Britain for all single men between the ages of 18 and 41. It was up to local 'Military Tribunals' to decide who was eligible for exemption.

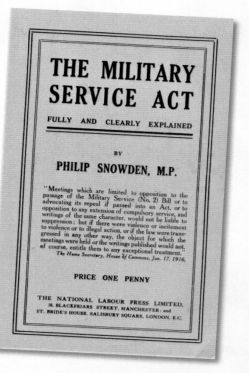

THE MILITARY SERVICE ACT

FULLY AND CLEARLY EXPLAINED

BY

PHILIP SNOWDEN, M.P.

"Meetings which are limited to opposition to the passage of the Military Service (No. 2) Bill or to advocating its repeal if passed into an Act, or to opposition to any extension of compulsory service, and writings of the same character, would not be liable to suppression; but if there were violence or incitement to violence or to illegal action, or if the law were transgressed in any other way, the object for which the meetings were held or the writings published would not, of course, entitle them to any exceptional treatment."
The Home Secretary, House of Commons, Jan. 17, 1916.

PRICE ONE PENNY

THE NATIONAL LABOUR PRESS LIMITED,
30, BLACKFRIARS STREET, MANCHESTER : and
ST. BRIDE'S HOUSE SALISBURY SQUARE, LONDON, E.C.

5 *Esther lived at 'Woodland Cottage' with her husband Joseph and five children. The family had moved from Burgess Hill c.1913, in which year her eldest son Leonard, a plumber's mate, had enlisted in the Army, aged 17. He became a driver with 67 Division Train, eventually returning home after a spell in 42 Hospital Salonica in July 1918.*

of Barcombe, appeared to answer a summons for being drunk and disorderly at the Railway Station at Lewes on February 4th. Defendant pleaded guilty and said she was very sorry.

Charles CARE, a porter at Lewes Station, said that at 8.20.p.m. on February 4th he saw defendant running after some paper boys. He asked her where she was going and she said "Wivelsfield." She was on the wrong platform and when asked for her ticket she produced a return half to Barcombe. Defendant fell and witness picked her up. He and Porter COLLINS put her in the 8.58 to Barcombe and while getting someone to ride with her, as she was not fit to travel alone, she got out. Witness put her back and she again got out and insisted on going to Wivelsfield. On taking her to the booking office for a ticket, she said she wished to send a telegram to her son. Witness wrote the telegram, after paying for which defendant had only a halfpenny left and still wanted the ticket. He last saw her going to No.3 platform where the collector summoned the station master. P.C. James MORRIS gave evidence of arrest, saying he saw defendant on the platform. She was drunk and put herself into the fighting attitude and obstructed passengers. The Chairman said that they would treat it as a first offence. Defendant would have to pay the costs 4s.6d.

and be bound over in the sum of £5, to be of good behaviour for six months. Defendant said she remembered nothing of the offence. She had not been well and could only recollect having a glass of port wine.

WHIST DRIVE – The Barcombe ladies connected with the Red Cross held another drive at the Reading Room on Tuesday evening for the purpose of swelling the funds for the soldiers serving at the Front. Twenty-five tables were engaged and the cost of use of the Reading Room is to be defrayed by the members of the local Stoolball Committee. The prizes were given by Miss Nancy FUNNELL, Miss Ethel RHODES, Mrs WALL, Mrs WELLS and Mr C.J.HOLLOWAY… The players were entertained by selections on a gramophone, kindly lent by Mrs DAY.

DEATH AND FUNERAL OF Mrs ASSER – Barcombe residents will be sorry to learn of the death of Mrs Amy Dinah ASSER, wife of Mr Frederick S.ASSER, which took place at her residence, Sussex Square, Brighton, last Friday. The deceased lady, who was well known in Barcombe and surrounding districts, and who had resided at 'The Lawns', Barcombe Mills, for over 20 years, was 55 years of age. She only left Barcombe Mills three or four years ago, but she

frequently visited the district. She had been suffering from an internal complaint, and was advised to undergo an operation, but whilst under it she had a seizure and died. Mrs ASSER leaves a daughter Kathleen[6] and son, Lieut. Richard ASSER, being attached to a Cycling Corps...

18th February (The first 'Mid-Sussex edition' of the *Sussex Express*) - PARCELS FOR SOLDIERS – The members of the Barcombe Red Cross Society are gathering the names and addresses of the local soldiers who are in the trenches. The purpose is to forward to each a parcel of goods from the proceeds of the two whist drives recently held in the district.

GOLDEN WEDDING – Mr & Mrs Stephen DIPLOCK, of 'Munster Cottage', celebrated their golden wedding on Sunday. They have been the recipients of many useful presents, and have received about forty letters of congratulation. They were married in 1866 at All Saints, Lewes, and afterwards resided at Spithurst for about three years. They then took up residence at 'Beaks Cottage', Longford, where they remained four years, and later occupied 'Longford Farm', which

---

6 *Kathleen Mary ASSER joined the Red Cross (-), in June 1918, aged 20, and was posted to the R.A.F. Hospital, Holly Hill, London NW3 as a full-time mess orderly (www.redcross.org.uk).*

they occupied for the lengthy period of 43 years. It was here that they celebrated their silver wedding, when they entertained about fifty guests. Mr DIPLOCK, who is 72 years of age, was born at Hamsey, and Mrs DIPLOCK, aged 71, is a native of Isfield. They have three children, one daughter and two sons, and have five grandchildren, one of whom is at present in France serving with the Army.

KILLED IN ACTION - The residents of Barcombe will regret to learn of the death of Private William H.BANKS,[7] who was killed by a shell in France on February 7th. He was serving with the 8th Royal Sussex Regiment, which he joined about seven months ago… A muffled peal of bells was rung as a tribute to his memory last Sunday, at Barcombe Church, and a similar peal will be rung again to-day (Friday).

ABOVE: 'Longford Farm', the home of Mr & Mrs DIPLOCK for forty three years. Postcard by Bliss & Co. of Lewes (Mike Green collection).

25th February - Mr MOON'S SUCCESSOR – Mr MOON will retire from the position of master of the local schools, after forty years' service, on March 31st.

THE MISSES DEALTRY – The knowledge that the Misses DEALTRY, together with their brother, Mr William J.DEALTRY, are

leaving Barcombe at the end of March has created keen regret amongst all residents. They reside at 'The Lawns,' Barcombe Mills, which was previously the residence of the late Mrs ASSER. The ladies are extremely popular, and one is secretary to the Barcombe Nursing Association. Interested in all matters connected with charity and the church, the Misses DEALTRY were district visitors.

DAMAGES FOR LOSS OF SHEEP – Arising out of a recent case of sheep-worrying at 'Church Farm', Barcombe, Messrs. J. & W.M.PORTER, farmers, were awarded damages of £72.13s.6d against Mr S.J.LAKER (of 'Holmbush'),[8] at Eastbourne County Court on Tuesday. On the night of December 15th two dogs

ABOVE: 'The Lawns', Barcombe Mills, home to the Misses and Mr DEALTRY and formerly to Mr & Mrs ASSER, from a contemporary postcard by Bliss & Co. of Lewes (courtesy Roger Newman).

---

7 For his biography, see vol.2.

8 Mr LAKER was the village scoutmaster (see 26th November 1915, also 26th May 1916).

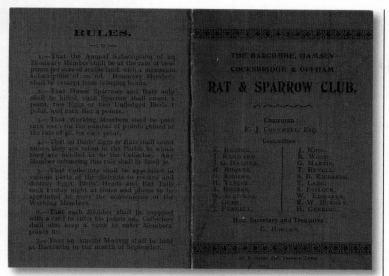

ABOVE: 'Rat & Sparrow Club' membership card. "Working members" would be awarded points, I for a sparrow and 4 for a rat and were paid each week at the rate of ½d. per point, a welcome supplement to the family income (courtesy the Cornwell family).

belonging to defendant, who lives near the farm, worried a number of Southdown sheep, with the result that 20 were killed and nine were badly wounded. Several witnesses were called on both sides, and counsel were engaged. His Honour decided that the plaintiff's case was fully sustained, and gave judgment in their favour with costs.

3rd March - WITHOUT A LIGHT – At Lewes Petty Sessions on Tuesday, John ELPHICK of Barcombe was fined 10s. For having been in charge of a bicycle without a light on the Offham road on February 17th.

FLOODS – The floods at Barcombe Mills, owing to the recent snow, appear more extensive and deeper than after the last heavy fall of rain. The river banks on either side have overflowed in many places.

RAT & SPARROW CLUB –At the Reading Room on Wednesday evening a number of farmers and others assembled for the purpose of resuscitating the old Rat and Sparrow Club, which became defunct about two years ago.

CHILD'S SUDDEN DEATH – Sympathy is extended to Mr & Mrs William TURNER of 'Half Yard Farm', Barcombe Mills, on the death of their little daughter, Emily which sad event took place on Tuesday morning. A sparkling little maid of eight years, Emily returned home on Friday evening from school complaining of not feeling well, and it was found she was suffering from measles. The child regularly attended Sunday School held at the Mission Hall, Barcombe, and she was a member of the local branch of the Girls' Friendly Society. The funeral will take place to-morrow (Saturday).

LOCAL WORK PARTY – The Work Party will shortly be affiliated to the Central Sussex Depot. It has done excellent work from its inception. From August 1914, the following garments have been made: 170 shirts, 48 aprons, 24 pillow cases, 24 oversleeves, 24 caps, 12 roller bandages, 13 belts, 23 pairs of mittens, 12 pairs of socks, 7 comforters, 4 cardigans, 10 pairs of slippers, 3 pairs of night socks, 1 dressing gown, and 3 pillows. Gifts in kind during 1915 were sent by the following persons: The misses DYKE, shirts; Mrs WALKER, flannelette; Lady GRANTHAM, felt for sailors' gloves, wool, and flannelette; and Miss GRANTHAM, wool.

WHIST DRIVE – A successful drive took place on Tuesday evening at the Reading Room, twenty tables being engaged. Mrs SPELLER and Mrs BEAUCHAMP were responsible for the organisation, and the proceeds, free of deduction for expenses, will be devoted to the local Working Party for the purpose of providing material for the making of garments for wounded soldiers...

10th March - AN OLD BARCOMBE RESIDENT – FUNERAL OF Mr JOHN BURDER – The remains of Mr John BURDER, who

ABOVE: 'The Beeches,' close to St.Mary's church. Home to the late John BURDER. "Photographed by Frank Cant, an itinerant photographer from Colchester" (courtesy the Riggs family).

passed away at Hastings on Friday, March 3rd, were interred on Wednesday afternoon at Barcombe Churchyard, the Rev. FARRAR officiating. Deceased, who succumbed to senile decay, was 83 years of age. He had resided for about 40 years at Barcombe, most of which time at 'The Beeches.' He had another residence, namely 'Codham Hall', Braintree, Essex. Mr BURDER was ever ready to subscribe handsomely to any deserving cause. When he first took up residence at Barcombe, he was, as he told a friend, practically a poor man, and property at that time being at a discount, his estate in Essex was yielding little profit. Being shrewd and far-seeing, however, he converted a large portion of the estate into a market garden, which being close to London, soon developed into a very profitable concern. Deceased had many friends, and was

much respected. The principle mourners were: Mrs BURDER (widow), Mr R.H.R.BURDER (son). Mrs LAMB (daughter), Miss Doris BURDER (daughter). Four sons could not be present owing to being abroad – Mr Talworth BURDER, Melbourne; Mr Percy BURDER, New York; Mr Lewis BURDER, on service in Egypt; and Mr Gordon BURDER, now on his way home from the Malay States to join H.M.Forces...

SCHOOLMASTER FOR 40 YEARS – PRESENTATION AT BARCOMBE - Despite the heavy snowstorm which prevailed on Tuesday evening, there was a fair assembly of residents and friends at the Mission Hall, Barcombe when Mr Alfred MOON, who had been head-master of the Church of England Schools for forty years, was the recipient of a testimonial. Having reached

his 65th year, Mr MOON's resignation according to the Education regulations, became compulsory. He was to have retired some little time back, but owing to the war, difficulties arose regarding securing teachers, and Mr MOON therefore, was asked to continue till the end of the present month. His first school was at Chipping Ongar, Essex; and it was in 1876 that he was instituted as headmaster at Barcombe School. In 1872 he received his certificate, and strange to relate, that is the exact number of children that has been admitted to his care and passed under his tuition. Interested in all matters connected with the village, Mr MOON has acted in the capacity of secretary for five or six clubs at a time, such as the Cricket Club, Barcombe and

ABOVE: Alfred MOON, who had been a widower since 1901, had three children; Alfred, Leonard (who died in Canada in 1913) and Elizabeth who continued to live with him after her mother's death. Alfred died in Barcombe in April 1928.

RIGHT: 'Hillside' home of the bride. Her father Thomas HEWETT (HEWITT) is listed as a florist in Kelly's 1915 directory, so probably supplied the tulips and forget-me-nots- for the bridesmaids' bouquets (Mike Green collection).

BARCOMBE.

District Agricultural Society, Village Reading Room, Juvenile Foresters, etc.

Previous to the presentation a lantern lecture was given by the Rector. The slides being thrown on the screen by Captain SHIRT…

The testimonial took the form of an illuminated address, a silver inkstand and a purse of gold containing £22.10s. The inkstand bore the following inscription:- "Presented to Mr Alfred MOON with an address and purse of gold on his retiring from the head mastership at Barcombe School 1876-1916;" and the address, which contained 189 names, bore the following wording: Barcombe Church of England School to Mr Alfred MOON – We the undersigned, managers, parents, and parishioners and, past and present scholars of the Barcombe Schools, hope that you will accept the accompanying ink-stand and purse of gold as an expression of our respect and esteem, and our appreciation of your valuable work as head master to our schools for forty years. It is given to few men to labour so long in one parish; and we pray that you may be spared for many years to spend a well-earned rest among those who have learned to value your friendship, many of whom owe you a deep debt of gratitude."

Lady GRANTHAM, in a neat little speech, when the gifts were handed to Mr MOON by two of his old boys, Mr Frank SMITH and Mr Harry DIPLOCK, said: "I am pleased to make this presentation of an illuminated address, inkstand, and purse of gold. I have known you for over 35 years and have always appreciated your work in the parish. I hope that you will live many years and thoroughly enjoy life." (Applause)...

TOMMIES' PARCELS - The proceeds from the two recent whist drives which were inaugurated by the lady members of the Red Cross have been spent in supplying 15 lots of goods for boys in the trenches and have been forwarded this week. The parcels consisted of many useful articles, wearing apparel, cigarettes, chocolate etc.

KILLED IN ACTION - We regret to chronicle the death of Private Frederick KING, who according to an authentic message, lost his life by a shell in France on February 24th. Private KING, who has two brothers serving with the Marines, Ernest and George, joined the 9th Royal Sussex Regiment nearly 18 months ago and previous to that worked for Mr H.GEARING, Sewells Farm. About 21 years of age, he was the eldest son of Mr & Mrs Walter KING of Holmans Bridge, Town Littleworth, Barcombe. Some time back he was wounded and, in consequence, was home for a short time.

WEDDING – A pretty wedding, which evoked considerable interest in the district, took place on Monday at the Parish Church. The contracting parties were Miss Annie Edith HEWETT, daughter of Mr Thomas HEWETT, of 'Hillside,' and Mr William G.LAWRENCE, son of the late Mr George LAWRENCE. The bride, who was attired in a fawn coloured costume, and wore a pink satin hat with ostrich feathers, and carried a sheaf of lilies and orchids with white streamers, was given away by her father, whilst her brother, Mr T.C.HEWETT, acted as best man. The lady was attended by three bridesmaids. Miss C. Emily HEWETT (sister), was clad in light blue, trimmed with black satin, and wore a black hat with blue roses, and carried a bouquet of yellow tulips. The two little girls, Miss Ida JONES and Miss Doris

HOLDEN, looked extremely pretty. They were attired in white, trimmed with blue satin and mob caps, with blue satin streamers and forget-me-nots, wore white shoes, and carried baskets of flowers of forget-me-nots and white tulips. The bridegroom's present to the bride was a gold locket, to the little girls gold brooches, and to Miss C.E.HEWETT a gold

pendant. After the reception, which was held at the home of the bride's father, the happy couple left to spend their honeymoon at Newton Abbot, Devonshire, the lady being attired in a navy blue costume and saxe-blue hat. The couple intended taking up residence in Cardiff...

17th March - CHAILEY TRIBUNAL – TEST CASES FROM BARCOMBE – In view of recent statements respecting the position of single men under 31 who are in starred occupations the Tribunal have had to revise to some extent their attitude in regard to the granting of conditional exemptions, which they have hitherto allowed to men, irrespective of age, who were proved to be indispensable in certified occupations.

Under these circumstances Mr F.J.CORNWELL's appeal on behalf of eight Barcombe men was practically a test case. Three of the men were under, and the remainder over, 31 years of age. The younger men were granted temporary exemption and the older men were conditionally exempted.

BARCOMBE WILL – Mrs Catherine Jane PATCHING of Spithurst, whose death occurred on the 31st January last, left estate of the gross value of £1,505.7s.4d. Mr Robert Alfred PENNEY of 82 Queen's Road, Brighton,

GREETINGS from "LOWTHER'S LAMBS."

I'm Thinking of YOU every Day.

I haven't got time to sit down and write,
And I thought perhaps you might grieve;
So I send you this card just to say I'm alright,
And longing to see you again when on "leave."
When the Empire's Call for more men to fight
For her honour—in me caused a thrill;
I felt fight I must or else I should "bust,"
So I'm at COODEN CAMP, near Bexhill.
The work it is hard— for we're marchin' all day,
And sometimes half of the night;
But we're hardening to it and getting quite fit.
And thank goodness for "grub" we're alright.
My duty calls me, as this picture shows,
To the Front where the fightin' is done;
And once "THE SOUTHDOWN'S" get grip on the foe,
There's no letting go till they've won.
So cheer up my dear, tho' parted we are,
And though I'm so far away;
My loved ones are ever first in my thoughts,
I'm thinking of YOU every day.

LEFT: A postcard published for 'Lowther's Lambs' to send from Cooden Camp.

merchant, and Mr William Clarkson WALLIS of Springfield, Withdean, merchant, are the executors.

NEW POLICE CONSTABLE –

P.C. WILLARD of Dallington arrived on Monday to take up duties. He succeeds P.C. Albert EDWARDS, who after about six years' service at Barcombe, has gone to Robertsbridge.

LANTERN LECTURE

– The first of a series of lantern lectures took place on Wednesday evening at the village Mission Room. The Rector, will continue these lectures each Wednesday evening throughout Lent, the subject being "The Life of Christ".

24th March –
SOUTHDOWNS IN THE FIRING LINE – After a long

period of training, the three Southdown Battalions of the Royal Sussex Regiment have realised their hearts' desire and reached the Front. By one of the accidents of warfare the enemy has drawn first blood. Within a fortnight of leaving the shores of England casualties occurred in the first and second battalions, the principal damage apparently having been caused by a shell which burst in the men's billets and took the first toll among "Lowther's Lambs" by the deaths of Worthing, Barcombe, and Bexhill men and injuries to several of their comrades. The news has caused a thrill of emotion to pass through hundreds of

ABOVE: 3rd Southdowns - '9 Section' of 'C' Company with their accordion-playing Corporal during training at Cooden Camp (courtesy Beryl Jackson).

Sussex homes, whose sons are in the battalions raised by Colonel Claude LOWTHER, M.P., men of Sussex who came largely from the coast resorts and the towns and villages of the eastern portion of the county, who were trained at Cooden, and who represented the earliest and most spontaneous response of the seaside county to the call to arms.

There are thousands of Sussex men in the other battalions of the county regiment, while in many other units of the British Army the county is well represented, but for reasons which it is not difficult to understand the Lambs seem to be more directly associated with the county's military efforts in this War, and typify the stubborn and unconquerable spirit of the men of Sussex.

The battalions, certainly the first and the second, were raised in the early days of the great struggle, when the shock of the War came suddenly upon the beautiful towns and peaceful villages of Sussex, and men of all classes eagerly rallied to the standard raised by a popular county gentleman, the owner of one of the stately ruins of England. For ardent patriotism, pure and undefiled, the recruiting of the Southdowns is probably unsurpassed in the whole country. The men did not want to be fetched. It was enough for them to know that old England was in danger, and they came in their thousands from counter and office, from mansions and the cottages of Sussex, married and single, rich and poor, placing their all on the altar of their country, without qualification or reserve…

BARCOMBE SOLDIER KILLED - PRIVATE C.H. PECKHAM - We regret to announce the death of Private

BARCOMBE SOLDIER KILLED.

PRIVAE C. H. PECKHAM.

ABOVE: Cecil Hugh PECKHAM, one of 'Lowther's Lambs' (Southdowns) to be killed by a shell explosion in the barn where he was billeted, within two weeks of leaving England.

Cecil Hugh Peckham, son of Mr & Mrs Joseph PECKHAM, of the 11th Battalion Royal Sussex Regiment (Lowther's Lambs). Private Peckham, who was 28 years of age, was a native of Barcombe and was at home about three weeks ago. He joined in September 1914 and only reached France on the 14th instant…

Previous to the war, deceased worked in the nurseries, and his special craft was carnation growing. He was one of the old boys of Barcombe School, and subscribed to the recent testimonial to Mr MOON the headmaster. His only brother, Charles, who joined the Army, is at present in training at Newhaven.

SCRIPTURE EXAMINATION – The Rev. Robert Blackden JAMESON, diocesan inspector of schools, visited the schools on Friday. Owing to an epidemic of measles about ninety children were absent, and it has since been deemed wise by the authorities to close the school for about a fortnight.

LANTERN LECTURE - The third of the series of lantern lectures in "The Life of Christ" was delivered by the Rector, Rev. H.W.FARRAR, on Wednesday evening at the village Mission Room. There was a good attendance. At each lecture the list of names of Barcombe men who have joined the Forces was read.

PRESENTATION TO MR MOON – The day before the School closed last week, Mr MOON was the recipient of several presents from the teachers, past and present, also the children and scholars. A number of the children's parents attended, as also did the Rev. Herbert W.FARRAR, the Rector, who spoke in eulogistic terms of Mr MOON's forty years' service. The present staff of teachers, Miss Ethel Mary ATKINS, Miss Gertrude WELSH (sister of Bert WELSH), and Miss Violet WILSON, also spoke and expressed their profound regret that their chief was retiring. The former teachers who subscribed to the presentation were Miss Agnes BEACH, Miss Margaret BEACH, and Miss Katie SAUNDERS. The presents comprised a handsome armchair and cushion, which was disclosed to the recipient by Miss Alice GANDER, a pupil; an album containing about 190 names, and a pipe together with tobacco, which were presented by the tiniest tot in the school, Miss May SCRASE. The album contained the following inscription: "Presented to Mr MOON as a token of respect, esteem, and affection, from teachers and scholars of Barcombe School, March 16th, 1916."

COURT "BARCOMBE" ANCIENT ORDER OF FORESTERS – The statement of accounts and balance sheet for 1915 have been issued, and the secretary (Bro. J.W. BRIGGS, P.C.R.), in his report remarks: The sickness during the year has been greater than in previous years, amounting to £126.12s.2d., as compared with £94.0s.2d. for 1914. The Court have lost by death one member and one member's wife. Three members have left during the year, and three have been admitted, the number at the end of the year being 148. (The Court have adopted new tables with a view to increasing the junior membership. The payments vary from one half penny per week, and it is claimed that the benefits are greater than any industrial company can offer. Under the new tables the junior members can be admitted from date of birth, and in event of death, or on attaining a certain age, a substantial sum will be paid. Adult members can be admitted from 16 years of age. A wide range of benefits can be provided for, payments varying from one penny per week upwards. The reduction

of contribution sanctioned by the E.C. early in the year is a great boon to those who have a membership of 10 years and upwards. At the end of the year 20 benefit members of the Court were serving in H.M.Forces. Several others have since enlisted, while a large number of others have attested. It is a pleasure to note that the members' surplus fund has been successful: four per cent, has been allotted as interest during the past year.

BELOW: Ancient Order of Foresters – An earlier Balance Sheet for 1894, showing an increase in membership from 25 in 1888 to 60 in 1894 (W.I. scrapbook, ESRO: WI 112/1/1, p.195).

ABOVE: 'Conyboro,' Lord MONK BRETTON's country house at Cooksbridge, on a postcard by Harry Tullett of Cuckfield.

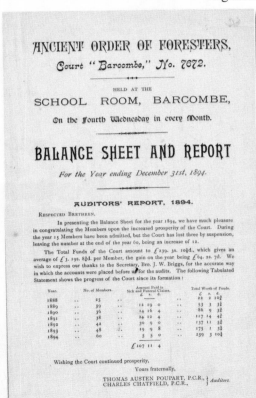

31st March - IN HOSPITAL – Signalling Sergeant William HAWKINS, Royal Sussex Regiment, is in Denmark Hill (London) Hospital. The Sergeant served right through the South African Campaign, for which he received two medals.

PARISH ANNUAL MEETING - ... The Rector inquired for his guidance, who was the parish doctor, but, strange to relate, nobody in the assembly could supply the desired information, and Mr F.CORNWELL promised to make enquiries. Questions were asked regarding the footpath which is to be made by the Barcombe Mills Station for use when the ground was flooded. It was pointed out that the Railway Company had placed notices at the Station, stating that terms which constituted the agreement entered upon between the District Council and the Railway Company, and it was therefore anticipated that the Company would shortly proceed with the work.

BURGLARS "CRACK" CONYBORO – LORD MONK BRETTON'S MANSION – Like most mansions of its kind, 'Conyboro' is embowered in tree and cannot be observed from the main thoroughfare. For some considerable time the family has been residing at their London address, Prince's-Gardens. Having heard of the burglary at 'Firle Place', however, where many miniatures and cameos, together with silver had been

Spithurst.   Barcombe. Sussex.

ABOVE: 'Church Farm', Spithurst taken over by David PARRIS in 1916 (Mezzotint postcard courtesy Roger Newman).

PLATELAYER KILLED AT LEWES – RUN DOWN IN A FOG – A fatality occurred on the London, Brighton and South Coast Railway about a mile from Lewes Station on Saturday morning, when Alfred SAUNDERS, aged 42, living at St. Nicholas Lane, Lewes, a platelayer, was killed by a passing train.

The inquest was held at the Fire Station, Lewes on Tuesday evening, and was conducted by the Coroner (Mr G.VERE BENSON). Mr C.BEST was foreman of the jury.

Selina Maria Ann SAUNDERS, widow of deceased, gave evidence of identification. She stated that she last saw her husband

BELOW: Frank & Jane SAUNDERS, parents of Alfred SAUNDERS, platelayer who was killed on the railway (courtesy Jo Newman).

stolen, the family deemed it wise to lodge all valuables with London and Lewes banks. The house, therefore, being stripped of its "riches," and the whole establishment being practically dismantled, the burglars were doomed to keen disappointment…

At the time of the burglary only the housemaid and under-housemaid were on the premises; and they knew nothing of what had occurred till 7 o'clock on the Monday morning, when Mr SAVAGE, the head gardener, found the front door of the mansion wide open…

7th April - ON LEAVE - Private H.WALLS, who has been at the front for the last eight months, and who is connected with the Motor Transport Section, is home on leave, as also is Harry

STEVENS, who is in the Marines.

FARM CHANGING HANDS – It has been arranged that a farm belonging to Mr William BENNETT is to be taken over by Mr David PARRIS, of 'Spring Barn,' Kingston, Lewes.

KILLED ON THE LINE – The two men, Mr Alfred SAUNDERS and Private F.ARCHER, who were killed on the railway, were well known in Barcombe. Mr SAUNDERS, who was a native, was a son of Mr & Mrs Frank SAUNDERS,[9] of Gladstone Cottages, Barcombe, who are the parents of 14 children. Private F.ARCHER, 2/5th Royal Sussex Regiment, resided for some time at Barcombe, and just previous to joining the Army worked for Mr BUNNEY (at the nursery).

---

9 Alfred's parents Frank & Jane were to lose another son, Frederick, killed in action on the Somme in November in the same year. (For his biography, see vol.2).

alive when he left home on the previous Saturday morning. He was then in his usual health. He had been a platelayer for 21 years.

Arthur RIDDLES, platelayer in the employ of the Railway Company, said he was in the same gang as deceased, who at 6.30 a.m. on Saturday was working at the 49 mile post when witness left him. There was a curve at the spot, which was between Lewes and Hamsey. The morning was foggy, and deceased would not be able to see a train until it was on him.

George STAPLEHURST, ganger in the employ of the Railway Company, stated that deceased was a member of his gang, but witness did not see the man before he commenced work on Saturday morning...

Charles Edward PEARCE, engine driver in the employ of the Railway Company, deposed that on Saturday morning he was the driver of the 4.18 train from Haywards Heath. It left at 5.57. Between Hamsey and Lewes witness heard the ballast flying and said to his mate "What's that?" Witness then

BELOW: S.B.RICHARDS, baker & confectioner – Advertisement from a 1918 issue of the parish magazine (courtesy Anne Pearce).

looked back but could not see anything. There was a thick fog. The train was travelling at a rate of from 30 to 35 miles per hour.

The Coroner – Was it safe to travel at that speed in the fog? – I could see the signals ten yards away. The witness explained that the fog was only a ground fog, and the signals were above it. He blew his whistle if he observed anything on the line. He did not distinguish anything and proceeded in the ordinary way to Lewes, where he reported that he had struck something. He could not find any mark on the engine....

The jury returned a verdict of "accidental death," expressed sympathy with the widow and relatives and handed their fees to the widow...The funeral took place at Lewes Cemetery on Wednesday afternoon, the Rev. Alexander David Charles CLARKE, Rector of All Saints, officiating. The mourners included – Miss Gertrude SAUNDERS (daughter), Mr & Mrs F.SAUNDERS (mother & father), Mr W.DAY (brother-in-law).

GENEROUS BAKER – British prisoners of war in Germany are continually

craving for English-made bread to be sent to them, and Mr S.B.RICHARDS, baker, has undertaken to forward, entirely free of cost, a 4lb. loaf to any prisoner in Germany whose home is either at Barcombe, Newick, Chailey or Hamsey. Relatives need only to send to Mr RICHARDS the full name, regiment, and address of the prisoners.[10]

CLERICAL ASSISTANCE – The Rector, the Rev. Herbert FARRAR, in a letter appearing in the current issue of the Parish Magazine, says: "The meeting with reference to the proposed Parochial Church Council, called for Wednesday, April 19th, will, I hope, be well attended. May I here speak of a matter which is giving me much thought and anxiety. Since I came to Barcombe I have paid (up to this date, March 21st, 1916, £140.19.1 out of my own pocket for clerical help in this parish to maintain the services in our two churches. Now I am sure you do not wish your Rector to bear this heavy burden alone. Let us meet and devise some way in which we may share this burden. I would here make a suggestion. The house known as 'The Residence' brings in a rent of £36 per annum. I propose printing the balance sheet of this each year and giving the net proceeds towards

---

10 *It is not known how many men from Barcombe and the surrounding parishes were taken prisoner, but at least one of the men on the war memorial, Claude ELDRIDGE, died whilst a P.o.W. (For his biography, see vol.2).*

the Clerical Assistance Fund. When repairs, insurance, and taxes are paid, this may average £30 per annum. This will be a start".

14th April - INEFFECTIVE SHUTTERS - At Lewes Petty Sessions on Tuesday, William Frederick DEAN was fined 5s. for having committed a breach of the Lighting Order at Barcombe on April 10th - P.C. WILLARD, who proved the case, said the shutters at the defendant's premises permitted light to come through into the street.

INVALIDED – Signalling Sergeant William HAWKINS, Royal Sussex Regiment, who has been in hospital at London for some time, arrived home this week. He has been invalided out of the Army, and is shortly being sent to a South Coast sanatorium to recuperate…

RAT & SPARROW CLUB – This Club became defunct, but a few weeks ago was revived, Mr George HOBDEN being appointed Secretary, and Mr Frank CORNWELL, Chairman. Mr REVELL of 'Delves Farm', has since been added to the Committee. A meeting of the members took place on Wednesday evening at the Reading Room, when membership cards were issued and subscriptions collected.

---

11 *William James CARTER and his wife Eveline arrived with a two-year-old son Philip Adrian.*

12 *The Women's Land Army was not formed until the following spring.*

ABOVE: 'Easter Dawn' – A postcard similar to the ones obtained by the Rector, which he had printed with a personal message (No.160 in the 'Home Words' series).

EASTER CARDS – The Rector, has procured coloured picture cards, one intended for sailors and the other for soldiers. They are of a sacred character, postcard size, and no doubt will be very acceptable this Eastertide to many of the sailors and soldiers. The Rector will be pleased to supply these cards gratis should anybody apply. The title of the picture is "Easter Dawn," and the wording on the card suitable for the sailors is: "The Rector of Barcombe will remember every sailor this Eastertide," and of that intended for the soldiers;" "From the Rector of Barcombe. At our Easter Communion we are praying for you."

21st April - NEW SCHOOLMASTER – Mr CARTER, who is from Flimwell, has taken up his residence in the village, and will commence his duties after the Easter vacation.[11]

WOMEN ON THE LAND[12] – A meeting in the furtherance of the scheme to influence women to help the farmers took place on Friday evening at the Mission Room. There was a good attendance. Miss Muriel GRANTHAM presided, and she was supported by Miss BRAND. Viscountess WOLSELEY was unavoidably absent, but her speech was read by Mrs BURROWS. Amongst others who spoke were Major W.W.GRANTHAM, Mrs W.W.GRANTHAM, the Rev. FARRAR, and Mr E.BOURDILLON. Mr VERCOE, of 'Banks Farm', remarked that his daughters and wife could all milk and do various descriptions of work on a farm, and he believed that women would prove successful helpers. Another speaker was Mr F.CORNWELL, who did not take such a sanguine view as Mr VERCOE.

PARISH COUNCIL MEETING – The annual meeting of the Barcombe Parish Council was held on Saturday evening at the Village Mission Room. Those present were Major W.W.GRANTHAM, Mr R.RHODES, Mr E.RHODES, Mr T.N.LADE,

Mr J.H.HAWKINS, Mr S.B.RICHARDS, Mr J.GURR, Mr F.W.BUNNEY, and Mr W.J.PARIS (clerk). On the proposition of Mr BUNNEY, Major W.W.GRANTHAM was re-elected chairman, and Mr E.W.BUNNEY vice-chairman. The Chairman thanked the members present, and said he regretted that, owing to other duties, he had been unable to attend all their meetings. Messrs. F.J.CORNWELL, R.RHODES and S.B.RICHARDS were re-appointed as Overseers, Mr R.RHODES on the Drainage Committee, and Mr RICHARDS was appointed School manager. Messrs. CORNWELL, BUNNEY and RHODES were re-elected on the Footpath Committee…

28th April - NO REAR LIGHT – For having been in charge of a bicycle without a red light at the rear at Barcombe, on April 12th, Miss Mabel KAY was fined 2s.6d. at Lewes Petty Sessions on Tuesday. P.C.WILLARD proved the case. Defendant said that, as she had almost reached home, she did not think it was necessary to re-light her lamp.[13]

VESTRY MEETING – …The Rector announced that Mrs SINGLETON had consented to act as Honorary Secretary to the Clerical Assistance Fund, for which the following sums had been promised: The Rector and Mrs FARRAR, £50; Lord MONK BRETTON £15; Mrs F.S.SHENSTONE £15; Major GRANTHAM £15; Captain

SINGLETON £5.5s. The net balance from the rent of 'The Residence' would be about £30 per annum, and this will also be given to the Fund. The Rector warmly thanked Lady GRANTHAM and Major GRANTHAM for their generous assistance in connection with the Mission Room. It was mentioned that all seats in the Parish Church were free after the bell had stopped ringing on Sunday morning, and all seats were free at the evening service.[14]

5th May - ON LEAVE - Private Fred KNIGHT, attached to the Royal Army Medical Corps, has been granted six weeks leave. He contracted typhus and for some time has been in hospital in Wales.

JUMBLE SALE – A jumble sale, which realised over £12, was held on Wednesday afternoon in the gardens attached to Lady GRANTHAM's residence. The proceeds are to be devoted to the Red Cross Society.

12th May - CHAILEY TRIBUNAL – On the application of John PORTER,

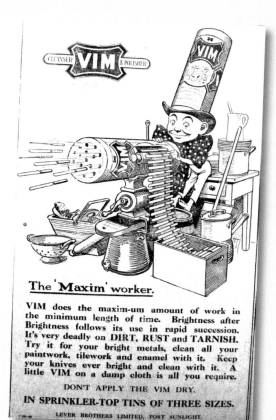

The 'Maxim' worker.

VIM does the maxim-um amount of work in the minimum length of time. Brightness after Brightness follows its use in rapid succession. It's very deadly on DIRT, RUST and TARNISH. Try it for your bright metals, clean all your paintwork, tilework and enamel with it. Keep your knives ever bright and clean with it. A little VIM on a damp cloth is all you require.

DON'T APPLY THE VIM DRY.

IN SPRINKLER-TOP TINS OF THREE SIZES.

LEVER BROTHERS LIMITED, PORT SUNLIGHT.

ABOVE: Vim 'The Maxim' Worker – Another Lever Brothers advertisement using military imagery, this time the 'Maxim' machine gun.

Henry SCRASE, 'Pond Plat', Church Road, carter and stockman, was granted conditional exemption.

13 *Mabel Eleanor KAY (30), was living at 'The Knowle' in 1911, with her widowed father Edwin, elder sister Beatrice, young nephew Edward and servant Minnie MARKWICK.*

14 *Pew Rents were an additional source of income in many churches from the early 17th century. Pews (which were boxed in and often lockable) could be rented and were allocated by the churchwardens in order of social precedence. Those who could not afford the rent would often be seated on benches in out of the way corners of the church (The Parish Chest, W.E. Tate).*

**SCHOOL MANAGERS'
MEETING** – A meeting
of the School Managers
took place last Friday
afternoon, the Rector
presiding. Others present
were: Miss SHENSTONE,
Capt. Mark SINGLETON,
Mr BOURDILLON,
Mr CARTER, and
Mr S.B.RICHARDS.
The schoolmaster's
agreement, relating to
his term of office, was
signed. The question
of having the boys
taught swimming was
raised, and the idea was
favourably received.
It was thought that
the stream joining
Barcombe Place was
a good position. The
question is to receive
further consideration
at the next meeting.
The master asked for
permission to allow the
infants to disperse five
minutes earlier than the elder
children. The request was
granted. It was decided that the
summer vacation, owing to the
long time the school had been
closed through the epidemic of
measles, should be curtailed.

19th May - ON LEAVE -
Private Abraham COLLINS,
Royal Army Veterinary Corps,
is home having been granted
a week's leave, and Private
Stanley WELLER, who was
wounded and in hospital at
Alexandria for a time, is also at
home.

LEARNING TO FLY – Mr
Frank BALLARD,[15] grocer,

etc., left the district on Monday
for Hendon, where he is to
undergo a course of training
under Mr Grahame WHITE,
with a view to entering the
Flying Corps. His numerous
friends wish him every success.

ABOVE: Frank BALLARD, from
his Royal Aero Club Aviators'
Certificate no.3413 (courtesy the
Royal Aero Club Trust).

**CRICKET CLUB'S
ANNUAL MEETING** –
The annual meeting of the
members of the Cricket Club
took place at the Reading
Room on Wednesday, Captain
SINGLETON (President)
acting as chairman. Others
present were: Major
W.W.GRANTHAM, Messrs.
A.MOON, G.HOLLOWAY,
C.HOLLOWAY, T.RABAN,
S.COX, J.SPELLER, and

S.B.RICHARDS (Hon.
Secretary)... It was pointed
out that this was owing to the
falling off of subscriptions,
many members having joined
the Army. The Hon. Secretary
observed that neighbouring
clubs were not running, and
it was unlikely that
subscriptions would be
as great as in previous
years. He thought that
if some arrangement
could be made with the
Trustees of the playing
fields regarding rent it
would be best for the
club to lay dormant for
the season, and simply
keep the ground in good
condition. Both Captain
SINGLETON and
Major GRANTHAM
thought it would be
a pity not to carry on
the club, for the sake
of the young lads of
the village, and it
was agreed that the
club be kept going,
both gentlemen promising
their support. – Captain
SINGLETON generously
promised a cheque for
the debt balance, also to
give his usual subscription
and pay too, his son's,
Lieutenant SINGLETON.
Major GRANTHAM
also kindly promised two
guineas – one for himself
and one for his son, Master
Ivor GRANTHAM. It was
proposed by the Major,
and seconded by Mr Alfred

15 *Frank (30) was the only child of High
Street shopkeepers John & Caroline
BALLARD.*

MOON, that Captain SINGLETON should be reappointed President…

26th May - CABBAGE PLANTS – Strong autumn-sown: Early, Late and Flatpoll Drumheads, Flockmaster and Enfield Market, 2s.6d. per 1,000; remittance accompanying small orders; bags charged unless returned. CORNWELL, Barcombe Mills.

CHAILEY TRIBUNAL - TEMPORARY EXEMPTION FOR BARCOMBE BAKER – S.B. RICHARDS asked for exemption for Isaac John ELPHICK, 'Pond Plat Cottages', Church-road, who was employed in bread-baking and delivery by motor van. Applicant agreed that a woman might drive the motor van, but he pointed out that ELPHICK was also engaged in the bakehouse. Exemption until August 1st was granted.

On the application of William EDWARDS, (his son) William EDWARDS, junior, 'Gallybird Hall Farm' was granted conditional exemption.

John Alfred PERKINS, 'Burtenshaws Farm', was granted conditional exemption.

On application of F.J.CORNWELL, Thomas WOODS, 'Scufflings Farm,' cowman, was granted exemption until 1st October.

On application of H.J.SPELLER, George John SPELLER, 'Place Farm,' Barcombe Cross, was exempted until September 1st.

On the application of

" For his Country's sake."

In Memoriam—Earl Kitchener.

Fearless, unflinching, he did his duty well,
His the Will that conquered savage horde :
Wedded to Empire—the World his Home,
In a Nation's Thanks—He hath his reward !

Stern, relentless, fighting as a soldier fights
Organiser of Vict'ry—he knew not the word Fail :
Onward, ever Onward, true Son of Britain's Might,
Imperial Soldier-Statesman ! Hail !!

L. Winton.

Born June 24th, 1850.
Died June 5th, 1916.

ABOVE: Earl Kitchener, the face on the recruitment posters, was killed when the ship on which he was travelling on a diplomatic mission to Russia struck a mine off the coast of the Orkney Islands on 5th June 1916.

George HOBDEN, conditional exemption was granted to Ernest Joseph Featherstone BROWN, Spithurst, threshing machine attendant.

NATIONAL EGG COLLECTION – For the wounded soldiers the school children have collected thirty-four eggs, and also 9s.10d. in pence for the purpose of purchasing more.

EMPIRE DAY – The celebration of Empire Day took place at 9 o'clock on Wednesday morning, when the flag was hoisted and saluted as the children marched past and the National Anthem sung.

BARCOMBE BANKRUPTCY – SEQUEL TO COUNTY COURT ACTION – STRONG COMMENTS ON SHEEP WORRYING – Some strong comments on the retention of dogs which were alleged to have worried sheep and caused considerable damage were made by the Registrar (Mr M.S. BLAKER) at the County Hall, Lewes, on Wednesday afternoon, when Sydney Joseph LAKER, of 'Holmbush', gentleman, underwent his public examination in bankruptcy.

The statement of affairs showed that the liabilities amounted to £145.14s.4d., and the assets were nil. Debtor alleged that his failure was due to judgement being obtained against him by the petitioning creditors. He had lodged a deficiency account showing that on April 14th, 1915, he had a surplus of £22. He had since received £40 for military pay. On the other side he returned his personal expenses at £40. The expenses of his illness were £50, and the judgement involved a total of £118 (£72 damages and £46 costs)…

Up to 1912 he carried on farming jointly with his wife at 'Hurst Wood', Buxted. His wife found the capital. Since then he had lived at Barcombe in a house of which his wife was the tenant. He had no occupation except when he was called up at the outbreak of war. From that time until he was invalided out in July 1915, he was a lieutenant in the Royal Garrison Artillery. As soon as he was fit for service again he was going to try to get another commission. At present he had no means. He was dependant on his wife…

Have you property at Barcombe? – No. Debtor further said he had no interest in a motor car which he had used…

A MATTER OF CONVENIENCE – Mr VINALL – In whose name has the licence for the motor car been taken out? – In my name, I think as a matter of convenience.

Yet the motor car has never been yours? – It is a matter of convenience.

Mrs LAKER pays the money and the licence is taken out in your name? – Yes.

Is there any special reason for that? – Because I have not got any money. It would be more convenient, if any accident occurred, for a man to be called upon.

You would be the one responsible for damages, and you conveniently, have not got anything? – No. It is not done for that at all. The arrangement was made merely in view of the possibility of accidents. Exceeding the speed limit is the thing one generally gets.

It is a curious state of

things? – There is no particular "funniness" about it.

Has the licence for that car always been in your name? – Yes, I think so.

You never buy anything for yourself? – Only tobacco. When I was in the Army I paid my expenses…

But the County Court Judge found against you. What guarantee do you give that these dogs will not break out again? They have been sold, I understand, to Mrs LAKER, and will remain at 'Holmbush.' What guarantee do you give to surrounding farmers that these dogs will not again cause tremendous loss? – They never did it…

NO ENDORSEMENT FOR DOG LICENCES – The

ABOVE: Mr Sidney J. LAKER, in an enlarged section of the Scout Group photograph (see 26th November 1915).

Registrar – I do not know how I can bind dogs over to be of good behaviour…

The Registrar described the case as a peculiar one, and

Charles David REYNOLDS

Able Seaman J/20103, killed in action 31st May 1916, aged 19.

Charles was the grandson of Mr & Mrs Isaac BRYANT of 'Gladstone Cottages' (now Weald Close). His mother Bessie, was born in Barcombe c.1873, and married sailor Charles William BRYANT at Portsmouth in 1896. Their son Charles David was born on 27th January the following year. Bessie and her sons moved to Stansted in Essex, where Charles jnr. and his brother Sidney attended primary school, before moving to the neighbouring Hertfordshire town of Bishop's Stortford.

On leaving school he worked briefly as an assistant gardener before following his father into the Royal Navy, aged fifteen. By November 1915 he was serving as an 'A.B.' (Able Boatman) on board H.M.S. "Queen Mary." He was one of 6,784 British and 3,058 Germans who died during the Battle of Jutland, when his ship sank in the North Sea, about sixty miles off the coast of Denmark. He is commemorated on the Portsmouth Naval Memorial, but not in Barcombe.

pointed out that the bankruptcy seemed to have been brought about as a result of an outbreak by dogs which were said to have destroyed sheep belonging to the petitioning creditors. That the Registrar remarked, was an unfortunate and disastrous occurrence…

The examination was closed, subject to a formal adjournment for the purpose of signing the notes.

2nd June - PROPOSED TROOP OF GIRL GUIDES

– Lady MONK BRETTON and Mrs BURROWS, 'Yewhurst', Spithurst, are endeavouring to raise a troop of Girl Guides in the district.

FAREWELL TEA – On

Tuesday afternoon the members of the local branch of the Girls' Friendly Society were the guests of the Misses DEALTRY, who had invited them to partake of tea at their residence 'The Lawns', Barcombe Mills. The Misses DEALTRY are leaving the district shortly to take up their residence at The Wallands, Lewes.

SEQUEL TO BICYCLE MISHAP

– At Lewes Petty Sessions on Tuesday, Frank STONE was fined 2s.6d. for having ridden a cycle without lights in Cooksbridge Road, Barcombe, on May 18th. P.C. WILLARD, who proved the case, gave evidence that when he was stopped defendant said: "I had an accident; I fell off my bicycle and bent the pedal. That made me late in getting home."

OTTERS SHOT

– Otters will abide where plenty of fishes haunt the river. During May Mr H.ROGERS of Barcombe, had the pleasure in shooting a large, bitch otter at Barcombe Mills, while Mr H.HILL of Ringmer, thanks to his keen scented sheep dog, had a similar pleasure in procuring two cubs, both of which were found in that portion of the Ouse which touches the Ringmer parish. Two or three otters were shot on the Ouse last year, and a similar number the previous year.

WEDDING

– A quiet wedding took place at St.Mary's, Barcombe, on Tuesday, the officiating clergyman being the Rev. FARRAR. The contracting parties were Miss Ethel Grace VERCOE, second daughter of Mr Hart VERCOE of 'Banks Farm,' and Trooper REDFERN, attached to the Yorkshire Dragoons, who is a native of Yorkshire. The best man was Trooper Allan VERCOE, Sussex Yeomanry, brother of the bride. The bride, who was given away by her father, was attired in a costume of wedgewood blue, and wore a hat to match. She was attended by her sister. Miss Ida VERCOE. After the ceremony a reception was held at 'Banks Farm', and later the newly-wedded couple left for Bridlington to spend their honeymoon... Amongst the many useful presents received were a cheque from the Major of the Yorkshire Dragoons, and also a cheque from Mr Hart VERCOE.

9th June - BARCOMBE BAKER'S HARDSHIP –

On the grounds of serious hardship, Charles John HOLLOWAY, bread baker was granted two months' exemption. It was stated that

ABOVE: A wartime wedding – The marriage entry for Trooper REDFERN and Ethel VERCOE of 'Banks Farm' in St. Mary's parish registers (ESRO: PAR 235/1/3/2).

30th June 1916 "The Day Sussex Died"

The 12th and 13th Battalions, supported by the 11th, were sacrificed in a diversionary raid on the Boar's Head salient at Richebourg on 30th June 1916 in an attempt to draw German attention away from the main Somme battle area further south. The Battle at Boar's Head lasted less than five hours, but the Southdowns Brigade lost 17 officers and 349 other ranks. Over 1,000 men were wounded or taken prisoner, and the 13th Battalion was all but wiped out.

livesofthefirstworldwar.org (IWM).

applicant had a married brother who was eligible for the Army. It was recognised that one of the two men would have to serve, and applicant was ready to do his duty, but he desired temporary exemption while his brother, owing to illness, was unable to work.

CHAILEY TRIBUNAL – William Thomas STEVENS was granted conditional exemption. On the grounds of domestic hardship, exemption until September 1st was granted to William Wilfred HARRIOTT, pianoforte tuner and teacher.[16]

16th June - CHAILEY TRIBUNAL – On the application of F.J. CORNWELL, conditional exemption was granted to Reginald HEASMAN. On the grounds of serious hardship, conditional exemption was granted to Albert STILL, insurance agent. On the application of George HOBDEN, conditional exemption was granted to William Charles HOBDEN, agricultural machinist.

23rd June - ANOTHER ECHO OF THE MORSE CASE – H.GEERING asked for exemption for John George AWCOCK, cowman and Matthew Thomas WADEY, cowman and carter, both of Barcombe. The cases came before the Tribunal because the men, whose ages were respectively 22 years and 20 years, had been removed from the list of exempted occupations. Captain Selby ASH said the conditions had altered recently because applicant had secured the valuable services of Mr VARNHAM, junior.

30th June - CRICKET – The Barcombe Club played its first match of the season last Saturday when its opponents were the R.A.M.C. of Brighton…

A NAVAL ASPIRANT – Thomas Luscombe REVELL, farmer,[17] was granted conditional exemption. Mr REVELL also asked for exemption for Richard BURCHELL, cowman and Samuel Henry GREEN, carter. Conditional exemption was allowed for BURCHELL. It was stated that GREEN had joined the Navy, and his case was adjourned in order that evidence might be obtained.

On the application of E.W. BUNNEY, conditional exemption was granted to

1st July 1916

The sound of artillery at the outbreak of the Battle of the Somme could be clearly heard on the Sussex coast. The noise of the guns routinely drifted across the channel and could be heard as far in land as London on some days. The sounds of fighting were particularly loud on 1 July 1916 as men rose from trenches to face the single worst day in the history of the British Army. By sunset, 57,470 men had become casualties, of which 19,240 were dead.

www.eastsussexww1.org.uk

16 William HARRIOTT was born in Hamsey in 1865 and had moved to Barcombe with his parents by 1871. In 1911 he was living in the High Street, and when completing his census return entered his occupation as; "Church Organist & Music Teacher" and his age as "35." The second of these facts was clearly untrue, as he was actually 45. The truth would catch up with him when he appeared before another Tribunal later in the year!

17 Thomas REVELL (31) farmed 'Delves' and 'Gallops.'

Horace William EPPS, foreman market gardener and florist.

7th July - CHAILEY TRIBUNAL – Harry GEERING, farmer, was granted conditional exemption. Conditional exemption was granted to Edwin George HOLLOWAY, baker. Mr H.J.HILLMAN supported the application. On the application of John GURR, conditional exemption was granted to Stephen James BAKER, cowman and Arthur AKEHURST, carter.

MARRIAGE – PETERS-BROOKSBANK – On the 2nd July, by special licence, at the Parish Church, by the Rev. FARRAR. William Alexander PETERS of the Malay States, late Lieutenant, Welsh Regiment, son of the late George Henry PETERS, of Craigmore, Yorkshire, to Constance Ruby, elder daughter of Mr & Mrs Edgar Musgrave BROOKSBANK of Barcombe.

DEATH OF MR F.S. SHENSTONE – OLD RESIDENT PASSES AWAY AT BARCOMBE – The death of Mr Frederick Smith SHENSTONE, MA, DL, JP, occurred at his residence, 'Sutton Hall,' on Monday morning, at the advanced

RIGHT: Mr Frederick SHENSTONE photographed in 1909 seated at his 'coach-and-four' with two liveried footmen. 'Horace' was Horace VERRALL his coachman, who later became chauffeur to Frederick's daughter Adela, owner of the first car in the village, a red Rolls Royce (ESRO: WI 112/1/1 p.30).

Frederick S. Shenstone

ABOVE: Frederick Smith SHENSTONE (1824-1916). Known as "The Squire" by W.W. GRANTHAM of Balneath Manor.

age of 92 years. Deceased, who was one of the principal land owners in the district, succumbed to bronchitis, which he developed the previous Friday. He had however, been in declining health for the last twelve months.

Previous to him purchasing the estate at Barcombe, which was in 1869, and which he has

greatly enlarged and practically rebuilt 'Sutton Hall', he managed the late Lord Dudley's industrial estates, as also did his father before him. It was about this period (1869) that he took the name of Shenstone, which is an old family name. He was the first Mayor of Dudley, which was fifty years ago, and only last year, when the Corporation of that industrial centre celebrated its jubilee, he received a telegram of congratulation from that body, who invited him to visit Dudley and receive the freedom of the town. Old age, however, prevented the deceased from accepting the honour, he not being able to travel the distance.

He was Captain of the Worcestershire Yeomanry for forty years, and had been a justice of the peace for Worcestershire, Staffordshire, and Sussex, and had also held the position of Deputy-Lieutenant for the two latter counties.

Liked by all who knew him, Mr Shenstone was careful and

F.S. "Rajah" "Milton"
Horace "Whiskey" "Charlie"

125

FIRST PRIZE awarded TRADES' EXHIBITION

LIFE-LONG
EXPERIENCE
AND STUDY
TO
PRODUCE
AND SELL
THE BEST
IN
FOOTWEAR.

BEAVER & ZUG
BOOTS
Of Every
Description.

FIELD BOOTS,
KEEPER'S ,,
POLICEMEN'S,
POSTMEN'S,
RAILWAYMEN'S
BOYS' & GIRLS'
SCOUT,
COLLEGE
BOOTS

SKULE
BOOTS
FOR BOYS
AND GIRLS.
MOST
RELIABLE
MAKES.

The Latest
Production :
STRONG
SERVICEABLE
BOOTS FOR
LADIES
DOING MEN'S
WORK 'Until
our Boys come
Home.'

REPAIRS BY
OUR OWN
WORKMEN
ON THE
PREMISES.

Note Address :

BOOT MANUFACTURING COMPANY, 206, HIGH STREET, SCHOOL HILL, **LEWES.**

GOLD MEDAL has been awarded to MANAGER of BOOT MANUFACTURING COMPANY, Boot Manufacturers and Repairers, 206, High Street, Lewes, for the Best Display of Footwear. He is undoubtedly an Expert in Footwear and Footwear Specialist. For many years he has made a successful study in producing and selling the most reliable Boys' and Girls' School Boots, Scout Boots, Postman, Railway, Farmer and Keeper Boots he has excelled. The latest production is strong, serviceable Boots and Shoes, extra strong uppers and soles, for Ladies who are doing men's work until our boys return from the Front. These Ladies' Boots and Shoes are made up to Size 8, and Men's up to Size 12. We are now manufacturing Children's Boots from best piece from Men's Army Boots and Men's Beaver and Zug Boots. BOOT MANUFACTURING COMPANY, as a progressive and up-to-date Firm, are thoroughly experienced men in every branch of the Boot Trade, capable of making the smallest Infants' Boots and Shoes up to the largest and strongest Men's. Their Branch is fitted up with all the latest machinery for making and repairing. Last year, from July 1st, 1914, to June 30th, 1915, 29,738 pairs of Boots and Shoes passed through their Repairing Department, representing work done to the daintiest Ladies' Dress Shoes to the strongest Men's Field Boots. Their 206 Branch is well stocked with every kind of Boots and Shoes, including Seamless and Scotch fitting, and the largest and best variety of Slippers in the district.

BOOT MANUFACTURING COMPANY, 206, High St., School Hill, LEWES.

LEFT: Boot Manufacturing Company of 206 High Street, School Hill, Lewes. "Strong serviceable boots for Ladies doing Men's work 'Until our Boys come Home'."

cautious and subscribed liberally to any object which appealed to him. He did many kindly actions and always unostentatiously. He was a staunch Conservative throughout his life, and was always deeply interested in all matters relating to agriculture, and was a great admirer of trees, many fine specimens of which he has grown upon his own estate...

About seven years ago he gave up his coach and four white horses, of which he was very proud, and with which he did a deal of travelling.

The Great War saddened him somewhat, but he would have all the news that could possibly be gleaned... He was also a lover of history, and his artistic taste is revealed by the beautiful statuary and pictures which bedeck Sutton Hall. Deceased's wife predeceased him by two years. He leaves one daughter, Miss Adela Shenstone, to mourn his loss...

14th July - CHAILEY MILITARY TRIBUNAL - LATE WORK FOR BARCOMBE BOOTMAKER – Henry STEVENSON,

bootmaker, asked for exemption. He stated that he was largely engaged in repairing boots for agriculturists. As they had only one pair of boots each a great deal of work had to be done after the men left their occupations in the evenings. The case was adjourned in order that applicant might submit a medical certificate.

BARCOMBE BUTCHER'S HARDSHIP - On the grounds of serious hardship, Charles MUGGERIDGE, butcher, was granted conditional exemption. The Applicant stated that he was the only butcher within a distance of 4 miles who sold foreign as well as home killed meat. As there was a difference of 6d per lb in the prices, his shop was a great convenience to the poor people of the neighbourhood. Nobody would buy a butcher's business now. If he had to serve in the Army he must put up his shutters and in consequence would lose the money he had invested.

Captain Selby ASH (Military Representative) expressed surprise that there was such a difference in the prices of foreign and home killed meat at Barcombe. The variation, he said, was not as marked at Lewes.

On the application of S.B.RICHARDS, conditional exemption was granted to Frederick TOMSETT, carter, Barcombe.

21st July - 'HOLMBUSH' – AUCTION OF HOUSEHOLD FURNITURE

– on Thursday, August 3rd at 12.30 o'clock. The excellent household furniture, including well-made Oak, Walnut and other Bedroom Suites, capital Oak Dining Room Suite, Dining Table extending to 7ft. 6in., Oak Writing Table, Easy and Occasional Chairs, Sweet-Toned Boudoir Grand Piano, in Ebony Case, Iron Frames Cottage Pianoforte, in Rosewood Case, Chesterfield, Handsome French 3 day Clock with 5 Sevres Plaques, Two Carved Oak Hall Chairs, with Rush Seats, and the outdoor effects and Poultry Appliances comprise: Nearly New Large Portable Match-Boarded Building, Excellent Span Roof Greenhouse 20ft. by 10ft. with Heating Apparatus, and numerous effects…
The residence is to be Let Unfurnished with immediate possession.[18]

STOOLBALL

– The result of the match between the school children and Ringmer's junior team: Barcombe had a full innings, and Ringmer lost three wickets. Barcombe score: Violet KING 3, Edith FARENDEN 34, Lena KING 97, Mildred

---

18 This sale resulted from the bankruptcy proceedings (see 26th May).

19 Henry REED (63) of 'Crink Cottages;' George HILLMAN (40) of 'Hayes Cottages;' Thomas BRADFORD (34) of School Path. Percy BROOK (39) of 'Crink Cottages.'

20 James Sexton FOORD (25) farmed at 'Bradness,' Longford.

ABOVE: Wounded men from the 5th Royal Sussex Regiment at Lewisham Hospital - Photographs of groups of men from Sussex regiments, were often published in the *Sussex Express* without any story or text attached. The caption often says something along the lines of "many of our readers will recognise faces…"

DIPLOCK 1, Mildred STANDING 5, Maud MARTIN 0, Barbara STANDING 1, Annie JONES 30, Kathleen RICHARDS 8, Ivy KNIBBS 4, Nellie TAPP 3, byes 16, total 202. Ringmer 106.

WOUNDED - The following men are reported wounded, Private Charles PECKHAM, whose brother Cecil was killed some little time back, Charlie MARCHANT, wounded on the shoulder and head, Private George FOORD, broken leg and Private Frank COPPARD.

CHAILEY RURAL DISTRICT TRIBUNAL

- Had dealt with about 750 applications for exemption from military service.

28th July - MILITARY SERVICE TRIBUNAL - Mr F.J. CORNWELL, a member of the Tribunal, asked for exemption for Henry REED, stockman; George HILLMAN, undercowman; Thomas

BRADFORD, thatcher and undercowman and Percival John BROOK, carter, all of Barcombe.[19] Applicant stated that his staff included old age pensioners, cripples and women. Conditional exemption was granted to REED, HILLMAN and BROOK and exemption until October 1st was allowed in the case of BRADFORD.

James Sexton FOORD, farmer,[20] asked for exemption for himself and James FIELDER, cowman. It transpired that applicant took his farm in September 1915. Conditional exemption was granted in both cases.

On the application of G. & E. RHODES, conditional exemption was granted to Arthur William RUSBRIDGE, carter.

H.GEERING asked for exemption for George BEARD, milk cart driver, Chailey and Leslie WADEY, farm worker, Barcombe. Applicant was

instructed to send BEARD for primary medical examination, temporary exemption till October 1st was granted to WADEY.

SUMMER HOLIDAYS – It has been decided to close the School for the summer vacation on Friday, August 4th, and re-open on the same date of the following month.

FOR WOUNDED TOMMIES – Barcombe residents never seem happy unless they are collecting for some charitable object, and their efforts are always beyond expectations. On Monday evening the inhabitants intend holding a meeting at the Parish Room for the purpose of fixing a date in August and raising the wherewithal to entertain over seventy wounded soldiers, who will be coming from Brighton and other districts.

BARCOMBE BOY WINS SCHOLARSHIP – Master Geoffrey TROWER,[21] who is aged only nine years, is undoubtedly a clever boy, in winning a scholarship. Master Geoffrey, furthermore, was adjudged best out of the fifty-five candidates, whose ages ranged from eight to twelve years. We congratulate Mr & Mrs H.TROWER, the parents of a bright and promising boy, who will soon be a pupil at Uckfield Grammar School.

4th August - BARCOMBE CHARITY TRUST – Probate of the will of Mr John BURDER of 'The Beeches,' who died on 3rd March at the age of 83, has been granted

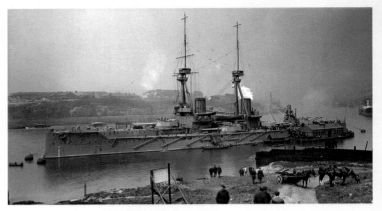

ABOVE: H.M.S. 'Superb' Wilfred BATTEN's ship, seen here leaving the Tyne, had taken part in the Battle of Jutland on 31st May 1916.

to Richard Howard Russell BURDER and John BURDER, power to prove being reserved to deceased's son, Lewis Algernon Wentworth BURDER, now serving in Egypt.[22] The estate was sworn at £21,718.15s.7d. The will creates a charity trust to be called the "John Burder Trust", to be administered by Mrs BURDER, and two members of the family.

CRICKET - Newick v Barcombe – This return match was played at Newick on Wednesday, resulting in a win for the home team by two runs. Tea was kindly provided by Mr T.BADEN-POWELL. Barcombe: H.WARNETT, C.GURR, J.WALL, P.TROWER, G.ELDRIDGE, A.COX, E.TAPP, H.WARNETT, H.FARENDEN, S.RICHARDS and W.SIZER.

DIES FROM WOUNDS - Private George FOORD, who at one time worked for Mr DEAN, butcher, and whose parents now reside at Blackboys, has succumbed to his wounds.

REPORTED MISSING - 2nd Lieut. T.E.BOURDILLON, Northants Regiment, is reported missing. He had only been at the Front for about five weeks. He came home from South Africa for the purpose of joining the Army.

MR S.B.RICHARDS wishes to inform his customers in Barcombe that, owing to the Government restrictions of petrol, and being shorthanded through his men joining the Army, he is compelled to curtail his (bread) delivery. He hopes that his patrons will assist him as far as possible and continue their support.

---

21 *Geoffrey Edward TROWER lived at 6 Gladstone Cottages with his three older brothers; Harrison Paul, William Arthur and Philip John. Their parents were Lois & Harry, carpenter & undertaker.*

22 *Lewis BURDER was born in Barcombe in 1883 and baptised at St.Mary's church. He attended Haileybury College, where he joined the cadet corps. In December 1914 he gave 'The Beeches' as his home address when enlisting with the Royal Horse Artillery. He was discharged to an address in East Chiltington in July 1919, suffering from malaria (TNA: WO 363). He later lived in Grand Parade, Brighton, where he died in 1949.*

DEATH OF SGT. W.HAWKINS - Sgt. W. HAWKINS succumbed to consumption at Portslade Sanatorium at the latter part of last week. Previous to the War he had been in the Regular Army but had been invalided out. At the outbreak of war however he had improved in health, so again offered his services which were accepted…

MEETING OF RESIDENTS – The meeting of the residents of the district, which was called for the purpose of making arrangements for the entertainment of wounded soldiers, took place on Monday evening at the Recreation Ground… The Rector presided.

It was arranged that the event should be held on Wednesday, August 16th, and if the weather was not propitious, on the following day. It was stated that items in kind would be preferred to money. Mrs RICHARDS, Mrs SPELLER, Mrs REECE, Mrs REYNOLDS, Miss Florence WALKER and Mrs J.FUNNELL undertook to attend to the catering; Miss Lena HOLLOWAY, the musical portion of the entertainment; Mrs MUGGRIDGE, a side show; Mrs SINGLETON, manage the games; Miss Muriel GRANTHAM, run a competition; Mr MATTHEWS, a new resident, kindly promised to pay for a band, and also to give 1,000 cigarettes; Mr BLAKER, cigarettes; the Rector, a subscription. Messrs. MUGGRIDGE and RICHARDS undertook to collect the goods and deliver same, and the former will control donkey rides. Mr REYNOLDS will make a quoit bed, and attend to same during the day; the Misses SPELLER and Miss Nancy FUNNELL will run competitions; Mrs KIRBY will have a stall containing drinks. It is expected that over 100 soldiers will attend, all of whom will come from the districts of Lewes, East Chiltington, Chailey and Newick.

11th August - ON LEAVE - Wilfrid BATTEN,[23] a member of the crew of H.M.S. Superb, is at home having been granted a well-earned leave.

FOR TOMMIES' SAKE - A military band consisting of 32 members, which is stationed at Seaford, has been engaged for next week, when about 200 wounded soldiers are to be entertained. The men are coming from Brighton, Lewes, Ditchling, East Chiltington and Newick.

WHIRLWIND'S CAPERS – Last week a whirlwind, travelling at a great velocity, was observed coming from a north-westerly direction towards Culver Junction. At a considerable height was revolving half a wagon load of hay. Here and there the whirlwind dropped some of the hay, but it travelled away with the major portion. It is presumed that it must have caught the top of a new haystack which was unthatched.

18th August - BARCOMBE FETE DAY – WOUNDED SOLDIERS ENTERTAINED – MESSAGE FROM THE KING – Though the wind was somewhat boisterous on

---

23 Wilfred BATTEN lived at 'Grange Villas'.

ABOVE: The Welcoming Party – Three carriages and a car wait at Barcombe Station to meet the wounded soldiers (Photograph by Meux of Lewes, Barcombe W.I. Scrapbook, ESRO: WI 112/1/1 p.96).

BARCOMBE AUG 16 1916.

Wednesday morning, and the scudding clouds threatened rain, the monarch of the day asserted himself, dispelled the clouds, and smiled pleasantly the whole afternoon. It was just the kind of weather that Barcombe residents desired, for they had no fewer than 180 guests – all war-worn, wounded soldiers. They were entertained on the Recreation Ground, and the inhabitants of the village turned out en masse for the occasion.

Barcombe people are noted for their kindness. They have no half measures when asked to subscribe for any good object, and always prove themselves very generous, as they did for Wednesday's function.

The soldiers invited were from the Pavilion, Brighton (30), Miss Pearson's establishment, Brighton (6), Eye Hospital, Brighton (9), Lewes Crescent, Brighton (24), Hill House, Lewes (33), St.Ann's, Lewes (15), Ditchling (20), East Chiltington (15), Newick (30).

Four wounded soldiers from a hospital at Hampstead were driven by motor by Miss WALKER, a local lady who is acting as a nurse.

The Rev. FARRAR acted as Chairman, and the following ladies and gentlemen (though the cost of the event is paid by the whole of the inhabitants of the village) were responsible for the various arrangements: Mrs WALKER, hon. Secretary; tea, Mesdames J.FUNNELL, HOLLOWAY, REECE, REYNOLDS, SPELLER and Miss F.WALKER; races, Mrs MUGGERIDGE, Miss V.WALKER and Messrs. C.MUGGERIDGE and CROWHURST, assisted by Masters POND, TAPP and WALKER; competition - sense of touch, Miss GRANTHAM; competition – weighing and smelling, the Misses SPELLER; concert, Miss L.HOLLOWAY, Mrs HAFFENDEN and Mr A.HOLDEN, stationmaster; band, transport of guests and photos, Mr H.B.MATTHEWS; tobacco and cigarettes, Mr A.BLAKER and Mr BALLARD; aerated waters, Mrs KIRBY; buttonholes, Miss MOON; fruit, the Misses HENTY and SMITH; ices, the Misses FUNNELL and Ethel RHODES; chocolates, the Misses T.HOBDEN and F.PECKHAM; matches, Miss Elsie RHODES; distribution of cigarettes, the Misses Doris HOLDEN, Molly MATTHEWS and Ruth NEWMAN; side

BARCOMBE AUG. 16. 1916

WOUNDED SOLDIERS "BARCOMBE" AUG. 16 -1916.

MEUX. PHOTO-LEWES.

ABOVE: Rev FARRAR in the centre of the gathering on the Recreation Ground, with the village school clearly visible in the background (along with a stoolball wicket and a bandsman's music stand in the back right of the picture). Photographed by Meux of Lewes (Mike Green collection).

shows ('Bashing the Boches', 'Aunt Sally', bowls, etc.) Mrs SINGELTON, assisted by the Misses DEAN, G.MacBEAN, RANN, TOWNER and VERCOE; croquet golf, Miss CARPMAEL; ring board, the Misses D. & K.RICHARDS; fortune telling, Miss ELPHICK; Kaiser Bill, Mr C.MUGGERIDGE; quoits, Mr REYNOLDS; loan of vehicles, Messrs. G.LLOYD, C.MUGGERIDGE, H.PERRY and W.MOORE, also Lady GRANTHAM, Mrs BURT BRILL, Miss LANE, the Rev. FARRAR, Mr W.F.DEAN, Mr A.BORRETT; tents, Messrs. CURTIS & Co. and Mr KING.

The band engaged, consisting of thirty-two members, was from the London Command Deport, Seaford, by permission of Lieutenant Colonel FOX-PITT, Grenadier Guards. The programme of music rendered was much appreciated. A sumptuous tea was provided, after which followed the concert, and the artistes from start to finish held a huge and attentive audience. Mr W.BUNNEY gave "Sussex by the Sea," and was well applauded; Miss F.RHODES, who possesses a sweet voice and proved a great favourite, was responsible for four songs, two of which were in answer to encores: "Flower of Empire's Manhood," "Laddie in Khaki, I'm waiting for you," "My Hero," and "When you come home, dear." Mrs F.BALLARD sang "The Carnival," which was much appreciated, as also was "The Break o'Day," rendered by Miss Nellie DEAN; Mr HARRIOTT, who accompanied himself on the piano, and who sings well, gave "The Old Umbrella;" Miss Violet KING sang "Michigan," and soon had the audience joining in the chorus; Miss Dorothy DREW varied the programme by dancing, her first dance being entitled "Faded Roses," and her second the "Society Cake Walk." She is a graceful dancer, and met with hearty approval; Miss Peggy SIMPSON is a sweet little maid, and, as most children, won her audience from the outset. She scored well with her song, "I'll make a man of you" and likewise with her dances. She is a clever little girl and may someday blossom into a Vesta Tilley and impersonate the Piccadilly Berties.

The comic element was left to Mr A.HOLDEN, Barcombe stationmaster and Miss L.HOLLOWAY, both of whom are really funny in their line. Mr HOLDEN gave

ABOVE: Wounded soldiers wearing "Hospital" or "Convalescent Blues" at Barcombe Station on the day of the Fete in their honour, 16th August 1916. (Photograph by Meux of Lewes, ESRO: WI 112/1/1 p.170).

"Stewed Prunes and Prisms," "It ain't all honey and it ain't all jam," "Archibald, certainly not," and "Standing at the corner of the street," each of which was greeted with hearty laughter and applause. Miss L.HOLLOWAY sang "The bell goes a-ringing for Sarah," and "Jenny Links," and on each occasion, particularly the first, the audience was moved to laughter. Miss HOLLOWAY is certainly quaint and original.

When the concert was over, Major W.W.GRANTHAM remarked that he was sorry he had not been in attendance earlier, so that he could have helped them. He proposed a vote of thanks to Mrs WALKER and her two daughters for their hard work in connection with the function. They had been working morning, noon and night to make it a success. So also had the Rector and Mr MATTHEWS, who was responsible for the band. Three hearty cheers were given, and

one of the soldiers replied on behalf of his comrades.

The Rev FARRAR, for the inhabitants, mentioned that he had two sons in the Army, one enlisted as soon as the War broke out, and the other did not wait long till he followed his example. One, however, he was sorry to say, was in his grave in Belgium. He would assure the soldiers who were present that the inhabitants of Barcombe were proud of them. He hoped that the time was not far distant when they would get to their own homes, but he would like them to always have a warm place in their hearts for the little place called Barcombe…

In reply to a message sent to the King, the following reply was received by the Rector: "I am commanded by the King to thank the Parish of Barcombe, Sussex, their guests, the 200 wounded soldiers, and the 150 men from Barcombe now serving, for their loyal message. His Majesty hopes that the wounded soldiers will

make a speedy recovery."

25th August - BARCOMBE TEACHER'S HARDSHIP – On the ground of serious hardship exemption was granted to William Wilfred HARRIOTT, pianoforte teacher & tuner.

PHOTOGRAPHED – The lady and gentleman workers in connection with the fete day, which was held to entertain the wounded soldiers, were photographed on Wednesday.

THANKS – Miss E.B.KNAPTON, matron of School Hill Hospital, Lewes sent the following letter of thanks to Mrs WALKER. "Will you kindly convey to the inhabitants of Barcombe the most grateful thanks of our wounded soldiers. I cannot possibly express their appreciation of the kindness and generosity of all those who helped to give the men such an exceptionally happy time. At the wounded men's request I send a thousand thanks to all."

CRICKET – The match which was played between Barcombe and Brighton Royal Army Medical Corps at Preston Park, resulted in a draw, and the return match was played at Barcombe last Saturday.

1st September - SCHOOLS RE-OPENING – The day school will re-open on Monday, and the Sunday school on September 10th.

FULLY SUBSCRIBED - Barcombe residents have displayed another instance of their generosity in subscribing towards purchasing an invalid chair for the use of wounded soldiers quartered at Brighton. The full amount has been procured and the chair will be one which wounded soldiers can wheel without aid.

8th September - QUICK RESPONSE - The cost of the chair, which is to be presented for the use of legless soldiers at Brighton is £5.17.6d. Bags held at the two church doors on Sunday August 20th realised £4.3.3d. Mr CORNWELL collected 18s, Mrs HEWETT 11s., so the total £5.12.3d is but 5s.3d short of the required figure.

WOUNDED – Private Sidney WALL, who joined the Bantams, but was transferred to the Sussex Regiment, has been wounded. The family has recently taken up residence at Crowborough.

GOOD LUCK – Mr Henry COTTRELL, the signalman at Culver Junction, after a wedded life of ten years, had the felicity on Tuesday of being presented with a little daughter.

LOCAL FLYER – Mr Frank BALLARD, desirous of becoming an aviator, has for the last few months been practising at Hendon, under the tuition of Mr Graham WHITE, and is now at Farnborough, having secured his certificate.

MILITARY SERVICE TRIBUNAL – BARCOMBE MAN IN THE DARDANELLES. An application for exemption was made on behalf of William Hart VERCOE, aged 18 years, stockman and shepherd, whose father stated that another son had been invalided home after 6 months service in the Dardanelles. Six months exemption was granted.

AFRAID OF THE COWS – Major W.W.GRANTHAM applied for further exemption for George John SPELLER, aged 20, horseman and stockman. Applicant's representative stated that 14 of Major GRANTHAM's men had joined the Forces, and difficulty was experienced, owing to shortage of staff, in meeting requirements. A girl who had been employed was afraid of the cows, and she only stopped one week. Two months' exemption was granted.

MRS. COX, of Mount Pleasant, Barcombe, who has three sons serving.

CORPORAL COX, R.G.A., France.

GUNNER COX, R.G.A.

PRIVATE COX, Royal Sussex, France.

ABOVE: 'Mothers of Empire' - Mrs COX of Mount Pleasant and her three serving sons: Cpl. COX, RGA; Gunner COX, RGA and Private COX, Royal Sussex Regiment.

15th September - AN EARLY VISITOR – At Lewes Petty Sessions, on Tuesday, Frances Mary ELPHICK was fined 5s. for a breach of the Lighting Order at 'Clovelly,' Grange Road – P.C. WILLARD deposed that at 12.20 a.m. on September 3rd he saw a bright light shining from an upstairs window at defendant's premises. Defendant stated that she had only just moved into the house.

THE RECTOR's SON - Mr S.G. FARRAR, son of the

Rector, has entered the Royal Military College at Sandhurst. Mr FARRAR was reading for Holy Orders at Lichfield when he joined the 16th Royal Sussex Regiment. He has served six months in the ranks and has now entered Sandhurst on a nomination from his old school, Dulwich College…

BARCOMBE AND THE WOUNDED – PRESENT OF AN INVALID CHAIR –

A public meeting was held on Tuesday evening at the Village Mission Room for the purpose of presenting an invalid's chair to the Royal Pavilion Hospital, Brighton, and giving a statement of accounts in connection with the successful Fete which was held last month, when about 200 wounded soldiers were the guests of the inhabitants. There was a good attendance, which included the local Boy Scouts. The chair was occupied by the Rector.

Mr H.B.MATTHEWS said he had received several letters of thanks, as also had Mrs WALKER, and he read one from the Matron of School Hill Hospital, Lewes, which stated that the men were still talking of the great treat they had had, and would always remember their visit to Barcombe.

The accounts, which showed a balance in hand of £5.12s., were then presented. They had been audited by Mr G.BOURDILLON, Mr Alfred MOON and Mr W.H.REECE, and it was pointed out that all bills had been paid. The statements were: Donations £10.10s.6d.; the boxes £5.18s.1d.; the Band Fund £5.1s.6d.; collections for cigarettes, £4.15s.8d.. The whole total collected was therefore £26.5s.9d. There were no fewer than 4,500 cigarettes purchased.

The Chairman then invited the audience to make suggestions as to what was to be done with the surplus cash £5.12s. Answering a question, he said that the invalid's chair cost £7, and Major GRANTHAM suggested that another chair should be purchased. Miss WALKER however, proposed that the money might be handed over to the Prisoners of War Fund for Sussex soldiers. Major GRANTHAM agreed with the proposal, and seconded it…

Mr MATTHEWS stated that when the soldiers were entertained he had a number of photographs taken, and 250 had been sold. He had promised, however, that the Red Cross Society would receive 1d. on each card, so he would have the pleasure in handing Miss WALKER £1.2s.6d. for the Society. There were a number of photographs left, and they would be sold at 1d. each...

The chair was then presented. It bore the inscription: "Presented by the inhabitants of Barcombe, September, 1916." Sergeant

ABOVE: FRIENDS OF THE WOUNDED - This photograph was taken on the Recreation Ground, by James Meux of Lewes and a copy of it presented to Mrs WALKER. It features some of the fete organisers, including Lady GRANTHAM (dressed in black, seated just left of centre), Ernest KING of the 'Royal Oak' (tallest man in the back row) and Rev FARRAR (back row, with a dark wide-brimmed hat). The village school is just visible in the background. (Photograph copied by Mike Green from an original belonging to Miss Violet KING).

HALLAM, acknowledging the gift, said he was pleased to receive such a handsome present for the wounded...

Mr MATTHEWS asked Major GRANTHAM if he would kindly make a presentation to Mrs WALKER, or her daughters on her behalf. The lady had acted as Secretary, and had done great work. A large number of the workers had assembled on the Recreation Ground and been photographed. He had one enlarged and framed, and he would ask Major GRANTHAM to present the same to Mrs WALKER.

Major GRANTHAM remarked that everybody knew how energetic Mr MATTHEWS had been, and how hard he had worked for the success attained in connection with the entertaining of the wounded soldiers. (Applause.) He had recently been turning over some of his father's letters and papers, and had found a programme which related to a dance at the Manor House, Lewes, on Tuesday, January 27th, 18—well, he did not intend to give away secrets, but his father was then in his twenties. However, he observed on the programme that his father's first dance was with a Miss GORRINGE, and his second dance, strangely enough, was with a lady whose name was

Miss ditto, and in the third dance, who could they imagine he chose as a partner? Well, the name on the programme was the same fascinating lady, Miss GORRINGE. (Laughter.) It showed that he was very nearly related to the present Mrs WALKER. Mrs WALKER being absent, the Major remarked that two daughters would perhaps equal one mother, and on the Misses WALKER coming forward he presented the photo and the Rector returned thanks on their behalf… After thanks to the Chairman, the meeting closed with the singing of the National Anthem.

22nd September - IN A PROHIBITED AREA – ALIEN'S TROUBLES AT BARCOMBE – The Bench were engaged for some time at Lewes Petty Sessions on Tuesday in dealing with cases in which defendants were summoned in respect of breaches of the Aliens restriction Order.

Antoinette KADLOVSKY, an alien, was summoned for having entered a prohibited area without the special permission of the Registration Officer.

Defendant pleaded guilty. P.S. GOODSELL deposed that at noon on September 6th he

called at 'Woodside,' where defendant was employed as a cook. He asked her what her nationality was. She said, "I am French; I came over from France in 1903. In 1912 I married a Russian Pole. He died in 1914.[24] I came here on July 4th this year." She stated that the only document which showed her nationality was her marriage certificate, which she produced. She added that she did not know she had to register; she thought that arrangement only applied to the sea coast and she had been told by the French Consul in London that she could go anywhere.

A fine of 5s. was imposed. Mrs Emma PEEBLES pleaded guilty to having failed to notify the presence of KADLOVSKY in her household... The Chairman said that as defendant had acknowledged that she knew the law, she must be fined £2.

ENGAGEMENT – A marriage has been arranged, and will shortly take place, between Cadet Gordon E.L.BURDER, Royal Garrison Artillery, son

---

24 *There is a marriage recorded between a Marie Antoinette MOURIBOT and Charles 'KADLEVSKY' in Norfolk in 1912. Charles died two years later, aged 33, and was buried in Sutton Road Cemetery, Southend, along with an infant son named Maurice.*

RIGHT: The New Register of Aliens – This notice had appeared the previous summer (*Sussex Express*, 25th June 1915).

LEFT: The "Simplex" Tractor, available from Culverwells, Cliffe Foundry, Lewes. The modern alternative to horse-drawn ploughs.

of the late Mr John BURDER of 'The Beeches', and Sallie, second daughter of the late Lionel DRUITT, M.D., of Mentone, Victoria and Mrs DRUITT, Girrahween, Tumbarumba, New South Wales.

ANNIVERSARY CELEBRATION – The members of the undenominational Mission Hall, also many friends, celebrated its anniversary on Wednesday. The Hall was erected about 19 years ago, and during the intervening period the congregation has much increased. Tea was served, about sixty persons participating. Later in the evening a public meeting was held, Mr ANSCOMBE presiding. An address was delivered by Mr W.TAYLOR. Other speakers included Mr McBEAN (Cooksbridge), Mr LARWILL (Lewes), and Messrs. LLOYD and VERCOE (Barcombe). The whole function met with great success, and was most encouraging to the principals.

CRICKET – Mr PIPER's XI (Lewes) visited Barcombe on Saturday, when they played the local team, which could only muster nine men for the occasion. Mr PIPER's XI won on the first innings by five runs…

29th September - ON LEAVE - 2nd Lt. A.BROOKSBANK, son of Mr & Mrs Musgrave BROOKSBANK, has been home on a week's leave and Private K.KNIBBS of 'Gladstone Cottages' has been granted ten days' sick leave.

DARK CURTAINS WANTED – At Lewes Petty Sessions on Tuesday, Mrs Priscilla C.GARDENER, a widow, was fined 2s.6d. in respect of a breach of the Lighting Order, on September 12th. P.C.WILLARD, who proved the case, said curtains over the window about which complaint was made were not sufficient to prevent a ray of light being seen on the highway. Defendant admitted that the light was rather bright, and added that she had ordered some dark stuff for the window.

ARRIVED TOO LATE – Private Lewis WHITBREAD, whose home address is at Spithurst,[25] and who has been at the Front for nearly two years, and was in the great battle of the Somme, arrived home just too late to see his sister, Eva Mary, before she died. The child, who was twelve years of age, was the daughter of Mr & Mrs William WHITBREAD and was the youngest of a family of twelve. She succumbed to heart failure, after ailing for a long time. Her funeral took place at Spithurst, the Rev. FARRAR officiating. Mr WHITBREAD is coachman and chauffeur to Miss SHENSTONE.

PUZZLE FOR POLICEMAN – At Lewes Petty Sessions on Tuesday, Henry DIPLOCK was summoned for having committed a breach of the Lighting Order at Barcombe. P.C.WILLARD said that at 9.45 p.m. on September 12th he saw bright lights shining from three windows at defendant's house. The windows were covered with light material, but were not sufficiently screened. When defendant saw the lights he said: "I did not think they were quite so bright. I thought they would just pass." Defendant told the Bench that he thought he had complied with the Order. He suggested that a representative of the Court should view the premises. He was willing to pay the expenses. A fine of 10s. was imposed. Defendant asked whether he would be allowed

---

25 The WHITBREAD family lived at 'Yew Tree Cottage.'

to use a storm lantern when he went to attend his cattle late at night. – The Chairman, Mr F.B.WHITFELD, said defendant should consult the local policeman.

6th October - STOOLBALL – The local club played Ringmer at Barcombe on Saturday, and the visitors were entertained to tea… The local members were easy victors.

HARVEST FESTIVAL – The thanksgiving services were held on Sunday at St. Mary's, also at St. Bartholomew's… The prevailing colours were yellow and white, and the gifts comprised a plentiful supply of vegetables and fruit, which has been forwarded to the Fleet, and flowers, eggs, etc., which were sent to Victoria Hospital, Lewes. There was a children's service in the afternoon, and the local boy scouts, with the Scoutmaster, Mr W.J.CARTER, attended. The Rector was the preacher in the evening, and the Rev. Haworth CORYTON, at the morning and afternoon services. The latter gentleman is chaplain to the Missions to Seamen, Rotterdam. He said one lesson the war had taught them was that nothing was too good for the men of the Merchant Service. They had never been deterred by

the constant danger of mines, submarines and prowling destroyers, from making one single journey, and only those who had been on the spot could have an idea of what they had been through. The crews of the "Brussels" and the "Lestres" which had been captured by the Germans, and now interned in Ruhlben, were constant visitors to the Institute, and the night before the speaker left for England twenty-eight of the crew of the "Brussels" were at the intercession service held in the seamen's church… The total collections at the services during the day amounted to over £8.

20th October - D.C.M. FOR BARCOMBE MAN - Barcombe is naturally proud that one of its men has been honoured. Private Sidney WALL is the recipient of the Distinguished Conduct Medal (D.C.M.) for carrying despatches under heavy shelling and machine gun fire. He is the son of Mr & Mrs WALL who have resided at Barcombe for the past 25 years and who have recently gone to live at Crowborough. Young WALL who is but 19 years of age, joined the Bantam Battalion[26] of the Suffolk Regiment about 12 months ago, but has since been transferred to the Lancashire Fusiliers. Several weeks ago he was wounded in the back, head and side and is at present in hospital at Liverpool. At one time he worked at Isfield Station, but just previous to joining the Army he was booking clerk at Sheffield

Park Station… Mrs WALL, his mother, is a Red Cross Nurse.

MILITARY SERVICE TRIBUNAL – Chailey Rural District Tribunal (including Mr F.J.CORNWELL) sat on Monday at the Guardians' Offices, Lewes. Among the cases heard were: Archibald Ernest BLAKER,[27] Fruit Grower, etc., asked for exemption on the ground that he was running the business alone. The application was disallowed on the understanding that the applicant would not be called up for service for 2 months. William Wilfred HARRIOTT, pianoforte tuner and teacher, was refused further exemption.

On the application of Mr F.J.CORNWELL, conditional exemption was granted to Thomas BRADFORD, milker, and Thomas WOODS, cowman was exempted until April 1st. F.L.ASSER sought exemption for Frank Albert SMITH, gardener, who had been passed for sedentary work at home. The Tribunal adjourned the case until men in the category in question were called up. On the application of H.GEERING, Leslie WADEY, milker, Barcombe, was exempted until April 1st, 1917.

PARISH COUNCIL MEETING – The meeting was held at the village Mission Room last Saturday evening, Mr F.J.CORNWELL acting as Chairman. Others present were Mr T.N.LADE, Mr R.RHODES and Mr John GURR. The Footpaths

---

26 *'Bantam Battalions' were created to allow men under the regulation 5 feet 3 inches (160 cm), but over 4 feet 10 inches (147 cm), to join the Army. They were named after the small aggressive fowl which became their emblem.*

27 *Archibald BLAKER (35) lodged at 1 Grange Road with Joseph & Mary STONE.*

Committee reported that the gate leading across the Railway Company's strip of land at Barcombe Mills had been fixed, and that the key had been left at the Station…

COWMAN's OVERCOAT STOLEN – At the County Hall, Lewes, on Friday, before Dr W.F.CROSKEY (in the chair)… Sidney HEATH, cattle drover, no fixed abode, pleaded guilty to having stolen an overcoat, valued at 5s., the property of John STEVENS, cowman, at Barcombe, on October 6th. Prosecutor gave evidence that on the day in question he hung up in the cooling house at the farm where he worked, the overcoat produced. He missed it at 1 p.m. It was safe when he went to dinner at noon. At that time prisoner was in the road about 30 yards from the cooling house. P.C. BATEMAN, stationed at Battle, deposed that at 11.30 a.m. the previous day he saw prisoner at Battle Workhouse and asked him if he knew anything about the missing overcoat. He replied "No," but added that he had an overcoat, and pointed to

RIGHT: FOUR SONS OF Mrs KEMP of 'Birds Hole' - Private Arthur Victor KEMP, R.M.L.I, H.M.S. Monitor; Private Hubert Ernest KEMP, Royal Sussex Regt.; Sergeant G.H.KEMP, Royal Sussex Regt.; Private Stanley KEMP, R.M.L.I., H.M.S. Woolwich (*Sussex Express*, 24th November 1916, p.7).

---

28 *The KEMP brothers were the sons of Thomas John & Eliza KEMP. Their father worked as a cowman on Sewells Farm.*

one. Witness remarked "That is identical with the stolen coat. How do you come to be in possession of it?" Prisoner answered "I walked with a man whom I did not know from Uckfield to Lewes, where he bought the coat for 1s. 6d. I was not there when he bought it. He was gone about four hours." Prisoner, who said nothing in defence, was sentenced to 21 days' imprisonment.

27th October - MILLER's LOADER WANTED – Capable and of good character; capital cottage and garden – Apply WILMSHURST, Barcombe Mills.

ON LEAVE – Frank Victor SMITH, Australian Contingent, is staying with Mrs PECKHAM, his aunt. He is the only son of Mr Frank SMITH, a native of Barcombe.

PROMOTION – Soon after war broke out Mr G.H.KEMP joined the Royal Sussex Regiment, and was wounded last August by shrapnel. His many friends will be glad to learn that he has been promoted to the rank of Sergeant. He has three brothers serving their country…[28]

OUR DAY – Barcombe's total collection for "Our Day" is again far in advance of those of her sister villages.

PTE. A. CONSTABLE, Royal Sussex, Nutley.

LCE.-CPL. E. V. CRISFORD, Royal Sussex, Catsfield Down (wounded).

PTE. A. V. KEMP, R.M.L.I., H.M.S. Monitor.

PTE. H. E. KEMP, Royal Sussex.

SERGT. G. H. KEMP, Royal Sussex.

PTE. S. KEMP, R.M.L.I., H.M.S. Woolwich.

Four sons of Mrs. Kemp, Barcombe.

ABOVE: Women Land Workers from Barcombe – Before the Women's Land Army was set up in 1917, the East Sussex Women's Agricultural Committee encouraged links between farmers and women willing to work on the land. These Barcombe workers wear smocks originally made for beaters at a shoot. Front Row: Mrs Lewis RICHARDS, Nellie JONES & Mrs CHATFIELD. Back Row (far right): Mrs SINGLETON (ESRO: WI 112/1/1 p.146).

3rd November - WOMEN FOR THE LAND – The East Sussex Women's Agricultural Committee has now linked up its activities throughout the country, where they are being efficiently carried on under the supervision of the Countess of Chichester (President), Viscountess WOLSELEY (Vice-President & Hon. Secretary) and the following district representatives and registrars to whom application should be made either by farmers desiring labour or women willing to work on the land: Lewes District representative, Miss Betty BRAND, 'Littledene,' Lewes. Registrar for Barcombe, Miss GRANTHAM, Barcombe Place.

WAR ECONOMY - A rather novel feature is being organised by Mrs SINGLETON, Miss GRANTHAM and the Misses WALKER. It is their intention to hold a "War Economy Exhibition" when demonstrations in rabbit, goat and bee keeping will be given, also intensive poultry culture. Prizes are to be presented for the most economical devices, cooking, carpentry work and home made toys etc.

It reached the splendid sum of £15.8s.8d., and the many lady collectors deserve to be congratulated… A brooch made from a portion of wire belonging to the Zeppelin L21, which was brought down at Cuffley,[29] was raffled and 50 tickets at sixpence each were sold. Miss WORSLEY was the winner. The lady workers were early on the scene, and a stall was placed in the village containing various items. In reality it was an open jumble sale, and the display of such articles as old and new hats, old clothes, fruit, flowers, a chicken, etc., soon found ready purchasers.

> *Barcombe ever tops the list*
> *Of villages when cash is needed,*
> *Be it concert, sale or whist,*
> *For Tommy's sake it's not unheeded*
> *Then here's to the noble band*
> *Of gentle ladies who are workers,*
> *Like their boys on foreign strand.*
> *They "do their bit" – are never shirkers.*

29 *The German airship (thought at the time to be Zeppelin L21, but later corrected as the Schutte-Lanz SL11) was one of sixteen from Germany taking part in the largest airship raid on England of the war. It was shot down by Lieut. Leefe Robinson of the R.F.C. (the first German airship to be destroyed over British soil). Leefe was awarded the Victoria Cross and a monument to commemorate the event was erected close to the site of the crash in June 1921.*

CLUB AND READING ROOM - A committee meeting took place on Monday evening at the Reading Room those present being Mr Alfred MOON, Mr Richard RHODES, Mr Ernest RHODES, Mr George HOLLOWAY, Mr S.B. RICHARDS and Mr J. REYNOLDS. It was pointed out that the caretakers were relinquishing the work and it was decided that applications would be invited. It was stated that Mr Archibald BLAKER who was on the Committee wished to resign owing to his having to join the Army. The resignation was accepted with regret. For the sake of the young members of the Club, it was decided that the bagatelle board should be re-covered and repaired and removed to the billiard room on the upper floor…

CHAILEY TRIBUNAL – W.F.DEAN asked for exemption for William Richard DEAN, aged 18 years, butcher. The case was adjourned on the understanding that the youth would attest and that the matter would be considered when he was called to the Colours.[30]

RUN OVER BY MILK CART – CORONER AND WAR TIME RISKS – A regrettable incident occurred on Wednesday morning, when Mr James BIGGINS, the well-known Brighton draper, of Preston Street, was run over by a milk cart and two hours later succumbed to his injuries at Lewes Hospital.

Mr BIGGINS resided at 'The Cottage,' Barcombe, and it was his habit to catch the 8.15 train for Brighton. As he was approaching the bottom of the hill coming from the village towards the station he was overtaken by a milk cart, belonging to Mr T.REVELL, of 'Delves Farm,' which was being driven by Miss Gertie BURCHELL, a girl who has been helping on the farm for the last two months, and which contained several churns of milk. Mr BIGGINS was extremely deaf, and it is evident that he did not hear the vehicle approaching, with the result that he was knocked down, and received fatal injuries.

Mr George HOLLOWAY, who is a member of the Red Cross, together with his wife,[31] hurried to the scene, as also did Miss Lena HOLLOWAY, Mrs Harry FUNNELL and Miss Florence RHODES. After receiving first aid, the unfortunate gentleman was conveyed to Lewes Victoria Hospital in Mr HOLLOWAY's motor. Mrs BIGGINS is in a delicate state of health, and has been so for the last two months.

THE INQUEST was conducted at St. Anne's Parish Room, Lewes, yesterday afternoon, by the Coroner Mr G.VERE BENSON. Mr W. WAGHORN was foreman of the jury. Laura Gertrude BIGGINS, daughter of deceased, gave evidence of identification. She stated that at eight a.m. the previous day her father left home to go to

---

30 *The 'Attestation' was an oath of allegiance to the King, signed by recruits prior to enlistment.*

31 *Edwin 'George' HOLLOWAY, baker and his wife Isabel lived at 3 Gladstone Buildings in the High Street. Lena, George's sister worked in Holloway's store and bakery.*

Barcombe.

ABOVE: 'Blacksmith's Hill,' the site of the accident, between the Forge (out of shot to the right) and the right-hand turn to Barcombe Station before the bridge (Vulcan series postcard).

Barcombe Station to catch the 8.13 train. His house was ten minutes' walk from the station... Gerald FROST,[32] a youth, living at Spithurst, said he was walking down 'Blacksmith's-hill' about 40 yards behind deceased, who was on the left side of the road. A milk cart passed witness. The horse was going at a trot. As deceased was crossing the road the milk cart ran into him. He did not think the driver could avoid the accident when deceased changed his direction. Witness obtained assistance…

DRIVER'S STORY – Gertrude BURCHELL,[33] living at 'Gallops Farm,' the driver of the milk cart, said she had been driving for the last fortnight. She was well able to manage the horse, and had it under control. On the hill deceased, who was in front of her, turned suddenly, and a shaft caught him in the back. Apparently he was unaware of her approach. Witness did her best to pull up… P.C. WILLARD said he rendered first aid and took deceased to the Hospital. At the scene of the collision the road was about 16 feet wide.

UNAVOIDABLE RISKS – The Coroner, in summing up, pointed out that to some extent the occurrence might be due to want of experience on the part of the driver, but he did not think she deserved censure. "We must nowadays," he added, "accept the little risks arising from want of experience, especially as

R. A. WALL, Royal Navy, Barcombe.

PTE. H. E. WALL, A.S.C., M.T., Barcombe.

PTE. S. WALL, Suffolk Regiment, Barcombe.

LCE.-CORPL. D. WALL, Royal West Kent, Barcombe.

DRIVER F. WALL, R.F.A., Barcombe.

PTE. G. BONES, Royal Sussex Regiment. Son of Mr. and Mrs. G. Bones, Crust...

ABOVE: FIGHTING SONS OF SUSSEX – This regular feature shows five sons of Mr & Mrs William WALL - Private Henry E. WALL, A.S.C., M.T.; Reginald A. WALL, R.N.; Private Sidney WALL, Suffolks; L/Cpl David WALL, Royal West Kents; Driver Frederick WALL, Royal Field Artillery.

women are so much needed on the land." The jury returned a verdict of "accidental death."

10th November - FLOODS - The river, owing to the recent heavy rain, has again overflowed the banks and the many fields around Barcombe and Barcombe Mills are flooded. In some part of the district the meadows resemble great lakes.

17th November - FIVE SONS SERVING – A photograph appeared in last week's issue of the 'Kent & Sussex Courier' of Private Sidney WALL, Suffolk Regiment, who has won the Distinguished Conduct Medal

for gallantry in the field. WALL won his distinction on August 25th, while serving with the Lancashire Fusiliers in France as a runner. He is the son of Mr & Mrs WALL of Crowborough, who formerly lived at Barcombe. They have five sons serving, and their photographs are reproduced.

---

32 Gerald St. John FROST (15) was born in Barcombe c.1902.

33 Gertrude BURCHELL (20) was born at Portslade in 1896. She continued to live with her parents Richard & Eleanor at 'Gallops Farm' (later demolished) until she married William BROWN, a Brighton railway porter, at St. Mary's church on 25th June 1917.

Their names and Regiments are: Private Harry WALL, 23 Mechanical Transport (France); Lance-Corporal David WALL, Royal West Kent Regiment (Mesopotamia); Driver Frederick WALL, 21, Royal Field Artillery (France); Private Sidney WALL, 19, Royal Suffolk Regiment (wounded and in Garston Hospital, Liverpool); Seaman Reginald WALL.

THE MORSE CASE – A sentence of three months' imprisonment, followed by a notice of appeal, terminated the Police Court hearing of the Morse case at Lewes on Tuesday evening.

The Military Authorities proceeded against William E.A.MORSE, 'Woolgar's Farm,' Chailey for having made false statements for the purpose of obtaining exemption for himself from the provisions of the Military Service Act… Major W.W.GRANTHAM prosecuted and Mr J.C.BUCKWELL defended.

Witness, Francis William VARNHAM, now working for Mr H.GEERING, Barcombe, said he was previously employed by defendant's father about five years… William Wilfred HARRIOTT, living at Barcombe, who used to visit defendant and his father frequently, said he had often seen defendant work in the market garden…

DANGEROUS ROAD – The fatality which occurred a fortnight ago was in

some measure owing to the disgraceful condition of the narrow road, which, at the bottom of a hill, and on either side has, particularly at this period of the year, mud to the depth of four or five inches, and extending for a yard or two to the centre. Persons can therefore, only use the centre of the road. The authorities ought to keep this main road clean, otherwise it is possible that more accidents will occur.

CANADIAN WOMEN ON FARMS – In a letter to Mr B.ROOKE of Barcombe Mills, Miss Annie BROWN, his niece, who is at Wolfe Island, Ontario, Canada, states that they are having awful weather, two feet of snow lying on the ground, and all the grain standing in the fields freezing. Help is so scarce that the machines cannot get round to thresh. The people in Canada are very much amused at the way people in England are talking about women milking cows. She herself often milks cows, and when they are short of help women have to turn their hands to all manner of work – rake hay, drive the horses, fork and clean out barns. In fact the women on the prairie have to do all sorts of men's work. There is scarcely any hay, owing to the terribly wet season. She was at first very lonely (she has been in Canada four years) but they have now a gramophone. All the bachelors for miles round come to hear the machine.

24th November - EAST SUSSEX APPEALS – W.W.HARRIOTT, piano tuner, appealed against the refusal of temporary exemption by the Chailey Rural District Tribunal. Appellant said he wished for exemption because his wife continued to be in ill-health. The appeal was dismissed.

THE SHORTCOMINGS OF WOMEN – George John SPELLER, stockman, Barcombe, who had been passed for service at home in garrison or provisional units, was exempted until January 1st, 1917. The employer urged that, having regard to the category for which he was passed, the man would render more useful service on the land. Captain SELBY ASH pointed out that men passed for service abroad or at home in garrison or provisional units were needed in the Army in order that men who were fit for general service could be released from duties in connection with home defence. The employer further stated that he had endeavoured to utilise girls, but his experience showed that they spoiled the cows…He milked cows which boys and women would not deal with. There were several kickers on the farm. Women were only of service for the purpose of milking "easy" cows.

The Chairman remarked that the point for the Tribunal to consider was whether the man was more useful where he was, or whether he should go into the Army. If he had to

ABOVE: Ypres After Two Years of War (Official War Photographs, Series 6, no. 47).

serve about 200 children might be deprived of their milk…

Frederick SMITH SHENSTONE, late of Sutton Hall, deceased – All creditors and others having any claims against or to the Estate... should send particulars in writing. The will and codicil were proved by Miss Adela Caroline SHENSTONE, William Frederick Alphonse ARCHIBALD, Esq. and Major William Wilson GRANTHAM…

ANOTHER AGE MISTAKE - BARCOMBE MAN'S ERROR – There was an echo of the MORSE case at Lewes on Monday when the curious fact that a witness had overstated his age was brought to the notice of the Chailey Rural District Tribunal.

The Clerk mentioned that William Wilfred HARRIOTT, music teacher and pianoforte teacher, Barcombe, who gave evidence in the MORSE case, had made applications for exemption, although it now appeared that his birth certificate showed he was born in 1865. That fact had been verified by the recruiting authorities. Mr E.C.KNIGHT – We cannot proceed against him for trying to evade military service (Laughter). Mr J.KENWARD – Lots of people said he must be 50 years of age… The Chairman wanted to know what the position was having regard to the fact that the military authorities had HARRIOTT's name on the list of men who were eligible for service.

Captain SELBY ASH (Military Representative) remarked that he supposed the recruiting authorities had sent the intimation as to age to show that nothing more could be done by them. The man had made an ass of himself or of the authorities (Laughter).

WHIST DRIVE – Mrs SPELLER is ever active and generous on behalf of soldiers and sailors. She organised a drive at which 92 persons attended, and engaged 23 tables. The proceeds, which will go to the mine sweepers, amounted to £3.11s.2½d. Major W.W.GRANTHAM distributed the prizes, which had been voluntarily provided by the ladies in the parish…

Mr J.BALLARD has received the following letter from

Drummer A.TAPP,[34] Royal Sussex Regiment: "I am writing this letter on behalf of the Drummers of my Battalion to ask you if you could manage to get, with the help of the residents of Barcombe who knew me, a pair of boxing gloves. We have been wanting a set for some time, but nobody knew who to write to 'till I suddenly thought of you: so I take the liberty of writing, and hope you will not be offended, nor think me asking too much. There is very little amusement for us, and a 'bout with the gloves' occasionally would make a good change when at liberty. I shall be very pleased to see old Barcombe again, and I hope it will not be long before I get the chance." Mr & Mrs BALLARD have had the pleasure in forwarding a pair of gloves.

DEATH OF MRS BIGGINS

– We much regret to state that Mrs Sarah Hastings BIGGINS, wife of the late Mr James BIGGINS, who only three weeks ago was knocked down by a milk cart and succumbed to his injuries a few hours later, passed away at her residence, 'The Cottage' last Saturday morning. The deceased lady, who was 73 years of age, died through heart trouble, but her death was no doubt hastened through the sudden death of her husband.

She had, however, been ailing for a long time. Having lost her father and mother within a month, much sympathy is extended to Miss L.BIGGINS, their only child. The family had only resided at Barcombe about twelve months, and previously lived at Brighton…

1st December - CHILD'S ENTERPRISE

– Miss Kathleen RICHARDS, aged 12, daughter of Mr & Mrs S.B.RICHARDS, initiated the idea of making tiny golliwogs from wool and selling them at one penny each. By so doing, Miss Kathleen has realised 5s.2d., which she has forwarded to a fund in aid of old soldiers.

BARCOMBE BOY'S SEA EXPERIENCE

- Fred DEAN, son of Mr & Mrs W.F.DEAN of Barcombe, is an apprentice on the sailing ship 'Falkirk,' a neat little barque which has just completed an eventful voyage, having, on the homeward journey, experienced terrific hurricanes. It was young DEAN's first voyage, and it was about fifteen months ago that he left England on the 'Falkirk' for Sydney. His own words can best describe his experiences: "It was whilst sailing round Cape Horn that we experienced frightful weather. We were sailing under lower topsails and several staysails, when the mizzen stay, unable to stand the strain, gave way. This was the beginning of a series of troubles, for a little later topsails and staysails were blown to ribbons.

The hurricane was increasing in velocity and strength, and shrieking and howling through the rigging like the furies of hell let loose. The shrouds, stays and numberless ropes on the ship made the wind, blowing so tempestuously, whistle and hum as though billions of bees were on the wing…"

READING ROOM ANNUAL MEETING

– On Wednesday evening the members of the Reading Room assembled for the purpose of having their annual meeting… The Hon. Secretary Mr MOON read the minutes and presented the 34th annual report, which showed a balance in hand of £3.2s.3d… Amongst others deserving special thanks were Major GRANTHAM, for placing the club room at the disposal of the members rent free; Lady GRANTHAM for gifts of newspapers and periodicals; Mr ARCHIBALD for gifts of valuable books; Mr BLAKER for magazines; Mr REYNOLDS for his interest in the management of the billiard table, and to all the donors of whist drive prizes throughout the year… Mr MOON, who had been Secretary since the club was founded 34 years ago, was re-elected secretary and treasurer.

BARCOMBE SOLDIER KILLED

- PRIVATE F.S. SAUNDERS - The many friends of Private Frederick S. Saunders, Middlesex Regiment will learn with regret that he has been killed. It will be remembered that his brother Alfred met his death on the railway line at Lewes about

---

34 Albert TAPP (21) was the son of Thomas Edward & Mary Jane TAPP of 'Street Hill,' Barcombe.

eight months ago. Private SAUNDERS, who was 28 years of age, was a native of Barcombe and son of Mr & Mrs Frank SAUNDERS of Gladstone Cottages…

8th December - LANTERN LECTURE – Mr BOURDILLON gave an interesting and instructive lecture on Tuesday evening at the Village Mission Room, his subject being "South Africa." The room was packed. Mr Victor BOURDILLON, together with the Rector, manipulated the lantern…

15th December - SHARE-OUT – The Slate Club share-out took place on Monday evening, at the Reading Room, when over 100 persons received £1.3s.9¾ d. each. This amount was larger than that of last year.

ON LEAVE - Sidney WALL, who was recently presented with the D.C.M., has been home on leave. Although his parents are now residing at Crowborough, young WALL spent several days at Barcombe.

PERSISTENT IRREGULARITY – At Lewes Petty Sessions on Tuesday an attendance order was made, with costs, against James TAPP, in respect of his son Cyril.[35] Mr A.J.GODDEN, Attendance Officer in the employ of the East Sussex Education Committee, stated that the case was one of persistent irregularity. The lad had attended for only four full weeks during a period of 34

THE GROUP SYSTEM

(1) IT IS SIMPLE AND FAIR.

Everybody is placed in his Group according to age, and whether single or married.

Single Men will be called first according to age; then Married Men—also according to age.

For any special reason a man may be put back and called up in some Group later than his own.

(2) IT RELIEVES YOU OF RESPONSIBILITY.

You may think your present work is more useful to the Country. If it is, the Local Tribunal, acting on behalf of the Government, will see that you remain at your work.

YOUR DUTY TO THE COUNTRY IS TO ENROL AND LET THE LOCAL TRIBUNAL DECIDE YOUR CASE.

BUT REMEMBER, LOCAL TRIBUNALS HAVE NO POWER TO ADVISE UNTIL YOU HAVE JOINED THE ARMY RESERVE SECTION B IN YOUR GROUP.

TO COME UNDER LORD DERBY'S SCHEME

ENLIST BEFORE 11TH DECEMBER.

'ABOVE: Derby Scheme' Deadline poster – Enrolment in the Army Reserve was required before a case could be heard at a Tribunal (U.S. Library of Congress, Reproduction No. LC-USZC4-11030).

weeks. He disliked school and his mother shielded him in every way.

22nd December - ANGLING – There is at present excellent fishing at Barcombe Mills. Last week Mr BAKER of Brighton hooked a fine specimen of pike, which turned the scales at 14lbs., and

on Saturday Mr J.ADAMS of Leighside Nurseries, Lewes, landed a similar fish weighing 9lbs. Roach, which are feeding well, are being caught freely.

DEATH OF Mr C.HOWELL – Mr Charles HOWELL, who was a native

35 *Cyril TAPP (6) lived with his parents James & Edith at 'Boast Cottage.'*

Your King and Country Thank You.

HOME WORDS No. 168

Christmas Greetings from *the Rector & Mrs Farrar* to

ABOVE: Rev. & Mrs FARRAR's Christmas Card for the men in service (Mike Green collection).

of Ringmer, but who had resided at Barcombe many years, passed away at his residence in Brighton on Sunday evening. Deceased, who was 54 years of age, succumbed after a week's illness, to bronchitis and heart disease. He was night watchman on the West Pier, Brighton. He leaves a widow, two daughters, and three sons, two of whom are in the Army…

WEDDING – A pretty wedding took place on Tuesday, the Rector officiating. The contracting parties were Miss Ida Florence WHITING, fourth daughter of the late Mr John & Mrs WHITING of Park Road, Lewes, and Mr William James MOORE, of 'Yew Tree Farm', Spithurst. The best man was Mr Edwin MOORE, brother of the bridegroom, and the bride was given away by her brother-in-law, Mr Albert PARKS. She was attired in a fawn-coloured costume, with a black velvet hat, trimmed with mauve. The ceremony over, a reception was held at 'Yew Tree Farm', and the honeymoon will be spent in London.

29th December - FEWER TRAINS – THE NEW WAR SERVICE – Consequent on the need for releasing the railways of the country to a greater extent for war traffic, considerable reductions are taking effect in the New Year. On the London & Brighton Railway many trains have been suspended and others altered in working… The following stations and halts are being temporarily closed for passenger traffic: Lewes Road, Brighton, Kemp Town, the Dyke, Ifield Halt and St. Leonards Warrior Square. On Sundays only Hartfield and Barcombe Stations will be closed.

Hull Daily Mail **28th December** –Violets and primroses have been gathered this Christmas at Barcombe Mills.

5th January - ON LEAVE - Drummer 'Bert' TAPP, son of Mr & Mrs Tom TAPP, is home on leave. It was to young TAPP that Mr BALLARD sent a pair of boxing gloves only a few weeks ago. He and his pals, so he states, had many a fine bout with them.

WAR ECONOMY - EXHIBITION AT BARCOMBE

– An event of great interest took place at Barcombe Schools on Wednesday afternoon, when a large number of people visited the premises to inspect the many war economy exhibits, which were varied in character, remarkable for conception of idea, praiseworthy from an economical point of view, and excellent in design and execution. Necessity is the mother of invention, and Barcombe residents must certainly possess a big bump of inventive genius, seeing that the whole of the exhibits were executed by local parties. The promoters of the exhibition were: The Misses WALKER, Miss Muriel GRANTHAM, Mrs SINGLETON and Mrs BROOKSBANK, and they are to be congratulated for the success which attended this function.

LIST OF AWARDS – There were 125 entries, and Lady GRANTHAM announced the winners and distributed the prizes (in categories including the following): Best articles made from old stockings; Darned stockings; Slippers made from old material; Best meatless dinner for a man, woman and two children, cost not exceeding 1s.; Fuel saving contrivance; Home-made toy; Poultry house made from old material; Anything made from old material by a boy or girl under 13 years of age; Anything made by a soldier or sailor...

Mrs SINGLETON, who had a stall containing war relics, did a nice business with hatpins. She had conceived the novel idea of making the heads out of fir cones, which she had gilded, and which looked remarkably pretty. The proceeds were in aid of Lord Roberts' workshops for Sussex men,[1] and it may be mentioned that Mrs SINGLETON has alone collected £23.3s.

12th January - A MISSING NECKLACE - UNLUCKY BARCOMBE SEARCH – A search at Barcombe for a valuable necklace involved an outlay of 5s. to meet a fine in respect of a breach of the Lighting Order, which occurred on December 23rd at the residence of Mrs Louisa H.BROWNE,[2] who pleaded guilty at Lewes Petty Sessions on Tuesday.

RIGHT: 1917 "Florin" – two shillings.

1 The workshops were founded in 1915, following the death in 1914 of Field Marshall Lord Roberts while visiting troops in France. Roberts, who had been awarded the Victoria Cross in 1857 during his service in the Indian Rebellion, had campaigned for more to be done for ex-servicemen, particularly the disabled. These workshops, including one at Chailey Heritage, produced basket ware, toys and furniture.

2 Louisa HARRISON BROWNE (55) had moved to 'The Firs,' Spithurst from Willesden, with her husband Joseph and daughter Kathleen (27).

East Sussex Agricultural Executive Committee.

District Committee.

Additional Acreage required in the *Chailey* District   Acres. (4)

Parish of *Barcombe*

Name of Farm	Name of Occupier	Total Acreage	Present Arable	Quantity already Recommended to be Broken Up by District Committee.	Additional Quantity Recommended by District Committee.
		Acres.	Acres.	Acres.	
Land Holmans Bdg	R Grover	14			
Croft Ham	Jas. Biden	13			
Land Spithurst	St John Frost				

LEFT: Barcombe Farms Survey for the East Sussex Agricultural Executive Committee, showing farmland at 'Holmans Bridge', 'Croft Ham' and 'Spithurst' (courtesy the Cornwell family).

P.C. WILLARD gave evidence that he was on duty at Spithurst, where he saw a bright light shining from an upstairs window at defendant's house. A light appeared to be close to the window which was only covered with thin curtains. When defendant ascertained that the light was too bright she lowered it. Afterwards she informed witness that her daughter had been searching for a necklace… The Bench imposed a fine of 5s. and defendant expressed her gratitude because she had been dealt with so leniently.

19th January - PARISH COUNCIL MEETING – Mr F.J. CORNWELL was voted to the chair. A letter regretting absence was received from Major W.W. GRANTHAM. The following letter from Mr S.A. WOODHEAD, joint hon. Secretary of the East Sussex War Agricultural Committee, was read: "In a letter from the Board of Agriculture & Fisheries, dated 19th December 1916, they ask all War Agricultural Committees to make enquiries of Borough and Urban Councils, also Parish Councils and Meetings, as to what steps they are taking to increase the growth of potatoes in 1917, and ask the Councils, etc., to send in to the War Agricultural Committee any requirements for seed potatoes. No grower is to be supplied with more than five cwts… It was decided to reply that the amount of seed potatoes known to be required was one ton…

SITUATIONS WANTED - FEMALE - Respectable middle-aged person requires situation as Working Housekeeper; small house or flat; Lewes or near; good references – Mrs WELLS, 'Skylark Villa'.

26th January - DEATH OF MR D.G. CROCKET – After undergoing an operation at a Putney hospital Mr Douglas Goldie CROCKET, of Spithurst succumbed rather unexpectedly on Sunday morning at the institution, and was buried in

---

Food self-sufficiency – Cultivation of Lands Orders

Following increased attacks by German U-Boats on merchant shipping delivering food to Britain, the threat of food shortages loomed. In a drive for greater self-sufficiency Parliament passed the first Cultivation of Lands Order on 19th January 1917, by which local committees, including the East Sussex Agricultural Executive were to carry out surveys of land under cultivation, with power to instruct farmers to break up pasture for growing more crops.

Draft copies of the survey for Barcombe survive in the Cornwell family archives. They are partially complete with 47 farm names or land holdings, occupiers' names and total acreage (as in the example shown here). In many entries the present arable acreage is noted, but information as to the additional land recommended for breaking up is missing.

F.J. CORNWELL was to receive an Order to break up further land at 'Broomlye Farm', Newick (see 28th November 1917).

the family grave at Highgate. Mr CROCKET was recognised as a clever artist, having, as also had his brother Harry, exhibited pictures at the Royal Academy.[3]

CHILD'S FUNERAL – The funeral of little Harry GEERING, only son of Mr & Mrs Harry GEERING of 'Sewells Farm,' took place at the latter part of last week. The boy was only six years of age, and has been confined to his bed for fourteen weeks. He was a bright little chap, and a great favourite. Much sympathy is extended to his parents and sisters.

DEATH OF MRS COLLINS – The widow of the late Captain Fred COLLINS passed away at her residence 'Collingwood,' rather suddenly on Sunday morning. Deceased, who was 76 years of age, had been ailing for many years. She led a quiet life and was well liked by all who knew her. She was the second wife of the late Captain, who was well known as the skipper of the 'Skylark' at Brighton. There is no family.

POTATO GROWING FOR WOMEN – Mr Frederick ASSER (miller, of 'The Lawn,' Barcombe Mills) sought exemption for Frank Albert SMITH (34), gardener, Barcombe Mills. The case had been before the Tribunal previously, and it was

---

3 *Douglas Goldie CROCKET (1874-1917) lived with his widowed mother Rose and his sister Margaret in a house rented from the Sutton Hall estate. His older brother Henry E. CROCKETT (1870-1926) was a watercolour artist.*

ABOVE: 'Collingwood,' complete with nautical flag post, the home of the late Captain and Mrs COLLINS, with 'Skylark Villa' marked 'X' to the right. Capt. COLLINS, who died in 1912, used to run pleasure cruises from Brighton beach encouraging trade with his call "all aboard for the Skylark." Postcard by the Mezzotint Co. of Brighton.

adjourned until the man, who had been passed for sedentary work at home, was called up.

The military Representative stated that the men in all categories were now being called up. The Tribunal were informed that the man was engaged mainly in fruit and vegetable growing, and he was also employed in keeping pigs and poultry. Mr F.J.CORNWELL remarked that the garden was large and very productive.

Mr L.G.VINALL: who supported the application, intimated that the employer was prepared to increase the production of the holding if he was allowed to retain the man, who, it was submitted, was more useful in his present occupation than he would be in the Army, or for purposes of substitution. It was mentioned that potatoes would

be cultivated in increased quantities in the open and under glass.

Mr WOOLLAND: Is there anything in growing potatoes under glass that a woman could not do after they were planted?

SMITH: I could not say.

Major TOWERS CLARK: But you have got to find the women.

Three months' exemption was granted.

DEATH OF AN OLD INHABITANT - LIVED IN 5 REIGNS - On Saturday the death occurred of Mr John PARSONS, at the age of 95 years and 9 months. He was born at Barcombe on April 28th 1821, and at the age of 28 went to Hastings, where he assisted in the erection of many churches and houses. He lived in five reigns. Mr PARSONS leaves one son, four daughters and six great

ABOVE: John PARSONS
(1821-1917)

grandchildren. He was buried beside his wife, who died in 1888. Deceased was a very genial man. He did not live to see his principle wish fulfilled – the end of the War.

2nd February - RECTOR OF BARCOMBE AND THE PROHIBITION CAMPAIGN

– In support of the Strength of Britain Movement – which has as its object prohibition of the selling of liquor during the war and for six months afterwards – a meeting, convened by the Mayor (Councillor A.E.RUGG, J.P.) was held at the Council Chamber, Lewes, on Monday evening.

In addition to the Mayor and Mayoress, those present included: the Rev H.W.FARRAR and F.J.CORNWELL… The results of the consumption of alcoholic liquor were known. Steps should be taken to prohibit the importation of malt, barley and other ingredients which were required for the production of such liquor.

The Rev. FARRAR, who at one time worked in Carlisle, gave some interesting conformation concerning the conditions which prevailed there and the considerations which probably led the Liquor Control Board to select the place as the scene of their experiment. He remarked that when he laboured in Carlisle, he felt it was his duty to oppose the renewal of a public house licence. The stand which he took on that occasion led to an attempt from certain quarters to depose him from the seat he occupied on the School Board. That was an indication of the feeling which was aroused at that time by intervention in such matters, but he knew that efforts which were made were carefully watched by men who had been informed as to the trend of opinion in the locality…

Mr MORRIS expressed the opinion that the nation should be ashamed because it had not followed the example of the King in the matter of abstinence. A blot on the national record was the fact that many young Canadians who came to England learned how to drink…

The Colonies were contributing to the fighting forces some of the finest specimens of humanity who ever walked. Was it right that traps should be laid for those young men when they came to England? …He had sent to the War the only two boys he had got, and the fact that their health had been good, although they had seen a considerable amount of foreign service, proved that alcoholic drink was not necessary.

BELOW: 'Alf,' a wounded Lance-Corporal of the Royal Sussex Regiment. According to a note on the back of this card it was given to a member of the HOBDEN family in Barcombe in February 1917 (courtesy Beryl Jackson).

9th February - SKATING

– There is some excellent skating to be had in the district. Lady GRANTHAM is allowing skating on the lake at Barcombe Place.

LETTER FROM ROYALTY

– The whist drives recently held on behalf of the Mine Sweepers' Fund has been acknowledged in the following letter to Mrs SPELLER: "I am requested by Princess Louis of Battenberg to thank you most cordially for your very kind subscription of £6.4s. for the Mine Sweepers' Fund. The Princess hopes that you will convey to all those who have contributed to this collection her most grateful thanks."

18th February - KNIGHTED -

Residents of the district will be pleased to learn that Mr W.F.A. ARCHIBALD, who was Master of the Supreme Court and nephew of the late Mr SHENSTONE, figures in the New Year Honours. Since his Uncle's demise, Mr ARCHIBALD, who a few months back resigned his Court duties, frequently visits Sutton Hall.

FREE LAND - The following

notice appears in the District - "In view of the importance of all possible waste land for the production of food, the Managers of Barcombe Schools offer, rent free for the first year and at an agreed rent afterwards, that portion of the unused ground not occupied by the school gardens and not already let, to anyone desirous of growing vegetables."

DEATH OF MISS BLISSET

– The death of Miss BLISSETT occurred on Sunday at her residence in Littlehampton. The deceased lady, who was about 90 years of age, was well known at Barcombe, having resided at 'Hill Brow' for about twelve years. She left the district to take up residence at Littlehampton about five years ago, when she was greatly missed. Miss BLISSETT was a patron of every good cause...

2nd March - FOR THE RED CROSS – FARMERS' GREAT EFFORTS

– Lewes Market was crowded during the greater part of Monday on the occasion of a highly successful gift sale, which was organised by the Lewes, Newick & Chailey Branches of the National Farmers' Union in aid of the British Farmers' Red Cross Fund…

About 300 lots were included in the catalogue, and the sale… was prolonged owing to the fact that many of the lots were offered several times…

Amongst the livestock sold was a "Fat cow" given by Mr F.J.CORNWELL which sold for £25. Further livestock included donations by Barcombe farmers H.GEARING, J.DUDENEY, H.VERCOE and J.S.FOORD. There was also agricultural produce and "many curious items" donated by Mrs H.VERCOE, Mrs SPELLER, Misses E. & A.SPELLER and W.J. MOORE of Barcombe.

FUNERAL OF Mrs MARKWICK

– Mrs MARKWICK, who died at Plumpton last week was buried at her native village, Barcombe, on Saturday, the Rector officiating. The bearers were Messrs. H. & J.FUNNELL, R. & E.RHODES. Deceased, who leaves two sons and one daughter, was 82 years of age, and her husband, the late Mr Sier MARKWICK, pre-deceased her by 16 years. About eighteen months ago she took a small farm at Plumpton, and on the first day she entered

ABOVE: Barcombe School c.1910 with the "School Fields" in the foreground that were to be made available for growing vegetables (courtesy Barcombe School).

her new abode she fell down the stairs and broke her leg. Previously she controlled 'Delves' and 'Gallops' Farms.

9th March - RURAL TRIBUNAL CASES - BARCOMBE FARMER'S STRUGGLE – Mr Hart VERCOE of Banks Farm, Barcombe applied for William Hart VERCOE, his carter and stockman, 18 and single. The man had been passed for general service. Applicant said that since the last application, when six months was granted he had lost one carter. His son had to take charge of a team which prevented his working to any large extent as a stockman.

ABOVE: The Women's Land Army was formed during March 1917, when the possibility of a food shortage was realised following German submarine attacks on shipping. Before the war Britain produced only 35% of the food required to sustain the population, relying on food imports by sea from around the British Empire.

ABOVE: The team of one-armed convalescent soldiers stand in front of the Royal Pavilion, Brighton, with the lawyers' team sitting in front. Major GRANTHAM is seated 4th from the left with the tree stripes on his uniform prominently displayed (photograph from the *East Sussex News).

Applicant said he was in a desperate strait. He had 230 acres, 110 of which were arable and was farming it with two men and two boys. The arable land had still to be cultivated. Conditional exemption was granted.

IMPORTANT WORK – A representative of the firm Messrs. CHATFIELD & Son of Lewes and Cooksbridge, applied for Edward AVERY, 26, ledger clerk, of 4 Gladstone-buildings. Temporary exemption until May 1st was granted, with power to apply again, the man being classified C3 and working in connection with English timber.

KILLED IN ACTION - We regret to state that Private Ernest KING of the Marines has been killed whilst in action.

JUVENILE THEATRICALS – Yesterday (Thursday) afternoon and evening the local school children figured in a musical war masque, entitled "The Empire's Honour." They attracted large audiences to the school, where the event took place… The performances were given in aid of the Prisoners of War Fund.

22nd March (*Eastbourne Gazette*) – STOOLBALL – Major W.W. GRANTHAM captained a team of lawyers in a game of stoolball played at Brighton on Saturday against a team of one-armed convalescent soldiers. Princess Louise was present.

23rd March - ON LEAVE - Private Reginald JESSUP, who has been for some time in hospital in Chelsea is at home on sick leave.

AT HOME – Master Sidney FARRAR, son of the Rector, and student at a training college, is now at home.

THOUSANDS OF FISH - Last Saturday Members of the Ouse Angling Preservation

Society visited the stock pond at Barcombe. Thousands of fish were obtained and transferred to the river.

MUNITION MAKING - Misses Emily, Lucy and Winnie, daughters of Mrs TOWNER of (Mount Pleasant) Spithurst and Miss Florrie MEWIES (Old Park) have left the district for London, where they are going munition making.[4]

OFF TO FRANCE - Mr Harry WELLER,[5] who has been building surveyor for the Chailey Rural District Council for twenty-two years, has joined the Sussex Road Making Battalion and expects to go to France early in April. He has the good wishes of his large circle of friends.

CHAILEY TRIBUNAL – W.F.DEAN sought exemption for William Richard DEAN, aged 18 years, butcher. Exemption until May 1st was granted, so that employer might find a substitute.

On the application of Mr F.J.CORNWELL, exemption until May 1st was granted to Henry Thomas FINCH, under cowman.

The Tribunal allowed the application of the Military Representative for the withdrawal of the certificate of exemption which was held by Albert STILL (Munster Cottages), aged 29 years, insurance agent.

LEWES DISTRICT EXEMPTIONS – The Military Authorities appealed against the granting by the Chailey R.D. Tribunal of conditional exemption for W.H.VERCOE, carter.

OUT FOR VICTORY.

THE MUNITION GIRL.
"England expects every woman to do her duty."

The Munition Girl - a postcard designed by *Punch* cartoonist Leonard Raven-Hill.

BOYS' FOOTBALL – Newick vs. Barcombe Schools - Some good play was shown, and there was a marked improvement in the form of the visitors. The home team won by eight goals to three… G.ELDRIDGE and J.WALL scored for Barcombe. After the match the teams were the guests of Mr T. BADEN POWELL at tea at

the Crown Hotel, Newick. Barcombe team: T.TAPP, goal; A.COX and H.GURR, backs; S.RICHARDS, H.WARNETT and H.SAUNDERS, half-backs; P.TROWER, G.FARRENDEN, G.ELDRIDGE, J.WALL and H.VERRALL, forwards. Referee, Mr W.J.CARTER.

30th March - THE VOLUNTEERS - A public meeting is to take place next Tuesday evening for the purpose of discussing the formation of a local detachment of volunteers. A number of men have already agreed to join the platoon and all are urged to avail themselves of the opportunity of being prepared in the defence of their homes. Colonel G.A.MONEY will attend the meeting and explain the duties and conditions of service and Major W.W.GRANTHAM will act as chairman.

4 *The TOWNER sisters, aged 25, 23, and 17 respectively, grew up at Mount Pleasant with their parents William & Mary and step-brother Frederick EDWARDS who was to be killed in action in September.*

Florence May MEWIES(18) was the daughter of Thomas & Annie who lived at Gamekeepers' Cottages, Newick Park, where their father was a shepherd.

5 *Harry WELLER (61) lived at 'Hog House' in 1911 and 'Finsbury Cottage' (location in Barcombe unknown) in 1917, must have been one of the oldest Barcombe man to join the forces. His duties in the Sussex Road Making Battalion would have been confined to planning repairs to existing roads and surveying any new roads that were required.*

LEFT: 1917 – The flag of the United States began to appear on postcards along with those of the Allies, after America entered the war on 6th April 1917, following U-Boat provocation.

6th April - PARISH MEETING

The only business before the meeting was the consideration of a letter received from the Chailey R.D.C., together with a supply of literature, on the subject of National Service. The Chairman, Major W.W.GRANTHAM, said he hoped that nearly every remaining man in Barcombe between the age of 18 and 60 would be giving in his name as willing to join the Volunteers at a meeting to be held later in the evening, and he wondered if anything further could be expected from the men of Barcombe. It was decided, on the motion of Mr R.RHODES, seconded by Mr HAWKINS, that in the opinion of the Parish Meeting any organised efforts to further the scheme of National Service in Barcombe would not be likely to prove successful. The distribution of the literature was arranged for.

VOLUNTEERS WANTED

- A large enthusiastic public meeting was held at the Mission Room on Tuesday evening for the purpose of discussing the formation of a local detachment of the Volunteer Forces. Major W.W. GRANTHAM was in the chair… The Chairman introduced Colonel G.A.MONEY, and in the course of a rousing speech said the meeting was not intended to see if a platoon could be formed in Barcombe, but for the actual formation of one, and hoped every eligible man in the room would give his name as a Volunteer. Several questions were asked and Volunteers were invited, with the result that 38 at once gave in their names as willing to join… It was decided that the enrolment of the men should take place at Barcombe Place on Thursday and arrangements were made for the drills to commence at once. It is understood that there are several others not at the meeting who have given in their names.

BARCOMBE MAN MUST SERVE

Albert STILL (30), insurance agent, appealed against the withdrawal by Chailey Rural District Tribunal of his certificate of conditional exemption. The appeal was dismissed on the understanding that the man would not be called upon to serve until May 15th.

THE PROGRESS OF RECRUITING

Mr F.J.CORNWELL sought exemption for William L.B. PLAYFOOT,[6] aged 25 years, carman, of 'Old Thatch Cottages,' who after being rejected three times, was passed for general service. The Military Representative said he understood that the authorities were now calling up men from the land for military service.

13th April - YOUNG SOLDIER'S DEATH

We regret to state that Private James KING, son of Mr & Mrs James KING of 'Woodbine Cottage,' Spithurst and grandson of Mr KING of 'Scufflings Farm' has succumbed to pleurisy and pneumonia at St. Albans where he was attending a training battalion. KING was only 18 years of age and only joined the forces a month ago. Previously

---

6 William PLAYFOOT was head gardener to Lt.-Col. MORLAND at Hurst Green before the war (Kelly's Sussex Directory, 1915), but by April 1917 was working for Mr CORNWELL in Barcombe. He joined the village platoon of the Sussex Volunteer Regiment the following week.

RIGHT: The Sussex Volunteer Regiment – A Great War "Dad's Army," featured on a Donald McGill postcard.

WE'RE READY TO THROW IN OUR WEIGHT

he worked for the Reverend Mr SCLATER of Newick Park. Great sympathy is extended to his parents.

THE BARCOMBE PLATOON - Appended is the first list of the Barcombe Platoon of the Sussex Volunteer Regiment: Edward G.AMER, Joseph AVERY (63), Ross BEATTY (56), Thomas BRADFORD (35), William J.CARTER (32, schoolmaster & scoutmaster), Charles CHATFIELD (54), Francis B.CORNWELL (17), Francis J.CORNWELL (53), James H.COX (65), Henry S.DIPLOCK (44), C. 'Harry' ELDRIDGE (17),[7] William ELDRIDGE (47), Rev. FARRAR (61), James GANDER (43), John GURR (44), George T.HAWKINS (66), Albert L.JESSUP (57), Herbert H.JONES (67), C. Richard KEMP (34?), Thomas N.LADE (45), George H. LONGHURST (51), Albert PARKS (41), George W. PASKIN (31), John A.PERKINS, William L.B.PLAYFOOT (25),

Percy F.RANN (17), Henry J.REED (41), Frank REYNOLDS (60), Richard RHODES (50), Sidney B.RICHARDS, jun. (16), Bertie SATCHER (44), Frank A.SMITH (40), John SPELLER, snr. (54), John SPELLER, jun. (51), C.J.SPINKS, William A.WALTER (53) and William A.WILMSHURST (30). Hon. Members: Major GRANTHAM (51) and Captain SINGLETON (67).[8]

VESTRY MEETING – This meeting was held on Tuesday evening in the Mission Room… The Rector referred to the encouraging work of the parish, and said that on Easter Sunday they had 165 communicants, and that over 150 of their men were serving their King and country…

CONCERT AT BARCOMBE – A highly successful concert was given on Thursday evening, in the Schoolroom, which was filled to its entirety, many people having come from the surrounding districts, including Lewes.

The proceeds, which must have reached a good figure, are to be devoted to the wounded soldiers, also to the prisoners of war…

The entertainment opened with the appearance of a musical quartet, consisting of the Misses ELPHICK and Private JESSUP, and was an excellent turn. This was followed by a song entitled "When the sands of the desert grow cold," which was rendered by Sapper OXBURGH, who possesses a good voice, and who had to respond to an encore…

20th April - CONCERT PROCEEDS – The concert which was given in the Schoolroom last week realised £10, which will be divided between Lady GRANTHAM's Working Fund and the Prisoners of War Fund.

SOLDIER'S FUNERAL - The funeral of the young soldier, Private James KING, took place on Monday afternoon at St. Bartholomew's, the Rector, officiating. Deceased

---

7 Claude 'Harry' ELDRIDGE joined the army later this year (see vol. 2).

8 Judging by the ages of the men (calculated from the 1911 census) this was very much a "Dad's Army." Another member of the Sussex Volunteer Regiment was the author, Sir Arthur Conan-Doyle, who joined the Crowborough Platoon. He would have been 57 in 1917.

had only just turned 18, and had been with the Training Battalion at St. Albans about a month. The coffin, which was shrouded with the Union Jack, arrived at Barcombe by rail on Friday evening, and was conveyed to Spithurst. The funeral was attended by many sympathisers and friends of the family. The bearers were: Mr James KENWARD, Mr Owen FUNNELL, Mr Richard RHODES and Mr Jack PERKINS, and the mourners were: Mr & Mrs James KING (father and mother), Miss Lily KING, Misses Florence and Edith KING (sisters), Mr James KING (grandfather), and Mr Thomas KING (uncle). Amongst others present were: Captain and Mrs SINGLETON, Mrs S.MARKWICK, Mrs MEWIES, Mrs Frank COX, Mrs H.FUNNELL, Mrs J.FUNNELL, Mrs G.HOLLOWAY, Mr T.RICHARDS, Mrs H.STEVENSON, Mrs G.STEVENSON, Mr E.KING, Miss HEWITT, Mrs E.ELPHICK, Mr W.H.REECE, Mrs James COX, Mr & Mrs J.GANDER, Miss WORSLEY, etc. The funeral arrangements were carried out by Mr H.TROWER.

COURT "BARCOMBE" A.O.F. (Ancient Order of Foresters)

– The statement of accounts and balance-sheet for 1916 has been issued, and the following is from the Secretary's report: "The sickness experienced during the past year has been more favourable than in the previous year, amounting to £49.12s.10d., as compared with £126.12s.2d. for 1915… At the end of the year 39 benefit members of the Court were serving in H.M. Forces - four members having lost their lives. The Court continues to subscribe to the Lewes Victoria, Sussex County, Sussex Eye and the Brighton Ear & Throat Hospitals...

ABOVE: Jack COX of Spithurst served in the 40th Siege Battery of the R.G.A. (photograph by J.G.Whorwell of Dover, courtesy Beryl Jackson).

27th April - ON LEAVE -

Private Jack COX, Royal Garrison Artillery, son of Mr & Mrs James COX, Mount Pleasant, Spithurst, is at home on sick leave.

CONCERT AT LEWES –

Miss Lena HOLLOWAY and Miss F.RHODES figured at a Red Cross Hospital concert held at 'The Shellys', Lewes, on Monday evening.

AIRMAN DESCENDS

- On Wednesday morning an aeroplane was observed circling over the district and eventually it descended near the Parish Church. The occupant proved to be Mr Frank BALLARD, son of Mr & Mrs J.BALLARD, who is attached to the Royal Flying Corps. On Wednesday morning he was ordered to take a two hours' flight. He had to descend owing to engine trouble, which was later repaired by two mechanics who motored down from the depot.

4th May - CHAILEY TRIBUNAL – BARCOMBE GARDENER EXEMPTED

- Mr F.S.ASSER sought exemption for Frank Albert SMITH, aged 40 years, gardener. It was stated that the man was engaged in producing foodstuffs. Additional effort to provide vegetables, including potatoes under glass, were now being made. Exemption until October 1st was granted.

BARCOMBE CASHIER'S RESPITE –

Messrs. CHATFIELD & Son[9] applied for exemption for Edward AVERY,[10] aged 26 years,

9   Chatfield & Son had a saw mill at Cooksbridge (Plans - ESRO: BMW A/13/11/1).

10   Edward AVERY lived at 4 Gladstone Buildings in 1917.

cashier, who had been passed for sedentary work at home. Exemption until October 1st was granted.

JOINED THE FORCES - Messrs. W.R. DEAN and Hart VERCOE joined the colours on Monday.[11]

ON LEAVE - Sergeant George H.KEMP, Royal Sussex Regiment, who has been at the Front for about eighteen months, and has been wounded, is now at home on leave.

WOUNDED - Mrs COLLINS, wife of Private COLLINS, has received word from Captain Gordon LALOR that her husband has been wounded. COLLINS is attached to the Army Veterinary Corps.

EGG COLLECTION - Mrs SPELLER inaugurated an egg collection for wounded soldiers, and the children of the local schools, up to the present, are collecting twelve to thirteen dozen per week.

PROGRESSING - Private Charles Alfred MARCHANT,[12] Royal Sussex Regiment, wounded eighteen months ago, and suffering from a fractured skull, is still at Whitchurch, Cardiff, and progressing as satisfactorily as could be expected.

11th May - CHAILEY TRIBUNAL - The Tribunal allowed the application of the Military Representative for the withdrawal of the certificate of exemption which was held by Ernest J.F. BROWN,[13] aged 22 years, threshing machine attendant, Barcombe.

The Tribunal arrived at a similar decision in respect of an application by the Military Representative for the withdrawal of the certificate of exemption which was held by Tooke LANE,[14] aged 39 years, who was engaged in farming etc. at Barcombe.

BARCOMBE MAN DIES OF WOUNDS –Mrs COLLINS has received information that her husband Private Abel COLLINS, Army Veterinary Corps, has been killed. Last week she had a letter from Captain Gordon LALOR stating that her husband had been wounded by a shell. The announcement of his death was received last Sunday…

PROMOTION - Mr Frank BALLARD, Royal Flying Corps, who was at home on leave last week-end and Lance Corporal F. HEASMAN have been promoted Sergeants.

SINGING TO SOLDIERS - Miss Lena HOLLOWAY and Miss RHODES journeyed to Seaford on Tuesday, where they entertained the soldiers. Both were well received.

NEST OF YOUNG MOLES – It is very seldom that a nest containing young moles is found. Mrs George OSBORNE, who is in the employ of Mr John PORTER, found a nest last week whilst weeding on 'Church Farm.'

VOLUNTEERS - On Sunday the local Platoon of Volunteers did duty for a number of hours. Next Sunday they will join the Lewes Volunteers on manoeuvres in the Uckfield district.

'ABOVE: Spot Cash' paid for 'Waste Paper' by F.J.Parsons Ltd, publishers and printers.

WASTE PAPER COLLECTION - Miss BURDER of 'The Beeches' is inaugurating a scheme whereby all waste paper in the district will be collected and sold on behalf of the Red Cross Society.

11 Both of these new recruits had been subjects of appeals against military service by their fathers.

12 Charles A.MARCHANT was born in Ringmer in 1889. He attested for the Royal Sussex Regiment on 5th September 1914 aged twenty four, giving his occupation as milkman and residence as Barcombe. He was wounded on the 7th July 1916 and discharged from the Army on 15th August 1917. The 1918 electoral roll gives his residence as 'Mongers.' He married Ellen Clarisa JONES of 'Spring Cottage,' Anchor Lane at All Saints, Hatcham Park, Deptford in March 1920, before re-joining the army.

13 Ernie BROWN was born in Fulham, and lived with George & Emily HOBDEN at Mount Pleasant.

14 Tooke LANE lived at 'Wootton Cottage' on Hamsey Road.

ABOVE: Munitions in France – Mr Charles Humbert, the "directeur" of *Le Journal* and advocate of mass shell production, at a depot in France.

AIDING THE CHOIR - The Choir in the Parish Church was at one time composed of boys and men only, but the War has so greatly depleted the body that the assistance of the following ladies has been secured: Mrs BALLARD, Miss FARRAR, Miss DEAN, Miss WELSH, Miss JESSUP, Miss HOLTER and Miss HOLLOWAY.

DEATH OF MISS AUSTEN – The death of Miss Rhoda AUSTEN took place on Tuesday morning at the residence of her niece, Mrs T.LADE, 'Mill Farm,' Barcombe Mills. Deceased was in her 80th year. She had always been active, and was out of doors last week, and was only taken ill the day previous to her demise. The butchering business now under the proprietorship of Mr MUGGERIDGE she conducted for many years, as did her father before her…

SALE OF WORK – The annual sale of work by the Barcombe members and candidates of the Girls' Friendly Society took place on Wednesday afternoon at the Reading Room, under the supervision of Mrs BURROWS of Spithurst. The various articles sold, which displayed excellent workmanship, included useful garments, such as woollen goods for soldiers, etc. There were also flowers, war cakes and biscuits made from non-rationed ingredients, and date jam made without sugar, and which can be retailed at 6d. per lb. The proceeds, which amounted to £5, will be devoted to the fund for sick members.

18th May - ON LEAVE - Second Lieutenant Alan FROST,[15] Royal Sussex Regiment, is home on leave from France.

WORKING IN FRANCE - Mrs A.PETERS, granddaughter of Lady GRANTHAM, is in France working at a canteen.

VOLUNTEERS From 9.30 a.m. to 5 p.m. on Sunday, the Volunteers of Lewes, Ringmer and Barcombe were on manoeuvres. They journeyed to 'Plashet Park', where they met the men of Uckfield, who were on the defensive, while the men of the other mentioned districts acted on the offensive.

BOY SCOUTS – Last week the Scouts, accompanied by their Scoutmaster Mr CARTER, marched to Lewes, where they did scouting work in conjunction with the Lewes troop, the venue being on the hills at Offham. On Wednesday evening they visited Landport Farm and practised tent-pitching, etc.

STOOLBALL – A stoolball match took place on the Recreation Ground, and was much enjoyed by players and spectators. The opposing teams had been arranged by Miss BURDER and Miss WELSH, and the latter lady scored well…[16]

25th May - ON LEAVE - Private Horace VERRALL, attached to the Motor Transport Service, is home on leave.

---

15 Alan St. John FROST (1896-1993) was the son of Ernest & Mary St. John FROST, of Spithurst. He appears on the 1918 Electoral Roll for Barcombe as a non-resident (military voter).

16 The team members are named in the original article.

EMPIRE DAY - Yesterday (Thursday) morning there was a short service at the School, conducted in the absence of the Rector by Rev. C.BURKE. The outside ceremony consisted of the hoisting of the Union Jack, marching past and saluting, the singing of the National Anthem, and cheers for the King. A patriotic address was given by Mr E. BOURDILLON, and later a short programme of patriotic songs were enjoyed. Amongst those present were Lady GRANTHAM, Miss Muriel GRANTHAM, and Miss FARRAR, and a number of the children's parents.

1st June - BARCOMBE BUTCHER RETAINED - The case of Charles Muggeridge, 33, a butcher of Barcombe, was one in which the Military Representative interposed. Mr MUGGERIDGE said that the conditions had not improved, for he was now doing all the killing himself without assistance. All the help he had now was received from his wife and a little girl.

---

17 *Edwin GARDNER is not named on Barcombe's War Memorial, and his connections with the area appear to be through his brothers Arthur in Barcombe and George at Cooksbridge. Edwin gave his birthplace and address as Brighton, when he enlisted in December 1915 at the age of thirty-six. He was a watch repairer by trade, married at East Preston, Brighton to Louisa Agnes PATTON in 1902. He served as private G/42021 in the Royal Fusiliers before transferring to the 7th Battalion, Queen's Own (Royal West Kent) Regiment as private G/18631. He was killed on 3rd May 1917 and is commemorated on the Bay 7 of the Arras Memorial.*

He had been passed C2. The application of the Military Representative was refused.

VISITORS - Both Barcombe and Barcombe Mills had their quota of visitors on Whit-Monday. The river was well patronised by those who, when opportunity affords, indulge in the pleasurable exercise of rowing.

ABOVE: Posted in Barcombe – A postmark on a halfpenny stamp attached to a postcard leaving the village Post Office on 21st May 1917.

NATIONAL FOOD ECONOMY – A meeting to hear a lecture on Food Economy took place at the Village Hall on Tuesday evening. There was a big attendance of the inhabitants. In introducing Miss HODGSON, Lady GRANTHAM, who presided, remarked that about three months back the honour of the people, which to English men and women meant so much, was appealed to, and they were asked to voluntarily reduce their consumption of meat, bread and sugar. Unfortunately, however, a good number of people disregarded the appeal, thinking they knew better than those in authority how much food there was in

the country. Then came the King's Proclamation, and now meetings and lectures were being held all over the country to try and teach people the use of substitutes. Poor people with large families must have bread, sometimes having no time to cook other foods, so it behoved everybody who had time and money to use substitutes. Miss HODGSON, who received an attentive hearing, said that if they did not economise voluntarily now they would have to go short later.

Many people were ignorant of the great scarcity. Substitutes badly cooked were, of course, nasty to the palate, and many people refused to eat them. Pulse foods such as peas, beans, lentils, took the place of meat. Lentils were the most nourishing, but required seasoning. The lady gave some excellent recipes. A vote of thanks was accorded on the proposition of the Rev. FARRAR, and seconded by Mr BOURDILLON, who mentioned that his children had been brought up in South Africa, where maize was termed mealey, and was the staple diet of the country, as rice was to Japanese and Indians.

8th June (*Sevenoaks Chronicle & Kentish Advertiser*) – **Private E. GARDNER** – In the death in action of Private Edwin GARDNER of Barcombe,[17] a well-known Sussex athlete will be missed. He made a reputation for himself twenty years ago in the South of England as a harrier, a cyclist and a pedestrian. He has taken part successfully in athletic gatherings at the Nevill Ground, Tunbridge Wells, and at Cross-in-Hand sports. He won the All-England Hill-Climbing Contest at Toys Hill, Brasted about ten years ago, and one of his most notable performances was on the Crystal Palace track in 1905, when he was second in the English Ten-mile Championship. His brother is Mr H.GARDNER of Tunbridge Wells.

CONCERT – The 'Reds and Blacks' (of Barcombe) gave a highly successful concert at 'Chyngton Hall', Seaford, on Tuesday evening. The entertainment was well attended, including a large number of Canadian soldiers. Those who took part were: Mr HARRIOTT, Miss DEAN, Miss RHODES, Miss Lena HOLLOWAY, Mrs BALLARD and Miss WELSH.

WEDDING – The Rector conducted the nuptials at the Parish Church on Tuesday of Miss Ethel Louise RANN, eldest daughter of Mr & Mrs Herbert RANN of Mount Pleasant and Driver Percival Evershed FROST, Army Service Corps, of Crowborough…

HINTS ON DOMESTIC ECONOMY AT BARCOMBE – Miss HODGSON gave some

excellent hints on how to economise when lecturing last week at Barcombe… Do not throw away water from rice or vegetables. The water in which vegetables have been boiled makes children grow, having bone-making properties… If rice water is not wanted keep to starch clothes. The blouse Miss HODGSON was wearing

ABOVE: Complete Victory – "If you eat less bread." Ministry of Food poster no.17.

on the evening of her lecture she had starched with the water boiled with the previous day's rice pudding… Everyone should have a stock pot and put in odds and ends. It must be boiled up every day or two, however… For making bread:

1 lb cooked rice, 2lbs of flour, teaspoonful of sugar. The rice should be boiled till perfectly soft, used when hot, and the liquid tepid. The bread should keep fresh for a fortnight if a cloth is kept over the crock. If a hard crust is not wanted, roll it up in a cloth when taken from the oven.

15th June - VERSATILITY AT BARCOMBE - E.J.FUNNELL sought exemption for Albert FUNNELL, aged 35 years, postman, Barcombe, who was also engaged in market gardening and poultry farming. Mr H.J.VINALL supported the application. It was stated that applicant, who had been recently passed for sedentary work at home, was willing to relinquish his postal duties and devote his whole time to work on the land.

IRREGULAR ATTENDANCE – At Lewes Petty Sessions on Tuesday, James TAPP was fined 7s.6d. for non-compliance with a school attendance order, which was issued in respect of his child, who had made 50 attendances out of a possible 62.

ON LEAVE – By a strange coincidence three soldier sons of Mrs Fanny STEVENS, of 'Thatch Cottage' have received leave at the same time. Their names are: Driver Charlie STEVENS, Army Service

ABOVE: Butcher W.F.DEAN "outside his first shop". The caption in the W.I. scrapbook also refers to his "artistry" (ESRO: WI 112/1/1, p.127).

Corps; "Plummer" STEVENS and "Colonel" STEVENS. Second Lieut. James DUDENEY is also on leave.

ACCIDENT TO A BARCOMBE BOY – KICKED BY A HORSE – A serious accident happened to a small boy named Stanley TAPP in the High-street, yesterday evening. The boy, who is the son of Mr & Mrs Thomas TAPP, residing in the district, was walking behind a horse which was being led by another boy, and when giving the animal a friendly pat, kicked him in the face and fractured his jaw. Fortunately

Dr RICHARDS was in the vicinity and promptly rendered first aid. The child's condition was such that Dr RICHARDS immediately ordered his removal to Brighton Hospital, and he was conveyed to that institution by Mr S.B.RICHARDS, the owner of the horse, and also of the motor in which he conveyed the boy.

SITUATIONS VACANT – LADS – BUTCHER requires good BOY, to assist generally, cycling and driving – Apply DEAN, Butcher, Barcombe (*Bexhill-on-Sea Observer* 16th June 1917).

22nd June - IMPROVING – The little boy, Stanley TAPP, who, as announced in our last issue, was kicked in the face by a horse, is progressing favourably. He is still an in-patient at the Hospital, Brighton.

CRICKET AT BARCOMBE – On Wednesday evening Barcombe engaged Laughton on the Recreation Ground connected with the former district. Each team had two innings and Barcombe, displaying great improvement in their playing, proved the victors by 75 to 74…

6th Battalion Sussex Volunteer Regiment – 'A' COMPANY – PARADES FOR WEEK ENDING 30th June: Sunday

24th, Parade at Drill Hall (Lewes) at 10.30 a.m. Dress: Marching order without packs. Barcombe and Ringmer Platoons to attend. Tuesday 26th, Parade at Drill Hall, 7 p.m., Inspection by County Commandant.

29th June - TITHE CLAIM – At Lewes County Court on Monday, Messrs. Powell & Co., agents for the Rev. FARRAR, claimed 19s.3d. from W.E.MORSE in respect of tithe rent charges.

DEATH OF MR SHOESMITH – The death of Mr E.D. SHOESMITH occurred on Saturday at the residence of Mr Alfred ROGERS, 'Longford Farm,' Spithurst, where he had been staying for the benefit of his health. Deceased, who was one of the principals of the firm of Messrs. Shoesmith & Sons, corn merchants, Western Road, Brighton, was well known at Barcombe, and it was his special wish that he should be buried at Spithurst. He had been ill health for a long period, and had borne his sufferings with great fortitude. He was very popular with his wide circle of friends, and was a keen defender of and fighter for the rights of the public. On more than one occasion his sense of justice prompted him to incur expensive litigation. Deceased was the prime mover in gaining a better goods train service, and for his action in the matter was the recipient of a testimonial and presentation. At one period Mr SHOESMITH was one of the school managers for Barcombe, and was that body's representative on the County Council…

BOY'S SCHOOL GARDENS – PRESENTATION OF PRIZES – An interesting little ceremony took place on Wednesday afternoon, when the boys of the School who have been cultivating little patches were awarded prizes of money for the best display of growing vegetables and neatness. The prizes, which were kindly given by Mr H.B.MATTHEWS,[18] a much esteemed (school) visitor in the district, were presented by the Rector. The judges were Mr JESSUP, head gardener to Lady GRANTHAM and Mr T.A.SIGGS (of 'Mission House'). There were seven plots to be judged, and each plot had been cultivated by two boys. The prizes were awarded on points for the condition of the following vegetables: Eight shallots, broad beans, dwarf beans, Brussel sprouts, savoys, runner beans, potatoes, kale, turnips, swede, peas, onions, carrots, parsnips, beetroots, lettuce and parsley. Plot 1, cultivated by Masters George FARENDEN and Harry SANDALLS, won 1st prize, which was 10s.; Plot 6, cultivated by Masters William KNIBBS and Hugh WARNETT, secured the 2nd prize, 6s.; and Plot 4, cultivated by Masters Philip TROWER and George CHATFIELD, gained the 3rd prize, 4s. Each plot was remarkably neat, and had produced a good display,

and much credit is due alike to the Master, Mr CARTER, and the boys.

The other of the boys did not go unrewarded, for Mr MATTHEWS generously handed each a small sum of money… One boy, Master Stanley TAPP, was absent, he being the little chap who was recently kicked by a horse. He is in hospital, but improving, and Mr MATTHEWS is seeing that he, too, will receive a present.

6th July – PROMOTION – Mr Theodore E.BOURDILLON has been gazetted Lieutenant in the Sussex Regiment. Mr Laurence SIGGS has been appointed signaller on H.M.S. "Broke," one of two vessels which recently made a splendid fight in the Channel.

RECTOR's SON GAZETTED – Mr S.G.FARRAR, son of the Rector, has passed out from Sandhurst, and has been gazetted to the Manchester Regiment. It was with this Regiment the Rector's eldest son was serving when he fell in action on Christmas Eve 1914, and was buried at Dranoutre, Belgium.

WALK TO LONDON – BARCOMBE BOY SCOUT'S DIARY – Two Boy Scouts have walked from Barcombe to London for the purpose of delivering dispatches to Lord MONK BRETTON at Prince's Gardens. These plucky lads, both fourteen years of age, were Philip J.TROWER[19] and Ronald GROVES. The latter

has, during the last week, gone to live at Pevensey. The two accomplished the journey in three days, staring on Wednesday and reaching London on the Saturday.

The following description of the journey is taken from a diary which was kept by young TROWER, who, it will be noted, is of an observant character, possesses artistic taste, and has a keen sense of the beautiful, traits which are rare in one so young. The diary has the true boyish ring, particularly so when he relates that "we had dinner sitting on the top of a sign post, and we carved our names on the wooden gate," also "we smuggled some bread and butter."

AN ELEVATED POSITION – "We started from Barcombe," relates the diary, "at 9.30 a.m., and at 11 o'clock we reached Newick, where we remained for nearly half an hour. We started off again for Sheffield Park, which was reached at 12.15. Here we thoroughly enjoyed the beautiful views along the road and over Newick End Common. We overtook Newick's ex-Scout Master, with whom we had a chat. I am now writing this on a bridge spanning the Ouse at Sheffield Park, where everything appears so pretty. We arrived at the Sheffield Arms at 12.40, and

---

18 Henry Burgoyne MATTHEWS lived at 'Skylark Villa.'

19 Philip John TROWER of 6 Gladstone Cottages, was the 14-year-old son of, the village undertaker Harry TROWER.

had our dinner sitting on the top of a sign post.

"A cattle driver, to whom we have been chatting, informs us that it is two miles to Danehill. We have now covered nine miles. Our dinner consisted of sausage roll and cake, which was very good. We left Sheffield Park at 1 o'clock, and walked through the most delightful wooded country until we reached Danehill. We have now covered eleven miles, and are standing opposite a church possessing a square tower. We went into a shop close by and inquired for the Scoutmaster, but there is neither Scoutmaster nor Scouts. We then went in 'Rogers', and they kindly gave us a glass of milk and some buns.

"Our backs to Danehill, we journey through lovely wooded land to Forest Row, 5½ miles away. In a thicket we come to a wooden gate, on which we both carve our names. We eventually arrive at cross roads, and pass the Red Lion Inn on our right, and Chelwood Gate and Common at the bottom of a long hill, with the various notes at the blacksmith's forge ringing in our ears. At present we are 3¾ miles from Forest Row, which we reached at 3.55 in the afternoon. We stay here only five minutes, and when we were half up a hill, which passes over a large common

with tall firs on either side, bits of Ashdown Forest, we halt here and have some grub. Later we passed an old curious-looking house, which I could not help thinking must have formerly been a monastery. Again we reach cross roads leading to

OUT FOR VICTORY.

THE BOY SCOUT.
Because he means to be a free citizen of a free country.

ABOVE: 'Out For Victory. The Boy Scout. Because he means to be a free citizen in a free country'. (Contemporary postcard by L. Hill Raven, Regent Publishing Co., London).

Hartfield, Holly Hill, Twyford, Crowborough Beacon and Plaw Hatch. It is downhill travelling from Chelwood, where we again have wooded country on either side of us.

A NIGHT AT FOREST ROW – "Forest Row is reached at 5.45 p.m., so we enter a shop and buy some buns at a cost of 3d., and eat some while resting at the station. From here we observe a fine church with pointed steeple. We enquire for the Scoutmaster, and were told to go to the doctor's house, where, after waiting some time, we were received, and are at present in the Girl Guides' Headquarters on the doctor's lawn. I think this is about the prettiest countryside I have ever seen, and I am thoroughly enjoying it.

"It is now 8.30, and we have been up to the kitchen and had supper as follows: Cup of Oxo, bread and butter, big plate of meat and salad. At ten o'clock we go to bed, but it is lightning and thundering so much that we cannot sleep for some considerable time. We are so tired, however, that sleep overtakes us, but we awaken again at four o'clock in the morning, and hear the rain pouring hard. At 6.45 we get up, and at seven o'clock we post our cards home. At 7.45 we breakfast, first taking a walk round the garden, cleaning our boots, and washing. We have porridge, fish, bread and butter, and tea. At 9.30 we pack up and prepare to leave the district, which appears to be a county town, with few shops, but a number of house, large and small. The weather, after the heavy thunderstorm, is simply lovely, and we find that we are three miles from East Grinstead, and it is our intention to reach Godstone to-day if possible… Ronald GROVES is helping a man who is mending a puncture beside a water trough given by public subscription. Ronald is now sewing a button on his front…

ANOTHER DICK WHITTINGTON – "… Blindly Heath is reached at four o'clock, and a man with whom we talked says that we can stay at his house for the night. We learn his name is Mr WOOD, and we accept his kindness, and are at present in his house, which, covered with Virginia creeper, is ideal. We have had tea in an arbour, and slept in a bed. Our arms are becoming sore and sunburnt…Some bells have just chimed, and I cannot but help think of Dick Whittington…

…They then reach Warlingham at 1.45 p.m., and later Kenley and Purley, which he describes is a large town, with big buildings and traffic galore. They journey on to Croydon, and there sought young GROVES' aunt, whom they eventually found. Here they received all they desired to eat, and had a good bed.

"We entered London," concludes the diary, "over Vauxhall Bridge, and we soon found our way to Lord MONK BRETTON's, where we delivered our message. We were kindly treated, and after having

dinner we went to the Albert and Victoria Museum, also Indian Exhibition. We should have liked to have stayed in London very much, but we left on the Underground Railway at 4.45 p.m., Victoria at 5.50 p.m., and arrived at Barcombe village again at 7.40 p.m.

Trees appear to have a great fascination for the boy, for they are mentioned many times in the diary, and the concluding words are: "Finished journey and enjoyed our little selves immensely. We saw plenty of copper beech trees in Surrey."

13th July – ON LEAVE – Private Richard DEAN, Hussars and Airman Frank BALLARD are home on leave.

HOLIDAYS – The summer vacation at the School will extend to five weeks, commencing on July 28th.

GOOD COLLECTIONS – Mrs SINGELTON, always an ardent worker on behalf of

ABOVE: Wedding Day photograph of Sergeant Bernard PULLINGER and Gertrude WELSH with her wedding bouquet (courtesy Anne Pearce).

soldiers and sailors, collected £10.10s. last Friday for the Lord Roberts Memorial Workshops…

RESIGNING – At the last meeting of the School Managers, Miss SHENSTONE, who has for a number of years so admirably occupied the position of correspondent, tendered her resignation, which was accepted with genuine regret. At the request of the Managers, however, the lady agreed to hold office till such time as another correspondent is appointed.

WEDDINGS - INTERESTING DOUBLE EVENT – Two exceptionally pretty weddings, both evoking great interest in the district, took place on Tuesday at St. Mary's Church, the Rector officiating at each ceremony. The brides are great friends, and the bridegrooms are both Sergeants in the Royal Sussex Regiment, and each has been the recipient of the Military Medal.

MISS WINIFRED DAISY FUNNELL & SERGEANT GEORGE T.DAVIES – The eldest daughter of Mr & Mrs Harry FUNNELL (blacksmith) was married by special licence early on Tuesday morning… The bride was attired in a blue shot silk poplin coat and skirt, wore a hat to match, and carried a shower bouquet consisting of white carnations, roses and lilies, amid an array of fern. The happy

---

20 *Bernard & Gertrude PULLINGER, set up home at 'Conyboro Lodge,' before moving to 'Handlye Farm.'*

---

couple are spending their honeymoon at Farnborough.

MISS GERTRUDE WELSH & SERGEANT BERNARD C.PULLINGER – Miss WELSH, only daughter of Mr & Mrs James WELSH, of 'Bridge Cottage,' Barcombe, who was wedded to Sergeant PULLINGER[20], fourth son of Mr & Mrs George PULLINGER, of Little Norlington Farm, Ringmer, is a teacher at Barcombe School, where she has been since she was eleven years of age, and is a very popular young lady in the district. Her brother Mr P.WELSH, acted as her best man. Miss WELSH was clad in a putty-coloured costume with navy silk facings, wore a Georgette hat to match,

BELOW: Silver travelling clock presented to the bride Gertrude WELSH on her wedding day (courtesy Anne PEARCE).

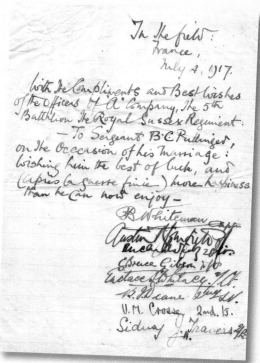

ABOVE: Congratulatory Letter from the officers of 'A' Company, 5th Battalion, R.S.R. "In the Field, France," to "Sergeant B.C. Pullinger, on the occasion of his marriage: Wishing him best of luck, and (apres la guerre finie) more happiness than he can now enjoy.

and carried a sheaf of lilies… There was a guard of honour, consisting of Boy Scouts, under the direction of the Scoutmaster, Mr CARTER, and at the reception hall there was a full display of bunting. Later in the day the newly-wedded couple journeyed to Brighton, where they are spending their honeymoon.

The presents were numerous, and above the names of the following subscribers, who presented Miss WELSH with a silver travelling clock, which was suitably inscribed, appeared the following: "Presented to Gertrude Welsh on the occasion of her marriage, together with a silver clock, by the Committee and members of the Barcombe Stoolball Club, July 1917."[21]

SUSSEX POULTRY CLUB – Amongst life members elected were Barcombe residents: Miss GRANTHAM and Mr H.G.WHIFFEN.

CHAILEY TRIBUNAL – The task of the Tribunal, at their sitting at Lewes, was considerably lessened by the fact that men engaged in agriculture were advised to apply to the War Agricultural Committee for certificates which, it was pointed out, should be produced so that the Tribunal and the military authorities might be satisfied that the men were not liable for service in the Army.

The case of William Lucas PLAYFOOT, aged 25, cowman of 'Old Thatch Cottages,' in which an application was made by Mr F.J.CORNWELL, was adjourned in order that the facts might be placed before the War Agricultural Committee.

20th July – NEW RESIDENT – Dr Samuel Allinson WOODHEAD, M.Sc., F.I.C., Principal of Uckfield Agricultural College,[22] will shortly be a resident of Barcombe, he having taken 'The Gables,' recently vacated by Mr & Mrs Edgar Musgrave BROOKSBANK.

HOME ON LEAVE – Mrs A.PETERS, daughter of Mr & Mrs BROOKSBANK,

ABOVE: 'The Gables,' Barcombe Cross, former home of the BROOKSBANK and new home to Dr & Mrs WOODHEAD (postcard by Harry Tullett of Cuckfield, Mike Green collection).

and grand-daughter of Lady GRANTHAM, is at present home on leave, and staying with her parents at Bexhill. She is attached to the Church Army Corps, and has been working in France. Lieutenant Sydney G.FARRAR, son of the Rector, left on Sunday to join the Manchester Regiment.

27th July – WEDDING – A pretty little war wedding took place last Saturday at Barcombe, the Rector officiating. The contracting parties were Miss Clara Ellen BANFIELD, elder daughter of Mr Edward BANFIELD, Church Road, and Private Henry MASON of Hawes, Yorkshire, who is attached to the Coldstream Guards…The couple spent their honeymoon in Eastbourne.

SCHOOL SPORTS – An interesting event took place yesterday and to-day (Friday), when Barcombe school children, together with their

parents and the inhabitants generally, heralded the summer vacation by holding a grand programme of sports on the Recreation Ground, also an exhibition of various forms of work constituting the

---

21 The names of 51 female subscribers and the curate, Rev. C.TOOGOOD, are listed. Amongst the gifts was also a salad bowl and cruet given by colleagues and scholars at the school.

22 Dr Samuel WOODHEAD (1873-1943) was a chemist and Public Analyst for East & West Sussex. While living in Uckfield, he became friends with local solicitor Charles DAWSON, "discoverer" in 1912 of the "Piltdown Man." Apparently Mr WOODHEAD was asked by DAWSON how bones could be chemically treated to make them look older, but didn't realise the implications of the question until after the "discovery" was published (Peter Costello, 'The Piltdown Hoax Reconsidered,' Antiquity, 1985 and B.G. Gardiner, Zoological Journal of the Linnean Society, 2003). DAWSON died in August 1916 and Samuel and his wife Eva continued to live at 'The Gables,' both taking an active part in parish affairs. Samuel died in 1943, having confessed to his wife about his unwitting involvement in the Piltdown forgery. Eva was President of Barcombe W.I. during the Second World War.

curriculum... Bee keeping and gardening were features which won their quota of appreciation and attention. After the exhibition, which was well attended, an instructive lecture on bee keeping was delivered by Miss BURDER (of 'The Beeches'), who had an attentive audience, including the boys who are studying the bee keeping industry…

All prizes, including those won at the sports yesterday, were distributed by Miss SHENSTONE of Sutton Hall (names listed)…

3rd August – REWARD FOR BUTTERFLIES – The following notice is posted throughout the district of Barcombe: "A prize of 5 shillings is offered to the person killing the greatest number of cabbage butterflies between the dates of July 28th and August 10th, and bringing same to 'The Grange.' The insects have haunted the district in swarms.

WEDDING – A wedding took place on Tuesday morning between Miss Alice STEVENS, daughter of Mrs F.STEVENS of 'Thatched Cottages,' and Airman Frederick Edward Else BROOKER,[23] son of Mr & Mrs Walter BROOKER, of Fisher Street, Lewes. The

---

23 *Fred BROOKER (32) was stationed at Roehampton Camp when he married Alice STEVENS (27). The newly married couple took over the tenancy of 'Thatch Cottage,' where Fred was living when he submitted his invoice for decorating the Billiard Room above the old village hall in November 1921 (ESRO: PAR 235/1/9).*

Rector officiated, and the best man was Mr William Thomas STEVENS, brother of the bride, who was given away by Mr James STEVENS. The bride was attired in a fawn-coloured costume, and wore a white hat. The bridegroom will shortly leave for Mesopotamia.

BOTTLING FRUIT, ETC. – Under the auspices of the East Sussex War Agricultural Committee, Miss SELLENS (from the Food Production Department, London), gave a successful demonstration on bottling fruits without sugar, also bottling vegetables, drying fruits and vegetables, pulping, and sulphuring, etc., at the Village Mission Room last Monday…

HOME ON LEAVE – Bombardier H.STEVENS, Royal Marine Artillery, after a short stay at home (for his sister's wedding), left the district again on Wednesday evening. Private B.COLLINS is home on leave, and Private CHATFIELD, Royal Sussex Regiment, having been wounded, is now in hospital in France.

CHAILEY TRIBUNAL – FARM HANDS' RIGHTS – It was stated that William Lucas PLAYFOOT, had now been granted a protection certificate by the War Agricultural Committee. A question arose as to what the position would be if the certificate was withdrawn at any time. Captain Selby ASH said in that event he would be liable for military service, but the Tribunal could protect them

by adjourning the cases so that they might be further dealt with if the certificates were taken away. The Tribunal agreed to this suggestion.

"RAID" ON BRIGHTON PIER – On Sunday morning the military authorities at Brighton, assisted by the borough police, carried out a round-up for recruits on the West Pier. The town is extremely full of holiday visitors, a large contingent having arrived on Saturday. The pier was crowded at the time of the affair, which was conducted between half-past twelve and one o'clock as the visitors were leaving. Parties of military and civilian police took possession of the exits, the unusual proceedings created excitement among the throngs of promenaders on the front. Women and children and elderly people were directed to certain turnstiles, through which they were passed, but young men apparently of military age were sharply challenged and ordered to remain, so that their papers could be examined. This process resulted in a large number of young men in holiday attire being held up. Groups of wounded soldiers and many men in khaki looked on with amused interest.

10th August - OFF FOR THE FRONT – Second-Lieutenant Sydney G.FARRAR, son of the Rector, passed out from Sandhurst, and was gazetted to the Manchester Regiment. He has been on his final leave, and

ABOVE: Ernie BROWN on one of HOBDEN's steam engines in the field behind 'Bye Law Cottage' Mount Pleasant (copied by Mike Green).

left for the Front on Thursday.

BARCOMBE SOLDIER KILLED - GUNNER L.H. STEVENS

- A letter from the Front was received by Mrs STEVENS of 'Thatched Cottages', Barcombe on Tuesday morning stating that her son, Gunner L.H. STEVENS, R.G.A. had been killed. STEVENS, who was 28 years of age, was one of eight brothers serving with the colours. Great sympathy is extended to his mother…

LEWES APPEALS

- THRESHING NOT COMLPLETED – The employer sought a review of the case in which exemption held by E.J.F.BROWN, threshing machine attendant, had been withdrawn.

Appellant stated that at the present time the man was engaged in sawing timber. Some of last season's threshing had not yet been done.

Mr WADMAN urged that it was important from an agricultural point of view that BROWN's services should be retained by his employer. The Chairman wished to know how Mr WADMAN reconciled his contention with the fact that the man had been engaged in sawing timber. Mr WADMAN pointed out that the control of the threshing rested with farmers. The man could not go to the stacks unless his services were asked for. The speaker added that the matter was important, and he asked the Committee to give it careful consideration. The man could not be replaced if he had to serve in the Army. He had been doing Government work when he was not engaged by farmers.

Exemption until October 1st, on the understanding that this would be final, was granted.

17th August – CRICKET

– A match was played last Saturday between Spithurst and Barcombe, the teams having been arranged by Master Worsley REECE and Master Malcolm WALKER. Spithurst won.

PROPERTY SALE –

'Collingwood House,' which was the property of the late Captain & Mrs COLLINS, the former being famous as a yachtsman at Brighton, was sold by auction yesterday (Thursday) by Messrs. Gambling & Sana. The highest bidder was Mr C.OVERINGTON of Isfield, who paid £700.

SOLDIER RECEIVES HIS DISCHARGE –

Private Charles Alfred MARTIN, Royal Sussex Regiment, brother of Mrs KEMP, who resides at 'Mongers Farm,' arrived home this week. In July 1916 he received severe wounds on the head by shrapnel. He was sent to a hospital at Whitchurch, Cardiff, which he left this week, having received his discharge from the Army.

4,000 BUTTERFLIES KILLED –

A money prize was offered by Miss WALKER, of 'The Grange', to the person who destroyed the largest number of cabbage butterflies in the district within a period of ten days. Needless to say local boys entered the competition with enthusiasm, and, judging by the number produced, they must have displayed tireless energy, for over 4,000 of the insects were taken to Miss WALKER. Master Victor KING[24] was a good winner, he having accounted for 1,395.

24 Victor Ernest KING, aged 12, was the son of Ernest KING, landlord of the 'Royal Oak.'

EXTRAORDINARY BEE HIVE

– Last year an exceptionally large swarm of bees made their hive on the front of Mr Harry FUNNELL's dwelling ('The Forge'). They got behind the tiles which cover the front of the house, and there they remained undisturbed till this week. They lived during last winter on their stock of honey, and this year they appear to have been particularly industrious in their process of manufacture, seeing that their store became so bulky that many tiles began to protrude, and finally came crashing to the ground. Bees hummed about in myriads, and it became dangerous to either enter or leave the dwelling by the front door. Eventually a bee expert, in the person of Mr OVERTON, of the firm of Messrs. Charles Thomas Overton & Sons, bee hive manufacturers, etc. of Crawley, was requisitioned and he found 30lbs of honey. It is believed that possibly another 20lbs could be found if more tiles were dislodged. Mr OVERTON found the queen, and after placing her in a properly constructed hive hard by the major portion of the swarm followed.

THE KING'S REPLY –

The first part of the War Anniversary meeting held in the Mission Room consisted of a short service conducted by the Rector, when the names of all those serving from Barcombe (154 out of a population of 1,277) were read by Mr E.BOURDILLON, who has four sons serving. Then the names of those who had made the great sacrifice were read, the audience standing as a tribute of respect. Captain SINGLETON read the 15th Psalm. The following patriotic resolution was then proposed by Major GRANTHAM and seconded by Mr F.J.CORNWELL, and seconded by Mr CORNWELL: "That on this, the third anniversary of the declaration of a righteous war, this meeting records its inflexible determination to continue to a victorious and the struggle in maintenance of those ideals of liberty and justice which are the common and sacred cause of the Allies." This resoloution was sent to the King, and the Rector has received the following reply: "Windsor Castle, 8th August 1917. Dear Sir – I write to acknowledge the receipt of your letter of August the 6th… I am commanded to convey through you to all who joined in the expression of these sentiments of loyalty. The Rev. FARRAR, Barcombe Rectory."

24th August - WOUNDED –

Private James MORLEY, Royal Sussex Regiment, son of Mr & Mrs J.MORLEY (of 'Culver Junction'), was recently gassed. After being cured he again entered the trenches and in a short time was wounded. He is at present in the Norfolk War Hospital at Thorpe, Warwick.

ON LEAVE –

Private Hart VERCOE, son of Mr & Mrs VERCOE, of 'Banks Farm,' has been granted final leave before proceeding to the Front. Private S.REED is on leave and Private Reginald JESSUP, Royal Sussex Regiment, who is suffering from an accident to his knee, is expected home this week.

EGG COLLECTION –

Miss Annie SPELLER (of 'Place Farm') has been acting as controller of the Barcombe Egg Collection, which has proved very satisfactory. The eggs are for the soldiers and sailors. The number collected from April 13th to the present date is 1,878, and most of these have been collected by the school girls.

VEGETABLE & FRUIT COLLECTION –

Organised by the Rector and a number of kind helpers, a vegetable and fruit collection took place on Wednesday evening, the depots for receiving being the Rectory and the Village Mission Room. Quite a big quantity was received, and it has since been sent to headquarters in London, where it will be distributed and dispatched to the Fleet and mine sweepers.

THE SWALLOW-TAIL BUTTERFLY

– ONE CAPTURED AT BARCOMBE – Several of our contemporaries during the last fortnight have given lengthy notices regarding the capture of the swallow-tail butterfly in Sussex during the present month, and entomologists have given their views on the rarity of the insect in the South of England.

The capture of two, however, has been recorded,

and the "Sussex Express" will add to the list by announcing that a beautiful specimen was caught at Barcombe last Saturday. The announcement will undoubtedly interest Mr Herbert S.TOMS, the naturalist, of Beaconsfield Villas, Brighton, who has asked for full data of any similar insects caught, so that a proper record could be made.

The Barcombe specimen was captured by Miss Gwen FUNNELL,[25] who has presented same to Master Malcolm WALKER of 'The Grange,' who is a collector of the insects. This particular butterfly was caught without injury to its wings or body, and it possesses beautiful colouring. With its wings outspread it measures about three inches, and independent of a deep yellow hue, has patches of blue and a red spot on each wing. It

ABOVE: The Swallowtail Butterfly featured on a Phillips' cigarette card issued in 1911.

is an exceptionally pretty insect and the swallow-tail adds materially to its beauty.

31st August – WOUNDED – We regret to state that Sergeant B.C.PULLINGER, whose parents live at Ringmer, and who was only married last month, has been wounded. Sergeant PULLINGER, as will

be remembered, married Miss WELSH, a popular teacher at Barcombe School.

BARCOMBE LADY DRIVER - Miss Winifred Margaret FARRAR,[26] daughter of the Rector, has been driving a business motor in London for the last twelve months, and has now joined the Women's Army Service Corps for either foreign or home service. It is expected that she may be drafted to France. This patriotic

BELOW: Sergeant Bernard PULLINGER (seated centre) with fellow wounded soldiers wearing "convalescent blue" uniforms (courtesy Anne Pearce).

25 Ethel Gwendoline FUNNELL, aged 21, was the daughter of Harry FUNNELL, blacksmith of 'The Forge.' She joined her mother in the local Voluntary Aid Detachment (V.A.D.) in October 1917, where she trained to become a nurse, serving until January 1919.

26 Winifred FARRAR (28) was born in South Shields, Co. Durham in 1888 and moved to Barcombe when her father became Rector in 1916. After the Great War she maintained her London connections, working as a clerk on the permanent administrative staff of the University of London. She was still working there at the outbreak of the Second World War, while looking after her widowed father at 'The Rectory.' She died in 1941, aged fifty-three and is buried in St. Mary's churchyard.

ABOVE: Miss Winifred Margaret FARRAR

young lady has gained the Royal Automobile certificate for driving and knowledge of mechanism (mechanics).

31st August 1917 - BARCOMBE OFFICER'S GRAVE IN BELGIUM - Below is a photograph of the grave of Second-Lieutenant Herbert Ronald FARRAR, Manchester Regiment, who

ABOVE: The temporary wooden cross marking the grave of the Rector's son who died on Christmas Eve 1914. The initials on the cross are, unfortunately incorrect.

was killed on Christmas Eve, 1914. He was the eldest son of the Rev. FARRAR (now) Rector of Barcombe, and was buried at Dranoutre, Belgium.

7th September - BARCOMBE MILK GIRL - Miss Annie JONES.[27] Although she is only 14 years of age this bright little Britisher of Barcombe, has been doing a milk round for Mr CORNWELL for a year. With her pretty face and engaging smile, she is welcome at every door.

21st September - KILLED - Private Frank FOORD R.G.A., has made the supreme sacrifice. Before joining the Army he was a gardener at Barcombe Place.

ON LEAVE - Trooper Dick DEAN, Hussars, son of Mr & Mrs William Frederick DEAN, arrived home last Friday, and returned to his Regiment yesterday (Thursday).

RETURNED TO FRANCE - Mrs PETERS, daughter of Mr & Mrs BROOKSBANK and granddaughter of Lady Grantham, has returned to France, where she has been working in connection with the Church Army Huts.

A NOVEL DEPARTURE – For the sole purpose of aiding Lady GRANTHAM's Working Party for the Red Cross, Mrs HOPWOOD[28] has adopted a novel idea in inaugurating the carriage of goods between Barcombe and Lewes every Tuesday at the small cost of 2d. for each parcel not weighing more than 6lbs., and not being more than 14 inches

MISS ANNIE JONES.

ABOVE: Miss Annie JONES (courtesy Doris Parker)

square. Mrs HOPWOOD has also undertaken to execute commissions.

SCOUTS – Fourteen of the local Boy Scouts visited Coneyboro', Lord MONK BRETTON's residence, last week, where they were entertained to tea. Five Tenderfeet were initiated as Scouts, and received badges. His lordship had prepared a treasure hunt, which was smartly carried out, and the winner was awarded a prize.

STOOLBALL AT BALNEATH MANOR – A stoolball match between Major GRANTHAM's XI, and men

---

27 *Photograph courtesy of Mrs Doris THOMAS (nee PARKER), Annie JONES's niece.*

28 *Mrs Clara HOPWOOD lived at 'Scobells Farm.'*

from the School Hill Hospital, Lewes, took place on Saturday. Mrs GRANTHAM kindly entertained the teams to tea. The scorer was Miss M.RIGDEN.

BARCOMBE CRICKET CLUB – The Barcombe Club annual meeting for 1916 was held at the Reading Room. Mr S.B.RICHARDS, the Hon. Secretary, in his report said that the Club had passed through a successful financial year, and not withstanding war conditions, several enjoyable games had been played with the Royal Army Medical Corps of the Eastern Hospital, Brighton, and local teams. The ground and tackle had been lent to junior teams on several occasions and every help given when possible. Those who were prejudiced against any form of recreation in these troublesome times must admit that the Club had not been run on selfish lines…

Major GRANTHAM said that he would accept the onerous responsibility of collecting the subscriptions on the understanding that the ground[29] should be kept going until "the boys come back." In the meantime the juniors could have the use of the ground to develop their talents.

25th September (*War Office Casualty List*) KILLED – Royal Field Artillery – 8953 Gunner W.EVANS of Barcombe.

28th September – BARCOMBE SOLDIER ATTACKED – On Saturday night at Brighton, Driver Frank STEVENS, attached to the Canadian Engineers, and son of Mrs STEVENS of 'Thatched Cottages,' was attacked by two unknown men, who dealt him a blow on the head with some formidable weapon which rendered him unconscious. Whilst in this state the culprits rifled the soldier's pockets and were successful in securing about 15s. in silver and coppers. Stevens, however, who was home on leave, had a number of notes in his possession, but these the men, evidently not having sufficient time at their disposal, overlooked, and promptly decamped when they saw some people approaching.

A crowd soon assembled, and an ambulance, which had been telephoned for, conveyed the soldier to the Canadian Hospital at Queen's Park, where he is now, it is stated, progressing as satisfactorily as possible.

It appears that Stevens has been twenty months at the front, and had been granted ten days' leave, the time expiring last Monday. He left Barcombe on Saturday for the purpose of seeing some of his soldier friends in hospital at Shoreham, and after so doing, and spending the evening in Brighton, was on his way to catch the 9.30 train for Barcombe when he was suddenly attacked. Stevens believes that the men were in khaki, and also that he met them a little earlier in the evening.

Stevens is one of seven brothers serving the colours, and only a few weeks ago one brother was killed while on active service.

HOME ON LEAVE – Private A. STILL,[30] who was well-known as an insurance agent in the district, is home on leave.

TRANSFERRED – Corporal W.E.HATTO,[31] who was recently home on leave, has been transferred from the Hussars to the Mounted Military Police.

CHAILEY TRIBUNAL – RELEGATED TO THE RESERVE - Mr E.W.BUNNEY claimed exemption for Frederick TAPP, aged 18 years, who worked in gardens at Spithurst, Barcombe. It was stated that, as a result of medical examination, the man had been relegated to the Reserve, and would be liable to a further call after February 28th next. The Tribunal decided to adjourn the case until after the date mentioned.

GARDENER EXEMPTED - Mr S.F.ASSER sought exemption for Frank Albert SMITH, aged 40 years, gardener, Barcombe Mills, who had been passed for sedentary work at home. It was contended that, owing to his state of health, the man was more usefully employed in his present occupation than he would be in the Army. Exemption until January 1st, 1918, was granted.

---

29 *The Cricket Ground was then next to Barcombe Place, on the land behind the current Village Hall.*

30 *Albert STILL (29) was living at 1 Munster Cottages when he enlisted at Chichester in May 1916.*

31 *William Edward HATTO lived at 'Old Thatch Cottage,' School Path with his wife Jane.*

17. "TOMMY" FINDS SHELL HOLES COMFORTABLE TO SLEEP IN

LEFT: 'Tommy Finds Shell Holes To Sleep In' (*Daily Mail* Series 3, no.17).

CLERK RETAINED – Messrs. Chatfield & Son, timber merchants, claimed exemption for Edward AVERY, aged 27 years, Gladstone Buildings, cashier and ledger clerk, who had been passed for sedentary work at home. It was explained that the firm were engaged in supplying home-grown timber in connection with Government contracts. Exemption until December 31st was granted.

NEW RESIDENT - Mr J. SCOTT-GARDENER, a solicitor, who has been invalided after three years' war service, has taken over the poultry farm known as 'Wootton Cottage,' and now named 'Belcourt'. Mr SCOTT-GARDENER was two years in France. He has served with the Duke of Wellington West Riding Regiment, also the Royal Marines.

KILLED IN ACTION - We regret to state that Private Fred EDWARDS, whose home address was Dallas Lane, and who was attached to the Royal Fusiliers, and previously of the Royal Engineers, has been killed whilst in action on the Western Front. Before joining the Army, EDWARDS was a carpenter at Barcombe Place.

2nd October - Weekly Casualty List (War Office & Air Ministry)

Royal Fusiliers, 16649 G. MATTHEWS, Barcombe.

7th October – James CROUCH, a former cowman of F.J.CORNWELL died in a Military Hospital near Ypres. He was married and living at St.Pancras Gardens, Southover, Lewes at the time of his enlistment in 'B' Company of the 1st/5th Battalion, R.S.R.[32]

12th October – ON LEAVE – Private Leonard CHATFIELD, son of Mr & Mrs Charles CHATFIELD, is at home on leave.

HARVEST FESTIVAL – Barcombe Mission Hall (undenominational) harvest thanksgiving services were held on Sunday. The speaker was Mr F.H.ANSCOMBE of Coolham, Horsham. On Monday evening there was a short service presided over by Mr A.McBEAN.[33] The amount realised from the sale of fruit, etc., including the Sunday offertory, amounted to £3.10s.6d. This sum is to be expended in the purchase of materials for the Ladies' Working Committee.

16th October (*Weekly Casualty List*) – Wounded - Driver F. WALL, 65370 Royal Field Artillery.

19th October - NOW IN FRANCE – Private Hart VERCOE, late of the Hussars, and now transferred to the infantry, has arrived in France…

ABSENTEE – At the County Hall, Lewes, on Saturday morning, William LEE, a gypsy, was charged with having failed to report under the Military Service Act. - P.C.WILLARD deposed that earlier in the day he arrested prisoner at Barcombe. Prisoner told the Bench that he thought he was 38 years old. The Bench fined prisoner £2, decided that he should be handed over to the military authorities and recommended P.C. WILLARD for a gratuity.

---

32 *Alison M.Benton, Men of Southover, Moira Publications, 1998.*

33 *Albert McBEAN was an orchid grower at Cooksbridge. His father James had founded the nursery in 1879, but it was Albert who decided to specialise in the breeding of orchids. A day at the nursery would begin soon after 6 am, with Albert leading his workers in prayer (www. mcbeansorchids.com).*

Surname Funnell.

Christian Names Ethel Gwendoline.   (Mr., Mrs. or Miss)

Permanent Address: Forge House
Barcombe. @ Lewes. Sussex

Certificate No.   **Age when engaged** 24 years.

Date of Engagement 24 Oct 1917 **Rank** Trainee   **Pay** £10 pm

Date of Termination 31. Jan 1919 **Rank** Nurse   **Pay** £1 11 10.

Previous Engagements under Joint War Committee, if any, and where _____

Dept. for References J. N. Dept.

LEFT: Ethel Gwendoline FUNNELL (24), daughter of Harry, blacksmith & wheelwright of 'Forge House' joined the British Red Cross as a trained nurse on 24th October 1917 (British Red Cross website: vad.redcross.org.uk).

Army Service Corps.

2nd November - NEW RIFLE RANGE AT BARCOMBE MILLS – A big muster was seen at Barcombe Mills on Sunday afternoon for the opening of a rifle range by General Sir Henry MacKINNON[34]. The range, which has been erected for the Barcombe Platoon of the 6th Sussex Volunteer Regiment, is on the top storey of the Mill, and the accommodation was kindly offered by Mr William A. WILMSHURST, who is proprietor of the establishment...[35]

The Platoons of Volunteers from Lewes, Ringmer and Barcombe, under the command of Colonel MONEY, had

RED CROSS DAY – This event was held on Saturday, and the amount collected, together with the sum realised by the sale of goods from a stall stationed outside the Post Office, was £19. The lady flag sellers were early on the scene...

26th October – 'THE BEECHES' – Sale of Well-Made Household Furniture & Effects, including: Iron and Brass Bedsteads, Bedding, Mahogany and other Chests of Drawers, Bedroom Suites, Toilet Ware, Chamber Organ with 4-octave keyboard, Mahogany Sideboard, Mahogany Dining Table, Mahogany Kneehole Writing Desk, Mahogany Dining Chairs, Antique Carved Screen, Carpets and Rugs, Glass, China, very large Copper Preserving Pan, kitchen and Scullery Requisites, also Set of Plated Harness, cob-size, Plough and Cultivator, Iron Roll, Garden Light, and numerous effects, which Messrs. J.R.THORTON & Co. have been favoured with instructions from the Executor of the late J. BURDER, Esq., to sell by auction.

30th October - Weekly Casualty List (War Office & Air Ministry) – Wounded – R. HOUNSON 28189 East Surrey Regt; H.E. WALL M2/048186

BELOW: Barcombe Mill, where the rifle range was located in the long attic on the top floor. The mill was destroyed by fire in 1939 (postcard by Edward Reeves of Lewes).

35 *William Alfred WILMSHURST, corn miller lived at 'Hayes Farm' with his widowed aunt Frances CORNWELL and her three daughters. He ran the large water mill at Barcombe Mills.*

34 *General Sir (William) Henry Mackinnon, GCB, KCVO (1852-1929) was appointed General Officer Commander-in-Chief for Western Command in 1910, retiring in 1916. He lived at Carlisle Place in London.*

assembled at the Mills, as also had the Lewes and Barcombe troops of Boy Scouts, under Assistant Scoutmaster SMITH (Lewes) and Scoutmaster CARTER (Barcombe). General MacKINNON inspected the Scouts, and to a number of the Barcombe boys he presented proficiency badges and service stars.

Addressing the Volunteers and Scouts, the General remarked that it had afforded him great pleasure to meet the men and boys. He always thought of the late Sir William GRANTHAM when he saw Volunteers in Sussex, for that gentleman's appreciation of the Volunteers was well known, and he would have been delighted to have seen how the Volunteer movement had flourished in the county. He was, he said, much struck by the splendid physique of the men, and was glad to know that the men of Barcombe had rifles and a certain amount of ammunition, which, though not in large quantity, was sufficient to make for greater efficiency. Continuing, the General said that the Volunteers had met with difficulties and discouragement, and were made to believe that they were not appreciated by headquarters. Now, however, the War Office knew their value, and appreciated them to the full. He trusted they would not only continue as Volunteers for the duration of the War, but would impress upon all men ineligible for the Army to join…

ANGLING – Good sport can be obtained by lovers of the rod at Barcombe Mills. On Sunday Mr Sydney FOSTER, of Lewes, hooked a fine pike, which weighed 13½lbs., and the same day Mr TROWER, of Brighton, caught a jack, which turned the scales at 7lbs.

DISCHARGED – Sergeant Jack ELPHICK, Army Service Corps, has, owing to heart trouble, received his discharge. He is a son of Mr & Mrs George ELPHICK, of 'Clovelly,' and, previous to joining the Army, he worked for a number of years for Mr S.B.RICHARDS. He joined as a private, but was soon promoted to Sergeant, and saw service in Gallipoli.

9th November - STOOLBALL MATCH TO-MORROW (SATURDAY) – What do the letters 'A.B.P.P.P.' stand for? Beyond telling us that they are connected with the stoolball match which is to take place to-morrow afternoon at the Dripping Pan, Lewes, we are entirely in the dark, and must leave it to be solved by our readers. However, a match is taking place at two o'clock, and the opposing parties will consist of wounded soldiers from School Hill Hospital, Lewes, and a team arranged by Major GRANTHAM. Admission is free, but there will be a collection on the ground for the purpose of purchasing stoolball sets for wounded soldiers.

BELOW: The Cultivation of Lands Order – This Order, dated 30th November 1917 by the East Sussex Agricultural Executive Committee required F.J. CORNWELL to "break up and properly cultivate as arable land" two fields of about 16 acres at 'Broomlye Farm', Newick within the next month (courtesy the Cornwell family).

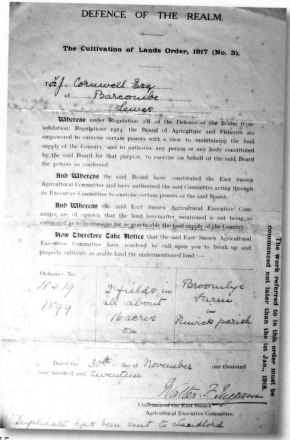

MAJOR GRANTHAM'S "CROCKS."

The Mayor of Hastings (Councillor W. Perrins), Miss Perrins and her collecting friends, and Major Grantham's "Crocks," who played a team of wounded soldiers at stoolball on Saturday at Hastings. The soldiers won by 162 to 64.

LEFT: Major GRANTHAM photographed with his team of "Crocks," including the Mayor of Hastings, Councillor W.PERRINS, Miss PERRINS and her "collecting friends."

end the soldiers won by 162 to 64. Private HILTON was top scorer for the winners with 71, and Major GRANTHAM for the losers with 24. Miss PERRINS, assisted by lady friends, took a collection on the ground on behalf of the Mayor's Fund for Christmas comforts for wounded soldiers in Hastings hospitals…

28th November (*Eastbourne Gazette*) OUTDOOR SERVANTS - WANTED - Man to work in garden; wages 25s., live out – Apply to Gardener, Barcombe House, Barcombe Mills.

30th November – SLATE CLUB – The members of the Slate Club attached to the Reading Room will receive their annual share-out on Monday, December 10th.

TRANSFERRED – Mr Dick DEAN, late of the Hussars, son of Mr & Mrs William Frederick DEAN, has passed the necessary examination and has now been transferred to the Royal Flying Corps.

ON LEAVE – Driver James BLACKMAN, Army Service Corps, son of Mr & Mrs Alfred BLACKMAN, of Mount Pleasant, Spithurst, has arrived home from Salonica. He has been in the East for three years, and was in the Gallipoli campaign.

16th November – OFFENCE AT BARCOMBE – Miss BROWN pleaded guilty to omitting to carry a red lamp on a cart of which she was in charge, at Barcombe, at seven p.m. on the 30th October. She said that she did not know that the light was necessary, and had not been used to driving in the dark... A fine of 5s. was imposed.

ON LEAVE – Private Jim EDWARDS[36] and Private Charlie PACKHAM are home on leave.

MISSING – Private Hart VERCOE, who joined the Hussars and was later transferred to the infantry, is, we regret to state, missing. Only recently he was drafted to France and word has been received from a sergeant that VERCOE went into action on October 25th and has since been missing.

23rd November – PROMOTION – 2nd Lieut. W. Ivor GRANTHAM, son of Major W.W.GRANTHAM, who is making satisfactory progress, after having been seriously wounded, has received promotion to the rank of Lieutenant.

24th November (*Hastings & St. Leonards Observer*) – STOOLBALL AT HASTINGS - MAJOR GRANTHAM'S "CROCKS" – There was a good attendance of spectators at the stoolball match played on Saturday at White Rock, Hastings by Major GRANTHAM's "Crocks" and a team of wounded soldiers. The Mayor (Councillor PERRINS) set the game going, and it was played out with considerable enthusiasm and a good deal of merriment. In the

---

36 *James EDWARDS, jun. (33) formerly a domestic gardener of 8 Gladstone Cottages.*

Home Produce - The GRANTHAM family of Barcombe Place turned the tennis courts on their front lawns to fenced plots for raising livestock as shown in these 'before and after' images.

ABOVE: Barcombe Place in a Mezzotint postcard posted in 1905.

RIGHT: photographs from the Barcombe W.I. scrapbook (ESRO: WI 112/1/1).

RETURNED FROM HOSPITAL – Private Charles OSBORNE,[37] son of Mrs Naomi OSBORNE, has been in hospital for the last six months at Windsor, suffering from a severe wound in the leg. He arrived home yesterday (Thursday).

SCHOOL BOYS' NEW DEPARTURE – The recent lecture by Mr SHARPE, the poultry expert, has interested the schoolboys, and they are now erecting a poultry house made from old desks, etc. The boys, whose vegetable gardens were very successful this year, have also two beehives.

DEATH OF MRS GEERING – The death of Mrs Jane Ann GEERING, widow of Mr Spencer GEERING, occurred on Monday at 'Seveirg Buildings', Lewes,[38] where she had resided for several years. Deceased, who was 73 years of age, and leaves two sons and one daughter, was well known in Barcombe, where, before her husband's demise, she resided at 'Sewells Farm,' now occupied by her son, Harry… After a service at Jireh Chapel, Lewes, to-day, the remains were conveyed to Barcombe, where the funeral took place.

LIGHTING OFFENCES – Miss Gladys STONE[39] was summoned for offences against the Lights on Vehicles Order

– P.C. WILLARD said that at 8.30 p.m. on November 15th he saw defendant driving a pony attached to a cart without a near side front light or a red rear light. He stopped her, and in reply to him she said that she did not think it compulsory to have two lights in front, and

37 Charles OSBORNE (27) worked a domestic gardener before the war, living with his mother at 'Foster's Cottages,' Clappers Bridge.

38 'Seveirg Buildings' (apparently the surname of the owner, Grieves, spelt backwards) was a large building in Lewes, on the corner of the High Street and Eastgate Street, where 'Boots' now stands.

39 Frances Gladys STONE (25) lived at 'Fir Cottage,' Town Littleworth with her parents Frederick & Alice.

RIGHT: Private William JONES of the Army Veterinary Corps, who was home on leave in early December 1917 (courtesy Pamela Godley).

that she could not get the rear lamp to burn. Examination showed the lamp to be without oil. A fine of 5s. was imposed.

7th December - SHARE OUT – The members connected with the Reading Room Slate Club will receive their annual share-out on Monday and the amount available for each member is £1.3s.11d.

HOME ON LEAVE – The following men are at present home on leave; Private William JONES, Army Veterinary Corps; Corporal Bob ESMOND and Dick DEAN, who is joining the Royal Flying Corps on the 17th inst.

NEW SCHOOL STOVES – East Sussex Education Committee were informed on Tuesday that the Managers of Barcombe Church of England School recommended that two new warming and ventilating stoves should be provided at a cost of £21.2s. to replace stoves which were entirely worn out and which were placed in the school in February 1904…

APPRECIATED WORK – Since the outbreak of was Mrs SPELLER and her daughter have been ardent workers on behalf of the soldiers and sailors. It was owing to their work that the men received Christmas plum puddings in 1915 and 1916, and their organising of a number of whist drives has been the means of

seeing to the many requirements of the mine sweepers. With the aid of a number of school children Mrs SPELLER and her daughter have collected 2,334 eggs for the wounded, and after finding that these delicacies were becoming unprocurable, Mrs SPELLER started to collect for the National Egg Collection for the Wounded, and in six days was able to forward to the authorities the handsome sum of £16.5s.2d…

FIRE BRIGADE EXPENSES – Expenses amounting to £10.0s.9d. (£42s.3d. for the services of Lewes Fire Brigade and £5.18s.6d. for the use of the engine, etc.), were incurred in connection with the attendance at a stack fire at Barcombe Mills Farm on November 9th.

14th December - ON LEAVE – The following local men are home on leave: Private

C.J.HOLLOWAY, Army Service Corps, Private F.COX, Royal Sussex Regiment (whose home is at Spithurst), and Sergeant F.HEASMAN, Royal Engineers.

RECTOR'S SON WOUNDED – We hear that 2nd-Lieut. Sydney G.FARRAR, Manchester Regiment, and T.M.B. (Trench Mortar Battery), was wounded at Passchendaele Ridge on the 5th inst., the bullet just missing his spine. He has arrived in England, and is in King Edward VII's Hospital for Officers, Grosvenor Gardens, S.W.1 and is going on as well as can be expected.

PAPER COLLECTION – During six months, March to September, a big quantity of paper was collected in the district. The organiser of the scheme was Miss F.M. Doris BURDER, and the amount of

Barcombe Mills, Sussex.

LEFT: The Station Inn, Barcombe Mills, venue for the inquest into the death of John MORLEY (Mezzotint Co. postcard, c.1910).

money realised by the sale of the paper was allocated as follows: War Hospital Supply Depot (Barcombe Branch) £5.5s.; Lewes Branch £5.5s.; British Red Cross Society £11.15s.

KILLED ON THE LINE – INQUEST AT BARCOMBE MILLS – An inquest touching the death of John Miles MORLEY,[40] a platelayer, in the employ of the LB&SC Railway Company, and who was killed by a fast train on the 5th inst., was conducted by the East Sussex Coroner, Mr Vere BENSON, at the Station Inn, Barcombe Mills on Friday afternoon. Mr Harry TROWER, undertaker, was chosen foreman of the jury.

William BLACKFORD, a platelayer (of 'Lower Barn'), said he was in the goods yard when the accident took place. The 10.46 train was at the platform. He did not see the Brighton to London train coming, but he heard it, and also heard the rattle of the beach stones, which convinced him that something unusual was happening. His view was obstructed owing to the down train, which was moving out of the station at the time. He with other men found the body.

David SANDS, a signal-porter (of 'Station House'), said he saw deceased a few seconds before the train struck him, and he was then working between the points. The train was punctual to time, and MORLEY was standing sideways when he was struck, and before the accident never seemed to notice the approach of the train. Another train was in the station, and owing to steam from the engine he was not able to see too well…

A juryman – He was travelling between 35 and 40 miles an hour, the wind was blowing south-east, and deceased, if working, was possibly stooping below the level of the platform, which would make it still more difficult for witness to see him. It was the coupling which struck deceased, because he found it bent when he examined the engine at Uckfield…

Mr CORNWELL, a juryman, said that fast trains often ran 60 miles an hour between Barcombe Mills and Isfield. He had timed them between the two whistles – one at Barcombe Mills the other when the train passed through Isfield.

This was refuted by the driver, who stated that they were allowed fourteen minutes to reach Uckfield from Lewes. The journey from Lewes to Barcombe Mills occupied six minutes, and the top speed could not be more than 45 miles an hour.

The jury returned a verdict of "Accidental Death," and attached no blame to the driver

40 John Miles MORLEY was born in 1857, the sixth of at least nine children of Miles & Sarah MORLEY of Spithurst. By 1881 he was working on the railway and boarding at 'Anchor Crossing' near the 'Anchor Inn'. On the day of his fatal accident he was sixty years old, unmarried and still living at the same address. He was buried in St. Mary's churchyard the following day by Harry TROWER, the village undertaker.

or his mate. They expressed sympathy with the relatives of deceased, as also did Mr DYBALL on behalf of the Railway Company.

21st December - BARCOMBE TICKET CASE – A

prosecution by the London, Brighton and South Coast Railway Company against a Barcombe woman for having travelled without having paid her fare failed at Lewes

BELOW: John MORLEY was buried by village undertaker Harry Trower, who was also foreman of the inquest jury. This entry from Trower's 'Funeral Arrangements' notebook shows that William BLACKFORD, one of MORLEY's colleagues, acted as one of four coffin bearers (courtesy Geoff Trower).

Funeral Arrangements.

Date. Dec 5th 1917

Ordered by Mr J. Morley
Address
Name of Deceased John Miles Morley
Address of Deceased
Age 60 Date of Death Dec 5th
Parish of Barcombe
Date of Funeral 8th Time 2.
Time at Cemetery 2.30
To be interred at St Mary's Barcombe.
Minister Required
Grave Instructions, &c.
Hearse Glass Coaches Carriages
Bearers 4 Cards Tea
Obituary Notices
Superintended by
Measurements, Instructions, &c.

Killed on the Railway at Barcombe
Mills Carried by Blackford, Funk
Chandler, A Saunders.

Petty Sessions on Tuesday. The defendant was Isabella BRUNTON, the wife of an Army schoolmaster.[41] Mr L.G.VINALL defended.

Ticket Collector UNDERWOOD gave evidence that at 10.33 a.m. on October 31st he was collecting tickets from passengers who came by train via East Grinstead. Defendant, who presented a third class single ticket from Barcombe Mills to Lewes, went to the booking office. On her return she explained that she booked the ticket on the previous Friday, when she intended to come to Lewes by the 4.9 p.m. train, but she did not do so as her husband arrived home on leave. Witness said "The date on this ticket has been rubbed out. Do you know who did that?" She replied "I did not. It may have been done in my glove." Witness saw in defendant's purse a return half of a third class ticket from Barcombe Mills to Lewes, dated October 29th, and he called defendant's attention to that. Defendant said the ticket belonged to a lady who did not return with it. Witness asked defendant why, if she thought the single ticket available, she did not use it when she came to Lewes on a previous occasion. She replied that

she did not then have the ticket with her. She added that, when she explained about the single ticket at Barcombe, she was told it would be all right. She then offered to pay the fare.

James FARENDEN, porter at Barcombe, stated that on the morning of October 31st he saw defendant, who showed him a third class single ticket from Barcombe Mills to Lewes, and asked him if it could be used from Barcombe Station. He was busy at the time and did not see the date on the ticket, but he told her it was available from either station at Barcombe… Without calling for the defence the Bench dismissed the case.

SHARE OUT – Members of the Slate Club attached to the Railway Inn, Barcombe Mills, had their annual share-out on Saturday evening. Thirty-five members received £1.5s.10½d. each, after which, together with a number of friends from Lewes and Brighton, they spent a musical evening in the smoking room.

CRICKET CLUB – The Rector presided at the A.G.M., which was held on Friday evening at the Reading Room. Others present were: Major W.W.GRANTHAM, Mr George HOLLOWAY,

41 William Colin & Isabella BRUNTON lived at 'The Larches.' Scottish-born William (51) had been appointed as an officer in the Corps of Army Schoolmasters at Colchester on New Year's Day 1900. He was still stationed at Colchester in 1911 when he married 'Bella' NEVILLE. By 1913 the couple had moved to Fort Road, Newhaven, before moving to Barcombe by the time of this incident.

Mr W.J.CARTER, Mr F.REYNOLDS, etc. It was pointed out that subscriptions were coming in satisfactorily, and that there was a balance to the good…

BARCOMBE VILLAGE CLUB – The AGM was held on Friday evening at the Reading Room, Major W.W.GRANTHAM presiding…

YOUNGER MEMBERS – The Hon. Secretary and Treasurer, Mr Alfred MOON, said that the Committee, in presenting the thirty-fifth annual report, desired to thank all subscribers to the Club for their support. It had been anticipated that in such trying times honorary subscribers would have decreased in number, but such was not the case. Ordinary members, too had responded well. The new rule of admitting members from sixteen years of age with probationers between fourteen and sixteen, had proved a success. The balance-sheet, which showed an expenditure of £41.18s.9½d., and receipts £40.13s.11d., left a deficit of £1.4s.10½d. This was accounted for by the purchasing of new lamps and the renovation of the bagatelle table, the combined cost of which was £6.7s.10d. Comparing the financial position of the Club with neighbouring village clubs there was little cause for complaint. Those who deserved the Club's best thanks were: Major W.W.GRANTHAM, who placed the Club at the disposal

ABOVE: Christmas 1917 – Cards show the American flag, following the country's entry into the war.

of the members rent free, Lady GRANTHAM, who gave gifts of newspapers and periodicals, Mr H.B.MATTHEWS, who gave whist drive prizes, Mr S.B.RICHARDS and Mr R.RHODES, who successfully carried out the various duties connected with whist drives during the winter months, Mr E.BOURDILLON and Mr W.J.CARTER, who had carefully rearranged the library, and Mrs PEEBLES for gifts of books; also all those who had assisted the Committee in the interest of the Club….

OFFICERS ELECTED – After a discussion on the supply of newspapers, which amounted to £3.18s.2d. per year, it was agreed that the Club should dispense with one of the penny daily journals…

AN ACT OF THANKFULNESS – Major GRANTHAM thanked all present, and said that it was always his wish to do all he possibly could for Barcombe, which they all loved. It was nice to see so many of the younger generation present, and he hoped that when they were older that their sons, and their sons following, would become members of the institution. He knew he voiced the feelings of all present when he said how sorry they were to learn that the son of the Rector had been wounded. They trusted that he would soon recover. He had a providential escape, and they hoped it would not be long before he would be back in Barcombe.

The Rev. FARRAR thanked them for their kind wishes and sympathy. When he received the first notification regarding his son he was unable to open the letter for some little time, so nervous was he lest it contained worse news. He was relieved, though naturally very pained, when he saw that his boy had been wounded. He would, as an act of thankfulness, be glad if they

ABOVE AND RIGHT: The soldiers of the Australian Imperial Force carved an outline map of their home country in the Downs above Hurdcott Camp.

would allow him to pay off the deficit of £1.4s.10½d.

24th December (*War Office Weekly Casualty List*) – MISSING, 20139 William Hart VERCOE, Royal West Kent Regiment.

28th December - FUNERAL OF MRS VERRALL – The wife of Mr Otto VERRALL (of 'Court Lodge Farm') passed away on Wednesday of last week, and was buried at Barcombe Churchyard on Saturday.

SCHOOL CHILDREN TREATED – The day the school broke up Lady GRANTHAM and Miss

WORSLEY (of 'Hill Brow') treated all who had been paying into the War Loan with fruit and cakes.

PRESENTATION – The school managers have presented a handsome writing bureau to one of the assistant teachers, Mrs PULLINGER (nee WELSH), wife of Sergeant Bernard PULLINGER (of 'Conyboro Lodge'), who was married last July.

WEDDING – A wedding took place last Saturday, between Miss Dorothy COX (21),[42] daughter of Mr & Mrs James Henry COX, Spithurst and

Richard CLARKE, of the Australian Contingent.[43] The best man was Mr George GARDNER and the bride was given away by her brother, Mr James COX, jun…

42 *Dorothy Ethel Annie COX was baptised at St.Bartholomew's, Spithurst on 14th June 1896 and lived with her parents at Mount Pleasant, Spithurst. Richard was still in the army in March 1920, when their daughter Peggy was baptised in the same church. The family emigrated to Victoria, Australia, where Dorothy died in 1984 (ref. Pat Broadhurst, Ancestry.co.uk).*

43 *Richard James CLARKE (31) was stationed at No. 4 Command Depot, Hurdcott (Convalescent) Camp on the Salisbury Plain at the time of his marriage (St.Mary's parish registers, ESRO: PAR 235/1/3/2).*

No.	When Married.	Name and Surname.	Age.	Condition.	Rank or Profession.	Residence at the Time of Marriage.	
470	December 22nd 1917.	Richard James Clark / Dorothy Ethel Anne Cox	31 / 21	Bachelor / Spinster	Soldier / —	Hurdcott Camp, Barford No. 4 Command. Spithurst, Barcombe.	Ro... / Ja...

Married in the _Parish Church_ according to the Rites and Ceremonies of the _Church of England_

This Marriage was solemnized between us, { _Richard James Clark_ / _Dorothy Ethel Annie Cox_ } in the Presence of us, { _James Henry Cox_ / _Fannie Funnell_ }

ABOVE: Marriage register entry at St. Mary's Church for Miss Dorothy COX and Richard CLARKE, of the "Australian Contingent" (ESRO: PAR 235/1/3/2).

ABOVE: 1918 'Souvenir de Belgique' – This embroidered silk postcard contained a "secret" pocket under the '1918,' in which the additional 'Best Remembrance' miniature card was concealed.

4ᵗʰ January - GOING TO FRANCE - It is announced that Miss Olive WALKER (of 'The Grange'), who has offered her services in the capacity of nurse, will shortly be going to France.[1]

WHIST DRIVE – On behalf of the Reading Room funds a successful drive was held on Thursday evening, the winners being: Miss WARNETT, Mrs CLARK, Mrs DAVIES, Mr FULLER, Mr GASSON and Mr HOLLOWAY.

HOME ON LEAVE - Sergeant J. PRATT, Army Veterinary Corps is home on 14 days leave.

NATIONAL DAY OF PRAYER – The day of Prayer and Thanksgiving was very earnestly observed in this parish. There were five services during the day – and each was well attended. At the 11 a.m. service in the Parish Church, the Barcombe Volunteers were present under Sergeant CARTER,[2] and presented a fine appearance… The services at St.Bartholomew's and the Mission Room were extremely well attended and of a very reverent and hearty nature. In the afternoon a united service was held in the schools, where many were unable to obtain a seat. The King's proclamation was read by Major GRANTHAM and the National Anthem sung…

SUNDAY SCHOOL TREAT - This happy gathering took place in the Motor House, Barcombe Place, and was an unqualified success. Many parents were present. The first part consisted of some highly amusing tableaux given by the clever family of Mr & Mrs RICHARDS and also Miss GRANTHAM… At the close the Rector voiced the thanks of all present for Lady GRANTHAM's kindness, and also for the clever performance of her grandchildren and daughter…

11ᵗʰ January - POTATO "BUTTER" – The Ministry of Food states that in view of the shortage of butter they have been carrying out experiments in order to find suitable and economical ways of eking out the available butter and margarine supplies by mixing in other food substances and so producing cheap and palatable substitutes. These experiments have shown that an excellent "potato butter," costing only about 5d. per lb. (or less if margarine is used) can easily be made in any household without special knowledge or apparatus…

FOUND DYING ON ROADSIDE – INQUEST AT BARCOMBE – Mr Vere Benson, East Sussex Coroner, held an inquiry at the 'Royal Oak' yesterday (Thursday) touching the death of a man

LEFT: 1918 Sixpence or "tanner."

---

1 Olive was the sister of Lieut.-Col. Frank WALKER, who was killed at Gallipoli in July 1916. Her sister Lilian had also volunteered to serve with the Red Cross the previous summer (www.redcross.org.uk).

2 Sergeant CARTER was also the village schoolmaster and scoutmaster.

known as Donovan, who was found on the roadside at Barcombe…

William HOBDEN of Spithurst, said that he was cycling last Monday evening, and just before reaching Clappers Bridge he saw deceased lying on the roadside. He dismounted and recognised the man as Paddy, who was working for witness's father… He loosened his collar and waist, then called on Mrs KING, who immediately went to the man's aid, and the police constable. Dr MACKWOOD of Newick, stated that he saw deceased on Wednesday evening… Death was due to loss of blood and heart failure. The jury returned a verdict of "Death from natural causes."

WAR TROPHIES – Few people are aware that there is a department of the British Expeditionary Force in France known as the inspectorship of War Trophies. One of its functions is the collection for the National War Museum of all objects of historical, romantic, or military interest which will serve to illustrate now and hereafter the intimate life of the Army in the field and in the air, and its particular exploits in battle. The bulk of the collection has been transported to London, and by the courtesy of the Director-General of the National War Museum, "The Strand Magazine" is enabled to describe and illustrate in its January number many of these objects…

ABOVE: Barcombe Parish Magazine, January 1918, bearing the Latin banner "In hoc signo vincemus," which translates as "In this sign we will conquer" (courtesy Anne Pearce).

18th January - FLOODS - The recent weather has been the cause of great floods in different districts, particularly Clappers Bridge, Longford and Barcombe Mills, the roads at certain periods being impassable.

NEAR AND YET SO FAR! - Even the most unpoetic Tommy longs to be at home, and nobody in the world knows the value of liberty like himself. Imagine rigid discipline for a long period and then suddenly to be told that you can have 14 days liberty - the very thing men are dying for! Thus it was with Gunner CLARK, Royal Garrison Artillery. He received leave and arrived in England on Wednesday, caught train for Lewes, but in some unexplainable manner was taken beyond his destination. He returned to Lewes, however, by another train and then proceeded to walk to Barcombe Mills. The night was

RIGHT: 'Where Bert is billeted in France' - a postcard of Fruges Watermill, Pas De Calais sent by Bert COLLINS to his family at home. The exact location has been scratched out by the military censor (courtesy Beryl Jackson).

dark and when near the dear old homestead he could hear the water rushing and surging across the road, so much so that he dare not attempt to ford such deep, rapid and threatening flood. He was obliged to turn back and wend his way to Ringmer, where he eventually enjoyed the welcome of a happy father.

19th January (*Bexhill-on-Sea Observer*) – **SMALL FURNISHED HOUSE** – (available) till April; sitting room, kitchen, scullery, 4 bedrooms, w.c., bathroom; five minutes from Barcombe Station; rent 25s. weekly – Apply Mr SPELLER, Barcombe.

25th January - FROM HOSPITAL - Sergeant John TAPP, whose home is at Spithurst, and who was the recipient of the Military Medal some while back, arrived home yesterday (Thursday) afternoon. He has been in hospital at Deal.

LORD ROBERT'S WORKSHOPS - Through the untiring energy of Mrs SINGLETON and her few helpers, the sum of £12.12s has been collected in the district on behalf of Lord Roberts' Huts. From the inception of the scheme, which is dear to the heart of the above mentioned lady, no less than £50 has been collected. Mrs SINGLETON has received notice that the £12.12s will be devoted entirely to the Sussex Workshops.

1st February – PALESTINE – Collections were made in the Churches and Mission Room on Sunday on behalf of the Relief Fund for Palestine and Syria. £12.13s.8d. was given.

COMMUNAL KITCHEN - A well-attended meeting was held in the Reading Room on Wednesday afternoon to discuss the question of starting a communal kitchen. The Rector presided supported by Mr F.J.CORNWELL (Vice-Chairman of the Parish Council) and many others. It was decided that a kitchen should be started. Mrs SINGLETON consented to undertake the management and Miss Muriel GRANTHAM to act as the Hon. Secretary and Treasurer. The Chairman pointed out the need of keeping before them the three 'P's' viz. No Pauperising; No Profiteering; No Patronising, and without class or distinction. Several present offered to be guarantors for certain sums, and at the close £10 was guaranteed, although it is felt that the movement should be self-supporting.[3]

15th February - ON LEAVE - Private HEMSLEY, whose home address is Dallas Lane, is at present home on leave.

CHILDREN'S WELFARE – An exceptionally large attendance of mothers with infants took place on Tuesday afternoon. The babies on this occasion were weighed, and the mothers enjoyed the usual hospitality.

3 *Plans to open the kitchen went ahead, with a later article saying that the kitchen was to open on Tuesday 20th February. A national, government-funded programme to combat wartime hunger began in May 1917, when Queen Mary opened the first "kitchen for all" on London's Westminster Bridge. In February 1918, the Ministry of Food instructed local authorities to set up "national kitchens" to provide a place in which "ordinary people in ordinary circumstances" could purchase a cheap, wholesome meal, during a period of food shortages (www.thegazette.co.uk).*

Date of		Cause of Discharge from Division or Ship	Character on 31st December, and on Final Discharge from the Service
Entry	Discharge		
11 Aug 15	1 Dec 15	Mis-statement as to age. R.M. Office memo	

LEFT: Bert COLLINS of Mount Pleasant, Spithurst, had originally enlisted in the Royal Marines on 11th August 1915, only to be discharged in December the same year due to a "mis-statement of age." At only 5 feet 2 ½ inches tall he appears to have become the mascot of his unit (service papers courtesy Beryl Jackson).

BARROW, Private Horace VERRALL and "Dodger" FUNNELL.

HONOURS - Lt. Col. A.C.R. SANDERS, son of Mrs SANDERS of 'Holmbush', recently received at the King's hands, the C.M.G. (Companion of the Order of St. Michael & St. George) and the D.S.O. (Distinguished Service Order). He has also been given the command of a Battalion on the Western Front, where has been for the last three years.

SCHOOL STOVE - On Tuesday East Sussex Education Committee decided that they would refund the Managers of Barcombe C. of E. School 95 per cent of £3.7s.3d which they paid for a second hand stove.

1st March - ON LEAVE - Driver P.FROST of the Army Service Corps, Mechanical Transport, son of Mr & Mrs FROST of Old Mill Farm, Crowborough and son-in-law of Mr & Mrs Herbert RANN of Mount Pleasant, Spithurst, is home on 14 days leave from the Western Front.

SALE BY AUCTION – At 'Wootton Cottage' – Messrs. J.R. Thornton & Co. have been favoured with instructions from Messrs. Gardner Bros. (quitting) to sell by auction on Thursday March 21st, 1918: 130 Head of Poultry, a Capital Pony, Poultry Appliances, and effects.

8th March - WHIST DRIVE – A drive, which was well attended, was held at the Reading Room last week on behalf of the local Volunteers.

ON LEAVE - Gunners B.COLLINS and Ernest

Ernest Nigel HURD, died of wounds 27th March 1918

Ernest was born in Barcombe on 27th October 1895, son of the village 'Bobby' P.C. Albert HURD and his wife Mary. He left the village the following year, when his father was posted to Forest Row and later to East Hoathly. Apprenticed as a motor engineer, he enlisted with the Royal Engineers in October 1914. He died in a Military Hospital at Rouen from wounds received in action on 25th March and was buried in the St. Sever Cemetery Extension, Rouen (source: de Ruvigny's *Roll of Honour*, vol.5, p.91).

RIGHT: Ernest's father, P.C. Albert E.HURD, Barcombe's 'Bobby' from 1894 to 1896.

22nd March - ANOTHER BARCOMBE MAN'S DEATH - The greatest sympathy is extended to Mrs STEVENS of 'Thatched Cottages', who has been notified by the Admiralty that her son Bombardier Henry STEVENS, Royal Marine Artillery, a member of the gun's crew serving on board the 'Clan MacPherson', has lost his life when the vessel was sunk by the enemy on the 4th instant. Mrs STEVENS, it will be remembered, had eight sons serving the colours, and this is the second son she has lost during the war, the first one, Leonard STEVENS, sacrificing his life last July.

HOME ON LEAVE - The following local men have been home on leave: Private Leonard CHATFIELD, Royal Sussex Regiment; Private B.COLLINS (just returned to his regiment); Bombardier Ernest STEVENS, and Private BLACKMAN of Spithurst.

AWAITING HIS COMMISSION - Sergeant George DAVIES, Royal Sussex Regiment, is at present home on leave, and awaiting his commission.

29th March - ON LEAVE - Seaman William FARENDEN.

19th April - BARCOMBE BUTCHER FOR THE ARMY – The National Service Representative sought withdrawal of the certificate of exemption which was held by Charles MUGGERIDGE,[4] aged 34 years, butcher, who had been

A **Profitable Pastime for WIVES**

The more we kill off our reserve stock of poultry, the worse becomes our national position and the only remedy is to INCREASE THE POULTRY POPULATION BY BREEDING MORE CHICKS. All classes of the community, in TOWN or COUNTRY, can take up this work with a certainty of making big profits, provided they make use of

HEARSON'S INCUBATOR

—the only incubator that hatches EVERY fertile egg.

English imports of eggs and poultry from foreign countries have been so much restricted by the war, that the demand now far exceeds the supply.

Interesting handbook "The Problem Solved" (104 pp. published at 1s.). Gratis and Post Free from:— Spratt's Patent Limited, 24-25, Fenchurch St., London, E.C.

ABOVE: Chick Breeding – "A Profitable Pastime for Wives."

placed in Grade 2. Applicant stated that he offered to enlist in the early stages of the war, and when he was informed that he would be passed for service he endeavoured to make arrangements in connection with his business, but was unable to do so. The application was granted.

SIX MONTH'S EXEMPTION GRANTED to Frank Albert SMITH,[5] aged 41 years, gardener, Barcombe Mills, who had been passed for sedentary duty.

10th May – BARCOMBE CLERK'S EXEMPTION - Three months' exemption was granted to Edward AVERY,[6] C3, aged 27 years, cashier, ledgers clerk, etc.

24th May – CONSCIENTIOUS OBJECTOR - A SOUTHOVER BAKER

– Before the East Sussex Appeal Tribunal, at Lewes, yesterday, Donald Richard CRUTTENDEN,[7] baker, aged 18 years, Grade 1, sought exemption on the ground of conscientious objection from combatant service.

Appellant said: 'I cannot shed human blood. Christ cannot fight for a place on earth, and I will not, because He has given Me a place in heaven. That is my country.' He added that he had been a conscientious objector for four or five years. He had

4 Charles MUGGERIDGE appears to have arrived in Barcombe c.1911, following his marriage to Daisy Doris ALLEN in the Brighton district. He rented an eight acre field (now part of the Recreation Ground) from the GRANTHAM estate, on which to graze his sheep, and is listed in the local trade directories as a butcher from 1912-1917. Following his military service he returned to the village as licensee of the "Royal Oak" from 1920-1933, with the telephone number of 'Barcombe 18.'

5 Frank Albert SMITH (1877-1947) lived all his life in Barcombe Mills. He was baptised at St. Mary's in 1877, the son of gardener William SMITH and his wife Ann. He followed his father's occupation, as did his son Fred. Frank lived at Garden Cottage, Barcombe Mills with his wife Mary Jane (nee FLEET) until his death in 1947. He is buried in St. Mary's churchyard.

6 Edward was the son of James and Lucy AVERY of 4 Gladstone Buildings, High Street, Barcombe. Born in Plumpton in 1890, he had been employed as a clerk to a timber merchants by 1911, while living with his parents in East Chiltington. During the war he moved to Barcombe with his parents.

7 Donald was born in Lewes, one of six children of William & Anne CRUTTENDEN of 61 High Street, Southover. He married Ellen PAUL in the Newhaven district in 1933, and died in Worcester in 1965.

been brought up in a family of Christians.

The Chairman, Major R.I. THORNTON: "That is a little hard on some of the rest of us." The National Service Representative, Major William Wilson GRANTHAM (of Balneath Manor): "It is, but conscientious objectors do not consider us." Appellant pointed out that there was no reason why, before the war started, he should state his conscientious objection.

The Chairman: "How old were you before the war started?" Appellant: "Fifteen years old." The Chairman: "Your opinions were fully formed when the war started?" Appellant: "Yes." Major GRANTHAM: "Are you ready to do ambulance work?" – "Yes."

"Are you ready to prevent the Germans killing your nearest and dearest? "I will leave that to the Lord..." After telling appellant that religion need not be introduced too much into the case, Major GRANTHAM asked appellant what he would do if Germans arrived at Southover and ill-treated his sisters.

ABOVE: Increase in Postage – The cost of sending a postcard inland doubled from ½d. to 1d. on 3rd June 1918.

Appellant: "I should count upon the Lord. He would give me grace. He has all the power."

The chairman pointed out that the Lord did not protect the women of Belgium.

Appellant was exempted from combatant service on the understanding that he would join the Royal Army Medical Corps.

7th June – A BARCOMBE ENCOUNTER

– SIGNALMAN BOUND OVER – There was a sequel, at Lewes Petty Sessions, on Tuesday, to a lively encounter which occurred at Barcombe on May 4th. James MORLEY, signalman of Culver Junction, was summoned for having assaulted Ernest HARRIOTT.[8] Complainant, living at 'Fir Tree Cottages', Cooksbridge, an estate labourer in the employ of Lord MONK BRETTON (of 'Conyboro'), gave evidence that defendant had threatened to "do for" witness because he had been with defendant's wife (Alice MORLEY).[9] Witness had denied that allegation. On May 4th, about 9p.m., defendant said he would settle with witness. He said "You have nothing to settle with me." After calling witness a liar defendant fixed him by the throat. Defendant said he would swing for witness or else "do time."

Cut out and keep this notice. Show it to everyone in your household.

Notes on Saving

No. 1.—How to save on Gas.

Do not light a burner until you need it for use.

Turn out the gas immediately when you have done with it.

Keep your burners and cooking utensils clean.

When boiling do not let the gas flare up round the sides of the pot or kettle ; turn the gas lower as soon as boiling point is reached.

Regulate oven flames to produce the right heat for your cooking.

Give early notice to the company of bad supply or defective stoves or fires.

Saving Gas means Saving Money.

Invest your Gas Savings in
War Savings Certificates

£1 for 15/6. £50 for £38 : 15 : 0. £500 for £387 : 10 : 0.

If you have not yet joined a War Savings Association, it is your patriotic duty to do so. Apply to the Secretary of your Local War Savings Committee, or write to the National War Savings Committee, Salisbury Square, London, E.C. 4.

Every Shilling saved and lent helps to win the War.

War Savings Certificates are a British Government Investment backed by all the wealth and power of the nation. Their purchase price is 15/6 each, and their value in 5 years' time £1 each—this is equivalent to compound interest at 5¼ per cent., free of Income Tax. You can get your money back in full at any time with any interest which is due. You can buy War Savings Certificates from any Money Order Post Office, Bank, or Shopkeeper acting as Official Agent.

ABOVE: NATIONAL WAR SAVINGS - 'Notes on Saving No. 1 - How to save on Gas.' One of a series of advertisements (the 'Swastika' was an ancient symbol of peace and good fortune, until adopted by the Nazi party prior to the Second World War).

Defendant – You are a false-speaking man.

William EDWARDS (55), farmer (of 'Gallybird Hall'), deposed that he was with complainant when defendant "took hold of him and shoved him about the road." Defendant used some very bad language.

8 At the time of this case, the complainant Ernest HARRIOTT (62) and his wife Maria (67) had been married for thirty six years and had three adult children.

9 The defendant James MORLEY (54) and his wife Alice (55) had been married for just over thirty years and had two adult children. Both defendant and complainant had been born in Barcombe, so are likely to have known each other for a long time.

Defendant stated that he said he would go to a field and settle the matter.

Witness – I did not hear that.

Frederick SHAW,[10] groom in the employ of Lord MONK BRETTON, said that there was some wild talk. He thought he had a little influence with both parties and he tried to use it.

Defendant – I did take hold of complainant. I told him I would come up to his field and settle the matter.

The Chairman, Mr Francis Barry WHITFELD (of Hamsey) – I wish you had settled it outside this court. Mr H.J. HILLMAN (representing complainant) – I asked defendant if he would apologise.

Defendant – I consider I have nothing to apologise for.

The Chairman – I suppose complainant is not in fear of his life?

Mr HILLMAN – I think he is. Defendant has hung about in the field at six o'clock in the morning.

Defendant – You do not think for a moment that I was going to commit murder?

In extenuation defendant pleaded that he had been in the service of the London, Brighton & South Coast Railway Company for forty years. He came to the court with a clean sheet. Defendant was bound over in the sum of £5 to be of good behaviour for six months, and he was ordered to pay 7s. costs.

21st June - WAR MEMORIALS - Is it necessary, or even desirable, that the character and form of memorials to those who fall in the fight for freedom should be decided now, before the fight is over? We ask the question because a number of communities in East Sussex are considering the question, and in some instances there is a considerable diversity of opinion as to the most suitable way of perpetuating the memory of the gallant dead. It seems to us that the matter cannot be satisfactorily settled if it is settled now. It may be taken for granted that every town and village will desire some permanent record of the sacrifice of its sons.[11] There will be a general wish for some memorial of a sacred character – the placing of some kind of feature in the Parish Church which will remind future generations that the heroes of to-day fought not for temporal gain or evanescent things, but for the eternal principles of righteousness and justice and for the sake of all that depends on Christian civilisation. A memorial of a more general and greater character will probably also be desired, but it is quite impossible to judge at the present moment what particular form it should assume.

While, therefore, there is no

10 *Frederick Harold SHAW was living at Conyboro Stables in 1917.*

11 *There were a small number of parishes (53 identified in 2013) in which all those who left to serve in the armed forces returned. They became known as "Thankful" or "Blessed" villages, a term popularised by Arthur Mee in his introductory volume to The King's England series of county guides (Enchanted Land, 1936). The only parish in Sussex to be able to make this claim is East Wittering.*

ABOVE: Bicycles were hard to come by during wartime due to the requirements of the Army. Rice Bros. emphasise this in their advertisement.

harm in starting subscription lists to-day, it would be a great mistake to fix and determine the particular nature of a memorial to be erected in circumstances which cannot be foreseen, and which might hamper the success of the efforts. This is a matter in which well-meaning leaders of local thought and anxious Committees should not tie their hands. The truth is that we do not know what the general and local conditions of life in England may be at the close of the war, and alas, we do not know how many names may yet have to be added to the sad and glorious Roll of Honour. It is conceivable that the nature of the Peace settlement may influence the minds of those who wish to set up local war memorials. When an astute person like Lord Mersey declares that it will be years after the war before we know which side has won, hasty action with regard to the determination of war memorials is to be deprecated.

Of one thing we may be

certain: that the period following the conclusion of peace will be a severely practical age in which nothing which is not useful will find a place. This will rule out suggestions for village crosses or obelisks, which, whatever their value as ornaments, do not serve any utilitarian purpose. The desire on the part of discharged men for clubs and recreation rooms where they can meet as old comrades in the great war points to the desirability of establishing a hall with club rooms in every village, where such an institution does not already exist. One Sussex village has already resolved on this form of memorial and it will probably have no reason to alter its decision. If agriculture is to be permanently restored, the social side of rural life must be developed. In this direction it should not be impossible to combine gratitude to the dead with a wish to improve the conditions of the living.

But we would still urge that the immediate adoption of a cut and dried plan as regards local war memorials is inadvisable. Many things may happen before the close of the war requiring a reconsideration of present day proposals, however excellent they may seem at the moment.

28th June - CRICKET A

match between Barcombe Boys & Newick Boys was played on Wednesday, the visitors winning by 25 runs. The display given by both sides was creditable, especially when the disadvantages of these days are taken in to account.

RECTOR'S SON MARRIED

– A quiet and pretty wedding took place by special licence at St. Anne's Church, Brighton on Saturday, when 2nd Lieut. Sydney Gelder FARRAR, Manchester Regiment, attached to the T.M.B. (Trench Mortar Battery?), son of the Rev. FARRAR, was married to Miss Matilda Agatha ("Millie") WOLVERSON, V.A.D., daughter of Dr. & Mrs WOLVERSON of Wolverhampton. Several of the bridegroom's military

Owen FUNNELL's Appeal to the Chailey Tribunal

This case serves as a good example of the staff on a country estate during wartime. He worked in the walled kitchen garden at Sutton Hall, living in an estate cottage, downhill from the "big house," at Longford.

The Tribunal minutes show that Owen's employer Miss Adela SHENSTONE appeared on his behalf to make the case for his exemption;

"Miss Shenstone said all the men had left except this man and her bailiff, aged 87, who had been on the estate 70 years. This man helped him in every possible way. The garden was over 2 acres and was cultivated for themselves. The surplus went to various houses and Hospitals at Eastbourne (1), Lewes (3) and Newick (1). Funnell's son, a boy of 14 was helping. This man was Kitchen gardener and Handy Man on the estate. The bailiff did the acc[ount]s." About 6 men employed on the estate; Bailiff, this man, gamekeeper, cowman. Boy and girl worked in the garden under this man. Estate about 22 acres, 3 cows."

(ESRO: DL/D/119/1).

Miss SHENSTONE was keen to emphasise that, "There was practically no pleasure garden" as this would have suggested that her gardener was involved in unproductive work. Temporary exemption was granted until 1st October, a decision which Capt. Selby ASH said "he should appeal." As the war ended just over six weeks after his exemption expired, it would appear that Miss SHENSTONE got her wish to retain Owen's services in her garden.

After the War and the death of the old bailiff, Owen took on that role while continuing to work as a gardener. He was still holding both of these positions when Canadian troops passed his home at 'The Lodge,' one of the gatehouses to Sutton Hall, to set up camp in the grounds during the Second World War. His employer, Miss SHENSTONE died in 1942 and he later moved to 'The Larches,' Spithurst, where he died in 1951, aged 78.

LEFT: Chailey Heritage - A soldier learns from a child resident. (From a photograph album entitled 'The book of Sir Robert Jones and his crippled children at The Heritage Craft Schools, Chailey.' ESRO: HB 131/118).

friends were present. The service, which was choral, was performed by the father of the bridegroom, assisted by the Rev. F.T.FREDERICHS, Rector of Acton Scott, Hereford…

5th July - BARCOMBE MAN'S RESPITE – CHAILEY TRIBUNAL – Exemption was claimed in the case of Owen FUNNELL, aged 47 years, Grade 1, kitchen gardener, Barcombe. It was stated that the man was employed in a kitchen garden which extended over two acres. Some of the surplus produce was sent to hospitals. The man also acted as assistant to the bailiff. Three months' exemption was allowed.

STOOLBALL - A stoolball match played at Balneath Manor, took place on Saturday between Major GRANTHAM's team and Wounded Convalescents from 'The Heritage', Chailey.[12] The Boys in blue won the match on the 1st innings.[13] Mrs KIMMINS made two brilliant catches. The teams were entertained to tea by Mrs GRANTHAM.

12th July - MISSING - We regret to hear that Private Claude ELDRIDGE of the Leicesters is officially reported as missing since May 27th.

AMERICAN'S OFFENCE - At Lewes Petty Sessions on Tuesday, Lawrence Arthur CARROLL was fined 10 shillings in respect of a breach of the Aliens' Restriction Order [14] at Barcombe. He had stated that he was of American nationality.[15] P.C.GOODSELL gave evidence.

26th July - AID FOR LEWES SHELTER – In aid of the funds of the Lewes Shelter, in connection with the Chichester Diocesan Purity Association,[16] a successful sale of work took place on Tuesday in the Church Hall, Southover… Stalls for useful and fancy articles, provisions, produce, baskets, etc., were in charge of the following ladies from the Lewes and Uckfield Rural Deaneries: … Barcombe: Miss SHENSTONE (of Sutton Hall), Miss MILLS and Miss WAGHORN.

2nd August - UNDRAWN BLINDS – Edwin PRATT[17] of 'Skylark Villa', pleaded guilty at Lewes on Tuesday to allowing an unobscured light to proceed from the premises at eleven p.m. on July 23rd. P.C.WILLARD stated the facts, and a fine of 5s. was imposed.

12 *The Chailey Heritage site was expanded with 'Kitchener Huts' for recuperating soldiers, built on the land of Major W.W.GRATHAM, Lord of the manor of Balneath.*

13 *A blue flannel uniform, which became known as 'Convalescent Blues,' was worn by those recuperating soldiers who were able to get out of bed. The jacket had a white lining and was worn with a red tie.*

14 *The 'Aliens Restriction Act' was passed by parliament the day after war was declared. It required foreign nationals to register with the police and imposed travel restrictions on them and their spouses, who automatically acquired their husband's nationality.*

15 *Mr CARROLL was born in New York in 1886. By the time of the above incident he was thirty-two, married and proprietor of the 'Riverside Hotel' (now the 'Anchor Inn'), Barcombe Mills. In August 1920 his son Gordon was born and he was fined £1 for riding a motor cycle in Uckfield without rear or near side lights (Sussex Express). Gordon was baptised at St. Mary's church on 21st November 1920 (ESRO: PAR 235/1/2/4).*

16 *The C.D.P.A. was founded in 1890 and undertook work with mothers and children, ran children's homes and arranged adoptions.*

17 *Edwin PRATT (1851-1952) was a taxidermist with a shop in Brighton, from where he was commissioned to prepare naturalistic dioramas of British birds for the Booth Museum. In his spare time he was an officer in Brighton's Boy's Brigade and in 1922 became Barcombe's scoutmaster, a post which he held for many years.*

CHAILEY TRIBUNAL – Six months' exemption was granted to Edward AVERY, aged 27 years, Grade 3, timber merchant's clerk and cashier.

9th August - DAY OF REMEMBRANCE - Sunday was fine, and consequently the congregations were large. There was an early celebration in the Village Mission Room, and the alms were given to the Prisoners of War (Sussex) Fund. The 11 a.m. service at the Parish Church was largely attended, the Barcombe Volunteers being present in strong force, under Corporal REECE.[18] The Rev. E.GRIFFITHS conducted the service and preached a thoughtful sermon on the subject of the day. In the afternoon a united service was held in the schools, which was largely attended by all denominations, the Rector presiding. Special addresses were given by Mr CROWTER and Mr G.LLOYD, and suitable lessons read by Major W.W.GRANTHAM and Mr F.J.CORNWELL. The collection (£5.7s.8d) was also handed to the Prisoners' Fund.

16th August - WEDDING - A wedding took place at the Parish Church on Thursday of last week, the contracting parties being Mr William Charles HOBDEN, only son of Mr George HOBDEN, Barcombe and Miss Alice Rose HEAD of 37 Haldane Road, Fulham.

A DOG'S EXEMPTION - For having kept a dog without a

---

18 *William Horton REECE (53) and his wife Christina lived at 'The Nest,' Spithurst.*

RICHARD'S NATIONAL HOME-MADE BREAD is guaranteed pure and made from the best Flour procurable, therefore easy of digestion and most nourishing. Try it of **S. B. RICHARDS, Baker & Confectioner,** Sole Agent in Barcombe for Dr. Allinson's Pure Whole=meal Bread. Special Value in Wedding Cakes, from 7/6. Noted for Self Rising Flour, Currant and Milk Bread. **CORN, COAL, COKE AND WOOD MERCHANT.**

ABOVE: S.B.RICHARDS advertisement from the January 1918 Parish Magazine (courtesy Anne Pearce).

license and for having failed to see that the animal was provided with a prescribed collar at Barcombe, Sydney B.RICHARDS was fined 8s.6d at Lewes Petty Sessions on Tuesday. P.C.WILLARD stated that the defendant admitted on July 30th that he had no licence for a sheep dog, but said he was not sure whether he had applied for an exemption for the animal. He also mentioned that the dog had broken its collar.

23rd August - ON LEAVE - Corporal E.DIPLOCK, Gloucesters, son of Mr & Mrs DIPLOCK, 'Mount Pleasant Farm', is home on leave. DIPLOCK, who has been serving in Italy, joined the Army four months after the outbreak of the war.

ANGLING - Good sport is to be had at Barcombe Mills. Fine specimens of various kinds of fish have recently been hooked, and last Monday, Mr WILSON, a well-known angler of Brighton, caught a trout, which turned the scale at 4lbs. On Saturday he caught one of the same specie weighing 2½ lbs.

CHILD'S SUDDEN DEATH - The death took place suddenly on Tuesday of Elsie Kathleen JONES, aged seven, at the residence of her parents Private & Mrs W.H.JONES, ('Rose Cottage', School Hill) Barcombe. She passed away within twenty-four hours of her illness. Deceased was the fifth daughter, and great sympathy is extended to the parents and family. The father, who is in the Army Veterinary Corps, was only home on leave a week ago…

CRICKET - Barcombe Boys v Newick Boys (return match on the Recreation Ground)… Barcombe XI again proving the stronger, winning this time by 39 runs. For the winners, the batting of G.FROST, C.BODLE and P.RANN deserves mention, as does the bowling of the first named and G.FUNNELL…

SCHOOLMASTER – The vacancy (at Ringmer) has been filled by the appointment of Mr CARTER, headmaster of the Barcombe Schools. There were about forty applicants for the post. Mr CARTER, who has been at Barcombe for two years… will take up his duties at Ringmer immediately after the engagement of a new master for Barcombe.

6th September - FIRE CHARGES - The charges of the Lewes Fire Brigade for their services at the stack fire at 'Avery's Farm', Barcombe on August 22nd, amounted to £26.9s.9d.

BARCOMBE SCHOOL – HOME EGG PRODUCING STATION REPORT - An intensive house was built and six pullets were bought at a cost of £2.5s. The pullets' egg production was as follows:- December 7 eggs, January 37, February 121, March 141, April 134, May 137, June 116, July 101 - Total 794. One pullet died in June. The other birds were sold on August 1st for £2.15s. Altogether 31 children received instruction in keeping poultry on this system and were entirely responsible for the management of the birds… after a substantial amount has been put by for the purchase of next season's birds, a balance remains. This has been proportionately divided amongst the 26 children at present on the school register, viz: 13 children receive 2s.6d., 2 receive 2s., 11 receive 1s.6d. (a total of £2.12s. was paid out, leaving £3.15s. in hand). Wm J.CARTER, Headmaster.

20th September - A PRISONER - Private Claude ELDRIDGE, son of Mrs ELDRIDGE, 'Croft Ham Cottage' is a prisoner in Germany.

27th September - A BARCOMBE LOSS - On

RIGHT: Sgt. William PYNE, best man (left), in the uniform of the Royal Flying Corps (forerunner of the 'R.A.F.') and his brother, bridegroom, Sgt. Thomas Henry PYNE, Royal Garrison Artillery (courtesy Muriel Pyne).

19 *For his biography, see vol.2.*

Tuesday Mrs SANDERS, of 'Holmbush', Barcombe, received official intelligence by wire that her son Brigadier-General Arthur Richard Careless SANDERS, C.M.G., D.S.O., Royal Engineers, had been killed in France on September 20th.[19]

CHURCH FARM – TO BE SOLD BY AUCTION – About 5 minutes' walk from Barcombe Mills Station and 3½ miles from Lewes. Messrs. J.R. Thornton & Co. have been favoured with instructions from the Executors of the late Mr J.PORTER (having let the farm).

DECORATIONS - Capt. Alec M. BROOKSBANK, North Stafford Regiment, has been awarded the Military Cross and Major Robert G. BROWNE, Manchester Regiment, the D.S.O.

WEDDING – A pretty wedding took place at St.Mary's on Saturday, the Rector officiating. The contracting parties were Miss May DAY, youngest daughter of Mr & Mrs George DAY of 'Willow Cottage' and Sergeant Thomas Henry PYNE, R.G.A. eldest son of Mr & Mrs Thomas PYNE of 112 Frensham Road, Southsea. The best man Sergeant William PYNE, R.A.F., brother of the bridegroom. The bride, who was given away by her father,

ABOVE: "Perfectly delightful here" – We "sit in the garden nearly all day, both enjoying rest." A message from a guest at 'Spithurst (boarding) House' in late September 1918.

was attired in a grey serge coat frock, wore a grey satin hat with tulle trimming, and a gold pendant and chain, a gift of the bridegroom. The presents included a silver butter dish from the scholars and teachers of the Mission Hall Sunday School, of which the bride had been a teacher.

HARVEST FESTIVAL - This festival was held on Sunday at St.Mary's Church, also at St. Bartholomew's, Spithurst... The collections, £6.6s.2d. at Barcombe, and £3.17s.10d. at Spithurst, were given to the Missions for Seamen and the Royal Agricultural Benevolent Institution. Three bags of vegetables were despatched to the Grand Fleet and mine sweepers, three dozen eggs to the wounded soldiers in France and fruit to the School Hill Hospital, Lewes.

AFTER TEN DAYS - Mr & Mrs Hart VERCOE of Banks Farm, Barcombe have received official intelligence that their youngest son, Private William Hart VERCOE, Royal West Kent Regiment, having been missing since October 1917, must be considered as dead. Private VERCOE joined the Hussars in May of last year and was transferred to the Royal West Kent Regiment. He had only been in France ten days when he was announced as missing.

4th October - INSPECTOR'S REPORT - Visit of 28th June to Barcombe C of E school "was satisfactory in the highest degree."

STRIKERS CONDEMNED AT LEWES – The Lewes Branch of the National Union of Railwaymen have passed a resolution deprecating the action of the strikers… The Branch have also intimated that they consider the employment

LEFT: Chailey R.D.C. Tribunal members of 7th October 1918 included Barcombe farmer Mr Francis J. CORNWELL and nurseryman Edwin W. BUNNEY (Chailey R.D.C. Tribunal minute book, ESRO: DL/D/119/1).

The Spanish Flu Pandemic – THE FACTS

1. Also known as the "three-day fever" or "grippe" it became known as "Spanish Flu" after it was first reported in the Spanish press.

2. Spanish Flu was a "pandemic" (a worldwide "epidemic").

3. It was an airborne virus, often spread by returning troops.

4. Estimates as to the number of people who died worldwide during the outbreak vary between 20 and 50 million (there were 15 to 20 million deaths due to the War).

5. 228,000 people died of Spanish Flu in Britain.

by certain Railway Companies of women in signal boxes and as guards constitutes a menace to the travelling public.

MAJOR GRANTHAM AND STOOLBALL - A match was played on Saturday between Major Grantham's team and that connected with the Princess Louise Military Orthopaedic Hospital, and resulted in the former being beaten by 56. After the match Lady GRANTHAM entertained the two teams to tea. Mrs KIMMINS presented Major GRANTHAM with a stoolball bat, which was handsomely painted with the arms of the Royal Sussex Regiment and which was from the Princess Louise Military Orthopaedic Hospital as a memento of his revival of the game of stoolball for the benefit of wounded officers and men.

SPANISH "FLU" AND GAS – Wonderful Cures by the Old Remedy – Veno's Lightning Cough Cure – Lance-Corporal A.J. Turner of the 4th Essex Regiment writes: "I was in hospital, and lying opposite me was a sergeant in the R.F.A., who had been badly gassed. It was awful to hear him coughing night and day. Knowing Veno's, I told him of it, and from the first dose all the fellows in the ward noticed a decrease in his coughing. In six weeks that same man proceeded to a convalescent hospital in my company. Two men and myself affected with Spanish "Flu" found instantaneous relief in Veno's."

THE REVIVAL OF STOOLBALL

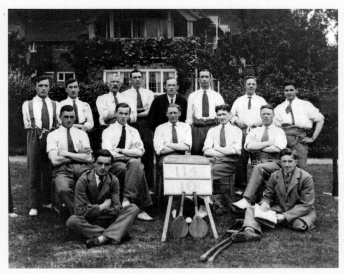

ABOVE: Stoolball team from the Princess Louise Orthopaedic Ward, Chailey (ESRO: HB 131/7).

Major W.W.GRANTHAM writes: "Thanks to the publicity given to my letter in your columns early this autumn, I am glad to be able to report that the revival of the very ancient game of Stoolball (it was played by, Among others, Robert Dudley, Earl of Leicester, in the reign of Queen Elizabeth at Wootton Hill) appears to have met with great success all over the country. I received applications for about 200 copies of the rules from nearly every county in England, from Scotland, Ireland, and Wales, from France and from Canada; copies of the rule have also been sent to India, Australia, and Japan. Thanks to the generosity of a few friends, I have been able to send stoolball wickets and bats to convalescent hospitals in France and Canada. On several Saturdays in each of the last six months I have arranged 16 matches in seven different parts of Sussex for officers and men from 12 convalescent hospitals, the last match of the year being played on Boxing Day in the Royal Pavilion Grounds at Brighton, and on no occasion has the weather or the condition of the ground prevented a match taking place. I am glad to say that no wounded officer or man (whether with only one arm or one leg) has received any damage in playing the game. I am hoping to be able to arrange another match (by kind permission of the Committee) at Lord's and also one at the Oval early in the Spring."

290 1918
October 7. I entered upon my duties as Headmaster here to-day
Adrian P. Bishop. Int B.A.
Very good attendance 120. On Roll 128.
E. Bourdillon, Esq. kindly welcomed me.

LEFT: Adrian P. BISHOP, the new headmaster, makes his first entry in the School log book on 7th October 1918 (courtesy Barcombe School).

PARISH COUNCIL – A meeting took place on Saturday, when there were present: Maj. W.W.GRANTHAM (Chairman), Mr F.J.CORNWELL, Mr W.H.REECE, Mr G.T.HAWKINS, and Mr S.B.RICHARDS. It was resolved on the motion of Mr REECE, seconded by Mr CORNWELL, that in the opinion of the Parish Council some extra cottage accommodation will be required in Barcombe, and the Council suggested that the Railway Company and the local authorities should provide cottages for all the workmen employed by them. A special parish meeting was also held, Major GRANTHAM being in the chair, and among those present were: Lord MONK BRETTON and Lady GRANTHAM. The chairman proposed, and Lord MONK BRETTON seconded, that a sincere vote of sympathy be conveyed to Mrs SANDERS of 'Holmbush', in the sad loss of her son. After considerable discussion it was resolved, on the motion of Rev. H.W.FARRAR, "This meeting wishes to record its opinion that the future of agriculture in Barcombe will require more cottages for the agriculture workers."

11th October – CHAILEY TRIBUNAL – William SAVAGE, aged 18 years, Grade 2, gardener in the employ of Lord MONK BRETTON, Cooksbridge, was granted three months' exemption on the understanding that he would continue to instruct allotment holders and that he would serve as an emergency special constable.

Frank Albert SMITH, aged 41 years, Grade 3, gardener, Barcombe Mills, was exempted for six months.

25th October - ON LEAVE - Private Harry COTTINGHAM[20] is at present home on leave.

ABOVE: Mr. Adrian Percy BISHOP, the new headmaster c.1920 (Barcombe W.I. scrapbook, ESRO: WI 112-11, p.163).

20 Harry COTTINGHAM (37) was a cowman, boarding with Charles PETTIT at 'Sole Cottage' before the war. His home in 1918 was 'Place Cottage', part of the 'home farm' of the Barcombe Place estate.

BELOW: School Log Book – entry recording the closure of the School from 23rd October to 18th November due to the Spanish Flu pandemic. The closure coincided with the declaration of the Armistice, which the headmaster Mr BISHOP appears to have added at a later date (courtesy Barcombe School).

Oct 23. The Rector announced to assembled school the closure till Nov. 4.

Nov 3. The S.M.O. ordered continuance of closure till Nov. 18 owing to the spread of the epidemic.

Nov. 11. Armistice declared. Last shot of the Great War fired.

Nov. 18. Re-opened with 115 on books. 100 present a.m. 101 p.m. Fires lighted for the first time. To economise fuel, they were well stoked at 8·30 a.m. & again at noon for the last time in the day. Blackberry money divided among the children. Returned blackberry tub to Newick Factory.

SCHOOL CLOSED - Owing to the influenza epidemic it has been deemed wise to close the school for a time.

WHIST DRIVE - A whist drive was held at the Reading room on Thursday evening of last week. It was arranged by members of the Stoolball Committee and the proceeds were in aid of the wounded. Seventeen tables were engaged.

ABOVE: Albert FUNNELL, Private FUNNELL's brother, in postman's uniform. In 1911 he was living with his sister Kate and brother-in-law Arthur OSMOND in the High Street (courtesy Helen Dick).

KILLED IN ACTION - Private George, Canadian Contingent, has we regret to state, been killed at the Front. The news was received by his brother, Mr Albert FUNNELL, a local postman.

RED CROSS DAY - The event was held yesterday (Thursday) and the lady workers were:Miss Muriel GRANTHAM, Miss GRAHAM-JONES, Miss BOURDILLON, Mrs GROSS, Miss Nancy FUNNELL, Mrs Harry FUNNELL, Mrs HAFFENDEN, Miss Lena HOLLOWAY, Miss WORSLEY and Mrs HOLTER.

DEATH OF MISS MABLE GLADYS ELDRIDGE – The second daughter of Private & Mrs William ELDRIDGE of 'Croft Ham Cottage', Barcombe, passed away at 21 Brunswick Square, Brighton on Monday. She contracted influenza, and finally developed acute pneumonia, to which she succumbed after ten days' illness.

DEATH OF MRS LUCY MANKTELOW of (9) Gladstone Cottages, aged 73, leaves 7 daughters & 4 sons.

DEATH AND FUNERAL OF MR VERRALL - At the advanced age of 87 years, Mr Alfred VERRALL passed away last Friday at 'The Lodge,' Sutton Hall, Spithurst. He had been employed on the Sutton Hall Estate for the lengthy period of over sixty years, first by Captain Richardson and afterwards by the late Mr F.S.SHENSTONE. Deceased, who was a native of Barcombe, leaves two daughters and one son. The funeral took place on Tuesday, the Rector, officiating.

1st November – PROCEEDS – Red Cross Day, which was held on Thursday of last week, realised £15.10s.6d.

KILLED – Private Bert WELSH, son of Mr & Mrs James WELSH, has been killed. He leaves a widow and three children in Canada.[21]

COMPENSATION – At Lewes County Court on Monday, Mrs Mary Ann RANN made an application under the Workmen's Compensation Act concerning a sum of £185 which had been paid by Major W.W.GRATHAM in respect of the loss of her husband,[22] who died as the result of an accident on a farm. His Honour Judge MACKARNESS decided that applicant should be allowed £4 per month for three years, and that £15 should be invested for the benefit of her son Ernest.

GALLANT CONDUCT – Private Selby REED,[23] Royal Sussex Regt., son of Mr & Mrs Henry REED of 'Crink Cottages,' has received the following tribute from the General commanding a division: "I have read with great pleasure the report of your Regimental Commander, also Brigade Commander, regarding your gallant conduct and devotion to duty in the field on the 8th and 9th August at Mallard Wood."

---

21 For his biography, see vol. 2.

22 Herbert RANN worked as a threshing engine stoker (1901 census) and was living at 'Mount Pleasant Cottages,' Spithurst when he was killed in an accident in October 1918. He was buried in St. Mary's churchyard, aged 53. Neither the accident nor his funeral appear to have been reported in the Sussex Express. His widow Mary Ann died six years later and was buried with him.

23 Selby REED, a farm labourer, was born in Barcombe in 1889.

ABOVE: William James CARTER (in the background) as headmaster at Ringmer School, where he introduced school meals (Ringmer History Study Group, photograph S4).

pleasure and encouragement, while it also confirms the high opinion held by us of your labours for Education in the best sense of the word. We wish you and Mrs CARTER many years of happiness in your new sphere at Ringmer."

5th November – PRISONER OF WAR – 19663 Arthur MEWETT, Royal Sussex Regiment[25] (*Weekly Casualty List*).

8th November - DEATH OF MAJOR BROWNE - We regret to state that Mrs BROWNE, who resides between Barcombe and Spithurst,[26] has received intelligence that her husband, Major R. Geoffrey BROWNE, D.S.O. Manchester Regiment, died on November 1st in hospital abroad, from the effects of influenza.

POPULARITY – The school managers have addressed a letter to Mr CARTER,[24] who has vacated the mastership of Barcombe Schools for a similar position at Ringmer, in the following terms: "We cannot allow you to leave without expressing our very sincere regret at your departure, and we are extremely sorry to lose your valued work in our schools and parish. The latest report of H.M. School Inspector must have given you and your colleagues the greatest possible

24 William CARTER's move to neighbouring Ringmer did not go smoothly. Soon after he arrived he caught "Spanish Flu." He recovered, but in December his wife Eveline (33) died during the birth of the couple's third child (ref. Anna Kay, One of the Best Schools in the District). The baby survived and was named Eveline after her mother. Now a widower with three children, William still found time after his school duties to form Ringmer scout troop and become their first Scoutmaster, a position he held until leaving the village in 1923 to take up a teaching job in Norfolk (Bexhill-on-Sea Observer, 23rd June 1923).

25 Arthur MEWETT served successively in the 3rd, 9th, 12th, 13th and 17th Battalions of the Royal Sussex Regiment during the Great War (R.S.R. Medal Roll, T.N.A: WO 329/1252 p.1801).

26 Mrs Louisa Harrison BROWNE lived at 'The Firs' (1918 Electoral Register, ESRO: C/C 70/203).

BELOW: Medical Treatment Card for Bernard PULLINGER of 'Handlye Farm' who was invalided from the 5th Battalion, R.S.R. on 31st October 1918 with wounds to the "head, arm, chest hand, etc." His treatment depended on his membership of the Cooksbridge & Hamsey branch of the "M.D." Friendly Society, paid for from his Army wages. He was to present this card to "the doctor or approved institution" of his choice (courtesy Anne Pearce).

Arthur MEWETT – A Barcombe man's experience of the Great War

Arthur and his parents moved from the coastal village of East Blatchington to 'Old Thatch,' ('Tudor Cottages'), Barcombe Cross in 1915. He spent most of his life with working horses. The following extract is taken from his biography, *An Uneducated Gentleman, Arthur Andrew Mewett 1897-1989*, written by his daughter, Mrs Joyce Knight (courtesy Jo Newman).

ABOVE: Arthur MEWETT (with his fiancé Mabel TURNER, inset top left) in his Khaki drill uniform while serving in the Middle East with the 17th Battalion, R.S.R. after the war (courtesy Jo Newman).

"In 1916, then aged 19, father got his wish and joined the infantry. Mr CORNWELL did all he could to keep him, but father was determined to go. He trained at Chichester and Newhaven Fort, and was soon posted overseas. He seldom spoke of his wartime experience, but he saw bitter fighting and trench warfare at its worst. Of the 12th Battalion of the Sussex Regiment (to which he belonged) only 74 able bodied men survived out of nearly 700. So many perished because they were ordered to perform impossible tasks, such as crossing swamps on duck boards with a full pack. He remembered vividly being so terrified in the heat of battle that one's hair literally stood on end. Food was scarce, but worst of all was the mud and frost in the trenches: the men's clothes froze to them and Father had frostbitten toes making it hardly possible to walk. He was on his way to a first aid post when he got a lift on a trolley load of corpses.

Due to the decimation of the 12th Battalion, the survivors were transferred to the 13th. He did once say he hated what happened to the horses; so many were killed or maimed, and they had to work so hard pulling gun carriages and other transport…

On 22nd March 1918 after fifteen months at Ypres and Passchendaele, both father and George KEMP (another Barcombe man) were captured whilst helping a wounded comrade. They then spent eight months as P.o.W's until the end of the war helping construct a rail road. The food was terrible, mostly black bread, and their guards didn't fare much better. At the time of the armistice the guards got drunk and the two men escaped, and found their way back to the British lines.

After a while they were sent to Turkey and Palestine because of unrest there. They did many guard duties in Jerusalem on the Mount of Olives and also in the Garden of Gethsemane. This period of his life he did talk about."

Arthur and Mabel married at St.Mary's Church in 1922 and settled at 9 Weald View.

WOMEN'S INSTITUTE

– A meeting was held at the Reading Room on Wednesday afternoon (6th November) for the purpose of forming a Women's Institute. It was decided that Lady GRANTHAM should act as President, Mrs OZANNE as Secretary,[27] and Miss GRANTHAM as treasurer.

MISSING - Inhabitants of Barcombe are much concerned as to the whereabouts of Miss WALKER, a lady who was staying with Miss BIGGINS, 'The Cottage,' Barcombe. It is stated that she is an Australian, and has been studying for the purpose of undertaking missionary work. She seemed in good health when she last left 'The Cottage', and her disappearance is a mystery.

15th November – BARCOMBE'S THANKSGIVING

– This village with over 175 men serving was deeply moved on Monday. The village was gay

BELOW: The minutes of the inaugural meeting of Barcombe W.I. held on 6th November 1918, "To consider the advisability of starting a branch of the Women's Institute." (ESRO: WI 112/2/1).

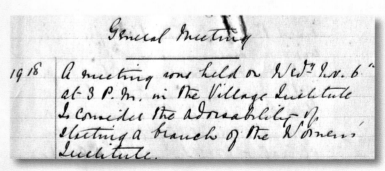

Armistice Day – Monday 11th November 1918

Surprisingly, the *Sussex Express* published four days after the Armistice was announced carried no front page headlines celebrating the end of the Great War. Instead, the newspaper carried the usual columns of text advertisements and auctioneers' announcements, the revenue from which would have supported the print run. The first mention of the cessation of hostilities, the most newsworthy story since the outbreak of war over four years earlier, appeared on page three and describes the initial scepticism, followed by relief when the news reached the nearby town of Uckfield:

ARMISTICE DAY - JOY AT UCKFIELD – The good news that the Armistice had been signed by the enemy was received on Monday morning, and spread rapidly throughout the town and district. At first its receipt did not provoke a great deal of visible enthusiasm, the feeling apparently uppermost in most minds being, "Thank God it has come at last." Needless to say, there was a certain amount of excitement, and while the news remained but rumour there was considerable hesitation in accepting it as fact, but an official intimation in the Post Office soon allayed the fears of the doubters. Then faces already light with anticipation were wreathed with joyous smiles, and it was only a matter of moments for the preliminary preparations of the celebration of Joy Day…

The residents of Barcombe appeared less reticent to believe the news and celebrate.

with bunting and flags. Bells were rung amidst every sign of rejoicing. In the evening a largely attended service was held in the village Mission Room, which was packed to the door. The Rector, presided, and was supported by those representing both church and chapel. A resolution was passed to the effect that one of the conditions of peace should be that no German prisoners be returned to Germany until every prisoner in Germany had been safely returned to this country.

27 Mrs Louisa OZANNE moved to 'Woodside' with her husband and son towards the end of 1918.

RIGHT: 'Peace Brings Him Back…' – An idealistic view of a young 'Tommy' reunited with his elderly mother. The process of demobilisation could take up to a year, with the early volunteers and men with valuable industrial skills being released first. Last to be released were the young conscripts of 1918 like the one featured in this Fred Spurgin illustration (Art & Humour Publishing Co. Ltd., London, Peace Series No.1036).

PEACE BRINGS HIM BACK TO YOU!

INQUEST AT BARCOMBE

– Mr G. Vere BENSON, East Sussex Coroner, held an inquest at the Royal Oak Inn, on Tuesday evening, concerning the death of Irene Muriel WALKER, aged 40 years, whose body was found in the river on Sunday morning.

Deceased's sister, Vera WALKER, who resides at Campden, Gloucester, stated that she was not surprised when informed that her sister had been suffering from a nervous breakdown, as she had previously suffered from the same complaint.

Margaret TURQUAND of Spithurst, said that deceased had been staying with her. For long periods she would sit doing nothing, and hardly ever spoke. She missed deceased on the morning of November 4th. P.C. WILLARD stated that he recovered the body from the river, and round the neck found weights of 14lbs., 7lbs,

and 4lbs. The jury returned a verdict of "Suicide whilst of unsound mind."

22nd November – THANKSGIVING SERVICES – Sunday (17th) was observed as a day of thanksgiving. The Volunteers, Women Land Workers and Boy Scouts attended the Parish Church. The service was conducted by the Rector, the Rev. Herbert W. FARRAR, assisted by the Rev. E.C. GRAHAM-JONES. Major GRANTHAM read the special lessons. The Rector gave a short address appropriate to the occasion, and read out the twenty-five names of those who had made the supreme sacrifice.[28] This

was followed by the hymn, "For all the Saints," and the service closed with the National Anthem, sung in unison with fine effect. The collection, amounting to £5.17s., was given to the Red Cross.

BELOW: NOTES ON SAVING - No.4. Tips include: "mashed potatoes can be used instead of suet for boiled puddings and instead of lard for pastry."

Cut out and keep this notice. Show it to everyone in your household.

Notes on Saving.—No. 4.

How to Save in the Kitchen.

Never waste good pieces of meat, fish, cooked potatoes, cooked rice or vegetables. Make them into rissoles, fish-cakes, soup, potato-croquettes or other savoury dishes.

Mashed potatoes can be used instead of suet for boiled puddings—instead of lard for pastry.

Don't fill the kettle when you only need a cupful of hot water; don't use the stove when a gas-ring will suffice.

A pinch of carbonate of soda in sour fruit lessens the amount of sugar required.

Egg-shells clean enamel; lemon rinds remove stains from the hands, and from brass and copper; tea-leaves clean bottles and lay dust.

Saving Waste means Saving Money.

Invest your Savings in
War Savings Certificates

£1 for 15/6.   £50 for £38:15:0.   £500 for £387:10:0.

If you have not yet joined a War Savings Association, it is your patriotic duty to do so. Apply to the Secretary of your Local War Savings Committee, or write to the National War Savings Committee, Salisbury Square, London, E.C. 4.

Every Shilling saved and lent helps to win the War.

NATIONAL WAR SAVINGS

War Savings Certificates are a British Government Investment backed by all the wealth and power of the nation. Their purchase price is 15/6 each, and their value in 5 years' time £1 each—this is equivalent to compound interest at 5½ per cent., free of Income Tax.

You can get your money back in full at any time with any interest which is due.

You can buy War Savings Certificates from any Money Order Post Office, Bank, or Shopkeeper acting as Official Agent.

---

28 *In the Parish Magazine of December 1918, the Rector also acknowledges, "all those who were 'broken in our wars' – the wounded, the blinded, the prisoners, and the sick."*

A united service was held in the Schools in the afternoon, when there was a large and representative gathering. The Rector conducted the service, and was supported by Mr CORNWELL, Mr LLOYD, Mr HEWETT and Mr SIGGS. Suitable hymns were sung and addresses given. The collection amounted to £5. The total sum given during the day, including St.Bartholomew's, Spithurst and the Mission Room, was £14.9s.8d., all of which was given to the Red Cross. Barcombe supplied 176 men for the Colours, and, as stated above, 25 sacrificed their lives.[29] Their names are: George Edward AMER, William BANKS, Alfred George BOTTING, Frederick Charles BOTTING, Robert Geoffrey BROWN, George Henry BUCKWELL, Herbert Abraham COLLINS, Frederick DAY, Frederick EDWARDS, Herbert Ronald FARRAR, Frederick GRANTHAM, Hugo Frederick GRANTHAM, William HAWKINS, Frederick

---

Frederick William HEASMAN

Gunner, Royal Garrison Artillery,
died 25th November 1918, aged 23.

It is with sorrow, pain and reluctance that we trespass upon the loss sustained by the death of this bright, happy soldier – just as it were in the "eleventh hour" of the war! One of the first to join up – and having gone through it all – then to fall through illness just at the close – adds a touch of tragedy to the pathos. To his widowed mother and her family we respectfully offer our heartfelt sympathy and prayers.

He is commemorated on both Barcombe and Hamsey's war memorials.

(Barcombe Parish Magazine, January 1919)

William KIRBY, Ernest KING, Frederick KING, James KING, Cecil Hugh PECKHAM, Charles William PECKHAM, Charles Herbert PRICE, Charles David REYNOLDS,[30] Arthur Richard Careless SANDERS, Frederick SAUNDERS, Henry STEVENS, Leonard Howard STEVENS and Arthur PLAYER.[31]

5th December (*Western Mail,*

Cardiff) – **DEATH** – LEWIS MATTHEW RICHARDS, J.P.[32] – On the 30th ult., at 16 Sloane Gardens, London, aged 57. Funeral Thursday, 5th inst., at Barcombe.

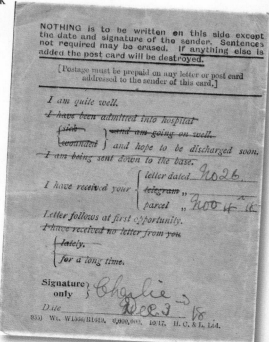

RIGHT: Men of Few Words – Field Service Post Cards were used by servicemen to send quick messages home without the need for a censor to check what they had written. This one was sent by "Charlie" to Miss Smith in London on 3rd December 1918.

---

29 *Further names would be added to this list over the following months.*

30 *See notes on Charles David REYNOLDS in May 1916. His name does not appear on Barcombe's war memorial.*

31 *This is the first mention of Arthur PLAYER., whose name, as it appears at the end of an otherwise alphabetical list, was probably a late inclusion by a relative of his who moved into the parish, or of a former resident of the parish who had sent news of the death to the Rector.*

32 *Lewis RICHARDS was the son-in-law of Sir William & Lady Emma GRANTHAM of Barcombe Place. He had married Gertrude Elizabeth GRANTHAM at St. George's, Hanover Square, London in 1899.*

6th December – JIBBING HORSE'S ANTICS – BARCOMBE BUTCHER SUED – WARRANTY DISPUTE – At Lewes County Court on Monday, before Judge MACKARNESS, the Southern Counties Dairies Co. Ltd. claimed £29.2s. from Charles MUGGERIDGE, butcher, as damages for breach of warranty in respect of a horse.

Frederick PARSONS, Sackville Road, Hove, Chairman of the Directors of the plaintiff Company, said that on May 29th at Barcombe defendant showed him the horse and some harness. Witness explained that he wanted a horse for a milk business at Southampton. Defendant stated that the horse was "the very thing," and he strongly recommended it. Witness replied "I am quite satisfied with your warranty, and I shall not examine the horse at all." Defendant gave a warranty to the effect that the horse was quiet to ride and drive, sound, and all right in every way. Witness had never before had such a warranty. He went for a drive a couple of miles behind the horse, which apparently travelled properly, but he remembered, after trouble began, how careful defendant was in handling the horse. Witness agreed, subject to the warranty, to buy the horse for £40, and some harness for £7. Defendant spoke about having to go into the Army, and as witness sympathised, he agreed to give a cheque promptly. On June

21at the horse was sent from Hove to Southampton.

HORSE WHICH WOULD NOT MOVE – Witness could scarcely believe the statement when he was told that the horse was a jibber,[33] but it would not move when it was tried at Hove. He had had several jibbers, but never one like the horse in question. On June 27th the animal was sold at Haywards Heath Market for 19 guineas…

Joshua ROSE, employed by the plaintiff Company at Southampton, deposed that on the day following its arrival at Southampton he tried the horse, with the harness and bit which came from Barcombe in a two-wheeled milk float. The animal refused to move, though it was tested for five days. On the sixth day the animal went about a mile in a milk chariot on a delivery journey, but witness had to fetch the horse back, as it refused to go any further…

NO JIBBING AT BARCOMBE – Other evidence was to the effect that while the horse was at Barcombe it never displayed any tendency to jib…

In giving judgement for the plaintiffs for the amount claimed, his Honour remarked that he had come to the conclusion that defendant

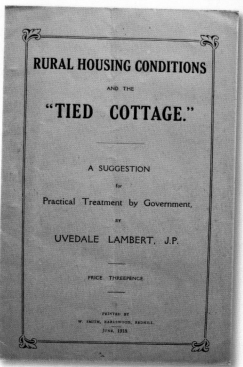

ABOVE: Rural Housing – A matter of concern for tenants and landlords alike. This pamphlet, published in June 1918, was bought by parish council member F.J.CORNWELL (courtesy the Cornwell family).

provided a warranty on insufficient grounds. He knew that the horse was required for the milk business which plaintiffs were carrying on… Unless the animal was a jibber there was only one explanation: that there was blundering on the part of plaintiff's men. The Court could not act upon that unless there was some evidence to support it…

7th December– HOUSING ACCOMMODATION – This meeting was held on Saturday,

---

33 A horse that jibs, i.e. refuses or stops short.

December 7th, at 3.30. p.m., in the Mission Room. The chair was taken by Major W.W. GRANTHAM, Chairman of the Parish Council… The need of more cottages was emphasized by all the speakers. The very important point was raised that such cottages should be built

near the roads so that children should get to school the more easily and with less chance of wet feet, also the better approach for tradesmen's carts, and above all the feeling of being less isolated from the life of the community. These and other points were dwelt upon and it was then decided to build a number of cottages for the increasing demands of agriculture and for the use of those engaged in the service of the community. The question of a good site and a supply of water was left to a committee who would be in touch with the agents of the sites and so build by mutual arrangement… (*Parish Magazine*)

17th December (*Weekly Casualty List*) – **PRISONER OF WAR RELEASED** - The following soldier who was a prisoner of war in Germany, has been released and has arrived in England. Gunner

ABOVE: Primroses & Violets on Raphael Tuck & Sons "Oilette" postcard no. 9611, first published in 1918.

166335 F. AVERY, Royal Garrison Artillery.[34]

20th December – WAR MEMORIAL –A large and representative meeting was held on Monday evening in the Village Mission Room, Major W.W.GRANTHAM, Chairman of the Parish Council, occupying the chair. He was supported by the Vice-Chairman, Mr F.J.CORNWELL and other members of the Council and many residents. The resolution that a war memorial be raised in the parish to those who had fallen and those who had served was carried. This was proposed by Mr CORNWELL, seconded by Mr MOON and supported by the Rector, Lord MONK BRETTON, Lady GRANTHAM, Miss SHENSTONE, Rev. GRAHAM-JONES, Mr

BOURDILLON, Lieutenant W. Ivor GRANTHAM spoke as to the different forms the memorial might take. It was decided to form a large and representative Committee to consider the various suggestions made and report at another meeting. There was an earnest wish expressed that some of the men serving should be asked to join the Committee.

28th December (*Yorkshire Evening Post*) - Violets and primroses have been gathered in a garden at Barcombe, Sussex.

34 Frank AVERY was the son of James & Lucy AVERY of 4 Gladstone Buildings. He had originally enlisted in the Royal Field Artillery in December 1915, served in England until June 1917 when his unit was sent to France. He was reported missing on 30th November 1917, but declared a Prisoner of War two weeks later (TNA: WO 363).

ABOVE: PEACE 1919 – An embroidered postcard showing a handshake in front of Allied flags.

10th January - GERMAN GUN - By kind permission of the authorities a German Gun has been temporarily lent to the village of Barcombe and was taken by road under the superintendence of Lieutenant Ivor GRANTHAM on Thursday of last week. By a curious coincidence six German prisoners left Barcombe Place Farm just as the gun was being placed in position. Among others to welcome it were Lady and Miss GRANTHAM, Mr & Mrs GROSS, Rev. FARRAR, Rev. C.E. & Miss GRAHAM-JONES, Mr & Mrs SPELLER, Mr & Mrs BISHOP (schoolmaster), Mr E.KING, Mr FIGG, Mr G.RHODES,

RIGHT: Captured – A 15 pound German Gun, on display outside Brighton Town Hall at the beginning of the war, photograph by E.Hilton.

THE PEACE

The effects of the war on the people of Barcombe did not end with the signing of the Armistice on 11th November 1918. After the euphoria of the long-awaited victory and the first peace-time Christmas for five years, there was now the wait for news of the return of loved ones who had been away on service or in captivity. There were also local jobs and housing to consider.

While the country awaited the conclusion of the peace negotiations. The Barcombe War Memorial Committee, along with parish meetings, continued to consider the ways in which the returning men should be honoured and how those who had died during the war would be commemorated.

Between February and April 1919 very few Barcombe articles appeared in the *Sussex Express*, suggesting that there was no parish correspondent for this period. In their place, general articles have been transcribed, reflecting local post-war concerns, including those of other parishes and the nearby county town of Lewes.

Mr JESSUP, Mr PECKHAM, Cadet DAVIS, Boy Scouts etc. The Rector proposed a vote of thanks to Major GRANTHAM for obtaining and carrying out the arrangements for its loan. The Major, in reply, referred to the gun having been captured just before the Armistice was signed by the New Zealand Division; he appealed to the good sense of the boys in the village not to treat it as the other guns had been treated elsewhere and said it partly depended on that

15 lb German Gun captured from the Germans. 3in Calibre. Placed in front of Town Hall, Brighton 20th Nov 1915. Phot. E.Hilton

205

how long the gun was allowed to remain in their midst. The National Anthem closed the proceedings.

31st January - SANDHURST SUCCESS - The Sandhurst passing out list contains the name of Leslie Burgoyne MATTHEWS to be 2nd Lieutenant in the Royal Sussex Regiment. This officer is the son of Mr & Mrs H. Burgoyne MATTHEWS of 'Skylark Villa', Barcombe and of Brighton.

21st February – UCKFIELD VOLUNTEERS – READY BUT NOT WANTED – … It was barely a matter of moments after that dread day in August 1914, when many of the men of Uckfield and district who could not join the Colours, determined to "do their bit" at home. Some were young men but many were well into middle age and they have conscientiously stuck to their self-imposed though patriotic task… And now with the happy prospect of Peace in the early future it appears that the Volunteers are to be disbanded and their equipment, with the exception of the uniform, has already been called in…

WOMEN LAND WORKERS – FUTURE IN EAST SUSSEX – The future work of the East Sussex Women's War Agricultural Committee was referred to at a meeting of the Committee at Lewes on Wednesday.

The Countess of Chichester, who presided, said the Committee were asked to carry

ABOVE: Cottages For Workers – Weald View, Barcombe, was not built until 1926/27 and named by Chailey R.D.C. in August 1927 (photograph courtesy Betty King).

on their work until further notice. It was vitally important that the Committee should keep alive some form of women's organisation from which assistance could be drawn in the event of any definite and active development of rural life. In connection with the agricultural side of the work of the County Council is was probable that shortly there would be many matters on which women should have opportunities of giving their views. If there was no representative body of women to which application could be made by the authorities it would be exceedingly difficult to obtain the right women to do work for which they might be needed.

28th February - THE HOMECOMING - Demobilisation is causing a difference in the appearance of the towns and villages in East Sussex. Less is seen of the man in khaki. Daily there are greetings between old friends who joyfully impart the mutual information that they have 'got their ticket' and are indulging in the luxury of leave before returning to their civil employment again. Some are already back in their old positions, others are filling those of men who can never return, and again there are numerous cases of men who have found Army life to their liking and have signed on for extended service. Steadily but surely the old order of things is being resumed, but with a difference. Better conditions of labour already exist and a healthier and happier condition of the worker prevails. It will not be long before the pre-war institutions such as local bands of music are re-organised and the depleted ranks of the Volunteer Fire Brigade will be replenished by the restoration of the younger men who have perforce had to engage in a fight more than with fires.

GARDEN VILLAGES - CHAILEY DISTRICT PLANS

COTTAGES FOR WORKERS – Visions of garden villages in various parishes in the Chailey Rural District are conjured up by the outlines of a housing scheme for their area which is being formulated by the C.R.D.C., who are so active respecting this matter that they will be prepared to meet as they arise problems which will have to be faced.

NEARLY 300 HOUSES ASKED FOR – After allowance was made for the houses which private owners so far have signified their willingness to erect the investigations by means of parish meetings showed that it was calculated that 266 new houses should be built, and these do not include 23 which the Council which to provide for their employees. It is estimated that the cottages will cost about £700 per pair…

VILLAGE COLONIES – The Council, who will endeavour to adapt the scheme, or parts of it, to the needs of different localities, will be guided by the expressions of opinion which were obtained at parish meetings. From these it was ascertained that the idea of village colonies was generally favoured in cases where several houses were required. Under such an arrangement houses will usually be built in pairs and will have plenty of garden space, though they will not be so far apart that the occupants will be isolated form their neighbours, the trading and social centres of the villages, or any institutions at which educational and other facilities may be obtained.

The type of new cottage which is generally approved is one in which there will be a commodious living room, about 15 feet long and 12 feet wide, and three bedrooms, with modern conveniences which can be provided without an exorbitant outlay. One improvement which will be welcomed is an arrangement by which the scullery will be situated so that steam will not penetrate to the living room. It is hoped that in each of the new cottages a bath will be provided, either in the scullery with a water supply from the copper, or on some other part of the premises.

RETAINING THE SUSSEX COTTAGE – The Council are fully in sympathy with the view that from an architectural stand-point the beauty of the Sussex cottage is an asset, and that, while in their housing scheme they must consider comfort in the interior of the dwellings and provide adequate modern convenience, the old style and character of the Sussex cottage should as far as possible form the basis of the exterior design. It is recognised that the countryside will be defaced if the houses which are erected under the new scheme are merely boxes of bricks which will not harmonise with rural surroundings.

March (*Parish Magazine*) – **THANKS** – The want of space prevents our printing two grateful letters of "Thanks" per Miss SHENTSONE: 1) From the Belgian Relief Committee to our school children and their Mistress, Miss ATKINS, for so many gifts of useful clothing made by our children for the little sufferers in that devastated land; 2) The other is a delightful letter from Mr Noble, in charge of the work for our brave sailors at Newhaven, expressing very grateful thanks for gifts of "woollies" for the mine sweepers and others sailing from that Port."

28th March - RATES FOR WAR MEMORIALS - … The proposals for local war memorials vary in different districts. The provision of certain kinds of memorials (e.g., in the form of recreation grounds, or buildings to serve as libraries or hospitals) is ordinarily within the statutory powers of a local authority, who would in such cases, no doubt proceed in the usual manner, but in other cases (e.g., where the provision of social clubs, or village halls, or institutions is suggested) sanction by the Board under the Local Authorities (Expenses) Act of 1887 would generally be required to authorise the expenditure.

April (*Parish Magazine*) – **BARCOME & HAMSEY NURSING ASSOCIATION** – SPECIAL NOTICE – After the first week of April no new

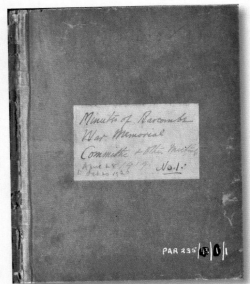

ABOVE: Barcombe War Memorial Committee minute book April 1919 – October 1920 (ESRO: PAR 235/43/1/1).

subscriptions will be received, and non-subscribers needing the nurse must pay for each visit.

PARISH COUNCIL - …A communication was read from Mr E.BOURDILLON, suggesting a better water supply, public wash houses and public slaughter-houses for Barcombe.

JAMES H.COX – In the death of James COX we have lost a valued bell ringer and a good parishioner. He was not spared to ring the "Peace" we are all longing for.[1]

18th April - FRAMFIELD'S MIGHTY DEAD - PAROCHIAL (WAR) MEMORIAL DEDICATED - The next year or two will see many memorials dedicated

---

1 *James Henry COX was buried in St. Mary's churchyard on 10th April 1919, aged 43.*

to the memory of the men who laid down their lives in the great war, and the first of these services, so far as the eastern end of Sussex is concerned, took place at Framfield on Sunday evening. The memorial is of pure white marble, and of very elegant design, and is suitable inscribed, but in view of the number of the fallen it has been very wisely decided to have them inscribed on a tablet inside the church and this will be done as soon as circumstances permit.

25th April - PRISONER OF WAR'S DEATH - Mr & Mrs ELDRIDGE, 'Croft Ham Cottage', have received official news from the German Red Cross that their son, Private Claude ELDRIDGE, died on October 13th, 1918 in a hospital at Novzen, France. Deceased went out on April 1st and was taken prisoner on May 27th 1918. No news was heard

BELOW: The Committee, named on the first page of the minute book.

of him until he wrote a letter which his mother received on 12th September and which he had written in July. This was the only communication. Private Eldridge had been working behind the lines since he was taken prisoner, and was not taken to Germany.

2nd May - WAR MEMORIAL MEETING – A well-attended meeting was held on Monday in the Mission Room. Major W.W. GRANTHAM took the chair and was supported by members of the Parish Council and leading residents, including

BELOW: Barcombe War Memorial – The printed notice announcing the outcome of the recent public meetings and the name of the Hon. Treasurer of the fund (ESRO: PAR 235/43/1/4).

> ## 'Red Triangle Club'
>
> The Red Triangle, symbol of the Y.M.C.A. became synonymous with the 'Clubs' they provided behind the lines in France. They were somewhere for off-duty servicemen to find light refreshment, a newspaper, notepaper and a warm and dry place in which to write a letter home. In Britain 'Red Triangle Huts' were set up near major London stations where, "Throngs of men would arrive… fresh from the front line in France with the mud of the trenches still on them, with steel helmets tied behind their backs and with rifles still in hand… they would flock to the huts while waiting for the trains..." (Sir J.A.Hammerton, quoted on www.worldwar1postcards.com)

BARCOMBE WAR MEMORIAL.

In reference to the above Memorial the following resolutions have been carried at successive Public Meetings of the Parishioners.

"That a War Memorial be carried out in Barcombe, in Memory of those who have fallen, and in thankful recognition of the courage and constancy shown by all who have served."

"That a Memorial to those who have fallen be placed in the Church or Churchyard, at a cost not exceeding £220, which sum shall be a first charge on the Memorial Fund, and that the main Memorial be in the form of a Parish Hall."

The Executive Committee appointed to carry out these resolutions has decided that the special Memorial to the fallen shall be placed in the Churchyard, the final resting-place for Parishioners of all Denominations.

The main Memorial, covering the whole of the original resolution, is naturally postponed until a certain amount of the Fund is raised and the cost of building is more normal.

The Hall, with possible future additions, is intended to be the Home of the Intellectual and Social activities of the Parish; thus rendering fruitful the Peace for which our men have died and helping to brighten the lives of their comrades who have returned.

The scope of the Memorial depends upon the support given by all members of the Parish, and the Committee earnestly appeal for your generous support.

A Committee has been appointed to undertake the collection of Funds, and Mr. E. Bourdillon has been appointed Hon. Treasurer.

EAST SUSSEX
PAR 235/43/1/4
RECORD OFFICE

Lord MONK BRETTON, Lady GRANTHAM, Miss SHENSTONE, the Rev. GRAHAM-JONES, Col. BICKNELL and others. The first business was the appointment of an Hon. Secretary. After an appeal for offers, the Rector consented to do the work.[2] Correspondence was read with reference to a Y.M.C.A. hut as part memorial. Mr E.BOURDILLON proposed and the Rev. GRAHAM-JONES seconded the following resolution: "That a permanent public hall be erected in Barcombe as a war memorial." Colonel BICKNELL spoke as to the probable cost of such a building. Lord MONK BRETTON dwelt upon the memorial being one which would directly commemorate the great sacrifice made by the fallen, and also as one worthy of those who had served. The Rector spoke on the same lines, and quoted the words: "A cross for sacrifice and a stone for remembrance." Mr FURNIVAL[3] proposed, and Miss SHENSTONE seconded. "That a permanent monument be erected and a branch of the Red Triangle Club be formed to carry out the object." This was lost. After further suggestions by Mr CORNWELL and seconded by Mr VERCOE, "That an obelisk, or other

---

2 The committee minutes (written by the Rector) suggest that he was reluctant to take on the role of secretary, but consented to do so after no one volunteered. He noted "that he might find himself opposed to what was decided upon, and so was to be free to resign the work to others." (PAR 235/43/1/1).

3 Osmer Gordon FUNRNIVAL (33) a schoolmaster and his wife Johanna had moved to 'Fernhill' from Ealing, West London.

suitable monument be erected at Barcombe, as a first charge upon the war memorial fund, and that a permanent memorial hall be erected in Barcombe to carry out the objects of the resolution carried at the first public meeting." This resolution then became the substantive motion, and was carried nem. con.[4] A warm vote of thanks to the Chairman and the singing of the National Anthem concluded the proceedings.

May (*Parish Magazine*)
BARCOMBE COUNTRY PRODUCE SOCIETY – A

general meeting of the Society took place on May 8th at Barcombe Schools. A very satisfactory report of the year's work was read, much pleasure being expressed at the increase of members (from 18 to 90) also of business…It was decided that a Show should be held early in September when it is hoped there will be a large number of entries.

9th May – FRAMFIELD's MEMORIAL HALL – Just

now, when collections for the provision of war memorials are daily to be met, a very surprising fact has established itself. The proposed memorials are all of

ABOVE: Sergt. Charles SAYERS, one of two men chosen to represent the demobilised servicemen on the War Memorial committee. Identified as 'no.53' in the July 'Peace Celebrations' group photograph (ESRO:WI 112/1/1 p.169).

them of a more or less useful and suitable kind and some of them are of a very elaborate nature, their cost running well over four figures. And herein comes the surprise. Committees approved the undertakings being well aware that the squire and a few other wealthy residents will subscribe handsomely, but they altogether under-estimated the giving inclinations of the remainder of the parish… It cannot be said that these people are mean, nor are they too poor

to give, but they have heard of a handsome heading to the list and much as they would like the memorial, say to themselves complacently enough, "The funds are coming in well, and little will be wanted from me." At Framfield it was stated at a meeting of the Memorial Committee that of about £1,500 required for the erection and endowment of a Parish Hall, £1,041 had been subscribed. The meeting was delighted. But it had a shock when told that of the sum mentioned £1,005 represented the gifts of 5 persons and that the remainder of the parish had contributed only £36. And yet Framfield badly wants that hall, and will be sorely disappointed if it is not theirs.

16th May - WAR MEMORIAL COMMITTEE

- This Committee met on Saturday evening. Lord MONK BRETTON presided in the absence of the Chairman, Major GRANTHAM, who wrote apologising for absence. The business chiefly consisted in the appointment of a sub-committee to consider the

---

4 *"nem. con." (with no one dissenting) unanimously.*

5 *Stanley Clement LLOYD (33) worked as a surveyor for West Sussex County Council, living at 'Gallybird' with his parents, Gerard, a gun maker and Annie, along with a live-in domestic servant.*

6 *Charles SAYERS, a bricklayer's labourer before the war, was born in Barcombe in 1886. He lived at Mount Pleasant with his widowed mother Julia COLLINS, uncle Benjamin and half-brothers Benjamin and Bert COLLINS (ref. 1911 census).*

Mr. Lloyd and Sergt. Charles Sayers, as representing the de-mobilized men – (the Rector as Secretary pro Tem) – and that this Sub: Committee be appointed to consider and report as to the Style, Position, and cost of the Monument and the proposed inscription thereon –

W.W. Grantham

19. VI. 19.

Monk Bretton

ABOVE: Demobilised men were to be represented on the War Memorial Committee by Mr LLOYD [5] and Sergt. Charles SAYERS.[6] Minutes of the meeting of Saturday 10th May signed later by Major GRANTHAM and Lord MONK BRETTON (PAR 235/43/1/1).

Barcombe Cross, Barcombe, Sussex.

ABOVE: Proposed War Memorial Site – The committee proposed this prominent position in the middle of the crossroads at the end of the village High Street (postcard by Arthur Homewood of Burgess Hill for sale by S.B.RICHARDS whose shop overlooked the site).

question of a site, the cost and inscription for a War Memorial monument for the fallen. The Hon. Secretary (the Rector) was asked to obtain from different firms such information and the meeting was adjourned.

23rd May - WAR MEMORIAL – Mr CORNWELL told the Chailey Rural District Council at their last meeting that it had been decided to erect a memorial for Barcombe village in the centre of the triangular space at the bottom of Barcombe street and he had been asked to apply for the sanction of the Council to

RIGHT: The High Street option - Miss SHENSTONE and Mrs PULLINGER's proposal recorded in the Rector's minutes of the meeting of 19th June 1919 (PAR 235/43/1/1).

the proposal. He explained that there was plenty of room for the memorial at this spot, and

it would not be an obstruction to the traffic. Mr PICKARD suggested that accidents might occur if it was not provided with a light at nights. The request was granted, subject to the approval of Highways Surveyor, plans of the proposed memorial to be approved by the Council before it was erected.

LEWES WAR MEMORIAL - The erection of a memorial on the School Hill site at a cost not exceeding £2,000, was approved at a public meeting held in the Town Hall last night… The design of the memorial is to be open to

19: June 19

A meeting of the Sub-Committee was held on June 19: 1919, 3-20 pm. When all the members were present —

Many Views, Plans, & Sketches of War Memorials were shewn by members of the Committee.

After due consideration —

Miss Shenstone proposed & Mr. Pullinger seconded that "A Cornish Cross, with Circlet, be erected at the" "Barcombe Village Cross roads, provided that" "permission for the same be obtained from the" "Authorities" — as an amendment —

Mr. Lloyd proposed and Mr. Charles Sayers seconded that "the War Memorial be in the form of an Obelisk" For 3 — against 6 —

A Second amendment was proposed by Mr. Cornwell Seconded by Major Grantham — That a granite structure, similar to the design prepared Mr. Bridgman of Lewes, be placed in the village — For 4 — against 4 — upon which the Mrs amendment chairman voting the gave the casting vote — upon this Amendment being put as the Substantive Motion, the same result followed — Mr. Cornwell and the Rector were asked to meet

LEFT: Signing the Treaty – Allied officers stand on chairs and tables to get a better view of the signing of the Treaty at 15.50 on 28th June 1919.

competition, and a premium of 50 guineas will be awarded for the one accepted… It should be in harmony with its surroundings and the ancient traditions of the historic town of Lewes, and the fullest

advantage must be taken of the ideal site which it is to occupy. Space must be provided for the inscription of about 300 names.

Mr A.M.PONTING moved as an amendment that the scheme be not proceeded with

unless a public convenience was provided underneath it. Councillor W.T.FOWLER seconded. The Mayor sarcastically remarked that perhaps somebody would go to the other extreme, and propose an aeroplane station on the top…

4th July – SIGNING THE PEACE TREATY – How Lewes WELCOMED THE NEWS – Lewes burst into bunting on receipt of the news that the Peace Treaty had been signed on Saturday.

With the official celebrations fixed for a month hence, there was nothing in the nature of a proclamation, and the event was not marked by any civic display

June 28th – The Treaty of Versailles

Signed in the Hall of Mirrors at the Palace of Versailles, the Treaty set out the peace terms which officially marked the end of the Great War. A formal state of war between the two sides having remained for seven months after the Armistice of November 1918.

The American public however, were opposed to the treaty, mainly because of the "League of Nations" that would be created. As a result, the United States did not formally end its involvement in the war until the Knox–Porter Resolution was signed in 1921.

After the Treaty of Versailles, further treaties with Austria, Hungary, Bulgaria, and the Ottoman Empire were signed. However, the negotiation of the last of these treaties was followed by the Turkish War of Independence, postponing a final peace treaty between the Allies and the newly formed Republic of Turkey until 24 July 1923.

As a result of the time taken to negotiate these treaties some war memorials date the end of the war as 1918, while others say 1919.

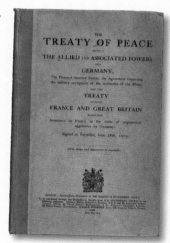

ABOVE: The Treaty of Peace, signed at Versailles.

ABOVE: 'Sutton Hall,' where the W.I. held one of their "summer gatherings." Postcard by Bliss of Lansdown Place, next to the 'Lansdown Arms,' Lewes (Mike Green collection).

or oratory… It is claimed that the first flag to be hoisted in the town was at the County Hall. Run up at 3.45 p.m., it apparently acted as a signal for

BELOW: Peace Celebrations – The Programme, as recorded by schoolmaster Mr BISHOP in the School Magazine (courtesy Barcombe School).

the rest of the inhabitants, and the main thoroughfares were soon gay with the British and Allied national emblems…

But it was reserved for the evening to see the impromptu rejoicings reach their climax. High-street became packed with exulting humanity, amongst which khaki was by no means absent. The old Lewes Town Band took advantage of the occasion to make a welcome re-appearance. When it was stated that the band has contributed no fewer than 18 members to the Forces, it will be readily seen that in themselves the musicians were evidence that happier times had arrived…

8th July (*Parish Magazine*)
WOMEN'S INSTITUTE – One of the summer gatherings took place at 'Sutton Hall', when the members were most kindly entertained by Miss SHENSTONE. Great interest was aroused by a lecture on the art of "Slipper making" by the Lady MONK BRETTON. Clever, thrifty and very ingeniously, the whole process was revealed and greatly appreciated…

11th July - PEACE THANKSGIVING SERVICES

– The services throughout the parish were extremely well attended. At the morning service at the Parish Church, members of the Parish Council attended. The Chairman, Major GRANTHAM, read the first lesson and the Vice-Chairman, Mr F.J.CORNWELL the second lesson. The Rector conducted the service and preached an appropriate sermon. The forms of Prayer were used and special hymns sung, amongst them Kipling's "Lest we forget" was given with fine effect.[7]

A united service was held on the Recreation Ground in the afternoon, over which the Rector presided, when excellent addresses were given and suitable hymns sung. The collections throughout the Parish amounted to over £20 and were divided between the Blinded Soldiers and the Widows and Orphans of Sailors.

25th July – BARCOMBE PEACE CELEBRATIONS

– The village was en fete on Saturday (19th July), and the Peace rejoicings were unmistakable. The day began with a cricket match, Soldiers v. Civvies, and the soldiers won. Then followed an invitation to dinner, when over 100 soldiers were entertained in a style which was as generous at is was possible to make it, which was greatly appreciated by the men. Lady GRANTHAM kindly lent her motor house to the Committee for this purpose…

Later on the men were photographed. Then followed a fancy dress parade through the village, which was clever and original. The sports for children came next, with over 28 events. The public tea was given to over 500 adults and children; in fact, to the whole parish. This too, was most successful, and was followed by sports for the adults. The rain came on later, but the resources of the Committee were not yet exhausted, for by the help of many willing hands a concert platform was erected in the large tent, kindly lent by Mr KING, of the 'Royal Oak', and an excellent programme followed, lasting three hours…

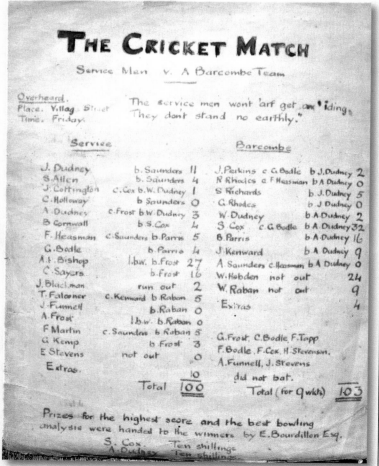

ABOVE: The Cricket Match – Service Men vs. A Barcombe Team. No sentiment was spared for the servicemen, someone was overheard saying; "The service men won't 'arf get an 'iding. They don't stand no earthly" (courtesy Barcombe School).

---

7 *The phrase 'Lest we forget' was popularised by Rudyard Kipling in his Christian poem 'Recessional' in 1897. This was later taken up as a hymn. Kipling, who moved to 'Batemans,' Burwash (about 20 miles east of Barcombe) in 1902, lost his son 'Jack' during the War.*

BARCOMBE PEACE CELEBRATIONS
19th JULY 1919.

"Honour to whom honour."

The Inhabitants of Barcombe Parish request the pleasure of your Company at

A DINNER

On SATURDAY, 19th, JULY 1919, at 1 p.m.,
on the occasion of
THE PEACE REJOICINGS,
to honour those who have served in the Great War, 1914-1919.

If you can be present, please reply by return of post on the enclosed card, and kindly bring knife, fork, spoon and glass

ABOVE: The Fancy Dress Procession – Group photograph and the prize winners. The best decorated house prize was won by Mrs HEASMAN of Grange Road (courtesy Barcombe School).

LEFT: An invitation to the Peace Celebration Dinner held at Barcombe Place. Attendees were asked to bring their own knife, fork, spoon and glass (ESRO: WI 112/1/1, p.133).

FROM ONE WHO COULD NOT BE PRESENT

Crink Cottage,
Barcombe Mills
July 17, 1919

Dear Sir,

Let me thank you for the kind invitation to the dinner on Saturday for the men of His Majesty's Forces, but having to return to my unit in Germany to day shall not be able to attend. I am very pleased by the way the inhabitants of Barcombe, as well as the Committee, is making the men their first consideration. I wish that the dinner as well as the proceedings during the remainder of the day will be a great success.

Yours truly,

S.CLARK

Gunr. S.Clark, 168454,
119 Heavy Battery, R.G.A., Germany

No.	Event	Class	Prize winners
1	100 yards	A Boys	G.Farenden A King H.Verrall
2	100 yards	A Girls	M.Diplock E.Manktelow I.Rann
3	Egg + Spoon	B Boys	J.Osmond C.Hobden D.Richards
4	Ditto	B Girls	D.Jenner H.Eldridge D.Jones
5	Potato Relay	C Boys	R.Richards F.Faulconer R.Maughan
6	100 yards	B Boys	F.Heasman S.Brooke C.Skinner
7	100 yards	B Girls	D.Jones A.Verrall D.Jenner
8	Obstacle Race	A Boys	S.King H.Verrall B.Eldridge
9	Ditto	B Boys	W.Barrow C.Durrant F.Faulconer
10	Egg + Spoon	C Boys	R.Maughan C.Tapp E.Skinner
11	Ditto	C Girls	— Honess — Honess M.Scrase
12	Sack Race	A Boys	H.Verrall S.Richards J.Kemp
13	Ditto	B+C Boys	D.Richards G.Constable J.Osmond
14	Wheelbarrow Race	A Boys	G.Farenden A King H.Verrall / S.Richards R.Skinner
15	Three-legged Race	A Girls	I.Rann A.Heasman F.Clarke / C.Tapp D.Willard E.Warnett
16	Ditto	B Girls	R.Kimblee D.Jones D.Jenner / E.Fuller A.Verrall E.Scrase
17	Ditto	A Boys	G.Farenden H.Verrall S.King / J.Richards E.Willard S.Farenden
18	Ditto	B Boys	J.Osmond R.Skinner W.Barrow / D.Richards S.Tapp C.Hobden
19	Thread Needle	A Boys + Girls	H.Verrall S.Richards S.Farenden / I.Rann E.Manktelow E.Beck
20	High Jump	A Boys	S.Richards G.Farenden H.Verrall
21	Ditto	B Boys	J.Poupart D.Richards J.Osmond
22	Egg + Spoon	A Boys	H.Verrall G.Farenden S.Richards
23	Ditto	A Girls	E.Manktelow A.Argent D.Willard
24	Leap Frog Race	A Boys	S.Richards D.Richards E.Willard S.Farenden
25	Slow Bicycle	A Boys	W.Faulconer J.Kemp / S.King E.Willard
26	Toddlers Race	Infants	K.Cox E.Heasman W.Hatto
27	Tug of War	A+B Girls	E.Harmer's Team
28	Tug of War	A+B Boys	E.Willard's Team

Our Concert

AFTER TEA, rain kept us under the tent, while the adults heroically finished their sports. Willing hands speedily erected a stage with piano complete, and the children opened the concert with singing competitions, the judging being left to the audience.

Song	"Won't you buy?"
Song	"The Woods + Groves"
Solo	"How beautiful are the feet of them—"
Round	"Hark! the bonny Christchurch bells"
Solo	"Good Morning"
Song	"Farewell"

A SPECIAL WORD of PRAISE must be given to George Farenden for his solo, so feelingly rendered, and also to little Violet Osmond who sang her little song quite unaccompanied. The list of prize-winners is as follows:—

Winners. Irene Rann, Flora Clarke, Ethel Warnett.

Ethel Manktelow, Elsie Beck, Ena Tapp.

George Farenden.

E.Miller; M.Towner; C.Smith; G.Farenden; E.Warnett; F.Clarke.

Violet Osmond (age 5)

Doris Jones, Edith Fuller.

The Rector, Rev. H.W. Farrar, and Mr. E. Bourdillon kindly gave out the prizes at school, after which the children were regaled with lemonade and a bag of sweets.

By The Way—

JULY 19, 1919 will live in the memory of all, rich and poor, young and old, as one of the happiest days of their lives.

All the village was "en fête", flags, bunting, flowers, pictures, and coloured lamps making a brave display.

The gentle rain which fell towards the close of the day in no way damped the enthusiasm of the merrymakers.

What rousing cheers greeted the hundred and forty brave fellows who marched de pa ... as on parade to the excellent dinner provided for them at Barcombe Place!

What pleasure it gave to all to see over one hundred children in fancy dress!

Who envies the judges' task?

How the tea, with mountains of bread and butter, and piles of cake, disappeared, when we got to work after the Sports!

After Thoughts

OUR BEST THANKS are given to

Mr S.Allen who whipped up the starters two races in front of schedule, thus enabling the long list of events to be run off without any waiting.

Mr. S.G. Richards, Mr.S.Cox, who kindly held the tape and acted as Judges of the 1st + 2nd Prize winners in each race, and also to Mr. R.Rhodes who spotted the 3rd winner.

Mr. W.Dudney, Mr.J.Beaney, Mr.J.Kennard, who gave the 3 winners their numbered slips, and bustled them off to the Pay-Table, presided over by Mr.E.Bourdillon, who untiringly handed out the Prizes.

Overheard. Late, very Saturday. "O-o-o, muvver, ain't it been a lovvierly day! I got a bigger 'eadache than what I had on Armistice night."

Mr. Spelter who ransacked his premises for rope, wire, sacks, ladders, poles, etc., thus putting no obstacles in our way in the endeavour to find obstacles for the obstacle race. (Is this a joke?)

Mr. King, without whose booth The concert and tea would have been considerably damped, if not extinguished.

Mrs. Jones, who kindly lent a gramophone, whose stirring tunes greatly enlivened the day's proceedings.

Mrs. Bishop, Montague Bishop and Angela Bishop who woke me up early to hoist the historic Union Jack over the school, a beautiful flag kindly lent by Mr. E. Bourdillon for the occasion.

ABOVE: Peace Celebrations - Four further pages form the School Magazine: (1) School Sports, The Boys and Girls prize winners; (2) The School Concert; (3) 'By-The-Way' and (4) 'Afterthoughts' (courtesy Barcombe School).

BARCOMBE SERVICEMEN O.H.M.S.

The Barcombe servicemen who attended the Peace Celebrations were photographed by Edward Reeves of Lewes (who is named on the Men's Club copy), probably in the grounds of Barcombe Place following the dinner in their honour. (See photograph on p.218).

There are two known copies of this photograph. A large framed copy, which used to hang in the Men's Club Room in the old village hall, is now in the new village hall. The other, smaller copy, is pasted into the Barcombe W.I. scrapbook. Each has a key to the names of those present, but there are a few inconsistencies between the two lists. The Men's Club version has 100 names, while the scrapbook version has names up to 97 (with gaps).

Some names can be confirmed by comparison with known images of those present, such as Major GRANTHAM, Rev FARRAR and Luther CORNWELL. (See Key on p.219).

The fact that some men have been wounded, can be seen by the presence of walking sticks (see the note on Lieut. W. Ivor GRANTHAM, No.77). Others appear too old to have served (at least in the regular services) so may have served with the parish's Volunteer Platoon. While the majority are pleased to be out of military uniform, the few who have chosen to wear theirs have been placed on the front two rows (except one, identified as Tom PYNE, who appears on the back row towards the right without a cap,). It is also interesting to note that most of the men have removed their hats (straw "boaters" appear fashionable), presumably at the request of the photographer, to ensure their faces could be preserved for posterity.

LIEUT. W. IVOR GRANTHAM
THE WHITE FEATHER INCIDENT

This story is taken from Ivor's memoirs, written for his niece Sheila in 1978. Writing about his recuperation following a serious injury in about October 1917, he says:

...About a year later your uncle was transferred from a military ward in The London Hospital at Whitechapel to a private Convalescent Home in Hove run by a lady in her own home on the front. Her "guests" – ten or twelve in number – were individually received by the butler at the front door on their arrival, and were then solemnly announced by rank and name to their hostess as she stood ready to receive them in the Drawing Room.
While sitting on the front one day near this Convalescent Home, dressed in mufti with his crutches on the ground beside him, your uncle was handed a white feather by a lady with a handful of such feathers, which left him amused but quite speechless.

The white feather was given to men of serving age as a sign of cowardice. Ivor GRANTHAM appears in the "O.H.M.S." Peace Celebrations photograph as 'No.77', his hand resting on his walking stick, two places to the left of his father, Major GRANTHAM. (Story courtesy the Grantham family).

"O.H.M.S." group photographed by Edward Reeves of Lewes on the day of Barcombe's Peace Celebrations. This image, reproduced from the original 10 × 8 inch glass plate negative, was recorded by the photographer as "Barcombe demob. group." The negative showed clear signs of retouching to "lighten the skin tones" of several of the faces, notably Alfred STEVENS (no.21) and Stanley EARL (no.7). This practice, reflecting the sensibilities of the times, was apparently common, but it is not known who would have requested it, the subject or the organising committee. At least four of the men are wearing silver, "wound badges" on their right lapel, while five others wear their regimental cap badges on the left.

A framed copy of this print, accompanied by a key and list of names of the one hundred men present, used to hang in the Men's Club room of the old village hall, is now in the new village hall. There is a second copy in the Barcombe W.I. scrapbook held at ESRO. The list of names below is copied from the village hall version, with Christian names added where possible (reproduced courtesy Edward Reeves, Lewes).

1   MUGGRIDGE, Charles
2   DUDNEY, Allan
3   ALLEN, S.
4   BUNNEY, Jack
5   GRIST, Herbert
6   TAPP, Albert
7   EARL, Stanley
8   WHITBREAD, Lewis
9   HOUNSOM, Robert
10 RANN, Albert V.
11 HOUNSOM, Harry
12 KING, Albert (jnr.)
13 REED, Selby
14 BEARD, G.
15 PULLINGER, Bernard
16 DIPLOCK, W.E.
17 DEAN, William R.
18 JESSUP, Reginald J.P.
19 DAVIS, George T.
20 COLLINS, Benjamin
21 STEVENS, Alfred
22 STEVENS, Ernest
23 COPPARD, Frank
24 AVERY, James
25 CHATFIELD, Charles
26 BROOKER, Frederick E.

27 WORSLEY, Edward R.
28 PYNE, Thomas
29 LONGHURST, George H.
30 SAYERS, G.W.
31 PARSONS,
32 ELDRIDGE, William
33 FARRAR, Revd.
34 KEMP, George H.
35 WARNETT, Edwin
36 COTTINGTON, Thomas
37 HOLLOWAY, Charles J.
38 KNIGHT, Frederick
39 MARCHANT, Charles A.
40 FARNES, B.
41 WALTERS, William A.
42 HEMSLEY, Frederick J.
43 DIPLOCK, Joseph
44 BLACKMAN, Frederick A.
45 VERRALL, Horace
46 KNIBBS, Alfred H.
47 CORNWELL, F. Burton
48 REECE, William H.
49 GURR, John
50 BURFIELD, E
51 VERCOE, Allan W.
52 FURNIVAL, Osmer G.

53 CORNWELL, Luther J.
54 FLEWELLING, Herbert
55 WELLER, Henry W.
56 SAYERS, Charles
57 COX, James or John
58 REED, Henry
59 COX, Fred
60 COTTINGHAM, Henry
61 BARRETT, Frank
62 WHITCHER, Frank J.
63 FAULCONER, Thomas F.
64 CHATFIELD, Charles L.
65 OSMOND, Arthur
66 PAYNE, Jabez
67 GREEN, Samuel H.
68 BECK, Sydney A.
69 HEASMAN, Frank
70 BLACKMAN, James
71 BLACKMAN, F. Alfred
72 BLACKMAN, Sydney W.
73 MORLEY, James
74 VALLANCE, S. (Capt.)
75 GRANTHAM, William W. (Maj.)
76 FARRAR, Sydney G. (Lieut.)

77 GRANTHAM, W. Ivor (Lieut.)
78 MARKWICK, Arthur
79 PUTTICK, George (jnr.)
80 MOORE, R.E.
81 BORLETT, James
82 SIMMONS, G.
83 COX, Charles F.
84 BEATTY, Ross W.
85 WARNETT, Edwin T.
86 TAPP, Wilfred T.
87 COLLINS, Bert
88 MARTIN, F. (Frank or Fred)
89 STEWART, Harold
90 BODLE, Charles W.
91 JESSUP, Albert L.
92 GRANTHAM, Alexander (Lieut.)
93 DUDENEY, James (Lieut.)
94 FUNNELL, Jack R.
95 SPELLER, George J.
96 DURRANT, J. Peter
97 MEADES, William J.
98 SAWYER, Jessie
99 BRYANT, William
100 STILL, Albert

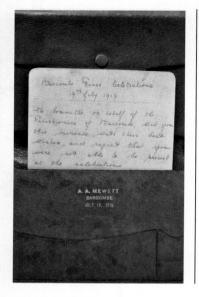

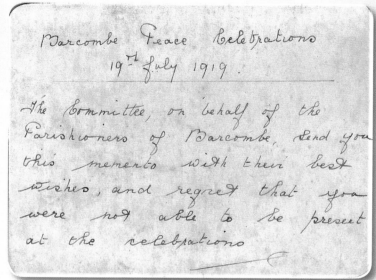

ABOVE: Wallet and accompanying card which were sent to Arthur MEWETT, one of 39 men still serving abroad with the Armed Forces at the time of Barcombe's Peace Celebrations. There is a note on the back of the card to say that it was "From Mrs SPELLER, Place Farm," suggesting that she may have sponsored the cost of the wallet (courtesy Jo Newman).

1st August – FETE AT BARCOMBE – Barcombe Foresters revived their fete on Thursday, when, favoured with lovely summer weather, a large number of people enjoyed sports and the usual "fair" attractions. Music was supplied by the Lewes Town Band, and in the evening dancing took place.

11th August – HOLIDAYS – The Correspondent said that he had received a communication from the Local Education Authority at Lewes stating that the children were to have six weeks' holiday this year, which was an additional week, by the wish of the King to commemorate Peace. The schools would thus re-open on September 15th instead of September 8th.

17th October – A PRESENT FOR SOLDIERS – At the last meeting of the Peace Celebration Committee it was decided that all Barcombe men serving in the Army, Navy and Air Service, thirty-nine in all told would receive a present. The form of gift is a handsome pig-skin wallet, each bearing in gold letters the name of the recipient, and accompanying same is a card with the following wording: "The Barcombe Peace Celebration Committee, on behalf of the parishioners of Barcombe, send you this memento with their best wishes, and regret that you were unable to be present at the Peace Celebration."

To be continued …

A second volume is planned to continue the Barcombe story from November 1919 to the unveiling of the war memorials in November 1920, along with detailed biographies of the thirty-six men associated with the parish who died, along with articles on how the village decided to commemorate their dead and provide for the living after the Great War.

LUTHER J. CORNWELL'S WARTIME DIARIES

◆

The eldest son of local farmer Francis J. CORNWELL and his wife Esther, Luther was born in 1895 at 4 Gladstone Buildings on the village High Street, while 'Crink House' was being built at Barcombe Mills. The following year the young family moved into the newly built house.

He attended Castle Gate School in Lewes followed by Uckfield Grammar School, where his 1911 report placed him 2nd in a class of ten pupils. His highest marks were achieved in religious knowledge, English, mathematics, science and woodwork.

Luther's diaries from 1912 to 1919 remain in his family, to whom I am grateful for the following notes and edited transcripts:

1912   *The war in the Near East has called for much attention. Turkey has been struggling for her life as it were against the combined forces of Bulgaria, Montenegro, Serbia and Greece. None knows where it will end. Some say in Armageddon.*

1913   The diary gives a detailed picture of life on a farm at the beginning of the century. LJC's social life consisted of visits to his grandmother and aunts at Hayes Farm, a weekly First Aid class and occasional parties.

ABOVE: Luther photographed in uniform with his cousins Lily and Hilda CORNWELL (courtesy the Cornwell family).

1915   The diary for 1915 was completed only until 16 April. LJC was serving in the Royal Army Medical Corps, stationed at Brighton General ("Kitchener") Hospital which received convoys of troops who had been wounded in the war in France.

He was experiencing a life completely different from that on the farm. This diary tells of route marches, drill, ward duties, scrubbing out, assisting at operations, transporting the wounded from Brighton station to the hospital. Perhaps the biggest change was living in a large town and having company of his own age.

LEFT: Brighton General or "Kitchener" Hospital, where Luther CORNWELL worked in 1915. (Postcard by Arthur Kingsley Pink of Dover Road, Brighton).

221

1917   This diary is rather thin. LJC continued his posting in Brighton until July, when he spent four weeks at home helping with haying. On 17th August he was transferred to Blackpool, in preparation for more active service. On 27th September he was told of his transfer to the Dorset regiment, and on the following day travelled to Weymouth. On 25th November, *"the funniest Sunday I have ever had,"* he embarked at Plymouth for the voyage to India.

Some Impressions of a Troop Ship

We boarded on a typical November afternoon, bitterly cold & trying to snow. Our luck is out and we get steerage in the aft of the ship. This is three flights down from the deck, a space of about 50 sq. ft. by 8ft. high for 120 men to live and sleep. My first experience of a hammock was quite a success, for having been up for about 17 hours, I was thoroughly tired.

RMS Ormonde is a brand new Orient liner on her maiden voyage. She is certainly a beautiful ship. We carry troops of all regiments: Black Watch, Seaforths, Royal Fusiliers, Devon, Somerset, Hants, Ox & Bucks, Suffolks, Wilts. Time passes slowly on board and one gets very bored at looking at nothing but sea. There is great excitement on board when a strange vessel is sighted, which is by no means often.

Christmas on Board RMS Ormonde

We started badly, the menu for breakfast being exactly as it had been all the voyage, viz. bread & butter & porridge. Several units refused theirs but got nothing else. During the morning we amused ourselves as usual and the prizes for sports held during the week were distributed by Brig. Gen. Dyer.

ABOVE: Cap badge of the R.A.M.C. with whom Luther was able to practise some of the first aid skills he had learnt after leaving school (courtesy the British Military Badges website).

ABOVE: Luther was transferred to the Dorsetshire Regiment in readiness for active service in September 1917 (courtesy the British Military Badges website).

LEFT: R.M.S. (Royal Mail Ship) 'Ormonde' in her wartime "dazzle" paint scheme. Originally commissioned in 1913 by the Orient Line to join its' fleet on the London to Australia service. Building was halted at the outbreak of war, only to be recommenced in early 1917 when troopships were in demand. She was completed with sparse quarters suitable for troops and officially requisitioned in October 1917.[1] (Image, State Library of Victoria).

---

1 *Ref. Reuben Goossens, ssMaratime website.*

Then came dinner & a good one it was. A fine bit of roast beef, cabbage, potatoes, gravy, Christmas pudding, beer, (minerals for teetotallers), mince pie, oranges & monkey nuts. In the afternoon most like pigs went to sleep. For tea there was bread and butter, jam, tea, cake and bully beef (incidentally this was kept for breakfast next day), and biscuits and cheese for supper. Altogether we were all agreeably surprised. In the evening I went to a carol service on the NCOs' deck, which was very nice.

1918 The regiment sailed via the Cape to Bombay, where the troops disembarked on 13 January 1918 and immediately travelled to Poona. In April they travelled to Egypt via the Suez Canal and spent the next nine months in Egypt and Palestine. On some parts of the march to Damascus in August troops were issued with one pint of water each per day.

1919 On January 18th LJC received a call to the demobilisation tent and started immediately on the homeward journey. He landed at Southampton on February 13th and after a brief delay through loss of papers he was able to travel home.

ABOVE: Luther CORNWELL in Tropical Dress Uniform, with his pith helmet displayed on a pillar, in front of a well-used makeshift canvas backdrop showing the Sphynx and a pyramid. Presumably taken during his time in Egypt (courtesy the Cornwell family).

LJC's volume of post in these army years must have been the envy of his fellow soldiers. He kept a meticulous record of the letters he received. Between 1st February 1918 and 12th January 1919 he received 58 letters from home (presumably written by his mother), between 90 and 100 from other members of the family (his father, brother, many aunts and some friends) and 48 letters from Ella ASHBY (whom he married in 1924). On his part he seems to have been a faithful correspondent, writing letters several times a week. He also sent large numbers of picture postcards, keeping a record of each card, so that no one received the same view twice.

Luther CORNWELL died in 1981, aged 85 years, having served as a Barcombe parish councillor for 7 years and Lewes district magistrate for 18.

◆

The homes and pre-war occupations of the men whose names appear on Barcombe war memorial and Foresters' plaque.

Map ref.	Name	Residence	Local Link
5	William H. BANKS	30 Brunswick Place, Hove	Father at Rectory Cottage
8	Alfred G. BOTTING	Half Mile Drove, Ringmer *	Father at Beaks Farm Cottages, Longford
31	Frederick C. BOTTING	Half Mile Drove, Ringmer*	As above
23	William T. BOTTING	Hadlow Down*	As above
26	Henry A. BROOKS	Gate Cottage, Balneath, Chailey	Worked for W.W.GRANTHAM of Balneath Manor
34	Robert G. BROWNE, DSO	Scobells Farm House	Home of his wife and widowed mother-in-law.
9	George H. BUCKWELL	Vuggles Cottages	Home of parents.
19	John E. CLARK	Lewes	
15	Herbert 'Abraham' COLLINS	Place Farm Cottage	Home
24	Frederick DAY	Willow Cottage	Home of parents (1918)
18	Frederick EDWARDS	Dallas Lane	Address of his widow (1917)
33	Claude H.W. ELDRIDGE	Croft Ham Cottage	Parents' home (1918)
1	Herbert 'Ronald' FARRAR		His father was Rector from 1916.
17	Frank FOORD	Mafeking (Byelaw) Cottages	Parents' home*
10	George F. FOORD	Mafeking (Byelaw) Cottages	Parents' home*
29	George FUNNELL	Canada	Brother Albert, High Street
2	Frederick W. GRANTHAM	Beeleigh Abbey, Maldon, Essex	Widowed mother, Barcombe Place
3	Hugo F. GRANTHAM	Beeleigh Abbey, Maldon, Essex	Widowed Grandmother, Barcombe Place
11	William HAWKINS	High Street, Barcombe	Home of widow (1918)

~ The Men Who Died ~

KEY:

Battn.	–	Battalion		Regt.	–	Regiment
Brig.	–	Brigadier		R.S.R.	–	Royal Sussex Regt.
Gen.	–	General		Sgt.	–	Sergeant

Occupation before the War	Rank & Regiment at time of death	Date of Death	Place died	Age
Gardener at River Lawns, Barcombe Mills	Private, 8th R.S.R.	1916.02.07	Maxse Redoubt, Somme, France	31
Farm Labourer*	Private, 1/5th R.S.R.	1916.06.28	Pas-de-Calais, France	25
Carter's Mate*	Private, 1st Royal Marine Light Infantry	1918.09.29	Pas-de-Calais, France	21
Farm Labourer*	Private, 8th East Surrey Regt.	1918.04.04	Somme, France	33
Farm Labourer & Carter	Corporal, 9th York & Lancaster Regt.	1918.06.15	Asiago, Italy	22
Soldier	Major, 1st Manchester Regt.	1918.11.01	Lyons Hospital, Rhone, France	37
Gardener*	Private, 2nd R.S.R.	1916.06.30	Pas-de-Calais, France	21
	Corporal, 23rd Middlesex	1917.09.21	Belgium	
Waggoner*	Private, 43rd Mobile Vet. Section, Royal Army Veterinary Corps.	1917.04.27	Pas-de-Calais, France	35
Under Gardener*	Gunner, 250th Siege Battery, R.G.A.	1918.04.25	Ypres (Ieper), Belgium	23
Carpenter	Private, 21st Northumberland Fusiliers	1917.09.09	Somme, France	32
At school*	Private, 8th Leicester Regt.	1918.10.13	Ardennes, France	19
School Teacher	2nd Lieut. 3rd Leicester Regt. (attached 2nd Manchester)	1914.12.24	Ypres (Ieper), Belgium	27
Gardener at Barcombe Place	Gunner, 352nd Siege Battery, R.G.A.	1917.09.01	Ypres (Ieper), Belgium	20
Assistant butcher to W.F.DEAN	Lance Corp., 7th R.S.R.	1916.07.19	Pas-de-Calais, France	21
Farmer in Canada	Private, 5th Battn., Canadian Infantry	1918.09.27	Pas-de-Calais, France	42
Army Officer	Captain, 2nd Royal Munster Fusiliers	1915.05.09	Pas De Calais, France	44
Military Academy	2nd Lieut., 3rd Essex Regt.	1915.06.28	Gallipoli, Turkey	20
Soldier	Sergeant, 9th R.S.R.	1916.07.31	Portslade Sanatorium	34

* As recorded in the 1911 census return.

The homes and pre-war occupations of the men whose names appear on Barcombe war memorial and Foresters' plaque *(continued)*.

Map ref.	Name	Residence	Local Link
35	Frederick W. HEASMAN	Forge Cottage, Cooksbridge	Home of widowed mother
13	Ernest KING	Holmans Bridge	Home of parents.
6	Frederick KING	Holmans Bridge	As above
14	James T. KING	Woodbine Cottage, Spithurst	Parents' home
28	William F. KIRBY	Acton, West London	Mother at High Street Bakery
20	Joseph Charles MILLER	'The Hall Lodge,' Wivelsfield Green	Parents at Bevern Bridge Cottages, Cooksbridge
7	Cecil Hugh PECKHAM	'Fern Cottage,' High Street	Home of parents
27	Charles W. PECKHAM	100 Hartop Road, Torquay	Parents at 'Fern Cottage,' High St.
36	Arthur PLAYER	Unknown	Unknown
25	Charles Herbert PRICE	Clappers Cottage	Home of widowed mother Esther (PARSONS)
30	Arthur R.C. SANDERS, RHC, CMG, DSO	Holmbush, Church Road	Home of mother Margaret
12	Frederick S. SAUNDERS	10 Gladstone Cottages	Parents' home
22	Henry "Harry" STEVENS	Old Thatch Cottages	Home of mother Fanny STEVENS
16	Leonard H. STEVENS	Old Thatch Cottages	Home of grandmother Fanny STEVENS
21	William H. VERCOE	Banks Farm	Parents' home.
4	Frank H. WALKER	'Erskine', High Street.	Mother at 'The Grange,' High St.
32	'Bertie' WELSH	Bridge Cottage	Parents' home

KEY:

Battn.	–	Battalion	Regt.	–	Regiment
Brig.	–	Brigadier	R.S.R.	–	Royal Sussex Regt.
Gen.	–	General	Sgt.	–	Sergeant

Occupation before the War	Rank & Regiment at time of death	Date of Death	Place died	Age
Gardener at Conyboro'	Gunner, Heavy Anti-Aircraft Battery, R.G.A.	1918.11.25	Field Hospital, Pas-de-Calais, France	23
Carter*	Lance Corp., 2nd R.M. Battalion, R.M.L.I.	1917.02.17	Pas-de-Calais, France	21
Worked for Henry GEARING, Sewells Farm	Lance Corp., 9th R.S.R.	1916.02.24	Hoogein, Ypres (Ieper), Belgium	23
Worked for Rev. SCLATER, Newick Park	Private, 22nd Training Reserve Battn.	1917.04.07	Hospital, St. Albans, Hertfordshire	18
Fitter's Impresser	Private, 1/23rd Battalion, London Regt.	1918.08.22	near Poziers	18
Gardener, 'The Hall Lodge,' Wivelsfield Gn.	Gunner, 210th Siege Battery, R.G.A.	1917.09.29	Belgium	31
Horticultural Nurseryman	Private, 11th R.S.R.	1916.03.19	Pas-de-Calais, France	20
Nurseryman	Private, 7th R.S.R.	1918.07.11	Hospital in Torquay, Devon	25
Unknown	Named in Sussex Express 'Thanksgiving Service' article, 22.11.1918	Unknown	Unknown	- - -
Soldier & Farm Labourer	Lance Bombdr., `A` Battery, 62nd Brigade, Royal Field Artillery	1918.06.03	Somme, France	37
Army Officer	Brig. Gen., Commanding 50th Infantry Brigade	1918.09.20	Pas-de-Calais, France	41
Labourer *	Private, 2nd Middlesex Regt.	1916.11.17	Somme, France	28
Farm Labourer	Bombardier, Royal Marine Artillery	1918.03.04	At sea off the coast of North Africa	40
Farm Labourer	Gunner 9th Siege Battery, Royal Garrison Artillery	1917.07.27	Ypres (Ieper), Belgium	28
Farmer's son	Private, 1st Royal West Kent Regt.	1917.10.26	Ypres (Ieper), Belgium	19
Army Officer	Lieut.-Col., 7th North Staffordshire Regt.	1916.01.07	Gallipoli, Turkey	46
Baker	Private, 119th Canadian Infantry (& 8th Reserve Battn.)	1918.10.01	Nord, France	35

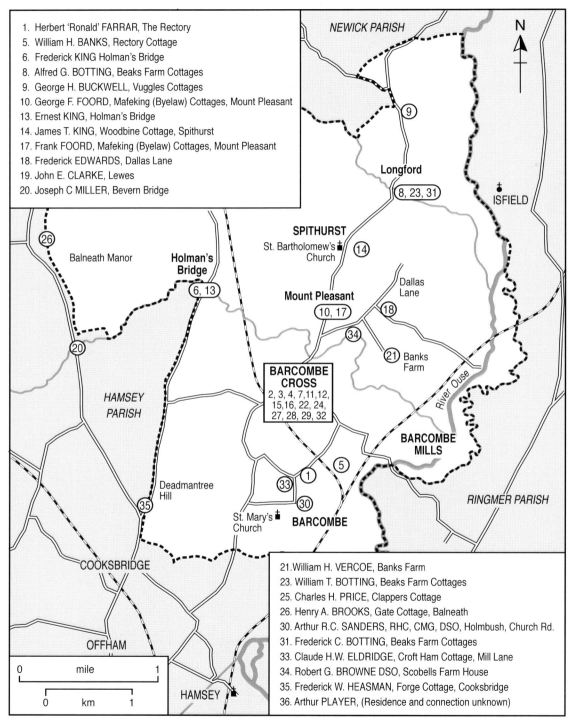

1. Herbert 'Ronald' FARRAR, The Rectory
5. William H. BANKS, Rectory Cottage
6. Frederick KING Holman's Bridge
8. Alfred G. BOTTING, Beaks Farm Cottages
9. George H. BUCKWELL, Vuggles Cottages
10. George F. FOORD, Mafeking (Byelaw) Cottages, Mount Pleasant
13. Ernest KING, Holman's Bridge
14. James T. KING, Woodbine Cottage, Spithurst
17. Frank FOORD, Mafeking (Byelaw) Cottages, Mount Pleasant
18. Frederick EDWARDS, Dallas Lane
19. John E. CLARKE, Lewes
20. Joseph C MILLER, Bevern Bridge

NEWICK PARISH

Longford

ISFIELD

SPITHURST

St. Bartholomew's Church

Balneath Manor

Holman's Bridge

Mount Pleasant

Dallas Lane

Banks Farm

BARCOMBE CROSS
2, 3, 4, 7,11,12, 15,16, 22, 24, 27, 28, 29, 32

River Ouse

HAMSEY PARISH

BARCOMBE MILLS

Deadmantree Hill

RINGMER PARISH

St. Mary's Church

BARCOMBE

COOKSBRIDGE

OFFHAM

0   mile   1

0   km   1

HAMSEY

21. William H. VERCOE, Banks Farm
23. William T. BOTTING, Beaks Farm Cottages
25. Charles H. PRICE, Clappers Cottage
26. Henry A. BROOKS, Gate Cottage, Balneath
30. Arthur R.C. SANDERS, RHC, CMG, DSO, Holmbush, Church Rd.
31. Frederick C. BOTTING, Beaks Farm Cottages
33. Claude H.W. ELDRIDGE, Croft Ham Cottage, Mill Lane
34. Robert G. BROWNE DSO, Scobells Farm House
35. Frederick W. HEASMAN, Forge Cottage, Cooksbridge
36. Arthur PLAYER, (Residence and connection unknown)

Map of Barcombe parish, showing the location of the homes connected with the men whose names appear on the village war memorials. Every corner of the parish was affected by the war.

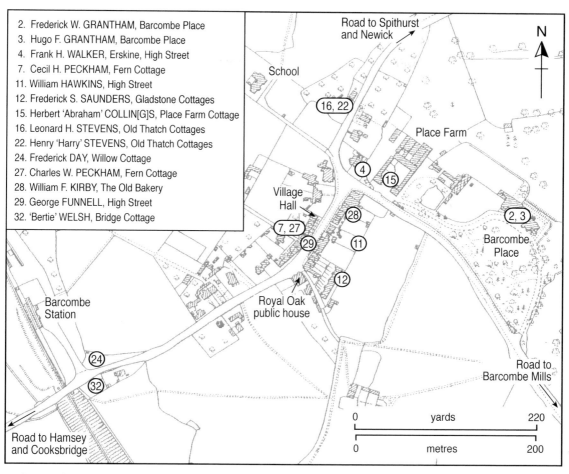

2. Frederick W. GRANTHAM, Barcombe Place
3. Hugo F. GRANTHAM, Barcombe Place
4. Frank H. WALKER, Erskine, High Street
7. Cecil H. PECKHAM, Fern Cottage
11. William HAWKINS, High Street
12. Frederick S. SAUNDERS, Gladstone Cottages
15. Herbert 'Abraham' COLLIN[G]S, Place Farm Cottage
16. Leonard H. STEVENS, Old Thatch Cottages
22. Henry 'Harry' STEVENS, Old Thatch Cottages
24. Frederick DAY, Willow Cottage
27. Charles W. PECKHAM, Fern Cottage
28. William F. KIRBY, The Old Bakery
29. George FUNNELL, High Street
32. 'Bertie' WELSH, Bridge Cottage

Map of Barcombe Cross village, showing the locations of the homes associated with the men whose names appear on the village war memorials. It was not just the men who were involved in the war, as the postcard below points out.

For further background reading on some of the topics covered in this book I can recommend the following books and websites:

General accounts of the Great War:

Arthur, Max, *Forgotten Voices of the Great War*, Ebury Press, 2003.

Barnett, Correlli, *The Great War*, Park Lane Press, 1979.

Blunden, E., *Undertones of War*, Cobden Sanderson, 1930.

Bridger, Geoffrey, *The Great War Handbook*, Pen & Sword Books, 2009.

Faulks, Sebastian, *Birdsong*, Hutchinson, 1993.

Hart, Liddell, *History of the First World War*, Faber & Faber Ltd., 1934.

Keegan, John, *The First World War: An Illustrated History*, Cornerstone, 2001.

Langford, William & Holroyd Jack, *The Great War Illustrated*, five volumes 1914-1918, Pen & Sword Books, 2014-2018.

Middlebrook, Martin, *Your Country Needs You*, Leo Cooper, 2000.

Paxman, Jeremy, *Great Britain's Great War*, Viking, 2013.

Price-Rowe, Catherine, *First World War Uniforms*, Pen & Sword Books, 2018.

Strachan, Hew, *The First World War*, Simon & Schuster, 2003.

Taylor, A.J.P., *The First World War*, Hamish Hamilton, 1963.

(Website) *The Long, Long Trail*.

(Website) The National Army Museum.

The Home Front:

Adie, Kate, *Fighting on the Home Front: The Legacy of Women in World War One*, Hodder & Stoughton, 2014.

Bilton, David, *The Great War Illustrated* – The Home Front, Pen & Sword Books.

Hetherington, Andrea, *British Widows of the First World War*, Pen & Sword Books, 2018.

Newman, Vivien, *Suffragism and the Great War*, Pen & Sword Books, 2018.

Sussex:

Baines, John A., *The Day Sussex Died*, Royal Sussex Living History Group, 2012.

Elliston, R.A., *Eastbourne's Great War*, S.B. Publications, 1999.

Grieves, Keith, *Sussex in the First World War*, Sussex Record Society v.84, 2004.

Harker, W.E., *Sussex: At Peace and War*, Southern Publishing Co. Ltd., 1918.

Harvey, B.W. & Fitzgerald, C. (eds.) *Edward Heron-Allen's*, *Journal of the Great War*, Sussex Record Society v.86, 2002.

Kimmins, G.T.H., Craft Schools and hospitals, Chailey [1904-1948], Chailey 1948.

Madden, Capt. C.H., 'The Volunteer Forces in Sussex,' *Sussex County Magazine* 13 [11], 1939.

Oowell-Edwards, H.I., *The Sussex Yeomanry & 16th Battalion R.S.R.*, Andrew Melrose, 1921.

Sussex Agricultural Express, newspaper copies available in the East Sussex Record Office archives at 'The Keep' and online at *FindMyPast* and *British Newspaper Library.*

West Sussex County Council, *Great War Britain - West Sussex*, The History Press 2015.

(Website) The International Red Cross – *Prisoners of the First World War.*

(Website) *The London Gazette.*

(Website) www.ww1photos.com

I would like to thank the following people for their support in the publication of this volume:

Tim Austen, Ray Gaydon, Mike Green, Brian Hewitt, Wally Hope, Alison & John Hutchins, Alex Lahood, William Nicholson, Nigel Raymond, Sue Rowland and John Sclater CVO.

Barcombe Garden Club (in memory of the gardeners who went to war).

Hedley, John & Barbara Cornwell (in memory of Luther and Burton Cornwell).

Dave Grantham, Esther Simmons and Ruth Woods (in memory of the Grantham family).

Muriel Hilder (in memory of Roy Hilder).

Beryl Jackson (in memory of the Hobden and Collins families).

Dr Andrew & Anne Pearce (in memory of Bernard & Gertrude Pullinger).

Where possible surnames and properties have been indexed under the spelling used by the householders in the 1911 census returns.